MORE JUNIOR AUTHORS

THE AUTHORS SERIES

📖 📖 📖

Edited by Stanley J. Kunitz and Howard Haycraft

AMERICAN AUTHORS: 1600-1900
BRITISH AUTHORS BEFORE 1800
BRITISH AUTHORS OF THE NINETEENTH CENTURY
THE JUNIOR BOOK OF AUTHORS
TWENTIETH CENTURY AUTHORS

Edited by Stanley J. Kunitz
TWENTIETH CENTURY AUTHORS: FIRST SUPPLEMENT

Edited by Muriel Fuller
MORE JUNIOR AUTHORS

MORE
JUNIOR AUTHORS

EDITED BY
MURIEL FULLER

NEW YORK
THE H. W. WILSON COMPANY
1963

Preface

THIS work is designed to be a companion volume to *The Junior Book of Authors*, second edition, revised, edited by Stanley J. Kunitz and Howard Haycraft and published in 1951.

MORE JUNIOR AUTHORS includes biographical or autobiographical sketches of 268 authors and illustrators of books for children and young people. The great majority are authors and illustrators who have become prominent since the publication of the second edition of *The Junior Book of Authors*, but several older writers omitted from the earlier work because information was available on them in Kunitz and Haycraft's *Twentieth Century Authors* have also been included; among these are James Thurber and Constance Lindsay Skinner.

As the first step in selecting names for inclusion, the editor compiled a preliminary list of approximately 1,200 names, drawing on the *Children's Catalog*, the *Standard Catalog for High School Libraries*, the pertinent American Library Association *Basic Book Lists*, suggestions from children's book editors, and other sources. These names were submitted to a panel of twenty-seven consultants, comprising children's and young people's librarians, school librarians, and other authorities on juvenile literature. The consultants were asked to vote on the list, and their votes provided the basis for the final determination of names to be included.

The editor and the publisher offer their grateful thanks to the following consultants for the time and thought which they and the members of their staffs gave to the voting on which the selection of names was based:

Virginia Chase, Head, Boys and Girls Department, Carnegie Library, Pittsburgh, Pa.; Mrs. Mary Peacock Douglas, Supervisor of Libraries, Raleigh Public Schools, Raleigh, N.C.; Edith Edmonds, Elementary School Librarian, Winnetka Public School Libraries, Winnetka, Ill.; Mrs. Margaret Alexander Edwards, Coordinator of Work with Young People, Enoch Pratt Free Library, Baltimore, Md.; Ruth Ersted, State Supervisor of School Libraries, State of Minnesota, Department of Education, St. Paul, Minn.; Lois Fetterman, Supervisor, Order Department, Library Section, Los Angeles City Schools Libraries, Los Angeles, Cal.; Mrs. Carolyn W. Field, Coordinator, Work with Children, Free Library of Philadelphia, Philadelphia, Pa.; Helen Fuller, Assistant Librarian in Charge of Work with Boys and Girls, Public Library, Long Beach, Cal.; Elizabeth M. Gordon (deceased), formerly Deputy Supervisor in Charge of Work with Children, Boston Public Library, Boston, Mass.; Mrs. Dora Leavitt Hay, Head Librarian, Seattle High Schools, Seattle, Wash.; Gladys L. Lees, Director, School Libraries, Tacoma Public Schools, Tacoma, Wash.; Helen B. Lewis, Supervisor, School Department, Cleveland Public Library, Cleveland, O.; Rosemary Livsey, Director, Work with Children, Los Angeles Public Library, Los Angeles, Cal.; Virginia McJenkin, Director, Fulton County School Libraries, Atlanta, Ga.; Jean A. Merrill, Director of Work with Children, Kansas City Public Library, Kansas City, Mo.; Elisabeth Morgan, Librarian, Carlsbad Mid High School, Carlsbad, N.M.; Mildred R. Phipps, Supervisor, Work with Boys and Girls, Pasadena Public Library, Pasadena, Cal.; Julia L. Sauer, formerly Head, Department of Work with Children, Rochester Public Library, Rochester, N.Y.; Marian Schroether, Children's Librarian, Waukegan Public Library, Waukegan, Ill.; Margaret C. Scoggin, Coordinator of Young People's Services, New York Public Library, New York; Ethna Sheehan, Superintendent, Work with Children, Queens Borough Public Library, Jamaica, N.Y.; Evelyn R. Sickels, formerly Supervisor of Work with Children, Indianapolis Public Library, Indianapolis, Ind.; Mrs. Frances Lander Spain, Director of Library Services, Central Florida Junior College, Ocala, Fla. (formerly Coordinator of Children's Services,

New York Public Library, New York); Jane D. Strebel, Consultant in Library Service, Minneapolis Public Schools, Minneapolis, Minn.; Frances Sullivan, Children's Librarian, Wichita City Library, Wichita, Kan.; Jean Thomson, Head of Boys and Girls Division, Toronto Public Library, Toronto, Ont., Canada; Marian C. Young, Chief, Children's Department, Detroit Public Library, Detroit, Mich.

Thanks are also due to the many children's book editors and publishers' publicity representatives who generously cooperated in supplying information and photographs. And finally the editor wishes to acknowledge a special debt of gratitude to the writers and artists who paused in their busy careers to write the stories of their lives.

THE EDITOR

More Junior Authors

Gladys L. Adshead
1896-

AUTHOR OF
Smallest Brownie's Fearful Adventure;
Brownies—Hush!; Brownies—Hurry!;
Brownies—It's Christmas!; Etc.

Autobiographical sketch of Gladys L. Adshead:

GLADYS L. ADSHEAD

I WAS born in England, in the rural county of Cheshire, in April and that in England is a beautiful month in which to be born. I came in with the lambs and other young things. The scent of may, the English wild hawthorn that encloses so many little pastures like white foam, was among my earliest memories. To smell it from an imported tree in Plymouth, Massachusetts, the other day took me back to all my lovely childhood memories of an English spring.

I was the oldest and my father was my dear companion. He took me on long country walks and with him I first learned to observe the beauties of field, flower, stream, and wood, to know and give character to the wild creatures. He discussed everything under the sun with me, so my active child mind tried to keep up with his thoughtful and imaginative one while my prancing feet kept pace with his stride.

On long winter evenings, by the blazing hard-coal fire, he would open his jacket. That was his invitation for me to sit on his knee, put my arm between jacket and waistcoat, lay my head on his chest, and listen to stories. I can still smell the tweedy smell and combined allurement of its impregnation of good pipe tobacco that belonged to these moments. I can still hear his heart beat and the tick of his big gold watch under my ear.

Dickens he read and all his favorite poems, things he enjoyed himself that he thought I could enjoy too. I thought him the best reader in the world.

It is wonderful to belong to the generation when Beatrix Potter's inimitable little books were first published. Each came my way and was appreciated as much by my mother and father as it was enjoyed by me. As my two brothers and a sister came along, I read the little books to them.

"Someday, Gladys," said my father, "perhaps you will write books for children."

I doubted I could do anything so difficult but entrancing. Secretly, I scribbled stories in old exercise books. Where they all went I am glad I do not know! At the tender age of ten, when the younger of my two brothers was born, I decided that when I grew up I would teach little children. So stories, storytelling, writing, children, and all the wonders and delights of nature always have been the fabric of my life. Although I was surprised as well as utterly delighted when my first book was published, I do not believe my father was surprised. He was inordinately proud, but being British he did not say so!

I went to private school and to college in England, but for years I have been an American citizen, teaching children, and writing for them. Now I am headmistress of an elementary school in Massachusetts and children are just as dear and as important to me as ever they were.

Adshead: *ADZ head*

Adam Allen

See *Epstein, Samuel*

Edward Ardizzone

1900-

AUTHOR AND ILLUSTRATOR OF
Nicholas and the Fast-Moving Diesel; Johnny the Clockmaker; Little Tim and the Brave Sea Captain; Tim to the Rescue; Etc.

Autobiographical sketch of Edward Ardizzone:

AS a young man in the 1920's I used to work in an office in the City of London. My job consisted chiefly of adding up figures and it was probably the dullest job that any young man could have. Six years of this was more than enough for me and so, very much against the advice of my elders, I threw it up, determined to make my living as a professional artist.

Since then I have painted many pictures and have had the good fortune to have achieved some reputation and to have had my works bought and exhibited by many galleries in all parts of the world.

In 1939, like so many Englishmen, I was in the Army, but soon I was transferred from my regiment to become an Official War Artist, and as such I followed the fortunes of the British Army in the North African and European theaters of war. I have traveled widely as well, going west as far as the United States, south to South Africa, and east to India and beyond.

Besides painting, I developed some talent for book illustration and have now illustrated over sixty books. However, on looking back on what has been for me a varied and interesting life, I think the works I am most proud of, and those which have given me most pleasure, were the stories I wrote and illustrated for my own children. The first of these stories was *Little Tim and the Brave Sea Captain.*

In 1957, *Tim All Alone* won for me the Kate Greenaway Medal. This medal is given by the British Library Association for the best illustrated children's book of the year.

Now I have been asked why all the Tim books have a background of the sea. This is easy to answer, for in fact the sea is very much in my blood. My paternal grandfather was a seaman and a master of a ship in the Mediterranean trade. My maternal great-grandfather, old Great-grandpapa Kirby, was the captain of one of the great sailing ships that sailed to China and back. In fact, my grandmother was born at sea off the Cape of Good Hope. Captain Kirby was an excellent amateur artist and kept a beautifully illustrated log of his voyages. He in his turn was the great-great-grandson of Joshua Kirby, who was an eighteenth century portrait painter and bosom friend of Gainsborough. So you see, art is in my blood too.

As for myself, I was born in China and I remember, as a little boy, the long voyage to England. Later, as a schoolboy, I lived in Ipswich, a small east-coast port, and there I spent many happy days playing about on the small coastal steamers and barges which arrived laden with mixed cargo and left with their holds full of grain.

Since then I have always been enamored of these little ships that sail our rough cold northern seas. It is no wonder then that when I invented my first stories for my sons, they were stories of the sea. Now my children are grown up, but I have grandchildren who will soon be old enough to have new stories told to them, and I would not be surprised if these stories were also of the sea.

EDWARD ARDIZZONE

Ardizzone: *ar dit ZOH nee*

Montgomery Meigs Atwater

1904-

AUTHOR OF
Ski Patrol; Smoke Patrol; Trouble Hunters; Cattle Dog; Etc.

Autobiographical sketch of Montgomery M. Atwater:

THE place where I was born is no longer on the map, a mining camp high in the Snowy Mountains near Baker, Oregon. When the veins of ore ran out, the miners left, and that was that. Since my father was a mining engineer, I grew up in a series of such places, always in the mountains. And all my books are in that setting which I know and love best.

For preparatory schooling, I went to Phillips Exeter Academy, and Lincoln High School in Seattle, Washington. It was my mother's idea that I should go to Harvard College, where I studied under that great teacher of English composition Charles Townsend Copeland. I did do some writing in the years after graduation but did not seriously think of myself as an author until 1939. I was snowed in that winter, in a cabin in northern Montana, completely alone except for my dog. I thought it was time to find out one way or the other if I really could write. The outcome was my first book, *Government Hunter*.

I was well started on a career as an author when World War II intervened. I served as an instructor in mountain and winter warfare in the ski troops, the 10th Mountain Division. Later, I commanded a reconnaissance unit in the 87th Infantry Division.

Most of my books have been about the Forest Service as well as the mountains. I long ago acquired a great respect for this organization which has done so much to preserve for us our heritage of forest and grass and water and wildlife. After the war I joined it, as an avalanche specialist. It made an ideal combination. In the winter I hunted avalanches and in the summer I wrote books. I'm still doing it. Many of the incidents in my stories are authentic. They either happened to me or to someone I know, or I heard about them by the campfires on many a lonely trail.

Richard Tupper Atwater

1892-1948

and

Florence Hasseltine Carroll Atwater

AUTHORS OF
Mr. Popper's Penguins

RICHARD Tupper Atwater was born Frederick Mund Atwater on December 29, 1892, in Chicago, Illinois. He changed his name officially in 1913. In 1907 he matriculated in the University of Chicago, and in 1909 was awarded the degree of associate in arts, and honorable mention for excellence in junior college work.

The degree of bachelor of arts was awarded to him in 1910, with honors in Greek, his major, and he was also awarded a scholarship for excellence in senior college work. He went on to the Graduate School and remained there until June of 1917, in the departments of Greek and Latin, without receiving a degree.

Mr. Atwater taught Greek at his alma mater, and Florence Hasseltine Carroll was a student in one of his classes. Eventually she became Mrs. Atwater. While on the staff of the university, Mr. Atwater wrote a show for the Blackfriars, the dramatic club, and also contributed to the column in the Chicago *Tribune* conducted by B.L.T. (Bert Leston Taylor).

After leaving the university, Mr. Atwater went to the Chicago *Evening Post,* where he wrote a column similar to that of B.L.T., which he signed "Riq." Keith Preston was the columnist for the Chicago *Daily News,* and when he died Mr. Atwater moved his column to that newspaper. His volume of verse, *Rickety Rimes of Riq,* published in 1925, grew out of his column. He also wrote a juvenile book, *Doris and the Trolls* (Rand McNally, 1931), illustrated by John Gee.

Mr. Popper's Penguins was published by Little, Brown & Company in 1938. It is a modern classic and became so almost overnight. The book was begun when one of the two Atwater daughters objected to the number of juvenile books with historical backgrounds. Before the book was finished, Mr. Atwater became ill and Mrs. Atwater completed it. The publishers say it has been a best seller almost since publication, and by the end of 1960 it had sold 176,000 copies. It has been translated into Italian, Dutch, German, Spanish, Swedish, and Japanese-Korean. It is an engagingly humorous tale of what happened when a mild little house painter was presented with an Antarctic penguin.

Margot Austin

AUTHOR AND ILLUSTRATOR OF
Brave John Henry; William's Shadow; Peter Churchmouse; The Three Silly Kittens; Etc.

SINCE 1939, Margot Austin has written and illustrated more than fifteen books. Her first one was *Bunny's Adventure*, which she declares is her great favorite. *Peter Churchmouse*, published in 1941, was unanimously chosen as the country's number one best seller of that year, and by April 1942 was in its thirty-fifth printing. Anne Eaton, in the New York *Times*, felt it had "the spontaneity of the child's own make-believe and a friendly bubbling humor."

Mrs. Austin writes of herself:

"I was born in Portland, Oregon, and studied at St. Mary's Academy there, as well as at the Emil Jacques European Art School in Portland. Then I went to New York City, where I studied at the National Academy of Design, the Grand Central Art School, and the Art Students League.

MARGOT AUSTIN AND YELLI

"In 1933, I married Darrel R. Austin, nationally known artist. We have one son, Darrel, born in July 1945. We now live in New Fairfield, Connecticut."

Since 1949, Mrs. Austin has written and illustrated the "Three Silly Kittens" page, as well as writing feature pages and doing many of the covers for the magazine *Jack and Jill*. In 1950 the book *The Three Silly Kittens* was published by Dutton. In 1956, her Churchmouse stories appeared in one volume which became a best seller in 1957.

Commenting on an earlier book by Mrs. Austin, *Barney's Adventure*, the late May Lamberton Becker wrote in the New York *Herald Tribune*: "Margot Austin is an illustrator with a distinctive style based upon disarming simplicity of spirit. She can draw children with instinctive tenderness, and animals with a child's sense of humor. She used both in this little fantasy of a brave tiny boy named Barney."

Margaret Ayer

AUTHOR AND ILLUSTRATOR OF
The Wish That Went Wild

ILLUSTRATOR OF
Anna and the King of Siam; Paddy and Sam; Golden Letter to Siam; Ranch of a Thousand Horns; Etc.

Autobiographical sketch of Margaret Ayer:

I WAS born in New York City at my grandmother's house during one of the periods when my parents were in the United States. My father was a doctor with a sense of adventure and during my childhood held positions in many foreign lands. He took the family with him, which made my education fairly informal, as we spent more time away from the United States than in it. However, this gave me a good background for my future work.

When my father decided to take a postgraduate course in tropical medicine in Philadelphia, I studied at the Museum School of Industrial Art where I was given a scholarship. My first published work was for the *Country Gentleman*, while I was still at school there. Later, I also studied in Paris and Rome.

There was some vague talent for art among my relatives, but I am the first one to work at it professionally. I have always

MARGARET AYER

wanted to as long as I can remember. My grandmother painted landscapes in oil in a ladylike manner. My aunts offered me some of these when I returned to New York and I most hastily refused them! When young, my aunts copied Gibson Girls in burnt wood and my father occasionally modeled a few figures which were very good, probably owing to his knowledge of anatomy.

My first recorded success was at five years of age when I drew a cow with all her equipment. At eight I drew palm trees which I remember as being very fine. Fortunately, none has survived. A little later my mother bought a paintbox for herself, with which she hoped to experiment sometime. After much begging she let me use it, though she had misgivings that I would mess up the paints. My picture was considered so good that I was given the box for my own. I have never had a gift that pleased me more.

When my father was Adviser in Public Health for Siam (now Thailand), I painted pictures which were sold at exhibitions in Bangkok, Penang, and Singapore. I saved a nest egg to take me to New York. A shipwreck added considerably to my funds. I had hopefully sent some pictures to a dealer in California. The ship struck a rock, the pictures were ruined, and I collected insurance!

When I returned to New York my knowledge of the Orient was a great help, for my first job was illustrating a serial on China for *St. Nicholas*. Remembering games of my childhood, I wrote and illustrated a book, *The Wish That Went Wild*. I have also had several short stories published. I intend to try and write some more but usually when I am about to start writing, a book by someone else turns up for me to illustrate. I have illustrated well over a hundred books, along with other types of work, including several books written by my sister, Phyllis Ayer Sowers.

I belong to the Society of Illustrators, the Women's National Book Association, and the Artists Guild, of which I was vice president. In the summer I go to Easton, Connecticut, where I own a home, three acres of land, 450 feet of river, and many large and beautiful trees. My husband, A. Babington Smith, works for a New York bank and my cocker spaniel, Taffy, does not work at all. We all move to New York in the winter and have a very pleasant life of two types which keeps us out of a rut.

Elizabeth Chesley Baity

1907-

AUTHOR OF

Man Is a Weaver; Americans Before Columbus; America Before Man; Etc.

Autobiographical sketch of Elizabeth Chesley Baity:

SHORTLY after *Americans Before Columbus* came out someone asked me, "When did you first become interested in Indians?"

"Why I've always been interested in Indians," I answered lamely. "Isn't everyone?"

The same was true of geology, paleontology, anthropology, and the game animals of Africa. It seems to me that being interested in such things is as much a part of childhood as measles, though in a nicer way. I've found children to have the same interests almost everywhere.

Growing up in Texas, one felt that Indians were just over the next hill. They had left behind them their flint arrowpoints, to become a part of the standard trading stock of an enterprising child. The dinosaurs, who obligingly left their footprints in some of the rocks at our place, had been gone a bit longer. And before them, strange sea animals had swum over what was to become

Baity: *BAY tee*

ELIZABETH CHESLEY BAITY

The next five books were produced in the South Sudan, just before the civil war which, to my sorrow, resulted in the death of one of my African co-writers. The last twelve were done in Tanganyika, a country which looks so like Texas that it was very hard for me to keep my sons, William and Philip, from patting lions on the head and saying, "Howdy, stranger!" when, after my job was done, we had a family safari. Bill and Philip have served nobly as fireside critics of my books. Now we want to write about East Africa, the zoo without cages.

Margaret J. Baker

1918-

AUTHOR OF

Homer the Tortoise; Homer Goes to Stratford; The Magic Sea Shell; A Castle and Sixpence; Etc.

Autobiographical sketch of Margaret J. Baker:

I WAS born in May 1918, at Reading, in Berkshire, England, a town of splendid toy shops, a ruined abbey, and a biscuit factory. My brother and I were always happy playing at motorcars in a small nursery warmed by a rosy gas fire, or making mud pies in the sunlit garden attended by a large bobtailed sheep dog. Most of all, we loved to listen to stories. My mother's throat often grew sore reading aloud to us so much. *Peter and Wendy* and *The Tailor of Gloucester* were our favorites, and *The Water Babies, Little Women,* Rudyard Kipling's *Puck of Pook's Hill* and *Kim, A Tale of Two Cities* and *Great Expectations,* and all the Nesbit books. The best of being read to was that we were never tied to any age group and our taste could range from Beatrix Potter to Dickens with little difficulty.

We lived in the country until I was about nine, when we moved to London. London was a treasure house. We wandered in the big stores which were as wonderful to us as Aladdin's cave. We caught tiddlers in the Round Pond in Kensington Gardens and threw silver sprats to the gulls calling and swooping in the gray winter sky. On wet days we explored the museums, sliding on the polished floors and pressing all the buttons on the working models in the Science Museum. I preferred the dolls' houses in

my home in Texas, leaving their bones to become fossilized in rock, or to end up ignominiously as doorstops. Naturally, one wondered why doorstops looked like fish, and what stone fish were doing so far from the sea.

When I was a child in Texas, I was like the little boy my New England uncle once told me about who wanted to be a whaler, "even if I only catch one whale a day." I wanted to discover unknown continents, if only one a month. But when I found virtually all explorers had been born boys, I wavered between wanting to be an actress, a writer or a missionary. It was a long time before that "last door opened," as we missionaries say. During the past few years, in a sense, I've been a "real, live missionary." That is, as the writer on the World Literacy and Christian Literature Team, I went forth to write little readers for grownups just learning to read. With the assistance of a varied collection of mission people and of native informants, some twenty-one little readers for adults have been produced.

We became the Swiss Family Baity in 1952, when my husband, a public health engineer, became a director in the World Health Organization. The first five of my readers were written in West Pakistan, where I found the tribal area just below the Khyber Pass strikingly like my native Texas and my Moslem colleagues quite congenial.

MARGARET J. BAKER

the Victoria and Albert Museum, and the embroidered waistcoat which was the same one that Beatrix Potter had drawn in *The Tailor of Gloucester.*

London was a friendly city, with scarlet open-top buses and fatherly policemen. Once we spent all our money on a birthday present for a relation and we had to walk home half across London. I went to a private day school called Roland Houses, in Rosary Gardens. There we read *The Waste Land* by T. S. Eliot, Keats and Shakespeare, and were shown the shimmering loveliness of *The Waves,* by Virginia Woolf I think it was her novels which first made me want to write. When I read *A Room of One's Own,* nothing seemed impossible.

I studied journalism at King's College in London for a while, and then we moved to Marlow in Buckinghamshire. Here I began to write in earnest, collecting a large number of rejection slips but on golden days articles were accepted.

When the war came we moved to Sussex. I drove a mobile canteen and writing had to be fitted in on my day off. I wrote adult short stories mostly, which appeared in *The Lady,* and other magazines. In 1943 a children's short story of mine was taken by *Child Life.* Its editor, the late Wilma K. McFarland, gave me great encouragement and I have been writing mainly for children ever since. At the close of the war I collected the stories which had appeared in *Child Life* and these were later published in

England in two volumes entitled *Treasure Trove* and *The Young Magicians.*

Homer the Tortoise and *Four Farthings and a Thimble* were my first books to be published in the United States. The first had the good fortune to be among the Honor Books in the 1950 New York *Herald Tribune* Spring Book Festival. *A Castle and Sixpence* and *Benbow and the Angels* have been dramatized as serials on the BBC television children's program. Altogether, I have written more than fifteen books for children.

My mother and I now live in Somerset in a cottage set on the Quantock Hills. We have four cats, two Pekes—Betsy Trotwood and Pippin Clatworthy—and two new tortoises, Homer and Flo. I write in a garden room. A honeysuckle grows up one side and a rose the other. It has three windows to catch the sun and the only noises are pigeons cooing, the baa of sheep, the call of a cuckoo, and at night an owl hooting in the apple trees. Our lane climbs to the top of the hills whose heather-covered slopes seem on a hot summer day to be close under heaven. It is their peace and loveliness I try now to share.

Rachel Baker

1903-

AUTHOR OF
*America's First Trained Nurse; Dr. Morton;
The First Woman Doctor;
Sigmund Freud; Etc.*

Autobiographical sketch of Rachel Baker:

I HAVE been called a writer for "young people." I write for people. In this country my biographies are often sold to the youth departments of libraries. In other countries my books have been translated for adults. One of my books, *Sigmund Freud,* published for young people by the original publisher, was reprinted in paperback for all types of readers. In my mind, there are no old or young readers, only readers.

I grew up in a whistle-stop town on the prairies of North Dakota, where the trains from the East to the West went through once a day, and the town throbbed for a moment with the vitality of their rumble. I was a child other children didn't play with because I was of a nationality different from that of the other children. As a result, I grew up with books rather than with children.

At home I read the many volumes of the *Oxford Encyclopedia of Medicine* in my father's bookcase. From this A-to-Z reading about medicine grew my interest in medicine, my work as a medical reporter, and finally my biographies of medical figures. From my aloneness in that North Dakota town came my need to know my racial origin deeply; the result, many years later, another biography, but not of a medical figure—the story of the refounder of Israel, *Chaim Weizmann: Builder of a Nation.*

I grew up in Dickinson, North Dakota. When I was nineteen my family moved to Minneapolis, where I attended the University of Minnesota, majoring in history. Before I was graduated, I went to Europe, where I rummaged in the British Museum in London, and satisfied my intellectual curiosity in Paris and in Berlin. Upon my return to America, I married a fellow student who taught me a great deal about writing. We founded a literary quarterly together. For half a lifetime we have taught writing groups. When our two children were small, I began to write, first medical articles, feature articles, then, in 1942, my first biography.

I have a life interest beside writing. With a woman handicapped by polio, I helped to found Resources Unlimited, a fellowship of physically handicapped and nonhandicapped people who study together in professionally taught groups. Their motto is "The only free bird is the mind." I believe so.

The great job in writing is to touch lives. I receive letters from India, Turkey, Iran, wherever my books have been translated. Books to me are bridges to other minds. I hope I shall always be able to build such bridges to reach others.

GLENN BALCH

Glenn Balch

1902-

AUTHOR OF

Tiger Roan; The Brave Riders; Wild Horse; Indian Saddle-Up; Etc.

Autobiographical sketch of Glenn Balch:

I WAS born in Venus, Texas, with a love for horses, dogs and the outdoors which I have never outgrown and hope I never will. This love has colored my whole life,

causing me to migrate to the land of high mountains and silver streams in Idaho, where I now live.

My desire to write developed early. I wrote my first short story at seventeen. It wasn't very good, and I know now that I owe a debt of gratitude to the editor of *Redbook* for rejecting it. It was about basketball, since at that time my main passion in life was to make the Baylor University team.

In addition to Baylor, I went to North Texas State at Denton, and to the University of Texas at Austin. Later, after my first book was accepted for publication, I did a term of postgraduate work in a course at Columbia University called "The Technique of the Novel." Oliver LaFarge was the instructor, and it was a lively and interesting experience.

Along the way I have accumulated a number of other unusual and interesting experiences which I draw on for source material in my writing. I did range riding and branding on West Texas cow ranches, and was a fire guard in Idaho for the Forest Service. I was snowbound in the high mountains for two winters, where I learned to drive sledge dogs and traveled on snowshoes and skis. I trapped marten, weasel, fox, badger and coyote, and hunted mountain goats on the high wind-blown ridges. The temperature got as low as 56 degrees below zero, and once I almost froze my fingers.

Balch: *BAWLCH*

During World War II, I spent four years in the Air Forces, and was in the China-Burma-India theater, where I was the commanding officer of a combat camera unit. Also I was in Alaska where, with a companion from the Coast Guard, I climbed the Hugh Miller glacier. In Alaska too I was shipwrecked when our boat hit a reef in Icy Strait.

But to me horses are more interesting than airplanes and boats. I have ridden ever since I can remember, and still do. I played polo, that fastest and most exciting of all horse games, for seven years. I have ridden on mountain trails and on the cavalry drill fields. And a lot of time I just rode, preferably where there were no roads or fences. One of my favorite places to ride is the big rough Owyhee country. Out there, on the long slopes, you can frequently get a glimpse of a wild horse—a real "slick," unbranded and yours if you're man enough to catch him. But that's not easy. Few things are wilder, or prettier.

I worked as a news reporter for five years, covering most of the regular "beats," from police court to the state legislature. I liked it, but I wanted to write fiction and magazine stories. So I quit and began free lancing. By getting up at five o'clock in the morning, I found that I could devote my afternoons to polo. For quite a few years the afternoons spent about all the mornings produced. But it was worth it, for I made the acquaintance of such game ponies as Jimmie Hicks, Queen Anne and The Hump-Backed Mare.

Along the way, I found time to get married, twice. And along with three delightful daughters and a son, I have produced some sixteen published books and a hundred or so magazine articles. And Freedoms Foundation at Valley Forge has three times given me George Washington Memorial awards for writings which were described as "outstanding achievement in bringing about a better understanding of the American Way of Life." I guess I'm pretty proud of the whole shebang.

* * *

Mr. Balch also received a Boys' Clubs of America Junior Book Award in 1951 for *Lost Horse*.

Laura Bannon

AUTHOR AND ILLUSTRATOR OF
Hat for a Hero; When the Moon Is New;
Red Mittens; Patty Paints a Picture; Etc.

Autobiographical sketch of Laura Bannon:

A FIRST copy of one of my picture books arrived in the morning mail. I unwrapped it with dread and hope. I dreaded the things that can so easily go wrong when as many as seven separate professional groups work to produce one small book. I hoped that, this once, the text, pictures, and format would be fitted together with the rightness of an egg in its shell. That proved to be too much to hope for but, still, it was something to work for on the next book.

My greatest single help in writing and illustrating books for children is the circumstance of having come from a large family. All eight of us lived out the noisy ups and downs of childhood on a hill overlooking Grand Traverse Bay, Michigan. I baby-sat my way through Traverse City High School, tutored my way through two years at Western Michigan State College, and did odd—very odd—jobs to earn my way through four years of training at the School of the Art Institute of Chicago. I painted on velvet, beaded lampshades, turned out designs for Christmas cards when the rent came due, did drawings of a sinus operation, and once

LAURA BANNON

I repainted a man's false ear to match his suntan.

I stayed on at the Art Institute to teach and, as a member of the Chicago Society of Artists, I was another exhibiting artist who exhibited far more than she sold. The stack of easel paintings grew. And with it grew my sense of futility. So much work of so little real use! I was more stimulated by the children's books I did on the side. They were used and I was paid for doing them.

Now I squeeze in time for an easel painting now and then but most of my working hours are spent on books for boys and girls. Many of the books are regional because I am so curious about out-of-the-way places. I become intrigued by a certain spot and then, sooner or later, I find myself, armed with colored chalk and a sketch pad, sitting on that spot—a houseboat near the Golden Gate Bridge, a llama trail in the Andes, a Seminole Indian camp in the Everglades, an island in Mexico where the huge butterfly dip nets are made, a Nova Scotia pilot boat bringing a freighter from the Bay of Fundy into Digby, a bathhouse in Japan.

Whenever possible I live native style in order to soak in the native point of view. The story plot is dreamed up after I return to my studio. Recently a breathy child voice spoke to me over the telephone.

"Is this the Laura Bannon who makes books? Well, that doll in your book is exactly what I have been looking for. Can I buy her?"

I remembered my disappointment in that particular book. Its parts had certainly failed to fit together like an egg in its shell. But now I feel better about it.

* * *

Miss Bannon has written and illustrated over twenty books, the first being published in 1939. Before that, she had illustrated two books, and altogether has illustrated five books which she did not write. Eight of her own books have been selected by the Junior Literary Guild, and two that she illustrated. One of her own books and one illustrated by her received awards from the Chicago Society of Typographical Arts, while one of her titles was an Honor Book in the New York *Herald Tribune* Spring Book Festival.

Hetty Burlingame Beatty
1907-

AUTHOR AND ILLUSTRATOR OF
*Little Wild Horse; Saint Francis and the Wolf;
Droopy; Thumps; Etc.*

Autobiographical sketch of Hetty Burlingame Beatty:

I WAS born in New Canaan, Connecticut, but have spent most of my life in New York State, Massachusetts, and Colorado. Most of the years have been spent either on a farm or a ranch, or as close to one as I could get. Loving horses most of all, I began drawing them as soon as I could hold a pencil and have been drawing them ever since, along with many other animals.

I went to school in Syracuse, New York, where I spent most of the time drawing animals on every piece of paper that came to hand. My other strongest leaning from the start was toward writing. In 1924 I went to the School of the Boston Museum of Fine Arts, where I studied sculpture and drawing, under Charles Grafly and George Demetrios, aided by two scholarships. In 1929 I went to Europe, where I spent two years traveling, and continuing my work in sculpture in Florence and Rome. After returning to the United States in 1931, I settled on Cape Ann, Massachusetts, and continued working in sculpture for several

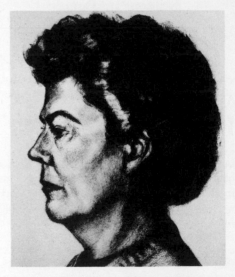

From drawing by Margaret D. Nelson
HETTY BURLINGAME BEATTY

years and exhibiting in many of the national exhibitions.

During these years I spent many happy evenings telling bedtime stories to my friends' children and drawing pictures to go with them. In 1946 I wrote my first children's book and illustrated it. I have been doing it ever since and thoroughly enjoying it.

Drawing seemed to come naturally to me from the start, but learning to read was something else again. I knew that stories came out of books and I loved them from the beginning. But whenever confronted with a page of incomprehensible type I simply composed my own story as I went along, solemnly turning the pages at what seemed the proper intervals. This led to considerable despair on the part of both my parents and teachers, but left me entirely happy with what I considered the process of "reading." I did, however, finally master the subject, and having done so became an immensely enthusiastic reader in all subjects. At one point, being short of new books to delve into, I remember reading an encyclopedia from start to finish with total fascination.

Five years ago I designed and built a little house near the top of Pigeon Hill in Rockport, Massachusetts, and have been happily continuing the children's books there, along with some serious adult writing.

NELSON F. BEELER

Nelson F. Beeler

1910-

CO-AUTHOR OF

Experiments in Science; Experiments with Electricity; Experiments with Atomics; Experiments with a Microscope; Etc.

Autobiographical sketch of Nelson F. Beeler:

I WAS born in Adams, Massachusetts, a small town in the Berkshire Hills. Since I was the youngest of four children, I have had to work hard, of course, to keep from being spoiled. All of my writing has been in the field of science. My early adventures with science were never very satisfying. Most of the stuff that the books said would be fun to use was either not available, expensive, or not acceptable to my mother. Part of the fun I have in working out experiments with my own children and my students is a holdover from the time when

I was anxious to try experiments but found them beyond my means.

My first scientific work was done when I was about ten. At that time I did quite a job on a zinc-lined sink belonging to my family. I cannot recall just how I goofed on that particular experiment but it very nearly wrecked a fine chemical career at the outset! I went to high school in Adams, then on to the state college (now the University of Massachusetts), to study chemistry. I worked my way through college cooking in a diner, waiting on tables, and doing a little exhibition Charleston dancing.

Right after college I began teaching high school in my home town and then spent ten enjoyable years teaching science in Nyack, New York. It was there that Franklyn Branley and I shared a small equipment-room office and from this headquarters we wrote for several years the science page for *Young America*, a publication then used extensively in the schools.

I taught science through the war years and was a civilian instructor in navigation and meteorology. After the war I went to Clarkson College of Technology in Potsdam, New York, to teach chemistry. When the teachers college, a unit of the State University of New York, offered me a position I snapped it up. I had kept on writing for children all this time and now I had a chance to do the two things I like best to do —teach science to college students and teachers, and work with children on their science problems.

I have a master's degree from Columbia University and my doctoral study at New York University deals with children's science books starting back with 1800. I still like to drop in at old bookstores with the hope of adding another fascinating old-timer to my collection. One of our jacket blurbs says that "the Beeler kitchen always bubbles with activity as Mr. Beeler and his four children test the experiments for use in his science books." Two of these "bubblers," Debby and Dick, are at college now. Debby plans to be a kindergarten teacher and Dick a mathematician. This leaves only Chuck and Linda to carry on the great scientific tradition at home.

We live in an old rambling house with lots of room for snakes, rocks, and such like, and space in the cellar to hold a marvelous collection of tin cans, bottles, candle ends, and bits of string which will one day become scientific equipment of great value. My wife, Marion, who was once a nurse, keeps us all clean and neat and well fed. She still finds time to work in a cancer lab taking care of mice. We call her Marion the Marvelous Mouse Minder. As a family we all like to roam the woods to picnic and fish, and then to come back home to read and read and read.

* * *

In 1962 Mr. Beeler was the recipient of the Thomas Alva Edison Foundation award for the best science book for children for *Experiments in Sound*. Most of his earlier books were written with the collaboration of Franklyn M. Branley, whose sketch appears elsewhere in this volume.

Harry Behn

1898-

AUTHOR AND ILLUSTRATOR OF
The Little Hill; All Kinds of Time; Windy Morning; The House Beyond the Meadow; etc.

Autobiographical sketch of Harry Behn:

ONE summer evening, thirty years ago, after a picnic, I wrote a little poem for my children called "This Happy Day." They liked it, and recited it, and asked for another, and another. As they grew out of childhood, I almost forgot about these

HARRY BEHN

poems; almost. Twenty years later they were published. How delighted I was to discover that other children liked them, too! Pamela, Prescott, and Peter had grown up, but soon there were grandchildren, and so, from time to time, I write another book for them. Now I am doing what I always wanted most to do but never mentioned to anyone, it seemed so improbable a career.

All my other jobs were interesting, and some very exciting. After I graduated from Harvard in 1922, where I was a member of Professor Baker's 47 Workshop, I started a little theater in Phoenix, Arizona. Then I was sent to Sweden disguised as a scholar. After wandering a while about Europe, I drifted to Hollywood where I wrote scenarios for several movies, including *La Bohème, The Crowd, Hotel Imperial, The Racket, The Big Parade,* and *Hell's Angels*. Then I taught at the University of Arizona, lived on a small ranch, organized and directed the university radio bureau, founded and edited the *Arizona Quarterly*, worked very hard for the Tucson Regional Plan, and I can't remember what else, all at once. With a burst of ambition, I organized a broadcasting company, sold it, and moved to Greenwich, Connecticut.

Here, my wife and I live in a beautiful house made out of an old barn in the middle of a lovely wood, and I write poems and stories for children. Greenwich reminds me of mountainous Arizona where I grew up.

I was born in McCabe, a mining camp, now a ghost town, but my earliest memories are of Prescott, with its Army post to guard us against the Apaches, or the Apaches from us, I'm not sure. But many of the people came from New England; there were pines and oak trees, and a real winter, and frogs peeping in the spring, just as they are today, here in Greenwich. I must go out now and see how much more the leaf buds have opened. . . .

Margaret E. Bell

1898-

AUTHOR OF

Daughter of Wolf House; Watch for a Tall White Sail; Love Is Forever; Ride Out the Storm; Etc.

Autobiographical sketch of Margaret E. Bell:

Lotte Jacobi

MARGARET E. BELL

ON December 29, 1898, I was born to young pioneers at Thorn Bay on Prince of Wales Island in southeast Alaska. My grandparents came to this island panhandle of the territory in the early 1880's. They were not seeking gold but came to settle and build in the salmon industry. One branch was a seafaring family. The other grandfather had the urge of his time, to travel to new places and find unspoiled ground. He left a cultivated background to travel halfway around the world and finally settle in Alaska which reminded him of "a wee bit of Scotland." Both families were Scottish, vigorous and romantic, bequeathing to me a mountain of writing material which I have been, and still am, mining.

My own childhood and youth in the Icy Strait country north of here provides still more Alaskan experience which, so far, I have touched upon in *Ride Out the Storm* and three early boys' books. I remember well my mother and my aunt pioneering in long skirts and hats and veils. They were not like the pioneers of the western states, for they traveled by ship and brought their finery and china teacups with them. Our part of the family, myself and a brother and sister with our parents and an uncle, lived at my father's salmon cannery in the wilds of this immense country. I, the youngest, came to love this life and even more to love the freedom that it gives and the wonder evoked by the mysterious and beautiful action of nature.

I was educated at the Annie Wright Seminary in Tacoma, Washington, and later at the University of Washington, spending my summers and vacations in Alaska during that time. I tried to settle into the conventional urban life of civilized places but I was not happy. I found myself repeatedly telling stories of Alaska life to youngsters. They would keep asking for more. Finally, I began writing the early boys' books. When the war came, I returned to the Northland, to Canada, Alaska, and the Aleutian Islands, to work in Army hospitals for the American Red Cross. I found that, indeed, this land is my great love. I like to write about young characters because I remember the intense living of every moment of my own life in such close communication with nature. During the years between thirteen and seventeen, first experiences come rushing at one. First decisions must be made, and every decision is a story.

I live now, by myself, in a cabin above the water's edge. I have time to watch the sea birds, the whales that come into the bay, the bears with their cubs, families of otter and mink, and the wild swans of the Naha lakes. My neighbors are homesteaders and fishermen and trappers. In the summer, vacationers and visitors come. Every two or three years I take a trip to New York to refresh myself with that mental food that only human beings in civilized places can provide. While there, I talk to my readers in the schools and the libraries and, armed with the stimulation derived from this, I return to write some more.

Now it is April again and the bears are coming out of hibernation. The wild geese and cranes pass swiftly over Naha Bay and the songbirds arrive daily. If I am lucky, I may come across a newborn fawn, for I know where a doe is awaiting her time on a little island at the mouth of the bay.

Ludwig Bemelmans

1898-1962

AUTHOR AND ILLUSTRATOR OF
Hansi; The Golden Basket; Madeline; Madeline's Rescue; Etc.

LUDWIG Bemelmans was born the son of a Belgian painter, on August 27, 1898, in Meran, a part of the Tyrol which was then Austrian territory. He attended school in Bavaria, first in Regensburg and later at a private academy in Rothenburg. Then he was taken out of school and apprenticed for two years to an uncle who owned several resort hotels in the Tyrolean Alps. At sixteen he set out for America, armed with letters to managers of various hotels in New York City. There he worked at the Astor, the McAlpin, and the Ritz-Carleton. His experience in these hotels provided the background for his adult sto-

Tony Venti
LUDWIG BEMELMANS

ries about the "Hotel Splendide." He also studied painting.

When the United States entered World War I Bemelmans enlisted. He described his experiences later in *My War with the United States*. After the war he planned to go to Munich to continue his study of painting, but remained in the hotel business until 1925, when he became part owner of Hapsburg House, a restaurant on New York's East Side. On its walls he painted all kinds of pictures, and even after he was no longer associated with the restaurant the murals remained. He also painted, on the window shades of his apartment, Tyrolean landscapes that reminded him of his birthplace. One day when May Massee, editor of children's books for Viking Press, was visiting Bemelmans in his home, she saw these landscapes. She persuaded him that he should write and illustrate a book for children. This was the origin of his first children's book, *Hansi*. In 1939 *Madeline* was published. His Caldecott Medal book, *Madeline's Rescue*, is about the same child. How he came to write both Madeline books, Bemelmans related engagingly:

"I had been in France, spending the summer on a small island called l'Île d'Yeu. While there, I had a bicycle and rode it to the beach and back. . . . I did not know there was a motorcar on the island. It was a motorized breadbasket that belonged to the baker of Saint Sauveur, the fishing village on the island. One day the motorcar came racing around a curve, hidden from view by pine trees. We met. I flew off the bicycle into the trees. . . . I was sufficiently cut up to go to the hospital in Saint Sauveur.

"The sisters in that small hospital wore large, starched white hats that looked like the wings of a giant butterfly. In the room next to mine was a little girl who had had her appendix out. In the ceiling over my bed was a crack 'that had the habit of sometimes looking like a rabbit.' That's the way I rhymed it, a year later, . . . for my first *Madeline*.

"Ever since *Madeline* . . . people have asked me for another. . . . Time passed, and I went again to Paris. I had a studio there, and I had a dog. I used to take long walks along the river Seine, and my dog liked to run down and swim in the river. One day as I sat there, some little schoolgirls . . .

passed in a long line. They crossed the bridge that is called Le Pont Royal. . . . Then the idea for a story came." [1]

The name of his most famous character was borrowed from his wife, the former Madeline Freund, whom he married in 1935. Their daughter, Barbara, was their only child.

[1] From *Young Wings*, former magazine of The Junior Literary Guild, book club for boys and girls aged 6 to 16. p 12-13. August 1953. Reprinted by permission.

Margot Benary-Isbert

1889-

AUTHOR OF

Dangerous Spring; Blue Mystery; Wicked Enchantment; Rowan Farm; Etc.

Autobiographical sketch of Margot Benary-Isbert:

MARGOT BENARY-ISBERT

I WAS born in Saarbrücken, but brought up in Frankfort on the Main, the old imperial city where the Holy Roman Emperors were crowned and where young Goethe grew up. It is a town with a stimulating background of history and legend. I can't say how early I started to tell stories to my younger sister and brother. As our mother died early and we were brought up by a succession of governesses, it seems that we had to make up a world of our own.

At ten or eleven, I started to write and have been writing ever since. My first short stories were published in magazines when I was nineteen. I went to high school in Frankfort, and after that to a convent on the Rhine for two years—finishing school, as one used to call it. There was much dancing with gay young officers in colorful uniforms of before-World-War-I times.

I planned to be an actress, a dancer, a painter in oils (as that did not need much drawing, my weak point), or a journalist. But life was always full of surprises for me. When I had started to study journalism at Frankfort University, the professor of ethnology asked me to be his secretary. There followed seven years at the Frankfort Völkermuseum, a wonderful time with much rich experience. One of my books for adults is about this time, *Mädchen für Alles (Maid of All Work)*. I met my husband at the museum and we were married in 1917.

Then came much traveling all over Europe, breeding Great Danes on the old place of my husband's family in Thuringia, bringing up our daughter, and in my spare time writing short stories and poems for magazines. From 1933 to 1945 I could not publish anything as I did not join the Nazi writers' organization. So I wrote only for our friends and read aloud to them in the long hours we spent in the bomb shelter.

In the spring of 1945 the American Army took over our town but after ten weeks left us to the Russians. We had had enough of one dictatorship and decided to go away and leave everything behind. First came a few months on Rowan Farm at our good friend Mrs. Almut's, then we settled in a little town in West Germany, near Göttingen and Kassel. For six years we lived in two tiny rooms. At last I had time to write again, and, as German youths were so much in need of encouragement and hope, I started to write children's books.

In 1952 we followed our daughter to this country and in 1953 my first book, *The Ark*, was published here. *Blue Mystery* is about our own family and the old house and garden in Thuringia. Some of my books have been published in England, Sweden, Finland, Japan, and South Africa. Since 1955 I have lived in California near my daughter and her family. I am now an American citizen.

Benary-Isbert: *BEN a ree ISS bert*

Jeanne Bendick

1919-

AUTHOR AND ILLUSTRATOR OF
*All Around You; How Much and How Many;
The First Book of Space Travel; The
Blonk from Beneath the Sea; Etc.*

and

Robert Bendick

1917-

CO-AUTHOR OF
Television Works Like This

Biographical sketch of Jeanne and Robert Bendick, by Jeanne Bendick:

BOB and I were both born in New York City, he in 1917, I in 1919, and we've known each other since our early teens. He went to DeWitt Clinton High School, to the New York University School of Engineering for a while and then, deciding he wanted to be a photographer instead of an engineer, to the Clarence White School of Photography. I went to the High School of Music and Art, when it was just starting, and then to the Parsons School of Design, where I studied illustration.

We were married in 1940, and Bob went to work at the Columbia Broadcasting System, as one of the first television cameramen in the country. This was before television stations were even broadcasting! When the war came, he joined the First Motion Picture Unit of the Air Force, and spent almost three years in the China-Burma-India theater, while I settled down to illustrating children's books, which was the thing I had always wanted to do. (Lucky me!)

It was during this time that I became interested in the new science of electronics. Doing research on the subject I was disappointed at not finding any simple books, so there didn't seem anything else to do but write one myself. Science has always been my great interest, and I have written a number of science books since then, in addition to illustrating almost sixty.

Since the war, we have moved back and forth from New York to California several times. Bob has worked in television and the movies, being the co-producer and director of the first two Cinerama pictures, producer of "Wide Wide World" for the National Broadcasting Company, and is now executive producer of "Today." I've kept busy too, averaging four or five books a year.

We have two children, Rob, Jr., and Candy. Rob likes to sail and Candy is half horse, but they both like to draw and write too. These days, I get most of the ideas for books from them and their friends, who seem curious about everything (which is, of course, the best way to be).

We live in Rye, New York, in a very old house right on the water. We especially like sailing, exploring, and doing things together. We have a large, shapeless, silly dog named Guido who takes care of us all.

JEANNE BENDICK

Bettina

1903-

AUTHOR AND ILLUSTRATOR OF
*Cocolo; A Horse for the Island; Carmello;
Castle in the Sand; Etc.*

Autobiographical sketch of Bettina Ehrlich, who uses only her first name as a pen name:

OFTEN I have wondered how I come to be so interested in children, having had none of my own, and I believe that an uncommonly vivid recollection of my own childhood accounts for it.

I was born in Vienna, Austria, in 1903, a delicate child who at the age of one and a half years could not yet stand on its legs.

Because of this deplorable fact my sister and I were taken to Grado, a sunny island in the northern Adriatic Sea. After one summer of roasting in its sands and bathing in its shallow sea, I walked like all children of my age. My father built a house in Grado and ever since I have spent every summer of my life there, except in the two wars. The ancient town, the fishing folk, and the scenery of this island have formed the inspiration and background for my books.

I had a passion for concocting pictorial stories from the age of five onward, using the same method as now: to draw and write at the same time. My mother, herself a painter, encouraged my love for the arts. My father, director of a coal-mining concern, invented exciting little stories, mostly about naughty children. It may be that the inheritance of these parental gifts made me a writer-illustrator.

When I was five years old I began to learn French and two years later started on English. For three years we had an English governess so that we spoke the language fluently, which proved a blessing later in life. My spelling, however, was always a headache to my governess.

I went to school in Vienna and got into trouble when once, during the geography lesson, I drew the French murderer Landru, who was being much talked about among adults, with his huge barrel filled with the corpses of his dead wives. Since then I have lost all interest in murder stories.

At the age of seventeen I entered art school (Wiener Kunstgewerbeschule) and later experimented in many techniques, lithography, etching, oils, water color, woodcut and linoleum cut. I spent two years in Berlin and one in Paris and exhibited in both cities.

In 1930, in Vienna, I married Georg Ehrlich, who was already famous as a sculptor and draftsman. We traveled much in Italy, which we both love. I printed my first two children's books on a hand press in 1932. Later, I began to print and paint on silk. At the International Exhibition of Arts and Industries in Paris, in 1937, I was awarded a silver medal for hand-painted silks.

In 1938, when Hitler had invaded Austria, we settled in London and later became British citizens. During the war, Chatto & Windus in London published my first books.

BETTINA

Many a night I took the pictures to the air-raid shelter. In 1947, several portrait commissions for my husband took us to the U.S.A., where Harper & Brothers were preparing my first American edition. We stayed in America for eighteen months and have retained not only the most delightful memories but also some lasting friendships.

When children come to my husband's studio to be portrayed, I usually entertain them with games and stories and find that I learn a lot from their reactions.

Hobbies? I collect small Greek terra cottas, I adore traveling, I love to sit with my husband on some beautiful Italian piazza doing nothing except drinking black coffee, smoking, and watching all that goes on.

Betty Betz

1920-

AUTHOR AND ILLUSTRATOR OF
*Party Book; Your Manners Are Showing;
Teen-Age Cook Book; Etc.*

BETTY Betz was born in Hammond, Indiana, where she says she was a typical teen-ager, taking part in all high school activities and in the student government. She was voted the most popular among eighteen hundred students and was crowned prom queen. At sixteen she became the women's Middle Western swimming cham-

BETTY BETZ

pion, and won the Illinois State title, breaking the world's record for the hundred yard free style.

She went to Sarah Lawrence College, and when she was chosen guest fashion editor for an annual college issue of *Mademoiselle*, her career was launched. Two pages of sketches and cartoons in that August issue enabled her to face art directors. After college, she became a fashion copywriter on *Harper's Bazaar*. Later, she wrote a monthly feature for *Seventeen* and for the *Woman's Home Companion*.

Miss Betz then turned to books. Her first was *Your Manners Are Showing*, a popular guide to etiquette for teen-agers. She wrote a syndicated newspaper column for teen-agers for six years and other books for young people came from these columns, all of the self-help or "how to" variety. She now designs clothes, greeting cards, stationery, jewelry, scarves, and scrapbooks. She has lectured from coast to coast and is in touch with young people everywhere.

While a college freshman, Miss Betz was sent by her parents with a missionary and his wife to Japan, where she lived with Japanese families. Years later she went around the world by plane, writing about youth in twenty-two countries. On this trip Miss Betz was awarded a citation from the French Government for helping children in the Montmartre district of Paris. In London she interviewed George Bernard Shaw, some-

thing veteran newsmen were unable to do. She sent bank firsthand reports of the way Poland and Czechoslovakia treated their young people, and the Communists criticized her violently in their publications. For her work on this trip she was presented with the Campfire Girls' highest award, the Wohelo. In 1950 she spent several months as a UN war correspondent in Korea.

Miss Betz is married to Frank McMahon, of Calgary, Alberta, and commutes between there and New York with her small daughter, Francine, born in 1957.

Elisa Bialk

1912-

AUTHOR OF
The Horse Called Pete; Wild Horse Island; Taffy's Foal; Jill's Victory; Etc.

Autobiographical sketch of Elisa Bialk:

CHICAGO is my home town. I was born there, grew up there, married there, and now, with my husband and two daughters, I live in one of its suburbs, Winnetka.

I cannot remember when I first started to write, because it seems as if I have always written. As a child I turned to it naturally, instinctively, growing into it as if it were a second skin. By the time I reached high school, writing was already a way of life. When I won a prize with the first poem I wrote, I concentrated on poetry for several years. The crowning achievement of this period was publication in *Poetry: A Magazine of Verse,* and a chance to know Harriet Monroe, who invited me to her poetry soirees and gave me some good advice. It was she who suggested that I try writing fiction because, she said, my poems showed "dramatic slices of life."

While still in my teens I began to sell short stories to national magazines. Also while in my teens, I wrote a novel, *On What Strange Stuff,* which was selected for publication by Burton Rascoe as one of two "discoveries" of the year. Magazine editor Herbert Mayes bought six of my short stories within several months; one of them, "The Sainted Sisters," was selected by Edward J. O'Brien for his annual *Best Short Stories* volume.

During this period all of my writing was done evenings, in my free time from the

Elisa Bialk: *ee LISS uh BAWLK*

and gratifying experience that it opened an entirely new field to me. I continued to write a book or two a year for children, keying each to the age of my daughters, and have had fourteen published. Now that my daughters are teen-agers, I have gone back to writing for younger children, and am at present concentrating on a series about a pony named Tizz.

ELISA BIALK

newspaper job I had taken after graduating from high school. I was the assistant editor and columnist of the *Lincoln-Belmont Booster,* now the largest community newspaper in Chicago. I also contributed poetry and short stories to the Chicago *Daily News,* and feature articles to the Chicago *Tribune.* Although I do not have a college degree, I carried special courses at Northwestern University whenever I could fit in the time. Later, I also taught an evening course in short-story writing, but I came to the conclusion that I could not write and teach. Each is a taxing job in itself.

With my marriage to L. Martin Krautter, an advertising executive, in 1934, my career became of secondary importance, although I have always continued free-lance writing in the background. This writing has taken various forms, accumulating in over two hundred published short stories and articles covering a wide range. I also wrote a play based on my short story "The Sainted Sisters," which was made into a movie by Paramount Pictures. For several years I wrote a monthly column for *Household* magazine.

To me, the most significant professional step I took was the decision to expand a short story I had had published, "The Horse Called Pete," into a book for children. I wrote it for my own two daughters, Elena and Libby, and found it such a pleasurable

Henry Billings

1901-

AUTHOR AND ILLUSTRATOR OF
Construction Ahead; All Down the Valley; Man Under Water; Bridges; Etc.

Autobiographical sketch of Henry Billings:

I WAS the youngest boy at an Episcopalian preparatory school in New England the year (1912) I entered the first form. I received more demerits, black marks, or whatever you want to call them, than any other student that year at school. Five years later I was asked to leave long before graduation. I had learned nothing and my teachers gave me up as hopeless. There followed two years of knocking around at odd jobs before I landed at the Art Students League in New York. At last I knew just what I wanted to do and despite the turmoil of the twenties and the depression that followed, I stuck to painting as the most important thing in my life.

During the war I was in the Air Forces making training films. When it was over, I tried my hand at illustrating children's books and, finding that editors were human beings, I had the audacity to attempt to write my own text. When I began, I had no idea that I could or would ever write on semitechnical subjects. I always had had a romantic admiration for the engineer. His railroads, his highways, his dams and bridges often seemed to me as beautiful as any contemporary work of art. That may have been my initial interest, but it was immediately followed by the problem of the why and how that made these complicated structures possible. My technical training did not exceed that of an average twelve-year-old. However, this gave me a good yardstick for understanding and I knew that once I had translated an abstract principle

HENRY BILLINGS AND GEOFFREY

into language simple enough for me to comprehend, my reader would have no difficulty.

Though I say I learned nothing at school, that is not exact, for I memorized the whole alphabet of boredom. It had been drummed into me how thin and flat the most fascinating subjects could become when crushed under the old pedagogical steamroller. Julius Caesar was an adventurer, not so many paragraphs of Latin prose. A bridge is not only an arithmetic equation, but also the balancing of dynamic and dangerous forces. If my books fill any need it is only because I have tried to make the obvious and commonplace as interesting as I could.

* * *

Mr. Billings added: "I consider myself a professional painter, not an author, and my painting career has covered more than a quarter of a century."

Since 1949, Mr. Billings has written and illustrated a book a year. He has a fine reputation as a muralist and painter, and has exhibited at a number of galleries. His wife, Augusta, is also a writer, and they collaborate on books. They spend most of their time on a hundred-acre farm in Rhinebeck, New York. He says they do not travel very much, being too busy carrying on "a hot and cold war with nature, trying to keep the farm in shape."

Ilse Bischoff
1903-

AUTHOR AND ILLUSTRATOR OF
*The Wonderful Poodle; Drive Slowly—
Six Dogs*

AUTHOR OF
Proud Heritage; Painter's Coach

Autobiographical sketch of Ilse Bischoff:

I WAS born in New York City. My father was German; therefore I learned to speak German before I did English. I read children's books in that language long before I tackled English ones. Two of these books, *Max and Moritz* and *Slovenly Peter*, are famous in translation. Their illustrations enchanted me as much as the verses and I think I must have, at the early age of five, wanted to draw amusing pictures for children's books. Certainly those drawings became the pattern of my ideal for illustrations because they have line, color, and humor.

I had a difficult time in kindergarten at first, as I couldn't converse with the children, but at last I learned English. Hardly had I achieved facility in it, than we went to Europe for a year, and I again spoke only German and had to relearn English when we returned. In that year abroad I saw the beautiful country, valleys, and streams which seemed to come right out of fairy tales. There I saw castles and moats and dungeons, the magic background of *Grimm's Fairy Tales*. The net result of speaking two languages opened another country's culture to me even at that time.

My childhood summers were spent in Rockland County, in New York State, in a house across the road from my grandfather's turreted Victorian one. I loved his big gloomy house, but best of all I loved his garden. When he took his grandchildren around its winding paths and pointed out favorite flowers and trees, he laid the foundation for my future love of the country and gardening. Now, in my own garden, I often start with delight when I see a remembered flower or tree. They seem a link to youth and my grandfather.

I attended Horace Mann School in New York City from kindergarten through graduation and after the diploma was in my hand I entered a new world, that of drawing and

Ilse Bischoff: *ILL zuh BISH off*

ILSE BISCHOFF AND COCO

were made from studies of all my poodles, which numbered five at the time. My dog life with these poodles and two beloved dachshunds appeared in an adult book in 1953. From letters I have received, it seems to have become general family reading for children and parents. I decorated the chapter headings but they can hardly be called illustrations.

I spend winters in New York City, and spring, summer, and autumn, unless I go to Europe, in an eighteenth century brick house in Vermont, with four dogs. There I have a studio built of old barn boards. While I paint, opera recordings resound through the high vaulted room. I change my garden every year, as most gardeners do, and hope that in the following year, as most gardeners hope, it will be the best ever.

painting. After attending the Parsons School of Design, I went to Paris to study. It was the first time I had been in any European country besides Germany and I fell in love with the French, their country, and above all the beauty of France's past. Some years later I went for further studies in Munich, where I turned from applied design to the fine arts. Later, in New York, I illustrated my first children's book which pleased me, *Hansel the Gander*. Many books and years passed between that one and the next whose illustrations I enjoyed drawing, *Gigi, the Story of a Merry-Go-Round Horse,* by Elizabeth Foster.

Through all those years it never occurred to me to write as well as illustrate books. But in 1940 I thought, "Why shouldn't I do just that?" I began to study writing in Professor Mabel Louise Robinson's famous workshop at Columbia University. As a result, *Painter's Coach*, the story of itinerant painters in the early nineteenth century, appeared. I did not illustrate it. I was working on *Gigi* at the time and was so impatient to see my first written effort on the bookshelves that I wouldn't wait for another season when I would have time to illustrate it.

In 1949, my first combined book of writing and illustrating a children's story came out, *The Wonderful Poodle*. The material for this story came from watching my own charming poodle Coco, and the drawings

Sonia Bleeker

1909-

AUTHOR OF

The Inca: Indians of the Andes; The Cherokee: Indians of the Mountains; The Seminole Indians; Indians of the Longhouse; Etc.

Autobiographical sketch of Sonia Bleeker:

AS I write, the broad Atlantic, now an emerald green, shimmers in the sun. We had quite a rainstorm last night that kept us awake half the night, but we were grateful for the rain. Our small vegetable garden and shrubbery needed it. We get very little rain here on the Florida Keys. Fresh water is piped all the way from Homestead—forty miles to the north.

Between our study and the ocean is a stretch of white coral sand, now pimpled with grass we planted two months ago, in the hope of starting a lawn. We built this house as close to the water as we dared. It's a two-story structure that faces the ocean. Upstairs, in our living quarters, we left an open (screened) space about a foot wide between the roof and walls. So the house is always full of moving air. In windy weather it is like being on a boat instead of the solid, cement block home it is. We purposely built a large house so we would have ample space to display our Indian collection of baskets, pottery, rugs, and beadwork. For too many years these have been packed away in moth-

SONIA BLEEKER

balls and we were deprived of enjoying them daily.

My husband, Herbert S. Zim, who is also a writer, has his desk opposite mine. He dictates some of his stuff on a dictaphone, but I write everything on an electric typewriter.

Living here in the subtropics on Plantation Key, midway between Miami and Key West, is "quite a piece" from my early beginnings. Although, as you can see from the above photograph, I'm not old, yet my life spans two very different historical periods and two countries. I was born half-a-globe distance away in White Russia and lived under the Czar. It was a "must" in our daily prayers to include the Czar and his family. We always said, "God save the Czar!" Then came the Russian Revolution and everyone seemed happy that we were on the way toward a democracy—like America. But events took a turn toward communism and so my parents managed to get us out of Russia.

I don't recall when I was not interested in the ways other people live, especially the American Indians. But I did not get a chance to see the Southwest and Indian country until I was almost out of college. We liked it so much we almost made New Mexico our home. We still spend some time there each year. The town where I lived as a child in Russia seemed no different from some of the pueblos in New Mexico and

Arizona. Perhaps that's why I feel so at home among the Indians. In Russia we used clay pots and pans, too. We watched the potters fire their pottery once a week. We baked our own bread, slaughtered our own sheep and pigs. We hauled water from the town well, just as they do in most of the pueblos today. We spun and wove our own everyday clothing, our linen and rugs. Instead of moccasins, we wore bast sandals.

After I finished college and wanted to do graduate work, it was a tossup between journalism and anthropology. I finally chose anthropology and entered Columbia University, studying under Franz Boas and Ruth Benedict. One day, while reading stories about Indians to my two boys, I looked for books that would tell how the Indians lived. There were very few such books for their age level (eight to twelve). A friend of mine, a publisher, suggested that I write such a book. We lived in New York at the time and used to visit friends at the Onondaga Reservation near Syracuse. I therefore began with a story of the Iroquois Indians. In all, I've written twelve books in the series of North American Indian profiles. Prior to writing my first Indian book, I worked for many years for book publishers, wrote some short stories, made some translations from the Russian, and, with Margarita Madrigal, wrote a little book on learning Russian, *An Invitation to Russian*.

I am very fortunate that here my liking for the outdoor life is so well met. My hobbies are swimming, sailing and fishing, camping, tennis and badminton. Someday I hope to set up a loom here on the patio to continue with my weaving.

Glenn O. Blough

1905-

AUTHOR OF

Soon After September; Wait for the Sunshine; After the Sun Goes Down; Not Only for Ducks; Etc.

Autobiographical sketch of Glenn Blough:

I WAS born in Michigan where the winters are cold, spring wonderful, summer a great growing time, and autumn beautiful with color and harvest. I lived on a farm until I was eleven, and perhaps that is why I have always liked animals, green growing things, the sky, and everything out of doors.

Blough: *BLOU*

After graduating from the University of Michigan, I began to teach science in junior high school and because I needed reading material in this field for my students that was not available, I began to write it myself. For a long time I wrote informational material for children and young people, and then for teachers.

One Sunday afternoon during my service in the Navy in World War II, I passed a pet shop in Boston. I looked in the shop window and soon several children joined me. We talked about the animals in the window and imagined some things that might happen at night when no one was around. As a result of this conversation, I wrote my first fiction book, *A Monkey with a Notion.* It was published in 1946.

After that, I wrote a little other fiction but I kept thinking that in addition to the textbooks in science for teachers and children I would like to do science books for children which they could find in their libraries and read just because they wanted to and not because their teachers had assigned them. Probably without my realizing it, my mind returned to my childhood in Michigan and I wrote the story of a tree which I had known well. It grew on the roadside halfway between my house and the house of my pal. We often met under it on summer afternoons and from there took off on exploration trips into fields and woods. The book, *Tree on the Road to Turntown,* was published in 1953 and was the beginning of a series of books about the world around us. There are now six of these books and four of them have been selections of the Junior Literary Guild.

I am a most fortunate fellow because I like my audience. I've taught children for years and have many close young friends. I like my subject. Science is so easy to find and is interesting to so many children. And I like to write. I find it fascinating to try to put my ideas down so that someone else will like to read them. It's nice to get letters from young people who have made discoveries through reading something I've written.

I now teach at the University of Maryland and live in Washington, D.C. I teach science to teachers who will teach it to children, and almost every day I am in schools where children are enjoying themselves through discovering the world in which they

© Bachrach

GLENN O. BLOUGH

live—the world of animals and plants and electricity and weather and astronomy, to say nothing of atoms and spaceships and earth satellites. There *is* a lot to discover and discovering it myself and helping others to do so is most enjoyable.

Vera Bock

ILLUSTRATOR OF
The Tangle-Coated Horse; The Oak Tree House; A Critical History of Children's Literature; Bow Bells; Etc.

VERA Bock was born in St. Petersburg (now Leningrad), Russia, where her Russian mother was a concert pianist and her American father an international banker. She learned to speak French, German and English at the same time as Russian, and she reads books in all four languages. At the time of the Russian Revolution, the American ambassador warned the family to leave Russia. They escaped on the last train, and made the long trip through Siberia and China, coming across the Pacific at last to the United States by ship.

Miss Bock writes of herself: "I drew pictures long before I knew it was 'Art.' I did not *make* it my career. I used it to earn a living, when that proved necessary. It became a career because it happened that enough people liked the way I drew pictures."

VERA BOCK

exception they are printed in several colors appropriate to the character of the book. The leading figure is usually the dominant motif. The artist's natural posteresque style and her ability to summarize graphically the book's content make her jackets not only attractive to look at, but from a sales standpoint, invariably invite closer inspection of the book."

Among the more than fifty books that Miss Bock has designed and illustrated are two of the beloved Andrew Lang fairy books— *The Arabian Nights* and *The Rose Fairy Book*. These have full-page, color illustrations.

Miss Bock's home is in New York City, but in the summer she goes to Maine. She also travels a great deal, both in this country and abroad.

She went back to Europe to continue her major interest, studying drawing and painting under European artists. In England she learned wood engraving, illumination, and heraldry. There she also became interested in printing and in the photo-engraving processes. All of this proved of the utmost value when she became an illustrator, for she was able to design books as well as illustrate them.

Her first book was *The Tangle-Coated Horse*, by Ella Young, a retelling of the Fionn Saga. It was not until 1939, ten years later, that she was able to put her practical knowledge of typography and layout to use in *The Girl Who Would Be Queen*, by Eric P. Kelly and Clara Hoffmanowa, which she both designed and illustrated. It became one of the Fifty Books selected that year. Since then, she has always designed the books she has illustrated.

Norman Kent, writing of Miss Bock's work in the *American Artist*, classes her with W. A. Dwiggins, Warren Chappell, and Valenti Angelo. He says of her books:

"Each is planned like a good house, with paper, type and decoration harmoniously interrelated. The crispness of her style with its clean line is ideally suited to adorn type, and in her selection and arrangements of the latter she has been most successful. . . . The first thing that impresses one is the excellence of her book jackets. Almost without

Franklyn M. Branley

1915-

AUTHOR OF

The Sun, Our Nearest Star; Big Tracks, Little Tracks; Lodestar; Exploring by Satellite; Etc.

Autobiographical sketch of Franklyn M. Branley:

SCIENCE and people are my two primary interests. As I think back, both of these interests came to the forefront quite by accident. My decision to enter the teaching profession was rather an enforced one, and was not one that was made early in life because of a driving desire to become a teacher. My interest in people grew very rapidly when I started my teaching career; it had to.

My first job was teaching nine-year-olds. When you are working with fourth graders you find that you are licked before you start if you don't like people. Those children almost caused me to leave teaching before I was fairly started, because I had not learned humility, nor had I learned to appreciate and respect people. Those fourth graders taught me more than I had picked up through all the preceding years of college.

Science was a newcomer in the field of elementary education during the years when I was gaining experience in the art of teaching. Many teachers in the elementary schools taught no science at all. This was a disturbing situation and so, together with another fellow, I wrote a pamphlet of directions for starting the teaching of science —a sort of how-to-do-it manual.

This writing venture probably was induced not only by the situation described above, but also by some sort of urge inside of me that demanded expression. While in college I had edited the school newspaper and also the annual of the senior class. My appetite was whetted during those years.

After writing the little pamphlet, I looked for other outlets, and I found them in many professional journals and also in journals for young people. My first few books were written in collaboration, and many continue to be done in that manner. But there are so many books to be written, youngsters are so anxious for information about any and all phases of science, that I have done books solo as well.

I was born in New Rochelle, New York, the youngest of four children. Most of my early forays into science were the kind that are frowned on by adults, such as burning the neighbor's clothesline with a red-hot poker. Throughout elementary and high school, science was just another subject, one that was not especially fascinating. My deep and driving interest in science stems from my early teaching days. When I saw how interested children were in science, I studied the subject more extensively myself so I could help them. My enthusiasm for science grows stronger continually; my wonder increases as I learn more about our world; and my faith in young people increases the more I live and work with them. I am convinced that there is nothing finer one can do with his life than devote it to opening up new horizons for all, and especially for youngsters. I only wish I knew more, and that I could write better, so I could lead young people more effectively to new frontiers.

* * *

Dr. Branley earned his B.S. at New York University, and his M.A. and Ed.D. at Columbia University Teachers College. In 1956 he was appointed Associate Astronomer of the American Museum-Hayden Planetarium, in New York City. Prior to that time, he taught in several high schools, including the Horace Mann School in New York City, and in the State Teachers College, Jersey City, New Jersey. The collaborator in

Robert B. Scallan
FRANKLYN M. BRANLEY

some of his early books, mentioned in his autobiographical sketch, was Nelson F. Beeler, whose sketch appears elsewhere in this volume.

Paul Bransom

1885-

ILLUSTRATOR OF
Wilderness Champion; The Biggest Bear on Earth; The Last of the Sea Otters; Etc.

Autobiographical sketch by Paul Bransom:

WHILE I have illustrated some forty-odd books about animals, only some of these were books for children. I have never written a book. I was born in Washington, D.C., evidently for the sole purpose of drawing animals, for that compulsion prompted my earliest efforts of expression and has persisted to this day.

Ever since I can remember, as a small child, my greatest delight and interest was in the company of animals and birds. Especially exciting were the excursions to our national zoo, then on the outskirts of Washington. Making pictures of animals and birds was the dominant interest in my life. This pattern was broken only once, when for a brief period between the ages of fourteen and eighteen I went to work in the office of a patent draftsman where I learned mechan-

PAUL BRANSOM

ical drawing—and also that this type of drawing was not what I was seeking.

Upon my arrival in New York I immediately discovered that there was an even bigger zoo—in fact, two of them! Also, through sheer good fortune, I found myself engaged by the New York *Evening Journal* to do a series of little comic drawings concerning the affairs of bugs, animals and birds, entitled "The Latest News from Bugville." During this pleasant assignment for a period of three years, I spent every spare moment at the zoos, sketching and working on animal drawings for myself. At length, I had collected a portfolio of pictures, covers and sample illustrations, which I took down to Philadelphia one fine day to show to the *Saturday Evening Post*. The art director of that great magazine, Mr. H. A. Thompson (bless him), received me with hospitable enthusiasm, placed all of my drawings around the room and went into an adjoining office. In a moment he returned with a brisk, friendly gentleman who briefly surveyed the pictures and pointed here and there, as he said, "We'll take this, and this, and this, and this"—four times!—and left the room. That was my introduction to Mr. George Horace Lorimer, who not only accepted four covers from my stock of samples but also some small drawings of animals which were used as decorative headings for some of the financial articles published in the *Post*. In

addition to all this, the editor told me they had a serial tiger story which they wished me to illustrate!

I don't know whether this is something of a record or not. Certainly in all my subsequent experience I have never heard anything like it. At any rate, that episode launched me upon the free-lance career of animal illustration which I have followed for so many years. Naturally, I have always had a warm spot in my heart for the *Saturday Evening Post* and though I have since illustrated many stories and sold a number of covers to that publication, it has been on the basis of strictly *one* at a time!

I must also say that about the time the *Post* started me on my way, my constant attendance at the Bronx Zoo attracted the interest of its first director, Dr. William T. Hornaday, and through his kindness and good offices I was accorded the rare privilege of a studio right in the zoo where I did a lot of my early work.

I am married and my wife shares my enthusiasm for animals and outdoor life. We have a studio home in the Adirondacks which for many years has been the source of much fine background material for my animal illustrations, but every winter finds us in New York City where I can have access to the zoo.

In recent years we have fallen in love with Jackson Hole, Wyoming, and in this fabulous place have acquired a little ranch and log cabin, seven thousand feet above sea level, at the foot of the majestic Teton Mountains. Out there, I have started an outdoor art school and, needless to say, in addition to superlative scenery there are plenty of wild animals around.

Vivian Breck

1895-

AUTHOR OF
*High Trail; Hoofbeats on the Trail;
White Water; Kona Summer; Etc.*

Autobiographical sketch of Vivian Gurney Breckenfeld, who uses Vivian Breck as a pen name:

A S far back as I can remember deciding to do anything or be anything in particular, I decided to be a writer. Because my father was a mining engineer, most of my early life was spent in remote mountain-bound mining camps on the west coast of Mexico. But I was not born there. For that event my mother insisted on returning to San Francisco.

Until I was ten years old, a pony, a pet fawn, a parakeet, and my parents were almost my only companions. When finally we came back to live in "the States," school was not easy. I was a jumbled child. I read too well for my age but had never heard of tag or hopscotch. But time and friends and understanding teachers at last managed to pour me into the American mold, so that I graduated from high school in Berkeley and then from Vassar. During these years I contributed to school magazines and took such writing courses as were available. But the everlasting need for cash in hand sent me straight from college into teaching. Writing was still a dream, something for the future.

After college, I returned to Berkeley to get a master's degree in English from the University of California—also a husband. Both before marriage and again afterward, when our two sons were in school, I taught English and history at girls' schools where small classes brought me very close to the high-school age, the age I like best to write for. I finally got down to business but it took a war to provide the necessary shove. A house in a university town, which for years has been full of "young adults" raiding the refrigerator, holding Scout meetings, studying, pulling up the rugs to dance, carrying on bull sessions at weird hours, listening to everything from Beethoven to jitterbug, takes on a tomblike quality when Army and Navy suddenly snatch away both its young men, half the family. I divided my time between nurses aiding and the typewriter.

The first result was High Trail, published in 1948. This story of a girl's adventure and courage in the Sierra Nevada grew directly from the many pack trips my husband and I had taken alone—and, when they were old enough, with our boys—where he was the wrangler and I was the cook. We couldn't afford the luxury of a professional packer so we learned about high-mountain camping the hard way. It was more fun, too. The favorite vacation for all four Breckenfelds has always been, and still is, the Sierra Nevada. We hope our three granddaughters

VIVIAN BRECK

will grow up to love every chunk of Sierra granite as much as we do.

Hoofbeats on the Trail sprang from one of our first trips with the Sierra Club, an unusually adventurous expedition over rugged terrain. My mother's ten years of life in Mexico developed into Maggie, a slightly older book than the others because it deals with the first year of a marriage.

White Water, published in 1958, is laid in still another bit of wild country, shooting the rapids on the Green River in Utah and Colorado, deep in those wonderful canyons of Dinosaur National Monument which were so nearly dammed up and lost to the American people. This introduced us not only to a world of new friends, but to a new sport, foldboating. Perhaps this explains why writing is so much fun. Everything in life is grist for the typewriter—joys, sorrows, friends, places, animals, and enemies, if any. And sometimes the most absurd incidents turn out to be the most valuable. Kona Summer, published in 1961, is about two girls in Hawaii.

My husband and I still live in the Berkeley Hills, in the house we built just before our younger son was born. From its windows we look straight out to the Golden Gate, to sunsets and Mt. Tamalpais. And through these same windows we have watched three bridges come into being across our beautiful San Francisco bay.

Howard M. Brier

1903-

AUTHOR OF

*Skycruiser; Skyblazer; Phantom Backfield;
Backboard Magic! Etc.*

Autobiographical sketch of Howard M. Brier:

BEING the son of a college president and author, and having an older brother who is a newspaperman and fiction writer, probably had a great influence in my becoming the author of books for young people. I must have been something of a nuisance as far as the family typewriters were concerned, for when I was still in grade school my father and brother bought me a used typewriter—mainly to keep me from pounding the keys of their machines.

I sold my first fiction story when I was seventeen and still in high school. It was a short dog story and the editor of *Boys' Life*, the Boy Scout magazine, thought it was good enough to publish. I believe he paid me fifteen dollars for my effort. Later, the same editor paid me a thousand dollars for another dog story, but many years had intervened. In fact, it was thirteen years before I sold another piece of fiction. During those thirteen years, which I call my apprenticeship, I was writing most of the time. I received bushels of rejection slips but this is not a new experience. Most people who are learning to write go through the same harrowing years of trial and error.

State of Washington Campus Studios
HOWARD M. BRIER

Aside from a trip to the Eskimo settlement of Aklavik, on the arctic coast of Canada, to gather material for my book *Sky Freighter*, my life has been devoid of excitement, but it has not lacked interest. I have found everything about my life interesting—my schooling, my work, my associates. I attended high school in Everett, Washington, a lumber city on the shore of Puget Sound. I received a bachelor of arts degree, and a master's degree, from the University of Washington, and wrote for the university daily and the campus humor magazine.

My newspaper work includes reporting, advertising, and circulation with the Everett *News*, the Everett *Herald*, the Seattle *Post-Intelligencer*, and the Seattle *Times*. Only recently I spent a summer on the copy desk of the *Post-Intelligencer* to remove some of the cobwebs, for my main job now is teaching journalism at the University of Washington. For eight years I was state director of the Keep Washington Green program, a forest-fire prevention campaign, and I have done other work in the field of public relations.

I began writing books for young people when I was a high school journalism teacher in the Seattle public schools. My daily contact with teen-agers made me aware of their problems and of their behavior. Watching a son and daughter grow up also helped. I knew that if I was to write books for young people the stories would have to be realistic, for a teen-ager is the hardest person in the world to fool. A story for the discerning mind of a high school reader must clear several hurdles—it must be interesting, it must move rapidly, it must be plausible, and it must not preach. Also, the fiction characters must be the kind of people young readers would like to know. A rather difficult order, but if one thinks writing for young people is easy, he might better take up plumbing.

Robert Bright

1902-

AUTHOR AND ILLUSTRATOR OF

*Georgie; Richard Brown and the Dragon;
Me and the Bears; I Like Red; Etc.*

Autobiographical sketch of Robert Bright:

I WAS born in Sandwich, on Cape Cod, but at six months my parents moved abroad where I was to spend my earliest years, particularly in the university town of

Göttingen. Here Baron Munchausen had lived and the philologists Jakob and Wilhelm Grimm had gathered their celebrated folk tales. It was a happy childhood, spent in an atmosphere of scholarship and of legend, and of much travel.

The First World War exploded this gentle way of life, but it could not destroy the memory. If I have turned so enthusiastically to the writing and illustrating of children's picture books it is, I think, because of a wish to enter again that child's world—if ever so briefly—and to invest it with the sort of stories that would have pleased me then, and that please me so much now, and that must therefore convey pleasure to children everywhere. For I have always imagined that there is nothing as contagious as delight.

Yet my discovery of this wish and this gift was a long time coming. My education, which was begun in Göttingen, continued in Andover and ended formally at Princeton. Here I joined the Press Club and thought to have found my career in journalism. This began as a police reporter on the Baltimore *Sun* and ended in France as a staff writer for the Paris *Times*.

I was married, had children, and for a number of years fancied myself cast for the profitable role of advertising manager in New York City. But I presently pulled up these little roots and settled with my young family in a tiny village outside Taos, New Mexico. Here in an adobe house, ringed around by fields and hills and kindly neighbors, and peopled by my wife, my children, my visiting friends, as well as by horses, goats, chickens, rabbits, cats, and dogs, everything at last came together.

A small figure in an oriental tapestry seen casually at the home of a painter neighbor gave me the idea for my first picture book, *The Travels of Ching*. The profound desire to write of my Spanish neighbors was the seed from which my first novel finally grew, *The Life and Death of Little Jo*. Thereafter followed more novels and many more books for children. While my novels seem to me like trees growing very slowly, my children's books are poems in words and pictures that seem to spring up like flowers overnight—sometimes as complete surprises, sometimes out of a wish, like the one made by my

ROBERT BRIGHT

children to really *meet* a ghost. And so, of course, a ghost had to be produced, and he had to be little and charming, the proper subject for a picture-poem, and with the proper sort of name. And that was *Georgie*, my first success.

Ruth Brindze

1903-

AUTHOR OF

The Gulf Stream; The Story of the Trade Winds; The Story of Our Calendar, The Story of the Totem Pole; Etc.

Autobiographical sketch of Ruth Brindze:

AS far back as I can remember—and I can remember things that happened when I was about three—I have always been entranced by books. I learned to read when I was quite young, which was a great relief to my mother because up to that time she frequently had to drop whatever she was doing to read to me. If she did not, I was a noisy, nasty pest.

When I graduated into first grade I was thrilled to discover that my classroom had its own library and that I could borrow any book I wished and keep it for three days. Some of the books really scared me—*Jack the Giant Killer*, for instance—but I borrowed *Jack* over and over again.

Brindze: *BRIN* zee

RUTH BRINDZE

the Gulf Stream. It seemed to me a wonderful subject for a book and to my delight *The Gulf Stream* won a first prize in the New York *Herald Tribune* Children's Book Festival and was also a Junior Literary Guild selection.

Many of the children's books I have written since, including *The Story of Our Calendar, The Story of the Totem Pole,* and *The Story of Gold,* developed in much the same way as *The Gulf Stream.* A subject aroused my curiosity, to satisfy it I did a tremendous amount of research, and my notes became the basis of a book. I think there will always be something I want to write about because I am curious about so many things.

I was born in New York City and now live in a nearby suburb. For pleasure I read, write, cook, garden,' and sail.

In addition to reading, playing ball and swimming, I enjoyed writing compositions about things experienced and imagined. During my high school days some books I read on the romantic aspects of newspaper work made me decide to be a reporter, and in preparation for a newspaper career I spent my last two years of college at the Columbia University School of Journalism. However, I worked on newspapers for only a few years and then began to write magazine articles and books.

My first book for children was *Johnny Get Your Money's Worth.* James Henle, then president of Vanguard Press, encouraged me to write it. We were discussing a manuscript on consumer buying I had recently completed when I remarked that someone should write a book telling children how to avoid the tricks of the market place. Jim suggested I tackle the job and *Johnny* taught me that writing for children is by no means easy but is a lot of fun.

My next book for boys and girls was *The Gulf Stream.* That book was really born in the air! I was flying back to New York from Florida where I had sailed in a small schooner along the Keys and had my first experience navigating in the Stream. When I saw the path of blue water again through the plane's window, I made up my mind to find out everything known about it. I studied many scientific works and the more I read, the more fascinated I became with

Margueritte Bro

1894-

AUTHOR OF

Sarah; Stub—A College Romance; Three—and Domingo; Su-Mei's Golden Year; Etc.

Autobiographical sketch of Margueritte Bro:

BRIGHT hours in my eighth grade were Saturday mornings telling stories to children in the St. Paul Public Library. Having been on crutches for two years, I had scads of time to read and invent. In grade school my favorite assignments were something called mental arithmetic and composition class in which we were shown a picture and told to write a story about it. Once I won a prize from a magazine for some tall tale about vegetables at a fair. Then at twenty, with college mostly behind me, I toured off on a Chautauqua circuit through New England and the East telling stories to children, plus—let my dozen grandchildren read this—teaching folk dancing.

Marriage to a Swede from north Wisconsin; graduate school; six years in China where two sons and a daughter were born; back at the University of Chicago writing plays and having one more son (after all, children born outside the U.S.A. cannot be President); traveling in South America; ten more years on a college campus getting to know the older young; around the world and

MARGUERITTE BRO

two years in Indonesia; roaming through the Far East and parts of Europe; back home, editing religious books.

Sarah came out of my own background in Minnesota where my father was then a minister; *Stub—A College Romance,* from the college campus where my husband was president; *Su-Mei's Golden Year,* from those happy years in China; *More Than We Are,* from a lifelong interest in inner growth—my own, that is, and the still young who can do something about themselves. Now I'm tinkering with a tale about a little Bali dancer whom I knew, gaily and sadly; and jotting down observations about the various ways in which teen-agers adjust to their parents' problems, including themselves.

What do I like best? Really? Children asking questions, sitting under an apple tree in bloom, swimming, reading, and a long sweet silence almost anywhere. Ah, yes, traveling on ships!

Winifred Bromhall

AUTHOR AND ILLUSTRATOR OF
*Belinda's New Shoes; Bridget's Growing Day;
The Princess and the Woodcutter's
Daughter; The Pony Tail
That Grew; Etc.*

Autobiographical sketch of Winifred Bromhall:

I WAS born and grew up in a midland town in England. I can't remember a time when I didn't like drawing, and was most fortunate in having a father who, although a schoolmaster by profession, was an amateur painter and certainly an artist in temperament. It was he who gave me my first paintbox and encouragement in what my mother considered, I think, a messy and somewhat unwholesome passion.

Like most children I liked drawing people and animals best, a fact borne out recently when I was one of the judges of a children's art exhibit. At least nine tenths of the pictures were of people—doing things, of course.

When I went to school again, I was lucky in having an art teacher who, probably to make teaching art to the young bearable, had a studio and illustrated children's books on the side. After being asked, one red-letter day, to go to tea to her studio with another promising(?) pupil, I decided there and then that this was the life I wanted. After a brief time at an art school in England, I came quite early to America.

After a few months in Boston I came to New York where I peddled drawings and got some work to do—at the same time having various part-time jobs—in a bookshop, the New York Public Library and, briefly and happily, in a pet shop. I was lucky, too, in being able to go back to Europe quite often.

To me, the nicest part of this children's book business is the letters one gets. Mine are, of course, from quite young children, nearly always written in pencil and rather grubby and for some reason always addressed

WINIFRED BROMHALL

to "Mr. Bromhall." My favorite is from, I am sure, the offspring of quite sophisticated New York parents. After rather condescendingly saying he liked my book he writes:

"In fact, your books don't bore me nearly as much as most authors' books do."

I treasure this letter for moments of depression.

I live—for the present—being by nature a rolling stone, in San Francisco and like it enormously.

Lynn Bronson

See *Evelyn Sibley Lampman*

Marcia Brown

1918-

AUTHOR AND ILLUSTRATOR OF
Once a Mouse; Dick Whittington and His Cat; Skipper John's Cook; Tamarindo! Etc.

Autobiographical sketch of Marcia Brown:

FROM my earliest memory, which is of myself running early one morning to get a picture book and asking my mother to read it to me, books and pictures have been very important in my life.

I was born in Rochester, New York, where my parents had both grown up, on the 13th of July, just in time to celebrate Bastille

Blackstone Studios
MARCIA BROWN

Day. My father was a minister, and we lived in a succession of small towns in New York State with the freedom to roam freely—first the woods behind our house in Clifton Springs, then the woods and fields around Otsego Lake near Cooperstown, and then the shores of the Hudson River near Catskill. Water was always important to me, whether vast Lake Ontario, Otsego Lake, or the beautiful and busy Hudson, where I learned to swim and loved to watch the constant river traffic—sidewheeler day boats that threw up huge swells, night boats like silver fish, tugs and heavy barges so sluggish they would be in sight all day long, tankers, freighters from all over the world, and our own boats, of course, for my sister and I made many of our toys. Now the sea—whether the Atlantic off Cape Cod, or the Caribbean, or the Mediterranean—has the same fascination for me.

Reading was the main entertainment of our family, the public library being a second home. Fairy tales—Andersen, Perrault, Grimm, and *The Arabian Nights*—were favorites and still are. Of course we drew—when we were very small on the "empty pages" of old magazines and then on large pads of drawing paper that appeared on Christmas and special days. My father painted one of our kitchen walls for me to use as a blackboard, where I drew by the hour. My favorite subjects were our cat Midnight and comfortable red barns with benign fairies hovering overhead like angels. When I was about twelve, I decided I would like to make pictures in books someday.

After graduating from Kingston High School, I went to New York State College in Albany. In the summers I learned to paint under Judson Smith in Woodstock. After college, I taught English for three years in Cornwall (New York) High School but decided I really wanted to paint and make books for young children. So I came to New York to live on the same Sullivan Street that is in *The Little Carousel,* to study painting under Yasuo Kuniyoshi and Stuart Davis at the New School, and to work in the New York Public Library. While working in the library for five years, I told stories from all over the world to the children who came from almost all over the world—Polish, Italian, West Indian, Czechoslovakian, Finnish, Chinese—and who help make New York the fascinating city it is.

I still live in New York City where I work on my books, when I am not painting, giving puppet shows, or traveling—to Cape Cod, where Skipper John found his cook, to Mexico, to the Virgin Islands, where Henry became *Henry—Fisherman,* to Jamaica, and more recently to Europe.

* * *

Miss Brown has twice won the Caldecott Medal for the "most distinguished American picture book" of the preceding year—in 1955 with *Cinderella* and in 1962 with *Once a Mouse.*

Laurent de Brunhoff

1925-

AUTHOR AND ILLUSTRATOR OF

*Babar's Cousin, That Rascal Arthur; Babar's
Visit to Birds Island; Babar's Fair,
Babar and the Professor; Etc.*

Autobiographical sketch of Laurent de Brunhoff, translated from the French:

LAURENT DE BRUNHOFF

THE first Babar book was created by my father, Jean de Brunhoff, in 1930. I was only a little boy of five then, and my brother, Mathieu, was a year younger. Our father would show us his sketches for the book and was extremely interested in our comments. One day he showed us the drawing of the little elephants singing in class, led by Cornelius. We asked him why the monkey Zéphir wasn't there. It was because he thought that the little monkey couldn't possibly sing in harmony with the elephants. Nevertheless, he added Zéphir, showing him looking in at the window.

Jean de Brunhoff drew on his own life in creating these picture books, and we were always delighted when we recognized a familiar landscape, or a person we knew. In a big winter sports scene, one person has fallen flat in the snow. We were sure it was our governess!

My father died in 1937. By that time I had already decided that I wanted to be a painter when I grew up, and Mathieu wanted to be a doctor. Our little brother, Thierry, who was only three, had no idea that he was going to be a pianist.

During the war I finished my schooling and in 1945 I rented a studio in the Montparnasse district of Paris and began to work seriously at painting. At the same time I composed my first Babar picture book. For without being fully aware of it, I wanted to carry on the tradition and revive Babar, the little elephant I had drawn so often for my own amusement. I began by drawing pictures around the idea of a story, and wrote the text afterward—the method I have used ever since. *Babar's Cousin, That Rascal Arthur* appeared in 1947.

I have never been able to paint and do Babar books at the same time. Only when a book was finished would I pick up my brushes and engraving tools again. I was beginning to turn to nonrepresentational painting.

Since 1947, I have published four Babar books. In *Babar and the Professor,* I have created some new characters based on my daughter and son (then five and three). They were quite pleased to recognize themselves and regard it as perfectly normal that they should be in the book along with Babar.

I also think about grownups, and not solely as a painter, as I have published a book of satirical sketches. But from living so long with Babar and his friends, I have given all my caricatures the heads of animals.

Laurent de Brunhoff: *lo RAHN duh bru NOFF*

Clyde Robert Bulla

1914-

AUTHOR OF

*Squanto; Benito; Three-Dollar Mule;
Riding the Pony Express; Etc.*

Autobiographical sketch of Clyde Robert
Bulla:

ALMOST as far as I can remember, I
wanted to write. I was born on a farm
near the town of King City, Missouri, and
my first school was a one-room country
schoolhouse. One day the teacher asked each
first grade pupil what he would do with a
thousand dollars, or some such amount. I
answered that I would buy a table. My
classmates laughed heartily and the teacher
was puzzled, but my answer really meant
that I wanted a desk or other flat surface on
which to write my stories!

My first piece of writing was a fragment
entitled "How Planets Were Born." The
ambitious opening sentence was, "One night
old Mother Moon had a million babies."
All through school I continued to write—
stories mostly, but plays and poetry, too.
After years of garnering editors' rejection
slips, I sold a magazine story, then several
more.

I went to the Southwest, where I lived
and wrote during a spring and summer.
When I went home to Missouri, I began a
novel and finished it the following year. A
publisher accepted it. On a wave of enthusiasm, I wrote two more. Novel number
one appeared and, almost too soon afterward
for coincidence, the publisher went bank-
rupt.

With far too many eggs in one basket (one
published novel, which was almost a total
loss, and two unpublished ones, which nobody wanted) I began looking for a job. I
found one on the local weekly newspaper.
For several years I struggled with the linotype, kept books, collected bills, and wrote
a weekly column. Several of the columns
came to the attention of a well-known writer
and illustrator of children's books. She wrote
to me, suggesting that I try writing a book
for children.

To show her I *had* tried, I got out the one
I had written a year before and mailed it
to her. The juvenile editor of a New York
publisher visited her that week end, took
the manuscript with her, and within a week
I had word that the book had been accepted.
This was *The Donkey Cart,* published in
1946. Since then I have written over twenty
books for boys and girls, as well as the
music for several children's song books.

My home is now in Los Angeles. Before
writing a story, I usually visit the scene of
it. This has led to a good deal of traveling.
I hope it will lead to a good deal more.

* * *

After Mr. Bulla gave the correct
pronunciation of his surname, he added
resignedly: "But over the years I've learned
to answer to Beulah, Buller, and even Bullie,
without much caring."

Bruce Campbell

See *Epstein, Samuel*

Natalie Savage Carlson

1906-

AUTHOR OF

*Hortense, the Cow for a Queen; Alphonse,
That Bearded One; The Talking Cat, and
Other Stories of French Canada; Etc.*

Autobiographical sketch of Natalie Savage
Carlson:

I WAS born October 3, 1906, in Win-
chester, Virginia. My first creative work
was published on the children's page of the
Baltimore *Sunday Sun.* It was only a para-

CLYDE ROBERT BULLA

NATALIE SAVAGE CARLSON

visited the Île de Ré, from which my French Canadian ancestors emigrated in the seventeenth century. I also made a pilgrimage to the village of Blosville, in Normandy, where my brother was buried after he lost his life in World War II. I like to wander through the Paris streets and explore the countryside. I also enjoy trying to speak French with the people. They can understand me but I can't understand them. I belong to a service women's group which works with the French orphans and aged people.

* * *

Mrs. Carlson added: "I don't think there will be any trouble about the pronunciation of my name, although a Chinese woman named Ng said that Carlson was the most unusual name she had ever heard."

graph long, but it was signed in real printed letters: "By Natalie Savage, Age 8." That taste of fame definitely decided my life's ambition. I've been writing stories ever since.

There was plenty of material to be found on the Maryland farm where I lived as a child. It was on the Potomac River about three miles from Harpers Ferry, West Virginia. I loved outdoor life as well as reading and writing. My happiest times were spent horseback riding, ice skating, practicing acrobatics, reading, and writing. My mother's people were French Canadians, so I was fascinated by the way they spoke and the tales they told. They are models for some of the characters in my French Canadian stories. My grandfather had run away from his home in Ontario and joined the Union Army during the Civil War.

There were eight girls in my family and when we moved to California in 1917, a baby brother joined us. In high school I became interested in elocution and loved to recite; now it terrifies me to talk before an audience. I worked as a newspaper reporter on a Long Beach, California, newspaper. Then, in 1929, I married a naval officer. I have two daughters and a granddaughter. As a service wife, I continually move from one place to another. I have visited every state in the Union.

Now I am living in France, near Paris, because my husband is stationed with the United States European Command. I have

Frances Carpenter

1890-

AUTHOR OF

Children of Our World; Tales of a Korean Grandmother; Pocahontas and Her World; Tales of a Chinese Grandmother; Etc.

Autobiographical sketch of Frances Carpenter:

ADMIRATION for my journalist father, Frank G. Carpenter, world traveler and pioneer syndicate writer of the turn of the century, was the compelling factor in my becoming a writer of geographical books for children.

A childhood love of fairy tales prompted my first folk-tale "book." It was written when I was ten years old, as a birthday present for my father, and it was entitled "Five Fairy Tales," by Frances Carpenter. Printed by my own hand, and bound in crinkly gray paper, tied with red ribbon, it was the forerunner of my seven later books of folk tales. The most enduring of these seems to be *Tales of a Chinese Grandmother*, which was published by Doubleday some twenty-five years ago.

Before my marriage I was fortunate enough to travel with my father, as his secretary, to many far corners of the earth. My Foreign Service husband, W. Chapin Huntington, enjoyed living in and visiting other lands as much as I did, and our two daughters were born in Paris.

FRANCES CARPENTER

So many thousand miles of travel, seeing for myself how people live in other lands, supplied a helpful background for writing my nineteen elementary geography books. These fall into two categories—supplemental books (like my father's gray-green *Carpenter's Geographical Readers* of the 1890's), the latest of my own being *Caribbean Lands,* published, like all of my geographical texts, by the American Book Company; and basic books, such as my recent third-grade home geography, *Our Homes and Our Neighbors.*

My pattern of living has included more than fifty summers in the Blue Ridge Mountains of Virginia. This is responsible for my interest in the early history of that state, and for my *Pocahontas and Her World,* published in 1957 by Knopf. I was lured from my fields of geography and folklore by my conviction that Pocahontas is too little appreciated by boys and girls of today. Usually she and her people are presented from the more severe point of view of the English strangers from across the ocean. In this book I have tried to tell how she herself must have felt about the happenings at Jamestown and along the rivers of her father Powhatan's empire.

One of my most continuous extracurricular interests has been Smith College, from which I was graduated, and which I have since served in various ways, including membership on its board of trustees. A second has been Children's Hospital, here in Washington, D.C., where I was born and where I have lived most of my life.

As I look back over forty years of writing for children, I am appalled at the thousands of hours I have spent at a typewriter. For me, being an author is hard work. Why do I do it? I honestly don't know. But I am afraid that I shall keep on just as long as my fingers can tap the keys or hold a pencil.

Harriett H. Carr

AUTHOR OF
Where the Turnpike Starts; Young Viking of Brooklyn; Against the Wind; Gravel Gold; Etc.

Autobiographical sketch of Harriett H. Carr:

NORTH Dakota's blizzard-bound winters, a mother-schoolteacher who read and taught me to read away the time, and a grandmother with fascinating stories of the generations of Carrs who had followed the American frontier from Massachusetts to Colorado in the gold rush days, directed my early interest to books and writing. Then when, at the age of eleven, a national magazine published a poem I had written, my career was settled: I would be a "great writer"!

High school literature convinced me that adjectives should be dropped! Rejection slips that came back with the short stories a college creative writing course encouraged students to submit (how the *Saturday Evening Post* must *hate* college creative writing courses!) made me skeptical of the whole idea. (I had been sent home to Ann Arbor, Michigan, where I was born, to assure my education.) So I secured a job as a reporter for the Ypsilanti *Daily Press,* was correspondent for the AP, UP, and INS, and it was exciting. Within a few years I became the first woman editor of a daily newspaper in Michigan, and was much too busy to think of anything beyond the 3:30 P.M. deadline.

From the little Ypsilanti newspaper I went to the Detroit *News,* then turned to the educational magazine field—staff writer for the *Michigan Education Journal,* associate editor of the *Michigan Vocational Outlook,*

HARRIETT H. CARR

editorial assistant for the *American Vocational Journal.* Very little creative writing resulted.

But with the last-named position I was back in the East where the Carrs had taken root when they came to the Colonies sometime in the 1600's. A packet of letters which my grandfather had written from Kansas Territory and the Shining Mountains of Colorado to his father in Still River, Massachusetts, fired my imagination. Here were the real pioneers who had made friends with the Indians, established trading posts, broken the soil of the Plains States, and mined gold! The creative urge was born again. Here were stories red-blooded young Americans would love as I did.

Gravel Gold was published in 1953. *Where the Turnpike Starts* recalls some of the stories my mother and grandmother told me of their pioneering days in Michigan. *Against the Wind* is true to memories of my childhood on the North Dakota farm my father homesteaded and which I still own. *Borghild of Brooklyn,* a Junior Literary Guild selection, might also be called a pioneering book—the story of today's pioneers helping to build a powerful, virile America.

Now I live in New York City and devote all my free time to writing books for young people.

Latrobe Carroll
1894-
Tough Enough; Tough Enough's Trip; Tough Enough's Pony; Digby, The Only Dog; Etc.

Autobiographical sketch of Latrobe Carroll:

I WAS born patriotically in Washington, D.C. But my mother, left a widow two weeks after my birth, soon took me to Denver, where we lived for many years. You enter Denver's state capitol by walking up a sweep of wide marble steps. After I had learned to read, I used to get books out of the public library, take them to the capitol steps and sit down and read them. My reading room's roof was as high as the sky. Sitting on stone, I read most of Jules Verne, just about all of *Grimms' Fairy Tales,* and an old-time thriller-shocker, *Wild Adventures Round the Pole.* This last one seemed especially real, since I read it on a wintry day with some snowflakes whipping along. My teeth were chattering, but I didn't leave my stair-step perch until I'd read the last word.

These books opened new worlds. Worlds of words. I used to tell myself that maybe— just maybe—I too would put words together, someday. Words on paper. Storybook words. Words that boys and girls would like. So I began to try.

My first efforts were reflections of vacations. Every summer my mother and I would go to a camp on a lonesome lake, high in the Rocky Mountains. The fishing was fine, but even better was my chance to get to know and love pets. There were two dogs— mountain mutts with informal ways. There was a pony to ride, and three fat, fish-fed cats. I tried to get my animal friends into stories. My tales were just eager gropings, but they helped to make a sort of emotional background for writing. Much later, my favorite subjects were pets and people living wide outdoor lives.

When I was twelve, my mother took me to Egypt, where we spent a winter in a desert hotel with five groups of pyramids in view. Next, for three years, I went to a Swiss school in Lausanne and then to a school in Munich, Germany. Between them, I learned enough to pass entrance examinations for Harvard.

While still in college, I sold my first fiction story to H. L. Mencken and George Jean Nathan's unconventionally distin-

LATROBE CARROLL

guished magazine, the *Smart Set*. After a hurry-up "war graduation," I served with the Army Engineers in World War I. When the fighting stopped, I got a job as first reader with a publishing house, then—briefly—was with the Foreign Press Service. Then I translated two thick books by Camille Flammarion, the French astronomer.

For nine years I was on the staff of *Liberty* magazine. I did editorial work and also wrote articles—among them interviews with Edna Ferber, Willa Cather, Harry Houdini, Katharine Cornell, and Clarence Darrow. While I was with *Liberty,* I married Ruth Robinson. When Ruth began to do books for children, her work interested me more and more. Mine interested me less and less, for I had slipped into a sort of editorial rut. At last I resigned from *Liberty* and joined Ruth in working on juveniles. I've never regretted the switch.

Ruth Carroll

1899-

AUTHOR AND ILLUSTRATOR OF
Where's the Bunny? What Whiskers Did; Etc.
CO-AUTHOR AND ILLUSTRATOR OF
Beanie, Pet Tale, Scuffles; Etc.

Autobiographical sketch of Ruth Carroll:

I WAS born in Lancaster, New York. When I was a year old, my parents took me to New York City. Later, they made a doll's house for me out of a square packing case. They gave me some dolls dressed quite as people dressed in those days. They sent me to a remarkable kindergarten. A teacher told us stories of King Arthur and his knights. That started me making up stories of my own: stories about my dolls and their house. I filled notebooks with them when I was older. In my tales, the dolls were knights and ladies, and the packing case was a castle. I was off on a path that led to imagining things—the path to storymaking.

I was led along still another path when my parents sent me to nature-study classes each summer in the Pocono Mountains, the path of science. I roved through the woods, discovering plants and wild creatures. When I went to St. Agatha's, an Episcopal school for girls, I wrote and illustrated pieces about worms, insects, and snakes for my surprised English teachers. I liked drawing better than writing. My illustrated stories about my dog, Johnny Baer, were published in the school magazine. One was elegantly entitled "The Smelling Dog."

I was graduated with honors from Vassar College, then studied art at the Art Students League in New York, and at many summer schools. One of my landscapes in oils was exhibited by the Philadelphia Academy, and several were purchased by the Newark Museum.

When doing portraits of children, I used to manipulate a puppet with my free hand and tell my models stories and make animal noises when appropriate, trying to keep them from getting bored and restless. They wanted shipwrecks, drownings, fires, airplane crashes, shootings. It was a challenge, holding their attention, even though I skipped catastrophes and mayhem.

After my marriage to Latrobe Carroll, I thought that working with children, trying to give them what they want and need, would be the most worth-while work of all. I wanted to illustrate children's books, but I couldn't pry a manuscript out of a publisher. Finally, I tried doing a story of my own—a story in pictures without any words—*What Whiskers Did.*

Later, my husband and I collaborated on many books. The idea for *Scuffles* came to me in a dream. I've often wondered what I ate for supper that evening. If only I could remember, I'd eat it again! *Where's the Bunny?* grew out of a request from a Vassar

RUTH CARROLL

professor of child study. She said there were no picture books that preschool deaf children could understand. She added: "Twos and threes love to participate and hunt for little hidden things and find them and point them out."

Our Tatum family series started after Latrobe and I moved to North Carolina to live. Now we ride horseback and hike through the Great Smoky Mountains, visiting mountain people and doing the work we like.

Helene Carter
1887-1960

ILLUSTRATOR OF
The Gulf Stream; The Story of Our Calendar; The First Book of Trees; The First Book of Tropical Mammals; Etc.

Autobiographical sketch of Helen Carter, written for MORE JUNIOR AUTHORS shortly before her death:

MORE years ago than I care to remember, I was born in Toronto, Canada, and I verily believe I arrived with a pencil in my hand, all ready to go to work. Even as a small child I was fascinated with all kinds of living things—dogs, horses, cows, raccoons, and cats. Most of all *cats*. These animals were all a part of my childhood. Frogs, too, played an important part. Very seriously, I made pants and jackets for the frogs which I kept in the rain barrel and tried to make them look like "The Frog Who Would A-Wooing Go." Mother did not share my love for these pets and would exclaim, "Oh-oh! Take the nasty thing away!" But I thought they were beautiful.

My growing years were torn between drawing and the violin, but at the ripe old age of sixteen I decided that the violin was out as a means of earning my living—which I was determined to do. So on my sixteenth birthday I was enrolled in the Ontario School of Art, where for four happy years I not only studied art but the theater also.

The school was quartered on the floors above the old Princess Theatre, which made it mighty easy to see all of the really great people of the stage—from seats in the top balcony for twenty-five cents. This privilege became, and has always been, a great source of pleasure and stimulation to me—just the memory of such people as Ellen Terry, Sarah Bernhardt, Forbes-Robertson, and Gertrude Elliott, Nazimova and many, many others.

After four years at the art school, I worked in the studio of a leading advertising agency in Toronto, where I learned the mechanics of reproduction and commercial illustration. The next stop was New York, where I studied at the Art Students League, both day and evening classes.

My first book assignment took me to Europe to illustrate *Two Little Misogynists*, by Carl Spitteler, a Nobel Prize winner in literature; also *The Three of Salu*, by Carolyn Della Chiesa. Several years later I made a second trip to do a book on Mont Saint-Michel, Avignon, and Carcassone, the three walled cities of France. All of these books are long since out of print.

For a number of years I collaborated with the late Dr. Raymond L. Ditmars, curator of reptiles at the New York Zoological Park. During this period I illustrated books on animals, insects, prehistoric animals, and reptiles. These were the beginning of a long line of nature books by other authors as well, including two by Ruth Brindze, *The Gulf Stream*, which won the New York *Herald Tribune* Spring Festival Award in 1945, and *The Story of Our Calendar*.

In recent years I have worked on a number of titles in the First Book series, published by Franklin Watts—*The First Book of Trees;* also *The First Book of Bees, The*

HELENE CARTER

First Book of Prehistoric Animals, The First Book of Gardening; and, more recently, *The First Book of Tropical Mammals.*

I am a member of the Women's National Book Association, and a life member of both the Artists Guild and the Society of Illustrators.

* * *

Miss Carter died December 31, 1960, in New York City, where she had lived and worked for many years. In private life she was Mrs. Helene Carter Silvey. She had served as secretary of the Artists Guild, and had been a member of the governing board of the Society of Illustrators.

Rebecca Caudill

1899-

AUTHOR OF
Tree of Freedom; Susan Cornish; House of the Fifers; Schoolhouse in the Woods; Etc.

Autobiographical sketch of Rebecca Caudill:

ONE of eleven children, I was born on a rocky farm squeezed between the Black Mountains and the Poor Fork River in Harlan County, Kentucky. Both my parents were teachers. My birthplace and its environs have served as background for many of my books. In many of them, too, there is an outcropping of my parents in one

character or another, for Caudill politics and philosophy provided plenty of drama, much of it hair-raising. In an impregnable Republican stronghold, my father was one of two Democrats. And among men whose favorite beverage was mountain dew, and whose favorite instrument for settling arguments was a Colt, he was a teetotaler and a pacifist who owned neither gun nor bottle.

In search of level land and better schools, my family left the mountains and eventually arrived in Sumner County, Tennessee, the garden spot of the Long Hunters. Here I grew up and attended high school. During this time I heard of college and decided to go to one. Having nary a penny to go on didn't strike me as an obstacle at all. I confided my intentions to an older sister who, during my senior year, enrolled me in a business school for correspondence courses in shorthand and typing. A letter from my high school principal to the president of Wesleyan College, Macon, Georgia, was answered with the offer of a stenographic job that would see me through four years of college. Wesleyan, the oldest chartered women's college in the world, was close to the century mark when I arrived to major in history, and I was the first Wesleyan student ever to work for her education. For this distinction I was called by my classmates a Yankee.

From Wesleyan I went to Vanderbilt University on a fellowship, and received a master's degree in international relations. Then, still penniless, I set out to see the world. I taught English to children of nineteen nationalities in Collegio Bennett, Rio de Janeiro, Brazil; I worked in an insurance office in Toronto, Canada; I edited a girls' magazine in Nashville, Tennessee; I traveled over most of Europe, including the Scandinavian countries and Russia. I was on the verge of signing a contract to edit a magazine in Turkey when I met another editor, James Ayars. We were married a few months later.

I have always felt guilty that every book of mine hasn't borne my husband's name as co-author, for without him I should never have written a book. He insisted from the beginning that part of me wasn't expressed except in writing, and he encouraged me to begin. He made it possible for me to write by being easy to live with. He is my severest and best critic of everything I write. We

Caudill: *KAW dle*

REBECCA CAUDILL

have had two children. A son, James, Jr., died in 1956. A daughter, Becky Jean, is a student in law school. We live in Urbana, Illinois, where my husband is technical editor for the Illinois State Natural History Survey, and where the magnificent University of Illinois library is handy for my research.

Frances Cavanah

1899-

AUTHOR OF

Two Loves for Jenny Lind; Abe Lincoln Gets His Chance; They Lived in the White House; Jenny Lind and Her Listening Cat; Etc.

Autobiographical sketch of Frances Cavanah:

EVER since I was a small girl living in southwest Indiana, I have been writing —or wanting to write. Much of my time has been spent being an editor instead, but if this work seems like a detour it is one I have enjoyed. My first ambition was to write plays, but after my graduation from De Pauw University I joined the staff of *Child Life* magazine. One of my duties as associate editor was to read the thousands of letters that poured in from the readers, and I soon began to realize how seriously children take their reading. If they liked a story or a book, they liked it very, very much. It really meant something to them, and I decided there could be no greater satisfaction than in writing for boys and girls.

Cavanah: *KAV uh naw*

After fifteen years with *Child Life,* I was the biography editor of an encyclopedia, and then became the director of a series of biographies called *Real People,* which are used in schools. In the meantime, I had edited several anthologies and written books and stories of my own.

In both writing and editing, my special interests have been history and biography. I was fortunate in having a seventh-grade teacher who gave me a special feeling for history, and I have loved it ever since. Aside from the fact that a knowledge of the past helps us better to understand the present, I enjoy trying to turn back the pages of time. My *Two Loves for Jenny Lind* told the story of the American tour of the famous Swedish Nightingale during the colorful 1850's. *Jenny Lind and Her Listening Cat,* for younger readers, while fiction, is the true story of how the great soprano got her chance. In *We Came to America* my purpose was to show America as it appeared to the succession of immigrants who have been arriving on our shores since the United States became a nation. *They Lived in the White House* told about the Presidents from the point of view of the children and grandchildren who knew and loved them. *Adventure in Courage: The Story of Theodore Roosevelt* and *Abe Lincoln Gets His Chance* were largely reminiscences of persons who had actually known them. From the time I can remember reading, I had been interested in Lincoln stories, the more so, perhaps, because I knew he had grown up in the county next to mine. Both of these famous Americans are heroes of two chapters in my latest book, *Meet the Presidents.*

As to personal information, I make my home in Washington, D.C., which is a fascinating place to live, and I appreciate the opportunity to do research at the Library of Congress. I like to travel, but late summer usually finds me returning for a visit to Petit Point, my niece's cottage west of Boston. Here, on a wooded point of land reaching out into a lake, I set up my typewriter on a picnic table in a breeze-swept "study." I have spent these past years writing and editing for a younger audience. Through my work I have made a host of young friends, some of whom I have known only through correspondence. I treasure their letters, such as the one from a fifth-grade girl, who had been studying a school history I had helped to write.

FRANCES CAVANAH

"Just think," her letter read, "if it hadn't been for you, I never would have known that Balboa discovered the Pacific."

Now I am looking forward to the day when my "honorary grandchildren"—Cynthia and Philip Nadelman, children of another niece—will be old enough to read my books.

* * *

Several of Frances Cavanah's books, among them *Our Country's Story*, have been transcribed into Braille, recorded as talking books for the blind, and translated into other languages. In 1952, her alma mater, De Pauw University, gave her a citation for attaining "distinction as a writer and editor of books for young people." In 1959, one of her books was cited by the Indiana University Writers' Conference as "the most distinguished work of literature for children" by a Hoosier author.

Betty Cavanna

1909-

AUTHOR OF

*Going on Sixteen; The Boy Next Door; Paintbox
Summer; Angel on Skis; Etc.*

Autobiographical sketch of Betty Cavanna:

A TYPICAL American small town is Haddonfield, New Jersey, where I grew up. Perhaps this accounts for my heroines, who are usually small-town girls. I have been

Cavanna: *kuh VAN uh*

involved with printer's ink since I was twelve. At that time, under the impression that I was much older, a Camden, New Jersey, newspaper editor hired me to cover the social news of my home town. Camden, incidentally, was where I was born. Throughout high school and Douglass College (where I majored in journalism) I was elbow deep in work for school papers and yearbooks. Following graduation from college, I worked for a year on a Bayonne, New Jersey, newspaper, and then entered publicity and advertising for the Presbyterian Board of Christian Education in Philadelphia.

Probably the reason I turned to teen-age novels rather than writing for small children or for adults is based on the fact that my brother and sister are ten and twelve years younger than I. During the long depression years I watched them grow and become familiar with every possible sort of teen-age crisis, both amusing and—at least momentarily—tragic. I like to think of novels for young people today as serious fiction based on realistic problems, not "written down" but written at the level of the teen-age mind. Teen-agers are people, young adults full of their own special kind of adjustments in living and needing an equally special understanding from the adults who help people their world.

After my husband's death in 1952, my son Stephen and I continued to live in Wayne, Pennsylvania. Since my recent marriage to George Russell Harrison, dean of the School

BETTY CAVANNA

of Science at the Massachusetts Institute of Technology, we have made our home in the Boston area.

* * *

Miss Cavanna has also written under the name Elizabeth Headley (her first husband was Edward T. Headley).

Jean Charlot
1898-

ILLUSTRATOR OF
*A Child's Good Night; A Child's
Good Morning; Two Little Trains;
. . . And Now Miguel; Etc.*

Autobiographical sketch of Jean Charlot:

MY training as an artist happened in Mexico, in fields only remotely related to children's book illustration, archaeology and mural painting. In the twenties, I worked for the Carnegie Institution of Washington, in the ruins of Chichén Itzá, in Yucatan, copying the bas-reliefs of haughty warriors and plumed serpents. In Mexico City, I did frescoes on the walls of public buildings, in the rather heroic manner that is the trademark of what came to be known as the Mexican mural renaissance.

I heard many a story from the lips of my Indian friends, stories meant for the young, but somewhat frightening by American standards, if not by the sturdier ones of Mother Goose. Mexican tales were full of peculiar creatures, prompt to devour delinquent little boys and girls; *nahuaques*, or sorcerers, could at will become wolves, or rare birds of prey.

My first illustrations published in the United States were for such oft-heard tales. *The Sun, The Moon, and a Rabbit*, in line and flat color, had a cool reception. Consensus was that its barbaric flavor was expected of Mexico but that American publishers would not stand for such crudities. That was in 1930 and since then crudity of a sort has become synonymous with sophistication.

To be tagged and pigeonholed by the book trade was another surprise. Not unagreeably, I became the fellow to contact when the story was about brown people, regardless of what country they came from. This enlarged my knowledge of geography. Dog fights and love feasts with authors and

JEAN CHARLOT

publishers have enlarged my knowledge of psychology. For stern criticism, there have been my four children, truly zealous to point to their father's shortcomings. As they grow up and enter their teens, something they are doing now with gusto, I may have to curtail my career as a children's books illustrator, and switch to the field of adult books.

* * *

A well-known muralist, born in Paris, Mr. Charlot has, since 1929, taught and lectured on art throughout the United States. He now lives in Honolulu where he is Senior Professor of Art at the University of Hawaii.

Richard Chase
1904-

COMPILER AND EDITOR OF
*The Jack Tales; Grandfather Tales; Hullabaloo;
American Folk Tales and Songs*

Autobiographical sketch of Richard Chase:

I WAS born near Huntsville, Alabama, on February 15, 1904. Summers, back then, we lived in a cottage on the west bluff of Monte Sano, where a neighbor, Miss Betty, and I often sat and watched sunsets together, finding in the sundown colors and clouds fairylands, and faces and figures of people and gods and demons. Miss Betty on

Jean Charlot: *ZHAN shar LO*

RICHARD CHASE

these occasions told me tales from Wagner's operas.

I walked a very long mile to a country school until I reached the fourth grade, and then graduated to Model T Fords which took me to school in Huntsville. At about the age of twelve, I boarded the little "jerkwater" branch-line passenger coach and went fearfully off to a prep school in Tennessee, where Latin, Greek, math, English, Greek, Latin were poured through my infant mind. Then college and more Latin and Greek. Oh, yes, I finally was granted a B.S. in the field of botany.

None of this "education" seems to relate to what has, over the past thirty-two years, become my Life Work. It was on a chance visit to Pine Mountain Settlement School, deep in the Kentucky mountains, that I heard my first ballad. The young'uns were waiting for an assembly to start and, without benefit of song books or teacher, a single voice began:

There was a little ship and she sailed on
the sea,
And the name of the ship was "The Merry
Golden Tree,"
And she sailed on the lonely lonesome waters
And she sailed on the lonesome sea.

And suddenly, at the second line, every child was singing: verse after verse telling the sad tale of the little cabin boy and the cruel captain. This chance visit happened to be on the school's Fair Day and so I saw my

first country dancing, a sword dance, and by midafternoon found myself dancing in a "Kentucky Set."

After that day, everywhere I went something relating to our heritage of English-American "old ways": ballads, songs, folk hymns, tales, singing games, country dances, morris dances, sword dances, The Mummers' Play—seemed to take hold of me. I learned of the work of Cecil Sharp, his founding the English Folk Dance and Song Society in England and America, his two thick volumes, *English Folk Songs from the Southern Appalachians*. I learned about Ralph Vaughan Williams and his symphonic work based on our folk music. And above all, I learned of the "living social uses" of all this lore by the Council of the Southern Mountains in its recreational activities with us eight million inhabitants of the Appalachian South.

The Jack Tales, too, I discovered by sheer chance. I was leading singing at a conference of teachers here in North Carolina, and one day Rebecca Jones, an aged "sweet singer" of traditional songs, came to sing for us. After this assembly, one of the teachers told me:

"We know a lot of old tales back home, handed down from generation to generation like you were saying about the old songs."

"What kind of tales?"

"Oh, mostly about a boy named Jack."

"Did he climb a beanstalk?"

"Bean *tree*. That's how we tell it. Oh, he got into a lot of scrapes with giants and all such, had to do certain things before he could court the girl, but he always comes out on top."

After seven years of following this lead, the Jack Tales got written down and "put in a book." I've done a lot of things besides just being a "book writer": told tales in schools, colleges, and universities; helped run "folk-game parties" in little schools and large; helped Methodist recreation workshops with these traditions; started a craft industry here where I live. Our first product, Gee-Haw Whimmydiddles, brings orders from gift shops clean out in Texas and 'way up north in Connecticut.

Now I am living in behind Beech Mountain (the Jack Tale country) in western North Carolina; and over in Boone, the county seat, I run summer-long folk festivals "of a Saturday from about three o'clock"; conduct a folk arts workshop at Appalachian

College; and direct the country dance scenes in our outdoor drama, "The Horn in the West."

Another book? Someday I hope to get on with my first "life ambition": the compilation of the finest of all traditional songs in the English language, from all possible sources and from all ages, "for living use" in schools, colleges, churches, communities.

Madye Lee Chastain
1908-
AUTHOR AND ILLUSTRATOR OF
Bright Days; Fripsey Summer; Dark Treasure; Emmy Keeps a Promise; Etc.

Autobiographical sketch of Madye Lee Chastain:

I WAS born in Texas on December 15, 1908. Some of the happiest days of my childhood were the summers spent on my grandmother's east Texas farm. To a small girl used to city life, all the new and fascinating sights and sounds and smells of a big old-fashioned farm were sheer delight —from the heady fragrance of the cape jasmine and honeysuckle in the hot Texas sun to the sharp, clean scent of scrubbed pine floors, the potatoes-and-pickles-and-spice-and-coal-oil smell of the huge old pantry, the savory aroma of fried chicken and hot biscuits.

From a very early age I loved to paint and draw, and remember illustrating Beatrix Potter's *The Tale of Peter Rabbit* (the effrontery of it!) when I was six years old. This was not in a spirit of competition, I'm sure, but was done out of love for the story.

When I graduated from high school in Dallas, my family and I moved to Atlanta, Georgia, where I went to college and to art school. Four years later, we came to New York, where I continued my art studies. For a short time I tried portrait work and exhibited paintings and etchings in group shows.

In 1936 I was married, and after the birth of my daughter in 1939 began to be really interested in the wonderful field of children's books. I was delighted with the wealth of good books and began to read to her as soon as she was old enough to listen. When she was five years old, I wrote and illustrated a little picture book about her. Subsequently, I wrote and illustrated four other small picture books, in addition to illustrating several

MADYE LEE CHASTAIN

books for other authors. However, I kept remembering those long, lovely summers of my Texas childhood and so finally wrote a book about them for an older age group. This was *Loblolly Farm*.

My own childhood experiences, people I knew, stories I heard, all seem to have found their way into one or another of my books. For example, I had been told many stories about my great-grandfather who had been a Mississippi River steamboat pilot for forty years. I became very interested in the history of the great river and its wonderful old steamboating days and this led to my writing *Steamboat South*, which ended in the old port of Jefferson, Texas, not far from Loblolly Farm. I visited Jefferson many times as a child and had been shown the old steamboat wharves which were still intact, although beginning to rot away in places.

My husband, Henry Kurt Stoessel, is an illustrator and designer, and our daughter, Roxana, studied woodcutting in college, her favorite art medium. We enjoy a great many things together, travel, the theater, art exhibitions, boating, music. We are all three members of a recorder group (recorders are the old English wooden flutes) which meets twice a month to play Elizabethan and Jacobean music (and sometimes "Red River Valley" and "Casey Jones"!). We live on a pleasant spot in New York City overlooking the Hudson River, with the other members of our family, Sugar and Spice, two beautiful and charming Siamese cats.

Madye Lee Chastain: *MAY dee LEE chas TAIN*

Joseph E. Chipperfield

1909-

AUTHOR OF

*Storm of Dancerwood; Windruff of Links Tor;
Wolf of Badenoch; Greeka, Eagle
of the Hebrides; Etc.*

Autobiographical sketch of Joseph E. Chipperfield:

PERHAPS in some ways I was one of the fortunate people who knew from an early age what I wanted to do with my life. My upbringing on a farm in Cornwall in the West Country of England did much to foster my love of the open air and for animals in general. The results of this background I carried with me into my school years, particularly into those formative years spent in a college in the south of England, where I developed a liking for the classics. I was fortunate, too, in that I went in for the study of Greek and Latin under the guidance of a priest famous in the Order of Redemptorists.

It was during this period that I began to travel a little. I visited Europe, and spent a considerable time in Ireland where, amongst other places, I stayed as a guest in the Trappist Monastery of Melleray. I had started keeping a scrapbook, and many of the notes I made about this time contained references to my many varied encounters with wildlife in unexpected places. These references were finally introduced into the books I came to write.

JOSEPH E. CHIPPERFIELD AND MAX

My first nature story appeared about this time, together with a short article on Melleray Abbey, which was published in the *Irish Monthly*. Then followed a novel, and soon afterwards, following a brief spell on a newspaper, I began to contribute regularly to a magazine devoted entirely to dogs, which association lasted for something like ten years. Many of the stories and serials I wrote during this period found publication in the United States, and led up to the books themselves. These may be classified in two groups—the dog books, and the pure nature books, narrated in a fictional manner.

Of the former, perhaps the closest to my heart is *Storm of Dancerwood*, because of all the books this is the one that is most autobiographical, and for the most part it is the tale of my own German shepherd dog, Max, and our long travels together in the West Country of England. It was during our many excursions over Exmoor that we encountered such animals as Huicie, the otter, and One-Eye, the seal. It was also while tramping the West Country with Max that some of the incidents in *Windruff of Links Tor* took place. In fact, most of the dog books contain much springing from these many happy journeys.

There now remain the nature books, such as *Greeka, Eagle of the Hebrides,* and those others with a distinctly Scottish background. In writing *Greeka,* I spent many weeks at different intervals studying a nesting site on the Isle of Skye. I was thus able to watch the young eaglets I had selected for my story, studying them from actual birth to flight. Much that happened to them during this period I have endeavored to tell in the book. I must confess that my many visits to the eagles' nest stand out as some of the most memorable occasions I have known. Because of them I learned to love more strongly than ever the sight of mountains misted with rain in the early morning, and the glimpse of landlocked stretches of water remote and silent, seeming to shiver a little as, behind the darkness, came the chill probing of the wind.

For the rest—hobbies! Just lazing by a stream or a Highland burn with my dog, Max, beside me in a like mood, both of us watching a run of salmon, or maybe glimpsing above the mountain's rim the slow turn of a hawk or an eagle. A grand life, and writing, a grand occupation!

Richard Church
1893-

AUTHOR OF

A Squirrel Called Rufus; Five Boys in a Cave; Down River; Dog Toby; Etc.

Autobiographical sketch of Richard Church:

I WAS born in Battersea, a suburb by the River Thames, in London. It was a rather dusty place, and I did not hear a blackbird sing until I was twelve years old and we moved to a village where the world was green with trees.

That taught me to love all living things, animal and vegetable. Ever since, whenever possible, I have lived in the country, and have written about it. For more than twenty years I have written a monthly essay for the *Christian Science Monitor,* always about the country life, either natural or human.

When I say human, I mean my fellow men. It takes poetry and storytelling to write about them! I have known them not only in the country but also in the town for I spent many long years as an official in Whitehall, where all the government offices have their headquarters. And somehow, nature crept in there also. At moments it was "red in tooth and claw," as it is said to be in the jungle.

But nature also knows loving-kindness and sweet provision, as I have found both in Whitehall and in the European countryside. When I had children of my own, and later grandchildren, I set out to tell them, in certain stories, about this double character of life in general. There are more such stories to come, I hope.

Now I live in a large cherry orchard, in an oast house with three towers that were once hop-drying kilns, and I look over the hills and valleys of Kent, which is called, and rightly called, The Garden of England. It is a quiet spot, except for the din of the bird choruses, and the steady tapping of my typewriter.

* * *

Mr. Church is the author of some fifty books, including *Collected Poems, The Inheritors* (Foyle Poetry Prize, 1957), *The Porch* (the Femina Vie-Heureuse Novel Prize, 1938), and *Over the Bridge,* the story of his early years (London *Sunday Times*

RICHARD CHURCH

Medal and £1,000 prize for the best literary contribution for 1955). The last title has sold more than a quarter of a million copies in England. *The Golden Sovereign,* a second autobiographical volume, deals with his life as a young man.

B. J. Chute
1913-

AUTHOR OF

Greenwillow; Blocking Back; Shift to the Right; Etc.

Autobiographical sketch of B. J. Chute:

I WAS born in Minneapolis, Minnesota, and grew up at our country home, Hazelwood, a big house in the middle of 250 acres of deep woods and a lovely place to live. My two sisters and I were tutored through the grade school years, and my first public school was West High in Minneapolis, followed by some evening courses at the University of Minnesota. Immediately after graduation from high school, I went into my father's real estate office, where I acted as his secretary for ten years, writing in my spare time. I sold my first juvenile short story in 1932, and my first adult story ten years later.

Because my early writing was all sports stories for boys, I wrote under my initials as B. J. Chute. My first name is Beatrice,

Chute: *CHOOT*

B. J. CHUTE

that novel, I found I could remember exactly how every plant and flower grew at Hazelwood and just how every animal and bird looked. An early interest in sports was responsible for my boys' stories and books, and the stories in *The Blue Cup* reflect a special interest in New York, with its policemen, children, Broadway types, and wonderful mixture of nationalities. I have always done a great deal of volunteer work in New York, especially with a shelter for temporarily homeless children in Spanish Harlem, and with the Police Department through Civilian Defense and the Police Athletic League, which supplies recreation for the city's children.

I like cooking (which includes making bread once a week), walking in the city, and, most of all, reading. The printed word still seems to me to be one of civilization's most wonderful gifts.

but I never use it, and my friends know me by my middle name, Joy. I have published hundreds of short stories for young people and adults, as well as five juvenile books and five adult books.

Both my sisters are well-known writers. Mary Grace (now Mrs. Frank Smith) writes under her initials too, as M. G. Chute, and her stories are published regularly in the *Saturday Evening Post,* among them the famous Sheriff Olson series. Marchette is a literary historian and biographer and has done biographies of Chaucer, Shakespeare, and Ben Jonson, as well as many books for young people. Most of our games when we were children were writing games, and I can't remember a time when I didn't write.

After my father's death in 1939, my mother and sisters and I moved to New York City. Mary Grace now lives near Boston with her husband, a son, and a daughter. My mother, Marchette, and I live in an apartment on Sixty-third Street near New York's East River, where we have a balcony from which we can see both ships and skyscrapers, and on which I can garden among window boxes. We have the additional company of a parakeet, a canary, and a large number of transient sparrows.

If I could trace any single influence on my writing, it would be my country background which shows most strongly in a book like *Greenwillow.* When I came to write

Marchette Chute
1909-
AUTHOR OF
The Wonderful Winter; Stories from Shakespeare
AUTHOR AND ILLUSTRATOR OF
Around and About; The Innocent Wayfaring

Autobiographical sketch of Marchette Chute:

I WAS born in Minnesota, at a place in the country called Hazelwood. My two sisters and I grew up there, in the middle of hundreds of acres that were full of birds and trees and rabbits and other useful things. When I grew up and wrote my first book of rhymes, I dedicated it to Hazelwood because it was such a wonderful place.

Whenever it rained, my sisters and I played indoors, and we had a whole series of very complicated games. We designed our own paper dolls and wrote schoolbooks for them, and in fact we did so much writing that it is not surprising we all grew up to be authors. My older sister is M. G. Chute, the short-story writer, and my younger one is B. J. Chute, who does books for children as well as novels and short stories and whose famous *Greenwillow* is a reflection of her childhood in the country.

We were all tutored through the grades, and because my mother is English we

Marchette Chute: *Mar SHET CHOOT*

MARCHETTE CHUTE

studied the history of England before we learned about George Washington. This is perhaps a good way to do it, since Washington was himself an Englishman, and this early training of mine may be one reason why so many of my books have English backgrounds.

I was especially interested in the first great English poet, Geoffrey Chaucer, and I specialized in his period, the Middle Ages, when I went to the University of Minnesota. Then, when I came to New York with my mother and sisters, I found the wonderful resources of the New York Public Library and decided I would like to write a story about Chaucer's England. The result was a love story for girls called *The Innocent Wayfaring*. Then I became equally interested in Shakespeare and his period and did several books on the subject. One of them was called *The Wonderful Winter* and tells the story of a boy who knew Shakespeare and acted in his company.

Over the years I have done seven books for grownups and seven for children. I illustrated some of them because I spent a year at the Minneapolis School of Art and know a little, although not much, about drawing. I like to do drawings, but I like writing much better.

I find New York a very pleasant place to live. There are fewer trees and rabbits in it but a great many more people. We live in

an apartment overlooking the East River, with gulls flying by the windows and a fine view of the new moon and the bridge and the midtown towers. Our balcony has a bird-feeding station on it, and a little yew tree, and the apartment is so full of plants that we might really be in the country after all.

Beverly Cleary

1916-

AUTHOR OF
Henry Huggins; Ellen Tebbits; Otis Spofford; Fifteen; Etc.

Autobiographical sketch of Beverly Cleary:

WHEN I was a little girl named Beverly Bunn, I lived on a beautiful farm in the town of Yamhill in the Willamette Valley in Oregon. Because Yamhill was too small to have a library of its own, my mother arranged to have the state library send out small collections of books. Once a week she acted as town librarian in a lodge hall upstairs over a bank. I remember how eagerly I waited for each new crate of books because I knew that a few children's books would be included.

When I was six years old we moved to Portland, where for the first time I had access to a public library. When I had learned to read, I made regular trips to the library. As I grew up, I read almost every book in the children's collection but I could rarely find what I wanted to read most of all. That was funny stories about ordinary American boys and girls. It seemed to me that all the children in books lived in foreign lands or were very rich or very poor or had adventures that could never happen to anyone I knew. I wanted to read about boys and girls who lived in the same kind of neighborhood I lived in and went to a school like the one I attended.

When I was in the sixth grade I wrote a story for my library class at school. The teacher liked it so much that she told me that when I grew up I should write stories for boys and girls. This seemed like such a good idea that I made up my mind that someday I would write books—the kind of books I wanted to read.

BEVERLY CLEARY

It seemed perfectly natural that I should also want to be a children's librarian and so, after finishing high school in Portland and graduating from the University of California, I studied library work with children at the University of Washington. Until I was married in 1940, I was children's librarian in Yakima, Washington. During World War II, I was the librarian in an Army hospital in Oakland, California.

Then one day I decided that if I were ever going to write a book I should sit down at the typewriter and write it. This is exactly what I did and *Henry Huggins* was the result. Although I wrote the book in California, the story takes place in the neighborhood I knew as a child in Portland. When I had written several books about Henry, Ellen Tebbits, and their friends, I was invited to speak at a junior high school. After my talk, several girls came to me and asked, "Why don't you write books like you write, only about our age?" This was the beginning of *Fifteen,* in which I tried to capture the funny and painful emotions that make up the important experience of first love.

My husband is Clarence Cleary and we are the parents of twins, Marianne and Malcolm. We live in Berkeley, California, in a house on the top of the hills overlooking San Francisco Bay.

Jack Coggins
1911-

CO-AUTHOR AND ILLUSTRATOR OF
Rockets, Jets, Guided Missiles and Space Ships;
By Space Ship to the Moon

ILLUSTRATOR OF
Fighting Ships of the United States Navy;
All About Rockets and Jets; Etc.

Autobiographical sketch of Jack Coggins:

I WAS born in a cavalry barracks in London, England, in 1911. My father served in a regiment of the famous Household Cavalry and my earliest memories are of the tall, scarlet-coated guardsmen with their shining helmets and cuirasses, the trumpet calls, and the magnificent, jet-black troop horses.

During the First World War I lived by the sea, where often we could hear the distant rumble of the guns in France. Warships and airplanes, sometimes German ones, were everyday things and through the streets of our little town marched many hundreds of thousands of men on their way to the ships, which would take them across the Channel to France. My favorite toys were lead soldiers and model boats. Perhaps it is no wonder that when I started to draw, my scrawly pictures all were battle scenes with ships and planes and bursting shells.

When I came to this country in 1923, I lived in Roslyn near Long Island Sound and had real boats instead of toy ones. I thought of being an engineer but as I have trouble adding two and two I went to art school instead. I now could paint pictures of ships as well as sail them.

When World War II started, I drew many battle pictures for *Life* and other magazines, and illustrated *Fighting Ships of the United States Navy.* In the Army I was assigned to the Army weekly, *Yank,* and sent back to Europe to draw battle pictures from real life. There I went up on bombing missions and down in submarines and saw a little of the war with all sorts of units: destroyers and PT boats and United States Army tanks.

Rockets always interested me and after the war the late Fletcher Pratt and I did *Rockets, Jets, Guided Missiles and Space Ships* and *By Space Ship to the Moon.* These were followed by other books and many science-fiction covers.

JACK COGGINS

I collect old guns and weapons, and my latest book is all about knights and armor *(The Illustrated Book of Knights)*. I live on a farm in Pennsylvania, where we have many animals and pets and my wife raises Toggenberg goats. When not painting or writing, I like to relax in my workshop. We make some of our furniture and many things we use around the farm. We have done a lot of building and our masonry work, while not professional, is certainly sturdy.

Occasionally I do a painting for the United States Navy and just recently spent a wonderful week on one of our largest and most modern aircraft carriers, the U.S.S. *Ranger*.

* * *

In 1958 Willy Ley revised *Rockets, Jets, Guided Missiles and Space Ships,* and the revision was published under the title *Rockets, Satellites and Space Travel.*

Carroll B. Colby

1904-

AUTHOR AND ILLUSTRATOR OF
Our Fighting Jets; F.B.I.; Military Vehicles; First Fish; Etc.

Autobiographical sketch of Carroll B. Colby:

THE trouble with writing an autobiographical sketch is that you either sound conceited as the very dickens, or as though you had done nothing worth writing about in the first place. This will probably sound like a combination of both.

I was born in Claremont, New Hampshire, in 1904, and attended school there until my thankful graduation from Stevens High School in 1922. From there I went to the School of Practical Art in Boston to learn to be a cartoonist and commercial illustrator. I graduated from SPA in 1925 and sailed to Puerto Rico to make my fortune as a free-lance artist. I was very successful, reducing my fortune to eighteen cents in a matter of weeks, so signed on with the United States Customs Service, then busily but rather fruitlessly engaged in trying to keep Puerto Rico as "dry" as the then prohibition laws futilely hoped to do. We accomplished rather vague success, but it did give me a chance to chase assorted smugglers for several months and pick up many anecdotes and much material for yarns later on.

Returning to the United States, via working my way north on a freighter, I took a position in Charlotte, North Carolina, as commercial artist and newspaper cartoonist for a short spell, then returned to Boston for more of the same.

In 1928 I met and married Lila Thoday (who knew little of what was ahead of her by way of trial and tribulation) and moved to New York to try to prove that two could live as cheaply as one. The proof was many years in arriving!

I learned to fly gliders in 1931, and so, becoming an overnight "expert" on aviation matters, began to write and illustrate articles on the subject for various aviation magazines. In 1937 I was offered the post of editor of *Air Trails* and *Air Progress* magazines, published by Street and Smith in New York. Carried out these chores until 1943, when I accepted the post of aviation editor for *Popular Science Monthly.* While in that capacity, I was accredited as a United States war correspondent, and assigned to the (then) Army Air Force, writing articles on arctic flying, survival, and search and rescue in Newfoundland and Labrador. I later went to Alaska to write similar articles. I left *PSM* in 1946 to free-lance and since then have "appeared" in over twenty-five national magazines.

I sold my first book, *Gabbit, the Magic Rabbit* (considered pretty "corny" by my two youngsters), to Coward-McCann in 1950. This was followed by *Our Fighting*

CARROLL B. COLBY

Jets the following year, and two nature books. Since then I have been very lucky, with a present total of nearly thirty-five books being published with quite pleasant success, about five a year. This includes a six-book series, which I have also illustrated, dealing with outdoor sports for the young sportsman. Those were particularly good fun to do, for I have hunted and fished in many places and camped in still others, from the arctic to the tropics, picking up (often the hard, cold and wet way) many things to pass along to the young outdoorsman.

Besides writing and illustrating the so-called Colby Books, I write and illustrate a daily feature appearing in a number of newspapers in the East. This is called "Adventure Today," and includes material on haunted houses, buried treasure, weapons, antiques, etc., a sort of escape valve for all the small and unimportant but interesting things I have picked up along my over twenty-five years of writing.

I think the secret (if there is one), of successful writing for youngsters is first of all to like writing, youngsters, and what they like. Fortunately, I like all three parts of the formula. It is not difficult to write about many things if you are interested in many things, and the fact that I have always tried to see and do for myself rather than obtain information secondhand, has enabled me to write enthusiastically and I hope accurately about many subjects. Fortunately, I was

brought up in the country where a fishing pole, jackknife, and a twenty-two rifle were standard equipment, along with freckles and missing front teeth, for all the young males. This enabled me to get to know the woods and the critters who live there. Such fine "neighbors" have always intrigued me and many of my books reflect this interest.

Although I now live within seeing distance (on a clear day) of New York, the woods about my home are still full of interesting folk wearing fur and feathers, so I have no trouble keeping alive that earlier enthusiasm for such guys and gals. Luckily my wife, a rabid camper, my son Fred, an outdoorsman, and my daughter Susan, an anthropologist, all share my interest and enthusiasm and curiosity about the outdoors and the things which most young readers enjoy reading about and looking at. No writer could have a more cooperative and tolerant gang to live with and work for than mine. To me, writing for youngsters *is* a wonderful "racket"!

* * *

In 1961 Mr. Colby had seven more books published. One is a book on animals, and a second is *Night People*, which deals with "all the folks who work at night while youngsters are supposed to be asleep."

Olivia E. Coolidge

1908-

AUTHOR OF
Greek Myths; Legends of the North; The Trojan War; Egyptian Adventures; Etc.

Autobiographical sketch of Olivia E. Coolidge:

I WAS born in Buckinghamshire, England. My father was a well-known newspaper columnist and part-time Oxford professor. He spent a good deal of his time in London or Oxford and seemed to meet all sorts of interesting people whom we never saw. For instead of living in one town or the other, which would have been convenient, our family was uncomfortably planted halfway between the two in a spot rather difficult to get at from either.

My parents wanted to live in the real country, and in a way we certainly did. There was no gas or electricity, no central heating, and no hot-water system in our house when I was a child. We grew all our own fruit and vegetables; and it was lucky that we did, as we had no car and had to walk three miles into town if we wanted to buy anything. Still, there were five of us children and we were allowed to run wild, so that we did not have a bad time; though I used to wish hard when I was at school that my parents would act just a little bit more like ordinary people. I sometimes wonder if my family does not feel the same about me, since having a mother who likes to write for children must be awkward.

In a way, I started writing at a very early age. My sister and I used to make up fairy stories and tell them to each other when we were put early to bed. One day we decided that we would make a book out of them, but there was a drawback. We were neither of us very good at our copybooks, and we did not see how we could ever write one whole story, let alone a collection, down on paper. Mother offered to help, but it soon turned out that a story which sounded splendid in bed or by candlelight in the nursery was less exciting when dictated very slowly to a patient grownup. I never tried writing a book again for quite a while, though I did write some tremendous long poems when I was about fourteen.

After I had been to school and to Oxford and had taught for a few years in London, I came over to the United States on a good, long visit which turned out to last the rest of my life. Naturally, I was too busy getting used to new scenes and new people and new ways of bringing up children to have much attention to spare for writing at first. However, because my own childhood was different from most people's here, I got in the habit of telling stories to groups of children around a fire, sometimes about things I had read. During World War II, I was teaching, and at the same time I was learning about what American children read, and what they don't like to read, and what they are missing. After the war, like all of us, I had time for myself. The very first thing I did with it was to write a children's book. I have been writing continuously ever since, not always for children, but generally so. I hope to go on doing much the same sort of thing for a very long time.

OLIVIA E. COOLIDGE

My husband works in New York, so we live in Connecticut, as deep in the country as we can get and be comfortable. Unlike my parents, I want a warm house, a good light, an easy chair, and lots of hot water. But we have a big dog as well, and pigeons, and flowers, and even a greenhouse. We have only four children between us, but they have always kept us busy. I rather think they don't read my books but I never ask them.

Barbara Cooney
1917-

ILLUSTRATOR OF

Chanticleer and the Fox; Christmas in the Barn; Peter's Long Walk; Where Have You Been? Etc.

Autobiographical sketch of Barbara Cooney:

MY twin brother and I were born in Brooklyn, New York, where we lived for two weeks. Along with two younger brothers, we were brought up on Long Island during the school year and in Maine during the summer. The latter is still Mecca for all of us, and we return each year if we are able.

My father was a stockbroker, but my mother was an artist. That I too am an artist is largely due to the tubes of paint, brushes, paper and other art supplies that were always available to my mother's chil-

Bradford Bachrach
BARBARA COONEY

dren. As far back as I can remember, I could always entertain myself by drawing pictures. I continued to do so during my school and college (Smith '38) years. Later I studied lithography and etching at the Art Students League in New York City.

At about this time I began illustrating and haven't stopped since. With one exception: when my brothers joined the Army during World War II, I joined the WAC. During this period I married Guy Murchie, with whom I had two children, a girl named Gretel and a boy named Barnaby. I am now the wife of Dr. C. Talbot Porter, a general practitioner in Pepperell, Massachusetts. Two more children have been added to the family: Talbot Jr., and Phoebe. We live in a rambling old house surrounded by broad lawns, tall trees and gardens. I couldn't ask for a pleasanter ivory tower. Possibly the term *ivory tower* is incorrect, for *ivory tower* doesn't generally connote hustle and bustle, which this house is full of.

I am now working on my fiftieth book. My being an illustrator is a highly satisfactory arrangement for me. Wives of country doctors catch only fleeting glimpses of their husbands. But I can be busy and happy working, still see my children even though I'm a "working mother," and be right on hand when my husband returns at night.

Although I am probably something of a romantic, I am quite realistic. I draw only the things I know about. Indeed, I am unable to draw any other way. I am always as truthful as I can possibly be. I draw from life whenever possible, and do not invent facts or "suggest" with a vague line something I am not sure about. In spite of this, my pictures don't look realistic; they always look like *me*, which bothers me. However, they are the truth—as I see it—and my attempt to communicate about the things that matter to me.

William Corbin

1916-

AUTHOR OF
Deadline; High Road Home; Golden Mare; Pony for Keeps; Etc.

Autobiographical sketch of William Corbin McGraw:

A S many writers have done, I sneaked into fiction writing by the back door—newspapering. Born in Des Moines, Iowa, I became an omnivorous reader at an early age and it seemed more or less inevitable that someday I should work at the writing trade myself. As I recall, I broke out in an adolescent rash of poetry—ghastly stuff, but anyway my mother liked it.

Recovering from this ailment in the fullness of time, I was graduated from Drake University in 1936, then went to Harvard for two years of graduate study. By this time I was writing short stories. These, while not as nauseating as my poetry, were obviously not going to bring me fame and fortune, or even a square meal. Accordingly, I went to work for the Athens *Messenger,* a daily paper in southeastern Ohio. This was after writing something over one hundred letters to publishers all over the country describing my inestimable talents.

The job was the beginning of a (sometimes) beautiful friendship between me and the newspaper business that lasted for fourteen years and took me from the *Messenger* to the Cleveland *Plain Dealer,* then to the Oklahoma City *Times,* and, last, to the San Diego *Tribune,* writing what must have

John O'Hara Cosgrave II
1908-

ILLUSTRATOR OF
*Wind, Sand and Stars; Come In; Carry
On, Mr. Bowditch; Let the Best
Boat Win; Etc.*

WILLIAM CORBIN

Autobiographical sketch of John O'Hara Cosgrave II:

I HAD the good fortune to be born in San Francisco, a city almost surrounded by water. My earliest recollection is one of dashing along a beach, splashing in the waves. Since then, whenever possible, I have been on the water or making pictures of it.

At the age of fifteen, I and three high school friends bought an old Navy whaleboat, named her *Moby Dick* and rigged her as a cat schooner, sailing her all over the large and often treacherous waters of San Francisco Bay. We had a shipwreck, a wild experience in a gale which nearly drowned us, and as many adventures as boys learning to sail manage to find. During vacations, the four of us got jobs on laid-up square-riggers, painting and working on the rigging. When the *Moby Dick* became worn out from hard use, I bought another whaleboat and rigged her as a ketch. She was called *Typee* and probably was the slowest boat on the Bay. The installation of a one-lung, make-and-break ignition engine made her a serviceable sailer. Every free week end was spent sailing up and down the rivers and over the bays.

At Lowell High School, I rowed on the crew, and we were the Bay champions for three years. I went to Marin Junior College which was very handy to the places where I kept my boat and afforded, as well, a long ferryboat ride as a bonus. After that, I went to the University of California, majoring in art.

In 1930 I left for Paris to study painting with André Lhote for two years. While there, I spent a lot of time wandering around the city sketching, and in the Musée de la Marine at the Louvre studying the models and pictures of ships. All the seaports of France fascinated me and I still have quantities of notebooks filled with drawings of ships and scenes of all the harbors I frequented.

I came to New York in 1932 and started doing book jackets, illustrating books, doing magazine illustrating and advertisements.

been millions of highly perishable words as reporter, feature writer, and daily columnist.

Somewhere along the line the romance began to cool and when my wife's first book for young people was published in 1951 I decided to try my hand at book writing. *Deadline,* a newspaper story for teen-age readers, appeared in 1952, and we decided to cast ourselves adrift upon the uncertain sea of free-lance writing. As an anchor to windward, we bought the twenty-three-acre filbert ranch in the Willamette Valley just south of Portland, Oregon, where we now live with our children, Peter, and Laurie, our two horses, two dogs, three (at the moment) cats, and one parakeet. We have yet to regret the move.

Bouncing around the orchard on a tractor provides relaxation of a rather strenuous nature from my writing chores, and the writing in turn provides relief from the bouncing. It's an ideal arrangement from a waistline point of view. Perhaps I should explain why I am William Corbin at the typewriter and William McGraw on the tractor. My wife writes as Eloise Jarvis McGraw and when my first book came out our publishers thought it would be less confusing all around if I had another name. Accordingly, I dropped the last .name and have used my middle name, Corbin, ever since. Now nobody is confused but me.

Since *Deadline* I have published three more books and some short stories.

JOHN O'HARA COSGRAVE II

Drafted in 1943, I endured a year in the infantry and the rest of the war in OSS. The State Department sent me to San Francisco to do charts and graphs for the beginnings of the United Nations. On the happy day of release, I tore home to Columbia Heights, in Brooklyn, New York. Ours is an ancient house, full of books relating to the sea, cookbooks (cooking is a hobby), pictures of ships, and all kinds of equipment for painting. A two-block walk puts me almost in the East River bay where I can revel in the shipping.

Summers are spent on Cape Cod, where my wife and I sail our Herreshoff Bull's Eye sloop, dig quahogs, and fish for scup in Buzzards Bay.

Harold Courlander

1908-

AUTHOR OF

Kantchil's Lime Pit; Uncle Bouqui of Haiti; The Tiger's Whisker

CO-AUTHOR OF

The Cow-Tail Switch; The Fire on the Mountain; Etc.

Autobiographical sketch of Harold Courlander:

THE first six years of my life were in Indianapolis, and the high spots were a flood which put the town half under water, Indians in war paint passing out handbills advertising their annual Hiawatha pageant, and putting nails on the streetcar tracks on Central Avenue. I also remember waiting on Central Avenue while my aunt hurled a freshly bought fish at me from the window of a passing trolley car.

My father was then a storekeeper (later he became an accomplished "primitive" painter at the age of eighty-five), and when his business failed he moved the family to Detroit, where I grew up and had my schooling. I suppose growing up in Detroit had something to do with awakening my interest in other nationalities and cultures. Not far from where we lived was a large Polish settlement; closer still was a Negro section; and across the street from my school was an orphanage maintained by German Lutherans. The first girl that mixed me up and made me feel foolish (age nine) was from a Hungarian family.

My formal education included an A.B. degree at the University of Michigan, followed by special graduate studies there and at Columbia. During the depression and drought years of the mid-thirties, our family bought a farm near Romeo, Michigan, and astounded our rural neighbors by our blithe and innocent approach to agriculture. We did everything wrong the first year, when practically no rain fell, and as a result had the only corn crop within five miles.

My travels have taken me to various parts of the United States, Canada, India, Africa, Haiti, Cuba, the Middle East, and Europe. I have worked for the United States Government as editor, writer, and chief of news and broadcast operations (Voice of America), and, during World War II, I was supervisor of news and features operations for the Office of War Information in Bombay. I have worked with the United States Delegation to the United Nations as press officer, with the United Nations itself as information officer, and with the Douglas Aircraft Corporation as historian of one of its overseas wartime projects.

Strangely enough, I have never thought of myself as a "junior author." My interest in young people's books is devoted to folklore materials. I have drawn heavily upon folklore and other "oral literature" of various cultures in writing adult books, as well. In presenting for children the folk tales of Indonesia, West Africa, Ethiopia, Haiti, and other regions of the world, I have had to be selective and I have tried to keep the language and imagery simple and straightfor-

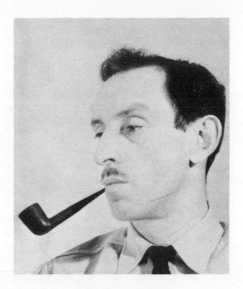

HAROLD COURLANDER

ward, but to me most of these tales are as suitable for adults as for children.

Unfortunately, despite their mature wit, subtlety, irony, and reflections on human foibles, folk tales are widely regarded as "fairy tales" in our culture, and relegated to some arbitrary age group, such as six to twelve. I have always felt that six to sixty and up would be more appropriate. The thing that interests me most about the Negro folk tales of the New World and Africa is their immediacy to life, in contrast to the European-type folk tale which has been perpetuated despite its amoral character and its frequent lack of meaning in terms of living.

In addition to the folk-tale collections for children, I have published two Negro folk plays, two books on the life and arts of the Haitian people, and a novel dealing with a dictator in the West Indies.

Margaret Maze Craig

1911-

AUTHOR OF

Trish; Marsha; Three Who Met; Now That I'm Sixteen; Etc.

Autobiographical sketch of Margaret Maze Craig:

I WAS born in Ridgway, a small town in northwestern Pennsylvania, January 16, 1911. During my teen-age years I longed for the glamour of city life, but when I started writing I was very glad that my background had been exactly what it was. Living in a small town it is impossible not to know a lot of people well and people, of course, are a writer's business.

I wrote my first novel when I was in the fourth grade. I wrote a whole *series* of novels. I referred to them as the Bobby and Betty books and they were intended as direct competition to Laura Lee Hope, who wrote about the Bobbsey twins. I wasn't as prolific as she, nor as successful commercially. None of my so-called novels was longer than a short-short story, nor did any of them see print.

I always knew that I wanted to be a writer, so when the time came for a college education I told my parents that I wished to major in journalism. My mother had other ideas. She believed that the only "proper" profession for a young lady was teaching, and she said, "If you study journalism what will you do for a *living?*" To this I had no answer, so I enrolled in a state teachers' college at Indiana, Pennsylvania, where, after four years, I received a bachelor of science degree. My major was home economics but I always earned my best grades in the English courses, particularly composition, which I loved.

For three years I worked as a home economist for an electric utility company and then I got married and began putting into practice the things I had been telling others to do. This wasn't as easy as I expected.

When my husband went overseas during World War II, I decided that the time had come to try writing for publication. I first experimented with greeting-card verse and sold nothing for months, but on the day I finally received a check for two dollars I wrote to my husband, then in the Philippines, and said, "Today I am a writer!"

After the verses began to click, I turned to prose. Some of my articles sold; many didn't, but it was the publication of my first short story which really charted my career. The story was about a teen-age girl, and its appearance in a women's magazine brought me a request for a teen-age novel. *Trish* was the result, and I enjoyed the writing of it so much that I have done nothing but this type of thing since.

I write about and for teen-age girls because I believe in them. I believe in them so much that I can't *help* writing about them.

MARGARET MAZE CRAIG

They are so wholly themselves—honest in their emotions, true in their actions—that to me they represent the most *real* of all people.

My most loyal fans are my husband, Roy, and our daughters, Judy and Jane.

Pers Crowell
1910-
AUTHOR AND ILLUSTRATOR OF
Beau Dare; Six Good Friends; The First Horseman; Cavalcade of American Horses; Etc.

Autobiographical sketch of Pers Crowell:

A LONG time ago, when I was a very young boy, I learned that horses are magic. They can make a boy or girl's blood tingle. They can make imaginations soar. The first time I realized this was when a boy in my town got four Shetland ponies—a little stallion and three diminutive mares. The owner rode the stallion and three friends of his choosing accompanied him astride the mares. My older brother often rode one of the mares. I was too young to ride then, but I shall never grow too old to forget those prancing horses with tossing manes and forelocks. I'm sure a pony must affect every child in the same way.

As a boy, I rode horses on the ranches near my home town in the eastern part of Washington State and on my uncle's farm in the Yakima Valley. I even considered becoming a cowboy until I lost my old ten-gallon hat. But school changes a lot of things. I graduated from Pasco High School, worked for a time as a stenographer for a railroad superintendent, then decided to follow an art career. I went to New York City and studied at the Phoenix Art Institute. Later, I attended Chouinard's in Los Angeles.

Illustration was my main interest, but like most young artists I had to start at the bottom. I went to Portland, Oregon, and worked at advertising art a number of years. During those early years in Portland, I adopted a hobby. You can guess what it was —horses! In a way, it was an accident that my love of horses and my art were brought together.

One day an artist friend of mine suggested, "Why don't you write and illustrate a book about horses?" This was a startling idea, but it turned out to be a fruitful one, for the product was *Beau Dare: American Saddle Colt.* It was fun to try to capture the magic of horses with words and drawings.

McGraw-Hill published my first book in 1945 and four others followed—all about horses. In addition to my own books, I have illustrated forty or more stories by other authors.

My wife, Donna, and I live on a small farm near Beaverton, Oregon. At one end of our house is my studio, where I write and illustrate. We have two collies, two cats,

PERS CROWELL

and a horse. Ebony, the horse, is our oldest animal friend. He is over twenty-one years old and has been my model for many, many illustrations. There is a lot of nice pasture here on our place—more than Ebony can eat. So the other day we decided Eb needed company. We're going to raise Shetland ponies. The wheel has really come full circle. We now actually have the stallion and three little mares!

Maureen Daly
1921-
AUTHOR OF
Seventeenth Summer; Twelve Around the World;
Patrick Takes a Trip; Etc.

Autobiographical sketch of Maureen Daly:

IN the winter of 1955-1956 I took a trip to Ireland, went up to the little village of Castlecaufield, County Tyrone, in the north, and knocked on a front door. It was opened by my Aunt Ellen, an old school-teacher and the same kind aunt who had accompanied us to the boat when my parents and (then) two sisters sailed for the United States. We girls were all under three when we left Ireland and until that winter I had never been back.

Yesterday I sat at the typewriter trying to work out a story about my visit back home. I mentioned the old, crumbling castle with the rooks nesting in the broken stones, the narrow, winding road that leads out of town to the horse market in Balleygawley, and the few back-hill farmers who still sit around the fireplace at night smoking clay pipes and talking about politics—or the trouble with "wee folk."

In almost everything I write, I seem to travel far for the subject—or else write microscopically about things that happen right at home. All during my childhood and high school days, "home" for me was the town of Fond du Lac, Wisconsin, right on the shores of Lake Winnebago. My first novel, *Seventeenth Summer*, and many, many short stories, were written about people and experiences from that town. All I changed was the names.

Contrarily, *Twelve Around the World* is made up of the true stories of young pepole from as far north as Iceland and as far south as French Equatorial Africa. To get

MAUREEN DALY

material for this book, my husband—writer Bill McGivern—and our two children, Megan and Patrick, spent twenty months traveling—an eight-day boat trip out to the Canary Islands, a night ride through the mountainous winter snows on the Orient Express train into Yugoslavia, an airplane ride at twenty thousand feet over the broad Sahara Desert and back again into the noise and bustle of New York City.

Besides writing fiction, I have been a magazine editor, and a police reporter for the Chicago *Tribune*. So a combination of training goes into my work: I like to make up stories—and I like facts, too. Now I try to see, feel, and find out as much as I can about any plot or subject. Then I begin to write.

*   *   *

When Miss Daly was sixteen, she wrote a short story, "Sixteen," which won first prize in a national short-story contest conducted by *Scholastic Magazine*. The story was selected for inclusion in the 1938 volume of the *O. Henry Memorial Award Prize Stories*, and was later reprinted in *Redbook*, eliciting a great deal of fan mail. In 1941, Miss Daly, then twenty and a junior in college, won the first Dodd, Mead Intercollegiate Literary Fellowship with the outline of *Seventeenth Summer*, which has since become a classic. For some years she was editor of the sub-deb department of the *Ladies' Home Journal*.

Helen Fern Daringer

1892-

AUTHOR OF
*Adopted Jane; Like a Lady; Pilgrim Kate;
The Golden Thorn; Etc.*

Autobiographical sketch of Helen Fern Daringer:

WHEN you come to think of it, everybody—that is, everybody who likes to read—grows up in two places at once. First, of course, there is the particular place where you happened to be born and where you live until you go away to college. For me that particular place happened to be Illinois—Mattoon, where I was born, and Danville, where my family moved when I was ten.

Towns like these are happy places. The country comes almost to the very doorstep, with lanes for bicycles, fields and woods for hikes and picnics, for flower hunting and nut gathering, streams for wading, a river for rowing and skating, hills for winter coasting, and roads that beckon to golden far horizons.

The "town part" of the town is just the right size for neighborliness and friendships, for school and Sunday school, for games and fun and work. There are streets where you feel as much at home as in your own yard, and streets which are "different," which you like to explore. Perhaps best of all, towns like these have libraries. For if you like to read, you live as real a part of your life in the books you read as within the walls of your own home with your family. Some inner part of you finds yourself sharing the life of storybook palaces, of log cabins and Crusader castles, of Indian tepees and of houses very like your own—some of them far away and long ago, and some no older than yourself.

So it is that the two places in which I grew up—Illinois and books—account for the stories I write. It was a long time before I knew that writing was what I wished most of all to do. I graduated from the University of Chicago, taught school and college, traveled in Europe and America, studied at Columbia University for a master's and a doctor's degree (one of those Ph.D. degrees, not an M.D.), taught again, traveled to China, Japan, Korea, Scandinavia, and Finland. Then one summer during the war, when I could not travel, I began just for fun to write a story, although I did not know just what it would be about. It turned out to be *Adopted Jane*, and it was such pleasure to do (but hard work, too!) that a year or two later I gave up teaching to have more time for writing. When a book is finished I go traveling, and some of the travels furnish backgrounds for stories of far places and distant times, Holland and England, for example, and Syria and old Jerusalem. I live in New York City.

Louis Darling

1916-

AUTHOR AND ILLUSTRATOR OF
*Penguins; Chickens; Greenhead; Seals and
Walruses; Etc.*

Autobiographical sketch of Louis Darling:

I WAS born in Stamford, Connecticut, April 26, 1916. Aside from a few years when quite young, I was educated and grew up there. After graduating from high school, I went to art school in New York for two years and studied privately for two more. After art school I worked in an agency for a short time and then enlisted in the Air Force in 1942. I served for about three and a half years as a photographer, two of these in Europe in a heavy bombardment group of the Eighth Air Force.

After the war I free-lanced in commercial art. My first book came through a friend

HELEN FERN DARINGER

LOUIS DARLING

who was scheduled to illustrate *The River Never Sleeps,* by Roderick Haig-Brown, but was unable to do so. The same publishers soon offered me another book, this time for children. Thus, quite by accident, I became launched in a career of doing exactly what I had always wanted to do, illustrate books. I started to write my own books because it seemed to me that there was seldom enough cooperation between author and illustrator. The best way to get this cooperation was to become the author myself. As the years have gone by I have done less and less commercial work and more and more books. The total is now well over thirty-five, six of which I have written myself.

The out-of-doors, hunting, fishing, camping, and natural history were the great interests of my youth. As I grew older this turned to an interest in the biological sciences and to the education of children in these sciences. My life has been pretty much a conflict between an interest in science and an interest in art. The science half was stimulated no end when I married Lois MacIntyre, a zoologist and scientific artist, in 1946. Fortunately, we have been able to bring the two parts of our lives together. All of the books I have written and many of those I illustrate are on the natural sciences. We have now commenced to write and illustrate books together.

Unfortunately, we have no children. Our year-round family consists of a female gold-en retriever, Natasha; a cat, Catherine; and a pair of mallard ducks. However, our numbers fluctuate wildly. In the spring, our many younger friends bring us every lost, strayed or stolen wild baby they come upon. Everything from hungry fledgling birds to salamander eggs that won't hatch arrives at our house. There is usually a batch of baby mallards, kittens, or puppies either on the way or growing up. We also teach biology in the Unitarian Sunday school and talk at local public schools when we have time. We have a small sailboat which serves as a pleasant means of getting to lonely islands where the beachcombing is best.

* * *

Mr. Darling did illustrations for *The Enormous Egg,* by Oliver Butterworth, and *Exploring Science,* by Jonathan Leonard. He regards these as the most notable books he has illustrated. With his wife he wrote and illustrated *Before and After the Dinosaurs.*

Laurent de Brunhoff

See *Brunhoff, Laurent de*

Dola de Jong

1911-

AUTHOR OF
*The Level Land; Return to the Level Land;
The Picture Story of Holland;
Nikkernik, Nakkernak and Nokkernok; Etc.*

Autobiographical sketch of Dola de Jong:

SOME time ago I was told that the high school in my home town of Arnhem, Holland, served as a fortress during the famous World War II battle of Arnhem. My son, Ian, then five, was much impressed when I told him this story, and, as he still had no concept of time, asked if I gave a good account of myself during the fracas and whether I escaped unharmed. After we had this muddle straightened out (which took, all told, about a week) I had sunk considerably in his estimation.

"You weren't even around," he said with the greatest contempt.

Indeed I wasn't. During the war years I lived in Tangier, Morocco, and in New York, and was very busy writing and broadcasting. I suppose that working on *The Level Land,*

DOLA DE JONG

I have written stories as far back as I can remember. My first children's book was published when I was eighteen, and was followed by nine more, three novels, and innumerable short pieces. Nowadays I am doing editorial work and am free-lancing for American and Dutch publications. I am working on another novel and I am employed by the United States Information Agency, broadcasting my stories about America to Holland and Belgium.

In 1947 I won the Literature Prize of the City of Amsterdam, and in 1955 I was elected to the Dutch Academy of Arts and Letters. I live in New York City.

Meindert DeJong

1906-

AUTHOR OF
The Wheel on the School; Hurry Home, Candy; Shadrach; The House of Sixty Fathers; Etc.

Autobiographical sketch of Meindert DeJong:

I WAS born in Wierum, Friesland, the Netherlands. Came to America at the age of eight, settled with my parents in Grand Rapids, Michigan, where I've lived ever since. Attended local parochial elementary and high school, and Calvin College also located here. Studied briefly at the University of Chicago. Graduated from Calvin College in the depression, 1929-1930, and with no jobs to be had, supported myself in rapid succession at all kinds of manual labor such as tinning and gravedigging; also was briefly a college professor. When the little, one-horse college in Iowa started paying us in scrip, I retired from professoring and became a poultry farmer.

While starving at that, wrote and sold my first children's book, *The Big Goose and the Little White Duck,* to Harper & Brothers, and have been with that house ever since. I've now had some fifteen-sixteen books published; have won the Newbery Medal; have been runner-up to it thrice; have won the Child Study Association Award, and the 1957 German Children's Book Award with the translation of *The Wheel on the School.*

I started writing children's books because during the depression the little magazines to which I was contributing my adult short

the book that everybody liked best, including myself, served as an escape from the worries about my family in Holland and the frustration I felt about mankind's stupidity. Though the family in *The Level Land* was a figment of my imagination, several members of that happy group have a great similarity to some of my relatives. Jan was much like my brother Jan who died in a concentration camp, Ruth reminds me of myself at that age, and Pieter Pim. . . .

It is a funny thing about Pieter Pim: I have written many times about a little boy who has the best intentions but being small, and thus having a particularly straight and narrow view of the world and his place in it, gets into all kinds of amusing situations. Already in Holland in the thirties there was such a little fellow. His name was Barendje Bas and every Sunday his adventures took up one whole page of an Amsterdam newspaper, *Het Handelsblad.* Grownups enjoyed him equally and as his popularity mounted, so did the circulation of the newspaper. The invasion of Holland and my flight to North Africa put an end to Barendje Bas but he reappeared in the United States first as Pieter Pim and lately in the flesh as my son Ian. Ian somehow is very true to the picture I designed of him long before he was born. It is strange indeed.

Meindert DeJong: *MINE dert de YOUNG*

MEINDERT DEJONG

Morgan Dennis
1893-1960

AUTHOR AND ILLUSTRATOR OF
*Burlap; Skit and Skat; Pup Himself;
Himself and Burlap on TV; Etc.*

Autobiographical sketch of Morgan Dennis, written for MORE JUNIOR AUTHORS several months before his death:

I WAS born in the South End, Boston. My mother was enthusiastic about music and we lived as close as possible to the New England Conservatory. My father had come to this country from England, as a shorthand reporter. He worked on the Boston *Globe* at night. After school, I got a job on the paper as office boy and it was a week before my father learned I was there. Among other jobs, I helped the cashier on pay day to hand out pay envelopes. I always peeked at the little penciled figures in the corner that showed what was inside. Wow! What those artists got! The cartoonist was making more than the managing editor! This was for me! All I needed to know was what kind of paper they used, what kind of ink and pen. The answer was Bristol board, Higgins Eternal, and a Crowquil pen, which, or its equivalent, I have used ever since.

From the *Globe*, I went to the art department of the Boston *American*, to the *Herald*, to the *Transcript*, where as illustrator I covered the shows with H. T. Parker, its famous dramatic critic. I did every kind of newspaper illustration, even a year as comic-strip man.

Working nights at the Vesper George School of Design gave me the "art bug." Later, I went to Provincetown to make pen portraits of distinguished artists who were painting there—Charles Hawthorne, George Elmer Browne, and others; but most exciting of all was my visit to the studio of William Bicknell, the etcher. That did it! For four months every year, for many years, June to October, I studied with Bick. The summer of 1923 I spent in southern Ireland doing a series of pictures and articles for the *Globe*, which paid my expenses. I also did a series of etchings, on the side, of Irish scenes and the people. On returning to Boston, I had an exhibition. Bostonians were not interested. It seemed I would never make a living at art.

stories died off like flies and left me with no markets. And since at that time I kept a pet goose on my poultry farm of interesting personality, high intelligence, and ornery temperament, I was persuaded by local librarians to write a child's book about him. I so did, it proved acceptable, and I've been writing children's books ever since. I got started writing because I was starving on that depression farm and there were no other jobs to be had for love or money—there was no money. Now I'm still writing children's books, and not starving—a decided and most comfortable improvement.

I'm a citizen. In World War II, I was a sergeant functioning as official historian for the Chinese-American Composite Wing of the Fourteenth Air Force. Our outfit was stationed in the general Chungking, China, area, at a little village named Peishiyi.

I've been trying mightily to think of something interesting to juice this up a bit, but I've no hobbies—those I had have long since deserted me—so my life consists of writing and nonwriting. When bored with nonwriting, I up and write another book—it's the one thing that gives things life and spice and interest and meaning. So I'll up and write another book.

* * *

In 1962, Meindert DeJong was the recipient of the International Hans Christian Andersen Award.

Dennis

It was at this low ebb in my career that the Macbeth Gallery of New York saw a Christmas card I had etched of my own Airedale, Bozo. They suggested I do a series of dog etchings. I did and they sold—yes, all over the world! A gasoline company adopted a pair of Scotties for a trade mark and according to their figures they reproduced that trade mark three hundred million times. I was becoming Dennis the Dog Man. Then followed an advertising account that's kept me busy drawing a little black-and-white dog for almost a quarter of a century.

I have written and illustrated several books for children and illustrated more books and magazine stories than I can begin to remember. Right now, I am writing another book and drawing more pictures, all about a dog and a houseboat. My wife, Margaret, and I live on a houseboat in Key West, Florida, and the name of the houseboat is *The Sea Dog*.

* * *

Morgan Dennis died October 22, 1960, in a New York bookshop. He had been an actor in a Key West theater group. One of his best-known dog portraits was of Fala, President Roosevelt's Scotty.

Wesley Dennis

1903-

AUTHOR AND ILLUSTRATOR OF
Flip; Flip and the Cows; Holiday

ILLUSTRATOR OF
Misty of Chincoteague; Halfway to Heaven; Etc.

WESLEY Dennis was born in Falmouth, Massachusetts. His father was John W. Dennis, an Englishman educated at Cambridge. He came to America as the member of a track team for an international sports event, met and married an American girl, Ida Morgan. He got a job in the composing room of the Boston *Globe*, and a little later moved to Falmouth. Mrs. Dennis wanted her son to be a clam digger or an assistant postmaster. That way, he would always be home at night for supper.

The boy obediently dug clams and did errands for his mother after school, but he had ideas of his own. One day he saw a newsreel that changed his whole life. It was of a polo game and young Wesley did not rest until he found out all about it. One

WESLEY DENNIS

old man told him the game was only for rich folks and that to play it a man had to have "a hull string o' ponies." It was undoubtedly the start of the boy's interest in horses.

Later, Wesley Dennis turned down the job of assistant postmaster in Falmouth because by then he knew he wanted to be an artist and paint horses. His older brother, Morgan, was already launched on his career of etching and painting dogs. For six years Wesley Dennis worked for the local store and then broke away to go to Boston, where he attended the New School of Design, and did fashion sketches for Boston department stores. By joining a National Guard cavalry unit, he had an opportunity to study horses and he learned—at last—how to play polo. He visited Cape Cod frequently during this period, and he also went to Paris to study for a while. He played polo at Coonamessett, where he met Dorothy Schiller Boggs, whom he married.

While on their honeymoon in Santa Fe, the newlyweds met May Massee, juvenile editor of the Viking Press. On their return to New York, Wesley Dennis called on Miss Massee to see if she had a book he might illustrate. She did not, but suggested he write one and illustrate it. The result was *Flip*, which he wrote in one afternoon and two dozen sentences, although it took him two months to illustrate it.

About that time Marguerite Henry had written *Justin Morgan Had a Horse.* She had seen *Flip* in the local library, and decided Dennis must do the pictures for her book on the famous Morgan horse. They have been a team ever since. She says of him: "He saw beyond hide and hair and bone. He understood and loved animals, and tried to capture their spirit, personality, and expression."

The Dennis family divides its time between Virginia, where Mr. Dennis is a fox-hunting squire, and Cape Cod. He has illustrated a book about a fox by Marguerite Henry, *Cinnabar, the One O'Clock Fox,* as well as her *King of the Wind,* which was awarded the Newbery Medal, and her *Misty of Chincoteague.* In the latter book, the author gives a sketch of Mr. Dennis, the illustrator who has done so much to make her books live.

© 1958 Francis de Regniers
BEATRICE SCHENK DE REGNIERS

Beatrice Schenk de Regniers

1914-

AUTHOR OF

A Little House of Your Own; The Giant Story; A Child's Book of Dreams; Was It a Good Trade? Etc.

Autobiographical sketch of Beatrice Schenk de Regniers:

ANYONE who has read *A Little House of Your Own* probably knows more about me than I am likely to reveal in an autobiographical sketch. Even some of the drawings in *A Little House of Your Own* look like me. A stranger who came into the large office where I work recognized me as the author because I looked like all the homely little girls with straight hair that Irene Haas drew for the *Little House* book. The tree house in that book used to be in my back yard in Crawfordsville, Indiana, where I grew up. I was born in LaFayette, Indiana, but I think of Crawfordsville as my home town.

When I was born I had an older sister and seven years later I had a brother. My sister's job was to take care of him and mine to entertain him. I used to make up stories to entertain him and myself. I think I find it natural to write for children because I remember so well how I felt and thought when I was a child. I even remember a dream I had when I was four years old.

My mother taught me to read by the time I was four, and though I have gone to school a great deal, I have a feeling that my parents had more to do with my education than my schoolteachers. On the other hand, my teachers never did anything to interfere with my education and that is why I am grateful to them.

I attended the University of Illinois, graduated from the University of Chicago, did graduate work there in child development, and took my master's degree at Winnetka Graduate Teachers College. I also studied (more or less) in France for eight months.

For a while, when I lived in Chicago, I was a member of a theater-dance group which I joined quite accidentally. We gave concerts at universities in the Midwest. But what I enjoyed most was doing dance pantomimes for school assembly programs. There I learned what a wonderful, creative, responsive audience children are.

Now I live in Manhattan with my husband and work as director of education materials for the American Heart Association. During the year I think about what I want to write, but I usually don't write it until I am on vacation—away from the city on an island or in a meadow. However, I did write part of one book, *What Can You Do with a Shoe?* on the subway while riding to work.

de Regniers: *de RAIN yay*

Sybil Deucher

AUTHOR OF

The Young Brahms; Edvard Grieg, Boy of the Northland

CO-AUTHOR OF

Mozart, the Wonder Boy; Joseph Haydn, the Merry Little Peasant; Etc.

Autobiographical sketch of Sybil Deucher:

I WAS born in New York City, although I spent much of my youth in Connecticut. Music was an intense childhood interest. At an early age, instead of playing out of doors, I would line up a row of stuffed animals, especially dachshunds, and for hours give them singing lessons, using a broad window sill as my piano.

Later, I began the study of the violin, and finally went on to be a professional musician. I have taught both music and dramatics, and am on the faculty of the Spence School in New York City.

After St. Mary's School, in Peekskill, New York, I went to the David Mannes Music School in New York City, and for a while studied at the Royal Academy of Dramatic Art in London. I lived abroad for many years, studying music, and while in Florence I was a voice pupil of Vannini.

In 1931 I began to think seriously about writing for young people, writing of the musical geniuses who have given the world so much joy with their music. What my co-author, Opal Wheeler, and I have tried to

SYBIL DEUCHER

Deucher: *doo SHAY*

do is find the way to a child's understanding of the master composers of the world, and to instill in young readers an enthusiasm for these men and their work. So we wrote many biographies of the great composers, as well as numerous books about the old masters among the painters. From the letters we receive, we feel we have succeeded in what we set out to do.

Babette Deutsch

1895-

AUTHOR OF

Heroes of the Kalevala; Walt Whitman, Builder for America; The Welcome; Etc.

CO-AUTHOR OF

Tales of Faraway Folk

Autobiographical sketch of Babette Deutsch:

NEW York is my native city. It has changed greatly since I was a child but I still love it more than any of the cities that I have seen since, here and abroad. There was so little traffic in the residential streets then that we needed no playground for hopscotch or marbles or red rover. It was in New York that I went to school and to college (Barnard).

I began composing verse before I knew how to write. One of the earliest of these productions ran thus:

I knew that the sky was blue
And I knew that the sun was gold,
But I never knew that the earth was round
Until I was told.

As a little girl I contributed verse to the *St. Nicholas League*. One of my poems was called "Vacation Down South." The line "Pappy'll play the teacher" was misprinted to read "Pappy'll pay the teacher." This troubled me very much but I didn't know what to do about it, and, to my distress, the mistake was there again when the piece was reprinted in *The St. Nicholas Anthology* many years later.

I was still in college when my work began to appear in adult periodicals, and in 1919, two years after graduation, my first volume of poems was published. Poetry has remained my chief interest, as some of the books I have written for boys and girls show. These include *Heroes of the Kalevala*, a retelling of the Finnish epic, and *Walt Whitman, Builder for America*, which won

Deutsch: *DOITCH*

BABETTE DEUTSCH

an award and was translated into Spanish for South American readers. In 1921 I married Avrahm Yarmolinsky, until his retirement chief of the Slavonic Division of the New York Public Library. We have worked together on a number of translations. We have two sons, one a lawyer, the other a biochemist. Often without knowing it, they helped me to write books for other young people. The younger gave me a good deal of information about biology and football that I used in writing *The Welcome*. Our older son is married, and he and his wife have three children: two sons and a daughter. *Tales of Faraway Folk*, which I wrote with my husband, is dedicated to the two grandchildren then on the scene.

Although I have written several books that are called juveniles, I believe that there is no such thing. There are good books and bad books. Only interest can decide when you are ready for a book. In writing for young people or for children, as in writing for their elders, I try to use words so that the experience comes alive. Some of the books that I wrote for adults are of interest to high school and junior high school students. Among these are my book of poems *Animal, Vegetable, Mineral;* a prose book called *Poetry in Our Time;* and *Poetry Handbook, A Dictionary of Terms*.

* * *

Miss Deutsch gives a course in twentieth century poetry at Columbia University, in the School of General Studies. She holds an honorary degree of doctor of letters from Columbia University and is a fellow of the International Institute of Arts and Letters.

Marguerite Dickson

1873-1953

AUTHOR OF

Bennett High; Stairway to the Sky; Turn in the Road; Bramble Bush; Etc.

WHEN she was twenty-six, Marguerite Dickson's first book was published, *From the Old World to the New*. It was an American history that was used in schools for thirty-five years. When she was seventy-two, Marguerite Dickson's first junior novel was published, *Bramble Bush*. At the time of her death, just short of her eightieth birthday, she had written seven books for older girls (all of which were published in that eight-year span, all written after she was seventy) and she had plans for several more books.

She was born Marguerite Stockman in Portland, Maine, November 14, 1873, of colonial American ancestry on both sides. She spent her childhood at Cape Ann and Springfield, both in Massachusetts. Her father, a physician, died while she was quite young, so at fourteen she went to live with cousins in Brooklyn, New York, on Columbia Heights, the scene of *Stairway to the Sky*. After teaching in Brooklyn, in 1900 she married George Dickson, also a teacher, and returned to New England.

After her husband's death, she resumed teaching to support her son and two daughters. Later, for ten years, she was director of the Character Education Department of the Women's Municipal League in Boston. When her older daughter opened a dance studio in Cambridge in 1934, Mrs. Dickson became secretary and registrar, and served in that capacity until 1946. Her second book, *Lightning Strikes Twice*, about a girl who wants a career as a ballet dancer, grew out of these years.

Two more books were set in the Maine village where Mrs. Dickson spent her summers for forty years—*Roof Over Our Heads* and *Turn in the Road*. The first was a semi-mystery, wherein a girl clears her dead father's name, while the second was about a girl who wanted to be a librarian.

MARGUERITE DICKSON

Mrs. Dickson's fifth book, *Stairway to the Sky*, was about a girl who worked in a bookshop and wanted to write, while her sixth, *Only Child*, told of a girl's adjustment to a difficult situation. Her last book, *Bennett High*, was published the year she died.

For nearly twenty years Mrs. Dickson was the guiding spirit of a creative writing group in Cambridge. Numerous books came from the members of that circle. She loved young people and gardening equally, and in Maine, she would sit in her birch grove and look at the bay, with the fog rolling in from the ocean like silver clouds.

For some time I made greeting card designs and sketches, and took them the rounds of the greeting card houses, sometimes selling my samples and sometimes receiving definite commissions. At the same time, I made up sample book illustrations and took them around to the children's book editors. In 1930 I was given my first chance to illustrate a book, *Mary Paxon, Her Book*. Doubleday published it in 1931. Since then I have done quite a bit of illustrating for children's books, magazines, book jackets, coloring books, etc.

Eventually I began to write and in 1946 my first book, *A Small Child's Bible*, was published by Oxford. In addition to the books listed above, I have also written and illustrated *The Boy Jesus; Bible Children; Brother, Baby and I; One Rainy Night;* and *The Story of Moses*. I collected the poems for *A Small Child's Book of Verse, Littlest Ones*, and *Poems of Praise*.

In 1934 I married Warren Hoffner. We lived in New York until 1949, when we moved to the country near Asbury Park, New Jersey. The children of the neighborhood keep me company in my studio and they are, if not my most severe, at least my most refreshing critics. They are often unknowing models and we all have a good time. They especially enjoy a coffee break after working hard at their drawing boards.

We have acquired quite a few cats, the number varying with traffic conditions and June moons. At present we have five, all dutifully loved and mauled by the children.

Pelagie Doane

1906-

AUTHOR AND ILLUSTRATOR OF
A Book of Nature; God Made the World; The First Day; One Rainy Night; Etc.

Autobiographical sketch of Pelagie Doane:

I WAS born in Philadelphia, where I went to art school and studied interior decorating. I also had a year of postgraduate work in the field of general art. I left Philadelphia in 1929 for New York, armed with a huge portfolio and high hopes. The art director of a lithographing house suggested I do some greeting card samples for them. When they bought five out of eight designs, I felt I was on my way.

Pelagie: *PELL a jee*
Doane: *rhymes with "tone"*

PELAGIE DOANE

du Jardin

Maurice Dolbier

1912-

AUTHOR OF

The Half-Pint Jinni, and Other Stories; Torten's Christmas Secret; The Lion in the Woods; Jenny, the Bus That Nobody Loved; Etc.

MAURICE Dolbier was born May 5, 1912, in Skowhegan, Maine, where he graduated from high school in 1929. Interested in acting from his high school days, he played the porter in the stage version of *Twentieth Century*, and carried a spear in Norman Bel Geddes' production of *Hamlet*. In pursuit of a theatrical career, he attended the Whitehouse Academy of Dramatic Arts in Boston, and went on the road with Shakespearean companies. He returned to Maine to work for WABI, a Bangor radio station, as announcer, then as educational and program director.

Mr. Dolbier was on the radio staff of the Providence *Journal* for several years, and in 1951 was appointed editor of its well-known book page. In 1956 he joined the staff of the New York *Herald Tribune*, where he alternates with John Hutchens as daily book reviewer, and edits a column of book news in the Sunday book review section.

The first of Maurice Dolbier's humorous fantasies for children was *Jenny, the Bus That Nobody Loved*. Originally written for radio, it was broadcast by the Columbia

Workshop in the United States and the British Broadcasting Corporation in England. It was later rewritten as a book and published in 1944. Among his other children's books are *The Half-Pint Jinni, and Other Stories*, a collection of humorous tales of magic, and *The Lion in the Woods*, a satire on the newspaper world which was described by *The Horn Book* as "a hilariously funny story."

Mr. Dolbier is married and has three daughters. He has written several plays for summer stock companies and is the author of a humorous book for adults, *Nowhere Near Everest*, a take-off on books about mountain-climbing expeditions.

Rosamond du Jardin

1902-1963

Double Date; A Man for Marcy; Showboat Summer; The Real Thing; Etc.

Autobiographical sketch of Rosamond du Jardin, written for MORE JUNIOR AUTHORS shortly before her death:

I WAS born in the small town of Fairland, Illinois, where my father taught school at that time. My family moved to Chicago when I was two and I grew up there, attending various grade schools and being graduated from Morgan Park High School. I was what amounted to an only child, my brother having died in infancy, but I was never lonely, never seemed to miss out on any fun, because my parents were such warm, hospitable people and made all my friends welcome. And when there was no one else around, we enjoyed ourselves together as a family. We all enjoyed reading and I have read a great deal ever since I can remember.

I began writing for my high school paper, but after graduation I worked in an office a few years and was married to Victor du Jardin. It wasn't until we had two babies, both under two years old, that I began trying to write professionally—a glaring example of poor timing! I used to write while the children took their naps and I began selling humorous verse and short fiction to newspaper syndicates. Next, I tried the magazine

MAURICE DOLBIER

Dolbier: *DAWL beer*

Rosamond du Jardin: *ROSE a mund doo JAR din*

ROSAMOND DU JARDIN

field and sold around a hundred stories to *Good Housekeeping, Cosmopolitan, Redbook, McCall's,* and so on. I had five adult novels published, most of which were magazine serials before they came out in book form. During this period I also did some radio writing, half-hour plays and a daytime serial. But from the start I particularly enjoyed writing stories about teen-agers, and so it seemed the most natural thing in the world that I should eventually write books for and about teen-agers. *Practically Seventeen* was my first, and during the thirteen years since it was published Lippincott has brought out thirteen other books of mine. Most of these have been published in foreign translations as well, in Sweden, Italy, and Japan.

In addition to writing three hours or so each morning, I keep house, play bridge and golf, bowl, love to read and to take walks. We live in the country and love it. Our household now consists of my husband and me, our enormous St. Bernard named Lana, and our nontalking parakeet, George. Our older daughter and our son are married now and we have four grandchildren. Our younger daughter is in college and wants to become a writer someday. We have a bookstore in Glen Ellyn, Illinois, near which we live. Our son works there, as does his father. Our older daughter's husband, formerly a successful commercial artist, is now a minister and they live in Indiana.

Readers often write to ask me whether the characters in my books are based on real people. They aren't. Perhaps they seem natural because, through my children and their friends, I've known (and liked!) a lot of teen-agers. And I try to have my imaginary characters talk and think and react to situations as real-life teen-agers might. A good memory of my own youthful feelings helps, too. And occasional incidents and settings from real life also help to lend reality to the books.

Robert C. Du Soe

1892-1958

AUTHOR OF

Three Without Fear; Sea Boots; Only the Strong; The Boatswain's Boy; Etc.

Autobiographical sketch of Robert C. Du Soe, written for MORE JUNIOR AUTHORS a few months before his death:

BORN in Los Angeles of pioneer parents and educated in the local schools and at Columbia University. I will never know what gave me the idea I could write though I have been working at it ever since I was a youngster in high school. There was time out for other things, of course, such as the Navy during World War I, but shortly after that I went to Honolulu where I worked on the local newspapers for several years. After that came a number of years of free-lance writing while living in New York, and moving around Europe from Italy to France and Belgium and then North Africa. Here I became interested in the old French Foreign Legion and wrote a lot about this famous organization before heading for Central and South America.

Hollywood came next, with screen writing at MGM, RKO, and Republic. Also, at about this time came the depression and there was no bread or beans to be had out of writing during this time unless one wrote on the dole. I have never been able to write on orders so I was no success at this. I have got to be honestly interested in what I am writing about or the results are no good.

It was about this time that I made the acquaintance of Pedro on one of my many trips down into Mexico and Pedro inspired me to write *Three Without Fear*. The actual writing was not done until I had served

Edward Eager

AUTHOR OF
Half Magic; Knight's Castle; The Time Garden; Magic by the Lake

Autobiographical sketch of Edward Eager:

ROBERT C. DU SOE

L IKE the children in my book *Half Magic*, I was born and grew up in Toledo, Ohio. But we were always going to stay in other places, and I have lived in Oregon and California and even Australia. I went to school in Maryland and to college in Massachusetts (Harvard).

After college I lived in New York City for fourteen years; then we moved to the country, to a house on a river in Connecticut, and here I hope to stay put, though I'd like to spend a year in England someday. The town where I live is very much like the town James and Laura move to in *Magic or Not?* and some of the things that happen to them in that book and *The Well-Wishers* are very like things that have happened to my son, Fritz, during the nine years since we came here.

As a child I was always reading, chiefly Oz books, and I alway knew I wanted to be a writer someday. But most of my writing has been for grownups, plays and songs for the theater, radio and television.

It was reading to my son that started me writing for children and my first book, *Red Head*, is about Fritz and how he hated his red hair when he was in kindergarten in

another hitch in the Navy during World War II. I never had any idea of writing juvenile fiction, not after all the hardboiled sea and war fiction I had turned out, but this little Mexican lad kept nagging at the back of my mind, so in order to get rid of him I put him into a book. This was after I had gone back into reserve and was trying to get adjusted once more to a normal way of living.

Well, the first book was such a success there had to be another and then another and they are still coming. Being a Navy man I was fascinated by our early sea efforts and especially the part taken in them by our very young boys and this subject came in for a share of my writing also in books such as *The Boatswain's Boy*.

It is my belief now that a child can be taught a great deal in a good book of fiction without letting the child realize that he is absorbing what you wish him to. If a boy suspects he is being preached to, he is through reading, but if you give him a story that will hold his interest and arouse his admiration for the hero he will want to be like him. This, of course, is true of an adult in a way but the younger mind is more susceptible and that is what I have tried to do. I have tried to give my young readers good entertainment and at the same time give them something worth while and authentic that they can retain.

EDWARD EAGER

New York and strangers would stop him on the street and say, "Hi, Red."

When Fritz was a little older I read him the wonderful magic books of E. Nesbit, which I had never known about and which I consider the greatest children's books in the world. These books have influenced my own magic stories.

Fritz is too old now for magic books, but I have found that I like writing for other children, and I hope to go on doing it for a long time.

Olive L. Earle

AUTHOR AND ILLUSTRATOR OF
Paws, Hoofs, and Flippers; State Birds and Flowers; Birds and Their Nests; Robins in the Garden; Etc.

Autobiographical sketch of Olive L. Earle:

OLIVE L. EARLE

IN my case, a natural bent turned into bread and butter. From earliest childhood, the world of living things has been my foremost interest. Nature study, as such, was unknown to me as a child. I think I absorbed some of the ways of creatures through my gills for I do not remember any preanimal age. My eldest brother (I am the youngest of eight children) had a room that we called "Ted's museum." In that sanctuary he told me about his huge elephant's tooth, his stuffed iguana, his rocks and minerals, and his fossils. I must have been about six years old when he taught me the grand words *ammonite* and *trilobite*.

But live animals were my great joy. The white rats that meekly allowed themselves to be harnessed to a cardboard cart. The rabbit that occupied my lap and could be stroked while I wrestled with a composition. I wish I had a rabbit now. There was a young eagle with a damaged wing to be fed and to be carried out of doors to his tree stump. There were a brother's pet lizards and snakes, a pivot-eyed chameleon, a dove that liked to sleep in my bed, and many, many others that, in succession, were the objects of my devotion. And, of course, the dogs, the horses, and the farm animals that I took for granted as part of the scenery.

There was wildlife, too. Nests to be found, and the growth of nestlings to be watched. There were water voles to see as

they dived from the riverbank, as well as the wily old trout forever almost motionless in his rocky pool. And each year there was the excitement of finding the first blossom of every wild flower.

All these memories come from my childhood in England, and they have been called on time and again when I am writing and illustrating. My approach has become a trifle more scientific, but all I do is colored by my affection for my intimate companions.

I was slightly educated at a private school where a visiting graybeard gave us weekly drawing lessons. I am glad now that he emphasized memory drawing. My father was a collector of fine paintings and probably, without knowing it, these helped me to appreciate good design. My formal art training was meager. When I wanted to study seriously, money was scarce and time had to be used for earning it in a variety of ways. In New York I had a brief period at the Parsons School of Design, and went to night classes at the National Academy for a few months. But I worked hard by the hit-and-miss method until, at long last, my work was accepted by a museum and used in encyclopedias and other such books.

I have managed to travel to see many of my subjects at home, and, at one time, studied tropical marine fishes energetically. At the moment, the wilderness garden surrounding an old house on Staten Island supplies me with endless material for study and is the background for the book on which I am currently working.

I was born in London, England. Soon I shall begin to boast of how long ago that occurred—but not yet! I grew up in the village of Horton Kirby, Kent. I became a United States citizen at the time of my marriage to the late S. H. Hannon. I am now the wife of Harry R. Daugherty, an artist. He is much interested in early American history but, fortunately for me, is also keen about dogs and other fauna. He is quite sympathetic to my world and most tolerant of my unhousewifely ways.

Walter Dumaux Edmonds

1903-

AUTHOR OF
The Matchlock Gun; Two Logs Crossing; Corporal Bess; Cadmus Henry; Etc.

Autobiographical sketch of Walter D. Edmonds:

MY presence in a book of children's authors is highly anomalous. For I have never written a book for children. My stories published as such were all originally written for adults and for the most part first saw print in adult magazines. This confession does not mean that I do not approve of children or of people who write children's books; it is merely a statement of fact, and having made it, I have only to report that I was born in Boonville, a central New York township about thirty miles north of the Mohawk Valley, in 1903; and in the summer months I invariably return to the house in which I was born.

When I was small, boats still inched along the Black River Canal, across the valley from our farm, carrying sand, potatoes, and lumber to the cities, and provided a mysterious backdrop of a different life to my own, which was entirely absorbed in the operations of the large dairy and general farm maintained by my father. Day school in New York City in the winters, and later two boarding schools were so much time put in; my existence centered at home; and when I finally entered Harvard and began to write, the canal and upstate New York inevitably appeared in the stories I handed in to composition courses or to the *Harvard Advocate*.

I have been writing about them ever since. The dairy herd of sixty head my father kept

WALTER DUMAUX EDMONDS

has shrunk to three cows; woods are reclaiming the uplands where he kept sheep; and we have bear and New York's own new breed of wolf about us. My own children have grown up, two of them have married, and now there are three grandchildren, and I have also acquired three stepchildren and another granddaughter there, so perhaps before long I shall be compelled to write a story especially for this third generation and thus become in fact a children's author.

* * *

Mr. Edmonds was awarded the Newbery Medal in 1942 for *The Matchlock Gun*.

Bettina Ehrlich

See *Bettina*

Fritz Eichenberg

1901-

AUTHOR AND ILLUSTRATOR OF
Ape in a Cape; Dancing in the Moon; Etc.

ILLUSTRATOR OF
Big Road Walker; No Room; Etc.

Autobiographical sketch of Fritz Eichenberg:

EXCEPT for a short time when I wanted to become a coachman (because I have always loved horses), I never wanted to be anything but an artist. This dates back almost to 1901 when I was born in the

Dumaux: *DEW moe*   **Eichenberg:** *EYE ken berg*

FRITZ EICHENBERG

ancient city of Cologne. I vividly remember how I hated school, but I loved to draw, to write, and to dream as much as I resented gym and arithmetic. *That* hasn't changed during the past fifty years.

Leaving school as early as possible, I tried to get an art education but being rather young was instead apprenticed to a lithographic printer. I still love to do lithographs.

I met up with the work of Goya and Daumier, who are still my idols, and wanted to study print making and the graphic arts. Instead, I spent a few miserable years in the advertising department of a big department store—before I had enough courage and money to put myself into the famous Academy of Graphic Arts in Leipzig.

There I studied under Professor Steiner-Prag and did book illustrations, lithographs and wood engravings to my heart's content. They are *still* my favorite media—which goes to show that one rarely changes one's early loves.

Then followed marriage, a family, and hard work as an artist-reporter for several German publishing firms. Again the arts of drawing and writing sustained me. Anti-Hitler cartoons made it advisable to look at the Atlantic from its other shores, early in 1933.

Sketching and writing my way through Guatemala and Mexico, I passed through New York City for a quick dash to Berlin and back, before arousing any undue attention.

The depression made the first years over here a little difficult, but never having lived during much easier times, I survived it, helped by many quickly acquired new and wonderful friends. To pick out a few great events:

My first American children's book, *Puss in Boots*, published by Holiday House, among the Fifty Best Books of 1937; my first teaching job at the New School for Social Research in 1935; my first full-fledged classic, Dostoevsky's *Crime and Punishment*, published by the Heritage Press in 1938, illustrated with wood engravings.

More than sixty books followed in the intervening years, children's books and classics, mixed in almost equal parts, keeping the artist in proper balance between the sublime and the slightly ridiculous. More demands to teach, to lecture, to write, to illustrate—and to serve on committees! Also a larger family—and more responsibilities.

More highlights: Illustrations for *Wuthering Heights, Jane Eyre, Richard III*, Edgar Allan Poe, *The Brothers Karamazov*, and many more books calling for wood engravings and lithographs.

The birth, shortly after World War II, of Timothy, who seems directly responsible for my first author-artist picture books, *Ape in a Cape* and *Dancing in the Moon*, published by Harcourt, Brace. Again the fine balance between the tragic and the cosmic sense of life, and a measure of satisfaction to be derived from the fact that one can remain true to one's earliest childhood resolutions.

First trip back to Cologne in 1956, to see the ancient city, destroyed and reconstructed, almost beyond recognition. Followed by a three months' survey of European art schools, prior to taking over the chairmanship of the Department of Graphic Arts and Illustration at Pratt Institute in September 1956. New experiences, new responsibilities, at this late stage, but exciting and full of promise for what is left of the future.

Mary Elting
1906-
AUTHOR OF
Wishes and Secrets; The First Book of Nurses;
CO-AUTHOR OF
Patch; The Lollypop Factory; Etc.

Autobiographical sketch of Mary Elting:

I WAS born in 1906 in Creede, Colorado, a mining camp high in the Rocky Mountains. After graduating from the University of Colorado (1927), I came to New York and got a job on the staff of *Forum* magazine. Except for a year that I spent studying at the University of Strasbourg, France, I've been at work in the publishing business most of the time since then. I was managing editor of *Golden Book* magazine; I've translated books from French and German, have done book reviewing, article writing, and book editing. Then, in 1943, I started writing books and stories for children. My name has appeared on more than a dozen books of which I was either author or co-author, and I've done a dozen or so more, either as ghost writer or under pseudonyms, one of which is Campbell Tatham.

Mary Elting, by the way, is my maiden name. My husband, Franklin Folsom, is also a writer for both children and adults, and sometimes the two of us work together on books. We live in Roosevelt, New Jersey, where our teen-age daughter, Rachel, goes to school. Our son, Michael, attended Antioch College. We are a family of enthusiastic travelers and campers-out, and we've spent a number of summers making long trips through the West, visiting national parks and monuments, hiking in the mountains, with headquarters in our tent-trailer, gathering material for books. The children always used to deny indignantly that they were tourists. They were researchers, they said, and they were more than half right, because our books usually reflect the adventures that we and they have had together.

We have found plenty of material close to home, too. My story *Wishes and Secrets* tells of boys and girls who live on poultry farms near the New Jersey Turnpike. In some ways it's my favorite among all the books I've worked on, because it seemed just to grow naturally out of the pleasant Sunday afternoons we spent visiting farmers and the

many trips we made to inspect the Turnpike when the men with big machines were at work building it. *The Helicopter Mystery* also has a New Jersey background.

Anne Emery
1907-
AUTHOR OF
Mountain Laurel; Sorority Girl; Sweet Sixteen; Senior Year; Etc.

Autobiographical sketch of Anne Emery:

I WAS born Anne Eleanor McGuigan (pronounced McGwiggan), in Fargo, North Dakota, on September 1, 1907. Since I was nine we have lived in Evanston, Illinois, where I went through grade school, high school, and Northwestern University. My father was on the faculty of the University of Illinois, and after my graduation from college he took the family abroad for a year —I have two brothers and two sisters. We spent most of the year in France, and I discovered that year that I wanted to write. There should have been material in that experience, but I couldn't seem to make any use of it then.

Back in Evanston I taught school for ten years, married John Douglas Emery in 1933, and now have five children: Mary, Kate, Joan, Robert, and Martha, who are attending the same grade schools I went to and taught in, the same high school, and the eldest is at my university. This repeating of the pattern in the second generation develops a sense of continuity and deep roots in the town that make its history and future important to all the Emerys, and our interests revolve around city planning, politics, historical society, and school boards, activities in which my husband participates freely. Most of my books have their setting in a town like Evanston, near Chicago and Lake Michigan. And in most of them one or another of the parents is active in civic affairs.

In 1941 the impulse to write reasserted itself, and this time the techniques for learning were clear. For a couple of years I wrote short stories, progressing from preschool material to teen-age stories, where I found the most interesting age level. I have many high school friends who like to talk about the things they are doing, and who

ANNE EMERY

could never believe that twenty-five years ago anything resembled life today. It is important to see things from the viewpoint of young people today, not from memory alone. Memory reminds me that the interior conflicts and uncertainties, the personal feelings and reactions of young people are the same in every generation. But standards differ, details vary, the social customs are changed, language usage is new. And customs are different between East and Middle West and West. One must learn these things at first hand, from the young people themselves.

All of my books have their initial inspiration in a personal experience, or that of one of my high school friends. One of my daughters is a musician, and it seemed only natural for someone in every book to be practicing music. Another daughter is devoted to theater work, and I have used that material in *First Orchid for Pat,* not as plot but as evidence of a girl's coming into focus on a goal.

My first story for girls was *Tradition,* which I wrote in 1946. The inspiration for the book came from a Japanese maid who was with me then, and with whom I discussed the problem of Japanese-Americans in being received in new communities. She said of the famous Nisei regiment in the Second World War, "I think our boys felt they had more to fight for than anyone else because they felt they had to prove their Americanism." I wanted our young people to understand something of that Nisei loyalty and the fine concept of Americanism that our Japanese-American citizens bring to their country and their neighborhoods.

With *Senior Year* in 1949 I began the group of books about the Burnaby family, stories about high school girls who had problems with going steady, high school sororities, friends of whom their mothers disapproved, all the things that confuse and puzzle and interest high school girls today, the problems they must learn to solve by themselves because no one else can solve them. I hope that some of the solutions these girls work out for their difficulties will suggest some answers to the girls who read the books.

Readers always want to know if these stories are true. They are true in the sense that some of the incidents have happened to real people, and many of them could happen to real people any time. Some incidents have been told exactly as they happened, others are arranged and combined to make a better story.

The characters are created from people I know: girls who have the same traits of impulsiveness or overcaution, self-confidence or uncertainty, ambition or lack of it, that my heroines have. The blend may be different, but the traits are the same, thank goodness, because high school girls are delightful and fascinating people just the way they are.

Beryl Williams Epstein

1910-

CO-AUTHOR OF

The Real Book About Submarines; Road to Alaska; Marconi, Pioneer of Radio; Etc.

Autobiographical sketch of Beryl Williams Epstein:

WHEN I was about seven years old I used to describe, in my head, almost every move I made, however ordinary—though trying, of course, to make myself sound extraordinary, as I imagined the heroines of grown-up books sounded. As I walked to the store for my mother I would be saying to myself, "She walked gracefully down the street, ignoring the admiring glances of those who saw her." There weren't really any admiring glances and I certainly wasn't graceful. But I thought then that the author of a book and a book's heroine must be equally romantic and glorified, and I had decided I would like to be both when I grew up.

Only one part of this foolishness lasted. I still describe things in my head as I see them or as they happen. But what I do now is to try to find the accurate words for those things rather than the romantic ones. Because I have discovered that the most ordinary objects and experiences can be most extraordinarily interesting if we look at them closely enough, or read about them in the words of somebody who can make us see them exactly as they are.

My husband, Sam Epstein—we work together on most of our books—agrees with me about this. When we wrote *The Rocket Pioneers on the Road to Space*, for example, we learned all we could about those brilliant and courageous men, and then tried to set down their life-and-work stories as clearly and truthfully as we could. And what pleased us most when the book was published was that people who had known some of those pioneers told us they thought the stories were accurate—and people who knew nothing about rocketry told us they thought the stories were interesting. If we really did write an interesting *and* an accurate book, then we did just what we hoped to do.

I was born in Columbus, Ohio, in 1910, moved to Passaic, New Jersey, with my sister, Dorrit, and our parents in 1918, and was graduated from Passaic High School and from New Jersey College for Women, now called Douglass College. Sam and I were married in 1938. And though we began writing books together even before that, we didn't give all our time to writing until 1941. I'd enjoyed the jobs I'd had before 1941. I'd worked part time in a library while I was still in school. Afterward I did reporting and editing on a daily newspaper, helped to write and edit guidebooks for the Federal Writers' Project, and then helped to edit a magazine.

Now I'm grateful to those jobs too. They taught me that a misspelled name or an incorrect date—in a library file, a newspaper story, a guidebook or a magazine article—can cause a lot of trouble. So all those jobs forced me to struggle for the accuracy we think is important in the kind of writing we do.

BERYL WILLIAMS EPSTEIN

Today, when Sam and I are writing about submarines (in *The Real Book About Submarines*), or the way a magician does his tricks (in *The Great Houdini*), or when I described a designer's ideas (in *Young Faces in Fashion*), it's always necessary to check our facts and then set them down as exactly as possible. Of course we usually become so fascinated by the facts, ourselves, that we want to cram more of them into a book than any single book could hold. Our chief difficulty, as writers, is cutting each manuscript down to proper length.

Like most writers, I realize I still have a great deal to learn. But by now, at least, I don't describe a foolish seven-year-old as "ignoring" admiring glances when I know no one is looking at her at all.

Samuel Epstein

1909-

CO-AUTHOR OF
The Andrews Raid; Francis Marion; The Rocket Pioneers on the Road to Space; The Great Houdini; Etc.

Autobiographical sketch of Samuel Epstein:

I WAS born in Boston but I can't claim to be a real Bostonian because my family moved to New York City when I was only about one year old. Ten years later we moved again—this time to the small town

SAMUEL EPSTEIN

of Stelton, near New Brunswick, New Jersey. We stayed there (with the exception of a year in Florida) long enough for me to be graduated from Rutgers University in 1932.

Jobs were scarce in 1932, so although I had studied journalism at Rutgers I was glad to take almost any work that came along. I became involved, therefore, in a series of jobs ranging from preparing catalogs for an engineering firm to teaching in a reform school. But writing was what I liked best, so I took the opportunity when it came along in 1936 and went to work for the Federal Writers' Project, then engaged in writing guidebooks for all the forty-eight states. I was an assistant director of the New Jersey project until 1942.

In the meantime I had met Beryl Williams, a reporter on the New Brunswick *Daily Home News*. Like many reporters she had always wanted to branch out into other writing fields. When we learned that a book publisher wanted a children's book about automobiles we decided to attempt it, even though neither of us had any experience with that sort of writing. We read dozens of children's books and then set to work. In 1937, after some false starts, our first book, *Tin Lizzie, and How She Ran*, was published under the pseudonym Adam Allen.

A year later Beryl and I were married, and by the time I entered the Army during World War II, we had written nearly a dozen books together. During the time I was away, Beryl wrote several books alone. But when I returned we resumed our collaborative efforts and have been working that way ever since.

We don't always collaborate, however. Beryl still writes books by herself and so do I—particularly the Ken Holt adventure series I write under the name of Bruce Campbell. I also keep up a connection of long standing with the New Jersey Agricultural Experiment Station, and the scientific writing and editing I occasionally do for that research center is among the most pleasant and stimulating work that comes my way.

We spend a good portion of each year out on Long Island, New York, where the salt water from Long Island Sound almost laps at our back door. It's a fine place to work. When a sentence refuses to be set down on paper I can always sit on our dock and discuss the problem with the clams and fiddler crabs. If an entire chapter refuses to be captured by the typewriter I can leave my work behind and go fishing until my jumbled ideas straighten themselves out.

There are always problems to solve in writing. Perhaps this is why Beryl and I like our work so much. But there are compensations as well. We're always learning new things as we move on from one subject to another. And we're always seeing new places too, because writing not only allows us to travel, it often forces us to move around to gather the material we need. We had to follow the railroad tracks from Chattanooga to Atlanta and learn all about that territory before we could write *The Andrews Raid, or The Great Locomotive Chase*. We prowled through the South Carolina back country when we were working on the biography *Francis Marion, Swamp Fox of the Revolution*. We went to Mexico to write *The First Book of Mexico*, and we crossed the Atlantic by freighter to learn all about those sturdy ships before writing a new Ken Holt mystery laid on a freighter in mid-ocean.

I estimate that the half-hundred books we've written have prompted us to travel some fifty thousand miles. We're looking forward eagerly to the next fifty thousand.

Loula Grace Erdman

AUTHOR OF

*The Wind Blows Free; My Sky Is Blue; Fair
Is the Morning; Separate Star; Etc.*

Autobiographical sketch of Loula Grace Erdman:

I WAS born near the little (very little) town of Alma, Missouri, on a farm where my father, his father, and his grandfather had lived. My mother's people, for several generations back, had lived nearby. So you see, I'm pretty well anchored in Missouri. I went to the country school where my father and my aunts and uncles had gone. The first day, I decided I was going to be a teacher when I grew up—the teacher looked so important and necessary while she was checking the roll!

Grow up I did, and in good time became a teacher. I attended Central Missouri State College, University of Wisconsin, University of Southern California, and finally took my master's degree from Teachers College, Columbia University, in 1941. I went to Amarillo, Texas, however, directly from the University of Wisconsin, and what a jump that was, both as to distance and type of country. I stood transplanting well—now I consider myself an adopted Texan.

I was teaching in junior high school in Amarillo when I first began writing, just for a hobby. I did short stories and articles for smaller magazines, among them the Becky Linton series for *American Girl*. The librarian at our school read them, told me I ought to do a book for young people. I said, "Oh no, not me." I never intended to raise my writing eyes as high as a book. But she insisted, even suggesting that I should do a career book. That was in 1942—the idea was beginning to catch on. I read a few of them, decided that I knew teaching, and I knew young people, so why not try a book about teaching? After many false starts and a great deal of work, I wrote *Separate Star*, which came out in 1944. It went over well, and I was not greatly surprised, because I had tried each chapter out on junior high school girls, and revised according to their suggestions.

In fact, it went over so well that I decided to do a companion book. I followed it with *Fair Is the Morning*, a book about rural schools, which came out in 1945.

LOULA GRACE ERDMAN

About this time I was asked to come to West Texas State College, at Canyon, which is seventeen miles from Amarillo, to teach English and creative writing. I accepted the invitation. It's a small college, and I love it there. I lived at the edge of the campus in a college house with young faculty members and their families around me. I now live in Amarillo.

Teaching in college gave me more time to write, so I embarked on an adult novel I wanted much to do. It was *The Years of the Locust*, which won the Dodd, Mead-*Redbook* Novel Award and was published in 1947. I told myself I was done with children's books forever. I wrote several adult novels, one of them *The Edge of Time*, which was laid in the Panhandle of Texas in the eighties. For this book I did a tremendous amount of research, and since my house was small, I had to keep all this material in orange crates under my bed. I got tired of barking my shins on those orange crates every time I made my bed, so I hauled one of them out and used the material for a book for young people called *The Wind Blows Free*. It won the Dodd, Mead-*American Girl* award. I still had one orange crate left, so I used it in writing the sequel, *The Wide Horizon*.

One of the nicest things about writing for young people is that they tell you when they like a book. I get many, many letters from them. They tell me about their school, their work, their families. They ask for the story of my life; they want my picture. They want to know if the things I wrote about happened; *truly* happened. They suggest sequels, even outlining possible plots.

Writing juveniles is not easy; each time I have finished one I have sworn: never again! But then, along would come one of those lovely letters from some young person half a world away, and I would forget my vow. Perhaps that's the way things should be. Perhaps, after all, one's readers should have a big hand in determining what one writes.

Eva Knox Evans

1905-

AUTHOR OF
Araminta; All About Us; Tim's Place; Why We Live Where We Live; Etc.

Autobiographical sketch of Eva Knox Evans:

I WAS born in Roanoke, Virginia, August 17, 1905. Father was a Southern Methodist minister, so we moved every few years from one Methodist parsonage to another. I have lived in sixteen different cities and towns in ten different states. My husband, Boris Witte, and I have lived in New Hampshire since 1946, a real record for me in staying put.

Father needed quiet on Sunday afternoons. Mother would give my two brothers, my sister and me a cup of sugar, some milk and cocoa to make fudge, and then the four of us had the long afternoon stretching ahead of us. Games were taboo on Sunday. We could read, but much more often, we wrote. Sometimes my older brother selected a topic and we had a competition as to who could write the best poem, essay or story. I never won. But it didn't bother me, because all I ever wanted to do was teach.

After graduating from teachers' college, I started on the wide road that led to twenty years of work with children. It took me into classrooms from Georgia to New York; into migrant labor camps from Florida to Texas; into rural schools in Alabama and Mississippi. It was a most satisfying journey.

In the middle of it, in 1935, I took a few cautious steps down a side path toward writing books. The little path has been pretty well worn by now, for, since 1946, I have worked only at writing. I like the side path, too.

Most of the Araminta stories were written during the five years I taught Negro children in the demonstration school of Atlanta University. Every child wants to feel a part of his own world, and he likes to get that feeling from his books, too. At that time— and it was a long time ago—the books about Negro children made them seem as if they belonged in the comic strips instead of in their own everyday world.

So I wrote *Araminta*. The children there helped me write it, and children have been helping me ever since. I couldn't write without them. Almost all of my books have been tried out on children. They make the best critics in the world, although my mistakes are not their fault.

While my writing started as an offshoot of my teaching, I must admit that now a blank piece of paper, a pencil lying idle, a silent typewriter, are all an intriguing challenge. I like experimenting with trying to write different types of books for different ages and kinds of people. I am forever taking notes on the way people talk and act; I scribble down ideas that come from my reading; I sometimes think of a good sentence about a bird or a mountain, and write it down in case I might need it later.

And always I keep thinking: "Someday, someday, I may write a truly good book!"

Katherine Wigmore Eyre

1901-

AUTHOR OF
Star in the Willows; Song of a Thrush; Children of Light; Lottie's Valentine; Etc.

KATHERINE Wigmore Eyre was born in Los Angeles in 1901, and has always lived in California. Her home is now in San Francisco. Her ancestry is English and her home had a decidedly intellectual atmosphere. The emphasis was on good reading, and she was encouraged to express herself creatively.

Although she had published articles, her first book did not appear until 1941. That was *Lottie's Valentine,* the story of an orphan who befriends a wounded carrier

KATHERINE WIGMORE EYRE

pigeon. Her best-known book is perhaps *Spurs for Antonia*. The locale is San Francisco and it won a California Commonwealth Club award for the best juvenile of the year by a California writer. It had a ranch setting, as did *Star in the Willows* and *Rosa and Randy*. *Susan's Safe Harbor* was also a present-day story.

With *Another Spring*, Mrs. Eyre turned to a historical theme, that of the ill-fated nineday Queen of England, Lady Jane Grey. Her next book also dealt with English history—*Song of a Thrush*, the story of Margaret and Edward Plantagenet, and their cousins, the little princes in the Tower of London. In *Children of Light*, Mrs. Eyre made use of the discovery of the Dead Sea Scrolls in the Middle East as plot and setting for a book about a young Arab boy whose discovery electrified the world.

Mrs. Eyre's first adult novel, *The Lute and the Glove*, likewise has an historical theme as well as an eerie quality that made it a best seller at once. It was dubbed "irresistible" and "a chiller." Her second, *The Chinese Box*, was also well received.

The Eyres have a son and daughter, and divide their time between their San Francisco home and Mr. Eyre's cattle ranch a hundred miles away. She admits to a preference for English novels. Her hobbies are traveling and gardening.

Louise Fatio

AUTHOR OF
The Happy Lion; The Happy Lion in Africa; The Three Happy Lions; A Doll for Marie; Etc.

Autobiographical sketch of Louise Fatio:

I WAS born in Lausanne, Switzerland. My mother is Swiss and my father was born in Southern France. I attended the public schools of Geneva, then went to a boarding school in Basel, German Switzerland, where I had some art training and learned to speak German fluently. I finished my education at the Collège des Jeunes Filles in Geneva.

I married Roger Duvoisin, with whom I collaborate on children's books, shortly before he accepted a position which was offered to him in America. Before World War II, with the help of two old local masons and a carpenter, we built a modern house in the beautiful hills near Gladstone, New Jersey.

When our two sons were still young, I began to help my husband with his work on children's books, contributing ideas and assisting him in some aspects of his art work. I also began noting ideas for future books, partly from the stories I invented for my own children. The idea for *The Happy Lion* came to me while I was sojourning in France before World War II. It began with the true story of a lion which had escaped from a circus in a small French town. The peaceful wandering of the well-fed lion through the streets of the town contrasted with the excitement he caused and was a natural subject for a book for children.

After the war my stories began to be published, with illustrations by my husband. The stories of the Happy Lion were translated into several languages and the first of them won the prize awarded by the German government in 1956 for the best book for children.

I am a voracious reader and an enthusiastic gardener. I love to see all sorts of pets roam about the grounds. At times, this assortment can include guinea hens, ducks, geese, bantams and other breeds of chickens, as well as cats and dogs. I even feed the raccoons which visit the house nightly, and I don't hesitate to get up in the middle of

LOUISE FATIO

the night to watch their antics with a flash-light.

But my great love is traveling. Every two or three years my husband and I take long automobile trips abroad and we have thus toured all the countries of Western Europe. We work during these trips, gathering ideas and documents for future books.

Harold W. Felton

1902-

AUTHOR OF

Legends of Paul Bunyan; John Henry and His Hammer; Bowleg Bill, Seagoing Cowpuncher; Pecos Bill, Texas Cowpuncher; Etc.

Autobiographical sketch of Harold W. Felton:

MY birthplace was in Neola, Iowa (the date was April 1, 1902). I had a won-derfully happy boyhood that left, I think, little to be desired. My father was a rural mail carrier and a farmer. No boy could have had a finer mother. She was such a good cook I can still smell the bread she baked every Thursday.

We lived in town, but we operated a farm and had a very large garden. One of the first tasks I had as a boy was to help my older brother harness my father's horses in the morning and unharness them after school and get a new team ready to drive two miles to the farm, where we would work until

dark. The trip home from the farm at night stands out in my memory. The whole family would sing and listen to my father tell stories. He had a special way with tall tales. He told us of the adventures of Baron Munchausen and Ali Baba. He told us Aesop's *Fables,* Bible stories, cowboy stories and oh, so many others. He was a good man with a poem too. I have often wondered how it was possible for him to know so many of them. The growl of a lumber wagon's wheels on a dirt road was wonderful back-ground music for either a poem or a story. Planting, cultivating, harvesting, canning, butchering, putting up the mincemeat and the sauerkraut all gave opportunities for stories.

I always had a dog. I always had a horse to ride. The horses best able to travel a mail route, twenty-five miles a day, rain or shine, in dust or mud or snow, were little horses with a lot of spirit and interesting brands. We called them broncs. A budding cow-puncher couldn't ask for more.

I think my first, firmest and happiest recol-lection is of my mother reading to me. There were plenty of books for all of us on birthdays and at Christmas and there was plenty of time to read them. There was plenty of time too for hunting, swimming, fishing and camping.

I went to the Neola public schools. At the University of Nebraska I earned an A.B. degree and an LL.B. In the summer, during my college years, I worked as a mule

HAROLD W. FELTON

skinner (driver of a mule team), as a farmer, and as an actor on Chautauqua circuits over most of the United States. Much of the time, while attending the University, I was stage manager of the University Theater, and later, an instructor in dramatics and public speaking. After college, a season of one-night stands on a lyceum circuit led me to believe I should practice law. After five years of private practice, I was employed as an attorney by the Government. I am still engaged in that work.

My wife and I have lived in New York since 1934. My books are the result of an interest I have in tall tales and folklore. I write a book for pleasure and relaxation, and never with a sense of work. I have plenty of work to do at the office. The moment writing a book begins to seem like work, I stop, and I don't start writing again until once more it appeals to me as a pleasant, relaxing activity.

CARROLL LANE FENTON

Carroll Lane Fenton

1900-

AUTHOR AND ILLUSTRATOR OF
Life Long Ago; Earth's Adventures; Wild Folk in the Woods; Etc.

Autobiographical sketch of Carroll Lane Fenton:

I WAS born on a farm in Iowa but spent my fifth to tenth years in Saskatchewan at a time when wildlife still was plentiful. Having no playmates near, I spent much of my time watching birds, coyotes, and other wild things. My favorite authors, as soon as I could read them, were Ernest Thompson Seton and Charles G. D. Roberts. At the age of eight I decided to become a naturalist and tried to write some nature stories in imitation of my hero, Seton.

Encouraged by a chum and a kindly librarian, I continued these interests after returning to Iowa. Then collecting trips to some rich fossil deposits near my home, plus guidance from an amateur paleontologist, led me to study fossils. In 1918 I entered the University of Chicago, determined to become a research paleontologist. Three years later I reinforced this decision by marrying Mildred Adams, another student, whom I had met at a Geological Society dinner.

We spent the next ten years at universities, producing two technical books and many papers published in technical journals. I even became associate editor of a scientific magazine, a position I still hold. But we found ourselves less and less happy in academic work and more and more interested in writing for both adults and children. My first popular book (on fossils) was published in 1933; it was followed by five volumes of nature stories written in collaboration with the late Edith M. Patch. Before this series was completed I had begun to publish independently, and in 1940 Mrs. Fenton and I collaborated on *The Rock Book*, for adults. This has been followed by children's books on geology, fossils, and biology, and a few volumes for adults.

I cannot remember when I began to draw, but fingers deformed by clutching a pencil show it was at an early age. I make all the drawings for our books while Mrs. Fenton provides the photographs. Drawing is relaxation as well as work, especially when it can be combined with recorded operas or chamber music. Pen work and Mozart or Vivaldi go together admirably.

Mrs. Fenton and I write about the natural sciences because we think them vitally important to children as well as adults. We also want the number of good authors to increase. This is why I have led workshops in nature writing at Arizona State College and have invited a few promising people to work with me as co-authors until they can go forth on their own. I also am acting as editorial consultant to the John Day Company, which publishes many of our books. Both the company and I want to find new authors and help them achieve publication with the least possible waste of effort and discouragement.

Mildred Adams Fenton

1899-

CO-AUTHOR OF
*The Land We Live On; Rocks and Their Stories;
Our Changing Weather; Etc.*

Autobiographical sketch of Mildred Adams Fenton:

I WAS born near West Branch, Iowa, and spent my childhood on a farm and in town. Two professors at the University of Iowa aroused my interest in geology and fossils. One of the professors also introduced me to Carroll Lane Fenton, a student who had already published two or three small papers. We were married in 1921, while both of us were undergraduates.

We spent the next ten years as students and research workers, devoting our summers to field trips on which we studied modern animals as well as ancient rocks and fossils. When my husband began to write popular books for children and adults, I acted as critic, research assistant, typist, and photographer. The next step was co-authorship, which began with a volume for adults and was soon followed by one for children.

Authorship is largely rewriting, and in this I do much of my work. Books on natural science must be up-to-date and accurate, requirements that call for checking of technical publications as well as independent observation. One must also say things in ways that enable readers to understand clearly and correctly. This often means that the manuscript must be read aloud to both adults and children, and that pictures must be shown to them. Only when text and pictures do their job correctly do we put them into a book.

Although we still have much to write about rocks, fossils, plants, and animals, we have begun to organize the results of trips to study prehistoric man in the Southwest and Mexico. I also assist Mr. Fenton in his editing and teaching, especially with beginning authors. We still write an occasional technical paper together, but these become fewer and fewer. Our job now is to write books that will stimulate children to become the geologists, paleontologists and biologists of the future, not to write technical works they would never see if they were not introduced to science.

Hans Erich Fischer

1909-1958

AUTHOR AND ILLUSTRATOR OF
The Birthday; Pitschi; Etc.

ILLUSTRATOR OF
The Traveling Musicians; Etc.

HANS Fischer was born on January 6, 1909, in Switzerland, the son of Dr. Kaspar Fischer and Emma Chevalier Fischer, both schoolteachers. As a boy he was a great observer of nature. Very early he started to make not only sketches of plants and animals but also caricatures of people around him. He completed his studies in the graphic arts at the art academies of Geneva and Zurich, and was a great admirer of Paul Klee, who was his teacher in Geneva.

In 1933 he married Bianca Wassmuth, also a student at the academy in Zurich. She was a hand weaver. They were com-

MILDRED ADAMS FENTON

missioned to decorate weekly the window
of a well-known sports shop in Berne. At
the same time Hans Fischer also made many
illustrations for the Swiss humorous magazine *Nebelspalter*, as well as assisting with
the commercial films of Pincheuer.

In 1937 he and his wife moved to Zurich
where he painted the scenery for Cornichon,
a group of young comedians and musicians
who presented satiric sketches of national
and foreign events and politics. At the same
time he continued drawing for magazines
and also worked in the field of advertising,
doing such things as posters.

Hans Fischer had always had a great love
for children and it was for his eldest daughter, Ursula, that he illustrated his first
children's book, *The Traveling Musicians,*
published in Switzerland in 1944. The
inspiration for his later children's books
also came from his own children. His
younger daughter, Barbara, in particular
begged her father to tell her stories and to
draw them. For adults, he had illustrated
the fables of La Fontaine and of Aesop.

Mr. Fischer had had numerous exhibitions
of lithographs and drawings in Switzerland,
in Paris, at the Biennale in Venice (1951),
in Sao Paulo (1955), and at the Chicago
Art Institute (1956). His children's books
are now published in Switzerland, the
United States, Germany, Yugoslavia, Poland,
and Japan.

His main occupation was his mural
painting, especially in Swiss public schools
where the children gathered around as he
worked. His largest mural however is at
Kloten, the international airport in Zurich.

Aileen Fisher

1906-

AUTHOR OF

All on a Mountain Day; Up the Windy Hill;
Over the Hills to Nugget;
Going Barefoot; Etc.

Autobiographical sketch of Aileen Fisher:

WHATEVER the pattern of stars above
Iron River, Michigan, in September
1906, I was born under a lucky one. My
father was well established in the affairs of

AILEEN FISHER

a mining and lumbering community. My
mother, a former kindergarten teacher, had
a head full of ideas for making life pleasant
for children. I had a brother to play with
and the activities of a small town to watch.

My biggest piece of luck, though, was my
father's decision, when I was five years old,
to buy a place in the country. He built a
large square house two miles from town,
across from where some of the first white
pine in the county had been cut a generation before. Even when I was a child lumbering activities were going on nearby, in
hardwood now that the pine was gone. My
brother and I used to follow the iced logging
roads to the landing and watch the lumberjacks. When I wrote *Timber!* I used this
Upper Peninsula setting I was familiar with.

From the day we moved into the new
house, I loved living in the country. My
father went in for farming in a mild way.
We always had horses, cows, chickens, dogs,
cats, and sometimes rabbits and pigs, and
even a lamb we raised on a bottle. We had
strawberries to pick (and potato bugs!), and
a river to swim in. Iron River flowed behind
our house, red-colored from mine water. But
half a mile upstream, above the iron-water
tributary, we found a swimming hole, deep
and clear. We walked back and forth to
school, even in the bitter cold of an Upper

Michigan winter. This country childhood set the pattern for my life, and keeps cropping up in my verses and books.

On my eighth birthday a sister was born, and I took immediate charge because she was, after all, my birthday present. Six years later another sister came along, but by that time my brother and I were almost ready to go to college. Still, things I had forgotten about my own childhood came back vividly through these two sisters.

I went to the University of Chicago for two years, then transferred to the School of Journalism at the University of Missouri. After receiving my degree in 1927, I worked in a little theater during the summer, then went back to Chicago to look for a job. I found one—an assistant in a placement bureau for women journalists! That fall I sold my first verses to *Child Life*.

For five long years I worked in Chicago, wondering every day how to get back to the country. The friend with whom I was living, a woman lawyer with a flair for writing legal articles, finally agreed with me that a city was no place to live. And so in 1932 we took a map and hunted for the perfect place. It had to be high country, near a university library, in a not-too-populous state. Our finger landed on Boulder, Colorado, and we couldn't have made a better choice. That summer we packed our books and typewriters and bought one-way train tickets.

In the meantime, my first book of children's verse had been accepted. Soon after we reached Boulder, word came that *The Coffee-Pot Face* was a Junior Literary Guild selection. So there were lucky stars over Boulder, too!

We lived in town a few years while looking for just the right acres in the country. Finally we found what we wanted in the foothills west of Boulder—a two-hundred-acre ranch with rocky meadows, and pine trees, and a view of Arapahoe Glacier. Here we live serenely without electricity and all the gadgets that go with it. Colorado has been the setting for four of my books.

* * *

In addition to stories and books of verse, Miss Fisher has written several volumes of plays designed for use, royalty free, by amateur groups.

Florence Mary Fitch
1875-1959
AUTHOR OF
One God: The Ways We Worship Him; Their Search for God: Ways of Worship in the Orient; A Book About God; The Child Jesus; Etc.

Autobiographical sketch of Florence M. Fitch, written for MORE JUNIOR AUTHORS shortly before her death:

THE quiet New England village of Stratford, Connecticut, was my birthplace. My father, who was minister of the Congregational Church, often told me that I answered the call of the church bell which was ringing at just that time, and he added: "You have responded to the call of the church ever since." Certain it is that I grew up in a home closely linked to the church, a home in which religion was the chief concern of life.

When I was three years old, we moved to Cincinnati, Ohio. Of the city I remember most vividly the large paved square where my sister and I could run in safety and where the German pretzel vender was always at her stall, the arcade with its array of fascinating shops, and the marvelous funicular car which carried us up to the surrounding hills.

One Sunday when Mother was not well, Father took us to church and seated us in the front pew. All went well until the sermon, in the middle of which the minister called out, "Florence, sit down," for I had chosen to walk back and forth on the seat of the pew. Another memory is of a wedding when I was a flower girl and carried a tall calla lily with its large cornucopia filled with tiny colorful blossoms.

Many Germans lived in Cincinnati and the public schools taught German. Here I discovered that two people can use very different words and still mean the same thing—a first lesson in understanding. I was seven years old when we moved to Buffalo, New York, our family home for more than thirty years. Here I grew up.

I graduated from Oberlin College, then returned to Buffalo, where I taught for three years. The next three years were spent in

FLORENCE MARY FITCH

graduate study in German universities and in long vacations of travel in Europe. After this I was called back to Oberlin, where I have taught philosophy and religion. This has been my home ever since. Three leaves of absence have given opportunity for further travel, including both the Middle and the Far East.

As a child I had been most interested in stories told by missionaries who visited in our home. Very early I became an internationalist. Travel increased my eagerness to understand other peoples. I came to appreciate the striving of men everywhere for a good life and their search for a God adequate to give life meaning. Two convictions have grown ever stronger: There is no place in the universe for more than one God; however varied may be our thoughts about God, the God we all seek is the same God or a delusion. And second: God is great and majestic beyond all of man's imaginings; no one can fully understand Him, but each man's knowledge may add something to our total understanding.

Differences in religion have divided people, but religion can become the greatest bond of union. If children learn to understand, they will not develop the hardened prejudices so difficult to remove.

No one expects a college professor to write children's books, but I have always enjoyed

young friends. So, when Beatrice Creighton, editor of Lothrop, Lee, and Shepard, asked me to write a book for boys and girls about the three chief forms of religious faith in our country, I was quick to respond. And other books have followed. The contacts which have resulted have been most happy for me. I have talked with groups of boys and girls from kindergarten through high school, as well as with their teachers and parents. I have found that children today, like myself when I was a child, are eager to know about God and to be friends with His other children of other lands and faiths.

Richard Floethe
1901-

ILLUSTRATOR OF
Song of the Pines; Mr. Bell Invents the Telephone; Ballet Shoes; Circus Shoes; Etc.

Autobiographical sketch of Richard Floethe (or Flöthe):

I WAS born in Essen, Germany. My father was an army man and he hoped to have me follow in his footsteps. However, my artistic bent seemed to be obvious from a very early age. I was always defacing my textbooks with pictures and receiving the customary scoldings for so doing. In preparatory school I did my first business in art. I sold landscapes and portraits to my schoolmates in exchange for much coveted sweets. This was during World War I.

When I got out of school I found Germany was out of an army. The military life was thus closed to me and I turned my serious thoughts toward learning to be an artist. I studied art in Munich and at the Bauhaus. I soon found that my talents and my interests led me to the graphic arts. One of my teachers at this time prophesied that I would eventually be a book illustrator.

I came to the United States in 1929 to visit a good friend who had preceded me here. I planned to stay one year. I have never left. I have become an American citizen, married an American girl, and am raising two very American sons. My wife says I have an American sense of humor. Anyway, I feel as if I belonged!

Floethe: *FLIRT a*

In 1934 I won the Limited Editions Club national contest for illustrators with my drawings for Charles de Coster's *Tyl Ulenspiegl.* Again in 1937 my illustrations for *Pinocchio* won another Limited Editions award. Since I have been in America I have illustrated over sixty books, mostly for children.

In the fall of 1956 it was my great pleasure to see published two books by my wife (Louise Lee Floethe), with illustrations by me—*If I Were Captain,* a picture book for small children, and *The Winning Colt,* a horse story for children from eight to twelve. This was the beginning of a collaboration which I hope will prosper through the years. Other titles written by my wife and illustrated by me are: *The Farmer and His Cows, Terry Sets Sail,* and *The Cowboy on the Ranch.*

During my years as an artist I have illustrated many subjects. I am probably happiest when drawing anything to do with boats and horses and farms. These things have been and are closest to me. Living in Florida as we do, close to the water, sailing is the hobby of the whole Floethe family.

Beside my illustrating, I am an instructor at the Ringling School of Art. I enjoy this contact with young upcoming artists and hope that I may pass on to them some of the experience I have garnered through the years.

Esther Forbes

1894-

AUTHOR OF

Johnny Tremain; America's Paul Revere; Rainbow on the Road; The General's Lady; Etc.

ALTHOUGH Esther Forbes, the historical novelist, writes chiefly for adults, her reputation as a "junior author" is securely founded on *Johnny Tremain,* a graphic novel about a sixteen-year-old boy in Boston at the beginning of the Revolutionary War, which has been hailed as "a live and clear and significant . . . picture of a great period in American history."

Esther Forbes was born in Westborough, Massachusetts. Her father was William Trowbridge Forbes, and her mother Harriet

ESTHER FORBES

Merrifield Forbes. After graduating from Bradford Academy, she was a student for two years at the University of Wisconsin. From 1920 to 1926 she was a member of the editorial staff of Houghton Mifflin Company, where she "discovered" the popular historical novelist Rafael Sabatini.

Miss Forbes took to literature quite naturally, as her mother too was a writer. As a child she read *Godey's Lady's Book* and numerous volumes on witchcraft, which she found in the family attic.

In 1926 her first historical novel was published, *O Genteel Lady!* This was also the year of her marriage to Albert Learned Hoskins, Jr., from whom she was divorced in 1933. *A Mirror for Witches* came next, possibly inspired by the fact that one of her ancestresses was accused of being a witch and died in jail. Not until 1935 was her third book published, *Miss Marvel,* followed by *Paradise* and *The General's Lady.*

Paul Revere and the World He Lived In was awarded the Pulitzer Prize for history in 1943, and the following year *Johnny Tremain* was given the Newbery Medal.

Miss Forbes lives in Worcester, Massachusetts, with a sister and brother. She likes dogs; also gardening, travel, and people, "in that order." She has been given a number of honorary degrees from various colleges and universities.

Françoise

1897-1961

AUTHOR AND ILLUSTRATOR OF

Jeanne-Marie Counts Her Sheep; Noël for Jeanne-Marie; Springtime for Jeanne-Marie; Jeanne-Marie in Gay Paris; Etc.

Autobiographical sketch of Françoise Seignobosc, who used only her first name as a pen name, written for MORE JUNIOR AUTHORS shortly before her death:

I WAS born in Lodève, in the south of France. I started drawing pictures at perhaps the age of four, maybe sooner. As my father was an officer in the army, I used to draw soldiers, soldiers, and soldiers—and horses, too, and, of course, my daddy in his uniform.

Then, I particularly liked to draw large families, of about ten or twelve children: Henri, Alice, Jeanne, Pierre, Lisette. . . . They all were supposed to be my own future children. . . . And I never was married and I never had *one* child. Such is life.

Later, much later, I entered art schools and special academies for design, where I learned layout and lots of other things. And later, I worked for a juvenile book publisher in Paris, who used to send all my drawings to America. I saw big packages of my drawings going to America. That gave me the idea of going over there myself. As I did

FRANÇOISE

Françoise: *frahn SWAHZ*

not have much money to pay for the trip, I won a scholarship and was sent to an American college with the idea in my head to meet publishers later on. And so it was.

Meanwhile, my parents bought a small farm in the south of France and there, when I came back from America, I had the opportunity of meeting little lambs like Patapon and little girls like Jeanne-Marie. In my studio in Paris I put them into picture books. In the south of France I found a shelter during World War II, and there I want to retire someday and live quietly with lambs, and dogs, and cats. That's my ambition . . . provided all my friends in America come to see me. If not . . . I don't know what I am going to do.

George Cory Franklin

1872-

AUTHOR OF

Monte; Tuffy; Wild Animals of the Southwest; Wild Horses of the Rio Grande; Etc.

Autobiographical sketch of George Cory Franklin:

I WAS born in Oswego, Kansas, March 24, 1872. My father, George Wesley Franklin, and George W. Cory (the man for whom I was named) were partners in the longhorn cattle business and brought several herds north from Waco, Texas. The Chicago fire (1872) brought financial disaster to the firm.

When I was four years old my family moved into the territory of the Ute Indian Nation in southwestern Colorado, locating on the Lake Fork of the Gunnison River, in what was called the Five Rivers country, which lies on both sides of the Continental Divide, where the Rio Grande, San Juan, Los Animas, Pine, and Gunnison rivers originate.

Mother's family had pioneered into the Western Reserve near Cleveland, Ohio, so as a girl she became accustomed to frontier conditions. She began teaching me to read at an early age; later, I attended school in Del Norte and graduated from the Presbyterian College of the Southwest. Later on, I took a course in engineering, which in-

GEORGE CORY FRANKLIN

cluded chemistry, and for several years practiced that profession.

During my childhood, the wild animals of the Rocky Mountains were my playmates. Deer fed on the slope in front of our house. On the low bluffs across the river lived a large flock of bighorn sheep. Lynxes and foxes could be seen from the doorway. On almost any moonlit night in winter, mountain lions could be seen hunting near the house. The only human playmates I had were the children of the Ute Indians. Around our fireplace at night I would listen to the experiences of trappers, hunters, and prospectors, all of which has had an influence on my stories.

For several years I wrote and sold to the outdoor magazines stories of the frontier and about cowboys I had known on the range. These stories were very popular. My first juvenile book was titled *Wild Animals of the Five Rivers Country* and won the Gold Award given by the Boys' Club of America. A publisher then asked for a book-length story about one animal and I wrote *Monte* (grizzly bear). *Wild Horses of the Rio Grande* followed. The next year *Pancho* (the story of an outlaw horse) was written. The demand for authentic stories of wildlife resulted in the publishing of fifteen books, several of which have been translated into French.

Don Freeman
1908-

AUTHOR AND ILLUSTRATOR OF
Beady Bear; Mop Top; The Night the Lights Went Out; Norman the Doorman; Etc.

and

Lydia Freeman
1907-

CO-AUTHOR OF
Chuggy and the Blue Caboose; Pet of the Met

Biographical sketch of Don and Lydia Freeman by Don Freeman:

I WAS born in San Diego, California, August 11, 1908, was graduated from the Principia High School in St. Louis, Missouri, and studied art under Joan Sloan and Harry Wickey at the Art Students League in New York City.

Creating stories with pictures for children has seemed a natural outlet for my love of the theater. Always I have been drawn to all phases of theatrical expression. For many years I reveled in graphic reporting of the Broadway plays for New York newspapers. Having come from California as a dance-band musician, I managed to study art in the daytime while playing trumpet in night clubs and at Italian wedding receptions at night. Gradually I was able to earn a living by sketching my impressions of the

DON FREEMAN

LYDIA FREEMAN

Broadway shows for the *Herald Tribune* and the New York *Times* drama sections. I suspect the then terrifying fact that I left my trumpet in the subway one night (because I was so engrossed in sketching the people sitting opposite me) had a lot to do with my turning to drawing as a means of making a livelihood!

Years later, I was successful in enticing a girl I had met in San Diego to come to New York and be my wife. Her name is Lydia and together we have enjoyed fully living in the city and now we are busy fitting ourselves into the Western scene. The presence of our son, Roy, probably has much to do with our enthusiasm for making up stories for young people. All our ideas seem to come directly from experiences we have had or at any rate we have observed happening to others close to us.

For instance, the story for *Fly High, Fly Low* stems from the experience we as a family have often had of living in a wonderful studio apartment only to have the building be removed from under us (after we have settled ourselves in for the duration). In my story two pigeons, Sid and Midge, have their perch on an electric light sign, a sign which in the course of events is taken down. However, as in our case too, they do not give up. They persist in finding the perfect perch. We once lived in Columbus Circle in New York but today if you were

to try and find that apartment you would discover in its place the gigantic Coliseum! And now we are far from the Circle, happily perched on a hill in California!

As for the books I have illustrated, I mention William Saroyan's *The Human Comedy*; also his *My Name Is Aram*, Brooks Atkinson's *Once Around the Sun*, and James Thurber's *The White Deer*.

Books of my own: *It Shouldn't Happen*, an Army satire, and *Come One! Come All!* the story of my coming to New York.

As for children's books, my wife, Lydia, and I collaborated on *Chuggy and the Blue Caboose* and *Pet of the Met*, a *Herald Tribune* Spring Festival Award winner. All my picture storybooks have been published by Viking Press. (What a privilege to have May Massee as my editor!). They are: *Beady Bear; Mop Top; Fly High, Fly Low; The Night the Lights Went Out;* and *Norman the Doorman.*

Lydia was born in Tacoma, Washington, January 13, 1907, and she is a landscape painter and at the moment is enjoying being a landscape creator by planting and growing things in our own garden. All her work is abetted by another nature lover, Roy, our son.

Ira Maximilian Freeman
1905-

and

Mae Blacker Freeman
1907-

AUTHORS OF
Fun with Science; Fun with Chemistry; Fun with Figures; Fun with Your Camera; Etc.

THIS husband and wife writing team has done much to bring science to young people. They were pioneers in home experiments that make otherwise obscure scientific facts clear even to the youngest child. They take all the photographs for their books, and combine these vivid pictures with text that is easy to read and understand. The two Freeman children pose for many of the photographs. The Freemans' books are entertaining as well as accurate, and have been termed "excellent," with "material very well presented."

Dr. Freeman is associate professor of physics at Rutgers University, and began his

IRA MAXIMILIAN FREEMAN

writing career with scientific papers and technical books. He is a fellow of the American Association for the Advancement of Science, and a consultant on physics films to Coronet Instructional Films. Mrs. Freeman's great interest, in addition to science, is the ballet, and she has written a book on the subject, *Fun with Ballet*. As a wife, homemaker, and mother of a son and daughter, she naturally knows a good deal about cooking, and has written *Fun with Cooking*.

MAE BLACKER FREEMAN

The Freemans lived for a time in Princeton, where they knew Einstein. Mrs. Freeman wrote *The Story of Albert Einstein* for young readers, "the scientist who opened the way to the atomic age." Dr. Freeman has written *All About the Atom* and *All About the Wonders of Chemistry*.

Frieda Friedman
1905-
AUTHOR OF
Dot for Short; A Sundae with Judy; The Janitor's Girl; Carol from the Country; Etc.

Autobiographical sketch of Frieda Friedman:

I WAS born in Syracuse, New York, where my father was in business. When I was six years old my family moved to New York City. When I entered school here my reading and writing made me eligible for the second term but my arithmetic was so poor that I had to stay after school to catch up. I still love reading and writing and I have never caught up on my arithmetic.

As a little girl I kept a notebook in which I wrote stories. They were all very sad stories. I remember that my mother's favorite, one which she made me read aloud to all the guests, was about a very poor *ten*-year-old. Her mother had to work for a living because her father had been dead for *fifteen* years.

I attended elementary school and Morris High School in the Bronx, then got my B.S. at New York University. I have taken postgraduate courses in writing at New York University and Columbia University. So you see, except for summer vacations, most of my life has been spent in New York City. That accounts for the sameness of background in my stories.

After graduation I had one job after another, all on brand new magazines or newspapers which folded up right after they opened. I spent one year on the New York *American*'s women's page, giving advice on a subject about which I know nothing—homemaking.

In 1930 I accepted a "temporary" job writing greeting-card verse for Norcross. I have been there ever since and for many years I have been editor.

FRIEDA FRIEDMAN

My first books were twenty-five-cent ones for very young children. Then I turned to the nine-to-twelve group. Three books—*Dot for Short, A Sundae with Judy,* and *The Janitor's Girl*—have won honorable mention in the New York *Herald Tribune* Spring Book Festivals. I have also written *Carol from the Country* and *Pat and Her Policeman.* Because I have a steady position, I don't find time to write as much as I'd like to.

I am unmarried. I learn about children from watching my nephews grow up and from listening attentively to my friends tell about their children, and the teachers I know tell about their pupils. I let them talk freely.

Elisabeth Hamilton Friermood

1903-

AUTHOR OF
Promises in the Attic; Jo Allen's Predicament; Hoosier Heritage; Etc.

Autobiographical sketch of Elisabeth Hamilton Friermood:

I WAS born and grew up in Marion, Indiana. Four generations of Hoosier ancestors have given me deep roots in my home state. My family was not well off; every penny had to be used frugally. However, I was not conscious of any lack in our way of living, my mother kept life so interesting for me. At an early age she introduced me to the magic treasures of the public library. Libraries have played a great part in my life. I know now that an imaginative, reading-aloud mother gives a child greater riches than all the gold of a Midas.

My father, Burr Hamilton, was a fireman, later fire chief. You will find him in the early chapters of *Candle in the Sun.* When I was five I used to sit on the curb in front of our house and watch for him to come by, astride one fire horse and leading another to exercise them. He would lift me up in front of him and give me a ride around the block. I can still remember the feel of the horse's back under my bare feet.

I was about thirteen when I found I could make up stories. My brother Tom, ten years younger, would say, "Tell me a story, Sissy." And "Sissy" has been telling or writing stories ever since.

When I was a senior in high school, a certain young man began walking home with me each afternoon. I have been keeping step with Harold Friermood ever since. For this reason I do not smile indulgently at high school romances and call them "puppy love." For me it was the real thing. I have described our high school days in *That Jones Girl.*

I received my formal education at Northwestern University and the University of Wisconsin. I served for seventeen years as a children's librarian in the public libraries of Marion, Indiana, and Dayton, Ohio. I am sure I learned more from the young people I served than from the universities I attended. Fitting young people into their proper sizes of books is an exciting and stimulating experience. Never a dull day when one works with youth and books.

It was while I was at Northwestern that I discovered I enjoyed writing descriptive letters to my mother. Later, when I was working in the Marion library, I sent my first story, "Little Jimmy Firewagon," to *John Martin's Magazine* and received ten dollars for it. The ten dollars I promptly used as a down payment on a typewriter, sure that I would soon make enough from stories to pay the balance. However, the first success was followed by a stream of rejection slips.

ELISABETH HAMILTON FRIERMOOD

These failures only served to spur me on. In the university I had become fond of the works of Thomas Hardy. In one of his novels a character says, "It's dogged as does it." This quotation I took for my motto. My first book was based on stories my mother told me about her girlhood in a log cabin on the banks of the Wabash River. I finished *The Wabash Knows the Secret* in 1941. In 1951, ten years, three complete re-writings, and seven publishers later, it was published! To succeed in anything one has to be persistent, aye, even "dogged."

My husband, Dr. Harold T. Friermood, is National Director for Health and Physical Education of the YMCA's. We have one teen-age daughter, Libby, who is my severest and most helpful critic. We live in Pelham, New York, a suburb of New York City.

Frances Frost

1905-1959

AUTHOR OF
Little Fox; The Little Whistler; Legends of the United Nations; Etc.

Autobiographical sketch of Frances Frost, written for MORE JUNIOR AUTHORS shortly before her death:

VERMONT is known as the Green Mountain State, and the small city of St. Albans lies between a circle of green hills and the windy waters of Lake Champlain. Here I was born and grew up. I drew pictures and wrote stories from the time I can remember. The stories were about princesses and towers and wicked ogres, or about pirates. I was daffy about pirates and for a long time was determined to become one, myself. I saved pennies in a coffee can to buy me a ship and run away to sea. I scorned the fact that there were very few lady pirates in the history of seafaring. Being a girl made it all the more imperative for me to be a particularly ferocious lady pirate—so I could beat the boy pirates! Needless to say, my piratical dreams disappeared in the sea mist of adolescence.

I was in high school when I finally determined to be a writer, and my English teacher encouraged me. I was still drawing, but poetry became my first love, and is to this day. I worked very hard at it; secured a textbook and practiced the various verse forms and rhyme schemes over and over. This self-discipline became very valuable in other forms of writing.

My greatest joy during my childhood was to visit my grandfather's farm in the Winooski Valley. There, with Camel's Hump against the sunrise, Mt. Mansfield against the north, and my grandfather's near wooded hills to the south and west, I absorbed every sight, sound, smell of the country. This delight in the outdoor world is evidenced in all my writing, or so I like to think.

I was not allowed to have animals at home, but at the farm there were plenty of creatures, tame and wild. There were the dog, several cats and a variety of kittens, big pigs and baby pigs (Grandpa gave me a baby pig, but I never could tell which one was mine because they were all alike—very pink with curly tails and frantic squeaky voices), horses and cows and calves. Up on the south hill lived a family of foxes, and rabbits and deer; and on the west hill were woodchucks and white-footed deer mice.

I went to Middlebury College, Middlebury, Vermont, for three years; then married and had two children; then finished college at the University of Vermont with a Ph.B. My son and daughter are now grown, and my son, Paul Blackburn, is also a writer.

FRANCES FROST

I have lived in New York City for the past twenty-five years, but I always love to return to Vermont and refresh my memory and perhaps find a new idea for another book for children.

Joseph Gaer

1897-

AUTHOR OF

How the Great Religions Began; The Fables of India; The Adventures of Rama; Holidays Around the World; Etc.

Autobiographical sketch of Joseph Gaer:

I WAS born far away and long ago; and the world of my childhood has since then completely disappeared. The little Bessarabian town I knew in my early boyhood had no paved roads and no motorcars, no radios or television, no sidewalks or electricity, and no one there had ever talked by telephone or traveled by train. The few considered rich had very little; and the many had much less. Yet no one felt insecure, since each man's ills were the concern of the entire community. Everyone in that town was deeply religious; and laughter and song were a great part of that religion.

Now, two world wars and fifty years later, I can still remember vividly the town and the people and their ways, who have disappeared and are no more. And among the people I remember most vividly is our Town Crier. He was a gnomelike, limping little man, with a pinched face and a pointed little beard, and a piercing, high-pitched voice. To all intents and purposes, the Town Crier was our newspaper. He announced the arrival of prominent guests in town, told the merchants when to close their shops for the Sabbath, when and what kind of fish arrived in the market place. We, the children, derived great pleasure in following him at a safe distance from corner to corner, where he stopped to repeat in a loud voice whatever was important at the moment. To annoy him, we would interrupt him with irrelevant questions or call him annoying nicknames. He would stop in the middle of a sentence, lower his voice to a whisper, and utter an agonized curse; then he would resume his singing advertisement where he left off.

Now, the Town Crier was not the only one we pestered with questions. I, for one, early developed the habit of asking questions. And I particularly delighted in any question that grownups had difficulty in answering. There was one question in particular that I discovered very early with which to annoy my elders. It was such a little question. And it seemed such a simple one. It consisted of only three little words, each word only one syllable, and each so common that everyone, even I at the age of six, knew exactly what it meant. Yet when I asked the question of my elders, they would look at me suspiciously as if I had tried to trap them; then they would look down at their shoes, clear their throats, hesitate for a long moment, and start feebly, "Well, you see, it is like this. . . ." Instantly I knew they were lost. Each one tried to hide his confusion in a different way. And my pleasure mounted.

As I grew older, the tables were turned, and the same question popped up for me to answer. This time I would look at my shoes or at the ceiling, wistfully, clear my throat, then start, "Well, you see, it is like this. . . ." I don't know why, but somehow no one could answer simply, "I really don't know." When I went to bed, I would lie awake and think of an elaboration on the answer. And when I arose, I started to write down the elaborate answers.

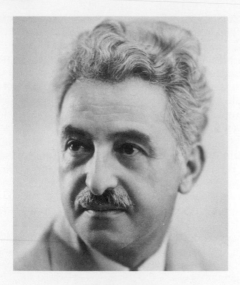

JOSEPH GAER

That is how I began to write. For I discovered that every book is, in a sense, an attempt to answer a question. And that all questions, if the inquiry is carried far enough, come back to the same question that has bothered me since childhood. And that is how I became a writer. And that is why you find my name here. Now my advice to young aspiring writers is to find a good question and try to give a plausible answer. They may want to start with an attempted answer to my childhood question, "What is life?" And the answer begins with, "Well, you see it is like this. . . ."

Flavia Gág
1907-

AUTHOR AND ILLUSTRATOR OF
*Four Legs and a Tail; Fourth Floor Menagerie;
Tweeter of Prairie Dog Town; Etc.*

Autobiographical sketch of Flavia Gág:

MY childhood was spent in the small German town of New Ulm, Minnesota. I was the youngest of seven children, and a lively lot we were. As our father was a painter, drawing came naturally to us. Evenings we sat around the big kitchen table, drawing pictures on any little scraps of paper we could lay our hands on.

I delighted in studying the children's fashion pages. One thing that always im-

pressed me was that all the little girls looked exactly alike! I thought to myself, "What a stupid artist. Why couldn't he make some of the children look a little different?" I always kept this in mind, and to this day I take special care to make all the children look very real and like distinct individuals.

My happiest vacations were spent at Grandma's farm, on the Minnesota River. How I loved running barefooted in the sunny hay meadow, and exploring the thicket of wild plum trees with a carpet of blue violets underfoot! I loved the barnyard too, my special delights being to switch the flies from the cow during milking and to dig big fat worms for the chickens. It was there that I developed my deep love for animals and the out-of-doors.

I lost my parents before I was nine. After that, my oldest sister, Wanda, packed us all off to Minneapolis, where she had been studying art. As we usually spoke German at home, we looked forward to improving our English in a large English-speaking city.

Up to the time I was twelve, I often wrote stories and painted colored pictures for them, making them into little storybooks bound with white thread. After finishing high school I went to New York where I worked as a stenographer. But office life was boring to me, and I spent more time sketching my fellow workers than tending to my job. Evenings I worked on a ridiculous "magazine" which I entitled "Fried Ice," of which I was editor, illustrator and sole literary contributor. I typed out all the stories— on the boss's time—and made elaborate covers in color.

Two years of office work was enough to take in one gulp, and I went to live with Wanda in her little country place in New Jersey. Here I indulged myself in writing, drawing, and composing songs to banjo accompaniment. With my sister's guidance and encouragement, I gradually worked into the illustrating and writing field.

New York is still stimulating to me, but always I have a great need for the country. My special likes are: children, animals, cooking, painting water colors, playing records, and studying French. Recently I have fallen in love with Florida. I visited a sister there and wrote another book, *A Wish for*

Gág: *GAHG*

FLAVIA GAG

Mimi, based on our lively family life in Minnesota. My childhood memories are so vivid that I was able to write about happenings during a bitter cold Minnesota winter, while basking in a sunsuit under the blue Florida skies!

Tom Galt

1908-

AUTHOR OF

Seven Days from Sunday; Rise of the Thunderer; Peter Zenger, Fighter for Freedom; How the United Nations Works; Etc.

Autobiographical sketch of Thomas Franklin Galt, Jr., who writes as Tom Galt:

WHEN young I wintered in St. Louis, where my two grandfathers had been prominent lawyers and politicians. In long summers in Michigan (where I had been born), I swam, sailed, canoed, built a water wheel in a stream, and with other boys made rafts on the lake, a log hut in the woods. My mother, a scholar and storyteller, inspired me to feel that the greatest profession is writing. While in school, I sold a joke to a humorous magazine, won a prize for an essay on science. In Harvard I took composition courses, wrote many short stories.

At eighteen I was a waiter one summer on ships in the Caribbean. Midway in college I took a year off, attended theater schools in New York trained for the musical stage. For a while I had a tremendously loud voice. Then I made a discovery: I had almost no sense of pitch. I went back to Harvard.

While still in college, I married. When I graduated, we chose New York as our permanent home, continued studying earnestly. The Depression had begun. Around us we saw much poverty, prejudice, the threat of war. We searched for something (even a little something) that we might do about them. My ideas interested a few friends, who asked me to teach ethics at the Fieldston School in the Bronx. Sitting with a circle of eight-year-olds, I discovered I could tell stories. My theater training helped.

During those teaching years, I also served as librarian of the lower school, bought the books, taught library techniques. But the children taught me about writing. Always when one asked, "What should I read?" I would go to the shelves and discuss books with him. I listened and learned. And I became president of a consumers' cooperative, gave lectures on ethics, have preached occasionally in churches and also in synagogues (I am nonsectarian).

In a world degraded by the savagery of war, I wanted to nurture sympathy among peoples. My wife and I studied Spanish, lived in Mexico, and at last I wrote a book,

TOM GALT

Volcano. It told the story of the new volcano at Paricutin. If my young readers gained some feeling for Mexican villagers, I had helped a little. More ambitiously then I attacked the war mania with two books on the United Nations and one on the beginnings of freedom of the press. Later I turned to ancient mythology, a rich source of understandings.

Having stopped teaching, I could put plenty of research into all these books. And I could study languages, live partly in Europe, travel round the world, meet professors, government officials, authors, and editors even in the Orient.

Ruth Chrisman Gannett

1896-

ILLUSTRATOR OF
*Miss Hickory; My Father's Dragon;
Hi-Po the Hippo; Etc.*

Autobiographical sketch of Ruth Chrisman Gannett:

SANTA Ana, California, was my birthplace, but I grew up all over southern California, an only and, like most only children, a lonely child. My best friend was my grandmother, who had grown up on a primitive Indiana farm and had the knack of making things take shape in her fingers— rag rugs and bonnets, principally. She taught me more than any of my art teachers.

Words on paper have always frightened me, but I learned early that one can tell stories with lines on paper, or even in the sand. At the University of California in Berkeley I had difficulty with Latin but found excitement in the art courses of Eugen Neuhaus, and, outside classes, in the palavers of poets, artists, and stage folk at the home of Porter Garnett. It seemed natural to go on, after an M.A., to teach art (and, unfortunately, a few other subjects) in the public schools of Orland and Hayward, California, and the students seemed to enjoy my classes even when the principals were shocked at their loud enjoyment.

In the early 1920's I came to New York, studied a bit with Best-Maugard and Winold Reiss, got a small job on *Vanity Fair*, and married an industrial designer, Egmont Arens. It was an exciting and overwhelming time and place. The city seemed full of great artists; I was frightened of it, and quit drawing. In 1931 I married Lewis Gannett, and the easiest way to communicate with his children was to draw pictures. A publisher saw some; I was invited to illustrate John Steinbeck's *Tortilla Flat* in 1934. A series of children's books followed; I think those I enjoyed most were Carolyn Sherwin Bailey's *Miss Hickory*, which won a Newbery Medal; Dorothy Thomas' *Hi-Po the Hippo*, which disturbed librarians; and the books by my stepdaughter, Ruth Stiles Gannett, *My Father's Dragon*, *Elmer and the Dragon*, and *Dragons of Blueland*.

Ruth Stiles Gannett wrote the first of the Dragon books before she became Ruth Gannett Kahn, and now she has five daughters and her brother has a batch of sons. I'd like to be able to tell them stories, both in words and in lines, that publishers would care to print in the future.

Zhenya Gay

1906-

AUTHOR AND ILLUSTRATOR OF
*Wonderful Things; Jingle Jangle; What's Your
Name? I'm Tired of Lions; Etc.*

Autobiographical sketch of Zhenya Gay:

IN the early part of the twentieth century, I was urged to study piano. For several years I practiced quite as diligently as any child would unless he or she was determined to become a very great musician. But gradually, thanks to my far greater love of drawing and painting, there was less and less time devoted to practicing and more and more given to sketching.

Formal education was rather sadly neglected but I had the wonderful opportunity to study anatomy and form under the sculptor Solon Borglum. Later, I attended day and evening classes at the studio of Winold Reiss, where the students drew and painted from models, worked on decorating projects, and altogether learned many phases of art from portraiture to mural painting.

My first "paying" work consisted of doing posters for moving pictures, black-and-white drawings for newspaper advertisements, and working with a theatrical costume designer. My first work in the publishing world was a lithograph portrait of Thomas Hardy for the

Zhenya: ZHAY nyuh

ZHENYA GAY

So in 1954 I gave up my New York apartment and moved me and my possessions to real country, near the foot of the Catskill Mountains.

At present I am working on ideas about my animal neighbors here in the middle of the woods and fields where I have a studio that is ideal. And I trust that any small readers of the words I've already written about the little fellows who live near me will continue to be amused by further adventures of small creatures in fur coats and feather cloaks.

Jean Craighead George
1919-

AUTHOR AND ILLUSTRATOR OF
The Hole in the Tree; The Summer of the Falcon; Etc.

CO-AUTHOR AND ILLUSTRATOR OF
Vison, the Mink; Vulpes, the Red Fox; Bubo, the Great Horned Owl; Etc.

Autobiographical sketch of Jean C. George:

frontispiece of a small edition of an essay on Hardy by H. M. Tomlinson and published by Crosby Gaige. This led to further illustrating of books for adults and of beautiful editions put out by publishers such as Knopf, a selection of Katherine Mansfield's short stories; Covici-Friede, the poems of Catullus; the Limited Editions Club, *Confessions of an English Opium-Eater* and *The Ballad of Reading Gaol*; and John Lane of London, *The Crime of Sylvestre Bonnard.*

Quite a few of my years have been spent abroad—Europe, Mexico, Central America. I began to wish that I could somehow tell of the people and animals I met and liked in other countries and in the States—and show them through drawings. I turned to children's books, in which I'd always been deeply interested but in which field I had feared I would never qualify for children's high critical standards. However, most fortunately for me, children seemed to like my work, for I've been illustrating books for them for quite some time. And in recent years I've discovered that a few little stories I've written have been acceptable to both my small audience and to my publisher.

Animals, both adult and, especially, baby ones, have seemed to me quite the most delightful things on earth and, from what children have told me, they agree. I decided that I would have more of an opportunity to acquaint myself with animals and their ways in the country rather than in the city.

I CAN remember very clearly being six, and deciding that when I grew up I would become an illustrator, writer, dancer, poet, and mother. I thought I would take up swimming and ice skating as hobbies. My parents thought this an ambitious program. However, they went along with it, and to further these careers they sent me to dancing school, provided me with a desk for writing and an audience, a home in winter where ice occasionally formed, and a home in summer with a swimming creek.

The painting I had to see through myself. I spent hours at this. I went on dancing and writing and painting and swimming and ice skating through Penn State College. During this exposure to learning I added politics and journalism to my career list, with science as a hobby. Finally one wise professor said to me, "Jean, you will have to make up your mind. You can't do all of these things well." This seemed to me to be sound advice, so I settled on two careers—painting and writing, with all the others as hobbies.

I had found I had things to say in paint and words; for all through my childhood my parents had taken the three of us (I have identical twin brothers) into the forests along the Potomac River outside of Washington, D.C., where I was born, to learn the

JEAN CRAIGHEAD GEORGE

ing our science and art into books. *Vulpes, the Red Fox* was our first venture, and this was such fun to do that we worked together to do five more animal biographies. John is now involved in scientific research, so I have turned to picture books for the ages of our children until my collaborator is free to work with me again.

The children are growing fast and have interests of their own, so I have gone back to school again. I am taking a course in painting at Vassar, writing between meal fixing and ironing, and have about decided that I was right when I was six. Housework and children are rewarding but not the whole answer. There is still time left over, so I think I will become an illustrator, writer, dancer, politician, and mother. Furthermore, Twig thinks she would like to be all these things, too, and it's fun to start all over again with her.

trees, flowers, birds, and insects, and to camp on the sandy islands, and to canoe and fish. Inadvertently I had learned much, and had come to feel close to the natural world. I still thrill to the memories of shooting the murky rapids of the Potomac on a big sycamore log, and jumping from boulder to boulder along the gorge. In contrast, there were the quiet intimate hours spent on the forest floor looking at insects, a garden of moss, or a bird. All this was easily converted into paintings and stories.

After leaving college, I studied painting for a while and then became a reporter for the International News Service and the Washington *Post*. This satisfied many interests and took me out of the attic into the world.

Meanwhile in Milwaukee, Wisconsin, John, my husband, had been living much the same type of life, only he was living and observing along the lakes of Wisconsin, and he was putting his material into scientific articles instead of stories. We met during World War II and were soon married. After the war we returned to the University of Michigan, where John completed his Ph.D., and where Twig was born. Becoming a mother was so nice that I went on with this career until now we have three wonderful children, Twig, Craig, and Luke.

We are now at Vassar College, where John is teaching ecology and conservation, and where we spend our evenings combin-

Helen Girvan

AUTHOR OF

Blue Treasure; Phantom on Skis; The White Tulip; Down Bayberry Lane; Etc.

Autobiographical sketch of Helen Girvan:

ALTHOUGH as an only child I often amused myself by making up stories, always about very large families, the idea of attempting to write them never occurred to me. I wanted to be an artist, a costume designer.

I was born in Minneapolis, but when I was six my parents moved to New York where, except for the summers, I lived until 1956. Originally my father's family came from England to settle in Maine and my mother's settled in Canada. Thus many of my early summers were spent in Canada with cousins, and the life of Quebec villages, where half the people are French and half English, became familiar. My relatives were all British but the French people were there, adding interest and something different. I never have lost my fondness for Canada and have often used the Quebec background in my stories.

My ambition to be an artist proved to be wishful thinking. After graduating from a junior college, I spent a year at art school where, even to me, it was soon apparent that I lacked the necessary talent. Then I took a

HELEN GIRVAN

secretarial course at Columbia, got a job with *Vogue*, and spent two happy and interesting years as secretary to the vice president and general manager of the Condé Nast publications. In that position I had the fun of seeing all the wheels go round. When I left, it was to marry an Englishman, Colin Gemmill Girvan. We moved to the suburbs and I began to write, short stories at first, but always stories for young people.

It was only a few years before we returned to the city, since my husband loved New York and so did I. Then our summers were spent in Connecticut, not far from where we now live. In 1956 we built a new home in the country and now stay throughout the year. We scarcely expected to see the thermometer say twenty-four below zero during our first winter but neither had we counted on the thrill of seeing two deer one morning not twenty yards from my bedroom window. From our breakfast table we could watch the many winter birds which came to our feeding stations, or see the red squirrel scurry down a pine tree and tunnel through the snow in play.

Unfortunately there are more interruptions in the country so that I have to be firm in order to make time for writing. I insist on spending all mornings in my study where I am working on another book. Art interests me as much as ever and I confess to missing

the exhibitions I attended so frequently in New York. I am also fond of the theater but we have an excellent summer playhouse nearby. Happily, I love to cook, especially meat dishes with wine. My husband and I dislike motoring but will go anywhere on a boat and wherever we go our small, beloved poodle goes along. She is the most engaging of the nine dogs I have owned and loved.

Rumer Godden

1907-

AUTHOR OF
Miss Happiness and Miss Flower; The Dolls' House; The Mousewife; The Fairy Doll; Etc.

Autobiographical sketch of Rumer Godden:

SOMETIMES I sit down and try and wonder what it would be like to be a person who does not write books; you see, I do not know, because ever since I can remember I have written.

I was born in Sussex in England but went to India when I was nine months old. We, my three sisters and I, were brought up in India, where we lived with our father and mother in a big stone house in a garden by one of the largest rivers in Bengal; it was two miles wide in some places. No children were ever happier than we. We had animals: a pony, mongoose, a cat who had kittens at least twice a year, dogs, rabbits, guinea pigs which we drove about in herds pretending we were David and Jonathan, and birds, including a talking mynah. We had Indian servants whom we loved, an Anglo-Indian nurse who told us stories. We sailed and fished, rode and danced, and we all wrote books.

Then there came a day, a very sad one, when we were sent home to England to school. It felt like the ending of the world to us—which it was, of that particular little world. I can remember the dreadful feeling of being closed in with many human beings, of not being allowed to go out of the school grounds, of the heaviness of our warm clothes—school uniforms then were made of serge—and the terrible feeling of wearing gloves for the first time. They were of brown kid, and we held our fingers out

RUMER GODDEN

stiffly because the gloves felt as though they would not bend. Everyone laughed at us and we were very miserable. As always when I was miserable or happy, I wrote more books; and I saved up my money when I was fifteen and published a book of poems. They were extremely bad and thank goodness not a copy sold.

After a while we learned to like England better and went through school, then back to India, after which I forsook writing for dancing; but very soon the writing came back, and my second novel was written in the intervals of working in my own dancing studio, for by then I had begun to be published. The first book was exciting; it was accepted and my first baby girl, Jane, was born in the same week. Later there was another girl, Paula.

I have always loved small things, which perhaps explains why I write books about dolls' houses, dolls and mice—even my handwriting is mouse-small. We have a dolls' house of our own, Observatory House, almost a hundred years old, and the dolls in it carry on a correspondence with another equally old family of dolls—the Shakespeares of New England.

* * *

In private life, Rumer Godden is Mrs. Laurence S. Foster, and lives in London.

Margaret Bloy Graham
1920-

ILLUSTRATOR OF

All Falling Down; Really Spring; Harry, the Dirty Dog; The Plant Sitter; Etc.

Autobiographical sketch of Margaret Bloy Graham:

I WAS born in Toronto, Canada. When I was a year old, my family moved to Sandwich, Ontario. My father, a doctor, became superintendent of the sanatorium there. Sandwich was a nice old town with lots of space to roam about in. It was on the Detroit River which was a source of endless entertainment to my brother and me. I loved being taken to the theater in Detroit and to the children's museum there. Summer holidays were spent with my grandfather in England or with my aunt in the United States. As a child, reading meant more to me than drawing, and when I grew older, reading became my favorite pastime.

When I was ten, we moved back to Toronto where I went to the Saturday morning classes at the art gallery. There we were never told *how* to draw, but were encouraged to draw things as we felt them. While in high school, I went to art classes taught by a sympathetic and encouraging teacher, and, as a result, my interest in sketching and painting grew.

After high school I went to the University of Toronto and majored in art history, with the vague idea of museum work or teaching as a career. I never considered that I might become an artist until one summer when I worked in the display department of a large store. The artists working there were encouraged to paint freely and expressively. It was exciting to do big canvases and for the first time I began to think of myself as a creative artist. After graduation I came to New York City to take a summer course at the Art Students League. Later, I decided to stay in New York if possible, but with no practical commercial experience it was difficult to get started in the art field. I became a silk screen apprentice, worked for a printer, was a ship draftsman during World War II, and later worked in the art department of a fashion magazine.

Finally, I began to do free-lance work. I did illustrations for magazines such as *Vogue, Glamour, Town and Country, The Reporter, House and Garden,* and *Seventeen.* The most complicated job I ever tackled was a painting of a cross section of the Secretariat Building of the United Nations for *Vogue.* In recent years I have concentrated on doing picture books with my husband, Gene Zion. I find that children's book illustration gives me great freedom for creativity and offers exciting possibilities to me as an artist. In my free time I enjoy painting and love to sketch on vacations.

Shirley Graham

1907-

AUTHOR OF

There Was Once a Slave; The Story of Phillis Wheatley; Booker T. Washington; Etc.

CO-AUTHOR OF

Dr. George Washington Carver, Scientist

Autobiographical sketch of Shirley Graham:

I WAS born in Indianapolis, Indiana, but because Father was a minister I grew up in a series of parsonages in widely different sections of the country. My four brothers and I learned geography and history in a very personal sort of way. We lived and attended public schools in Detroit, Chicago, Nashville, Colorado Springs, Spokane, and Seattle. Our paternal grandfather was the son of an escaped slave who had settled in the Midwest, while our maternal grandfather was a Cheyenne Indian who had crossed the Mississippi River to settle in Illinois. My father was a marvelous storyteller. He made wherever we were an exciting place because of what had happened there in the past and what could happen in the future. He gave us a sense of adventurous living, of having a share in a Great Plan in which Bad as well as Good served a constructive Purpose.

I never planned to be a writer. Music was to be my field and I was taught to read music along with my first words. But though I played the piano for Sunday school and in other assemblies, when I had to stand up to reach the pedals, I "earned" my first dollar through writing. It happened this way: I was nine years old and we were living in Nashville. The morning paper (I do not

SHIRLEY GRAHAM

remember its name) carried a limerick contest. The only detail I recall was that the contestant had to make up the last line of an unfinished poem. I believe a new poem was offered each week. At any rate, without telling anyone, I completed one of the poems and mailed it in to the newspaper. Two or three days later my family was astonished to read my name in the paper *as a winner!* My proud father took me downtown to the newspaper office where I was presented with a crisp, new one dollar bill. From that time, I continued "to write."

In the eighth grade my dramatization of Longfellow's "Evangeline" was produced by the class. An "editorial" written in an English class in the high school at Colorado Springs actually appeared in the evening paper of the city, and I was class poet of my graduating high school class in Spokane. Shortly after this, my father journeyed to Liberia, to take charge of a mission school there, and I was put in school in Paris.

When I entered Oberlin College in 1931 as an advanced student, my mind was already cramped with totally unrelated masses of diversified, multitudinous, variegated, bilingual, but utterly fascinating knowledge. Oberlin brought some form and organization to what I had learned. Even there, however, I broke out of the decorous routine by writing the words and music for a music drama (based on African melodies and rhythms) which was produced in the Cleveland Stadium.

The Americans of whom I have written in the past fifteen years are all deeply rooted in my own background. Frederick Douglass —*There Was Once a Slave*—used to visit my great-grandfather's farm in Indiana. This farm was one of the underground railway stations for runaway slaves. When I was teaching in the South, Dr. George Washington Carver, in his green-black alpaca coat, was a familiar sight. I have walked with him through the woods near Tuskegee. *The Story of Phillis Wheatley* was a tale first told to me by my father when I was a little girl. For years I have wanted to tell the Indian's side of our American heritage. I had that opportunity in *The Story of Pocahontas*.

When I was a little girl movies were not commonplace and television was unheard of. But I had books. As I write now, I try to reach out to my readers as the books which I loved reached out and held me. And I know it was the people in the books which made them so precious. The great city of Chicago becomes something very personal and warm when one knows Jean Baptiste Point de Sable, its founder. It is my hope that my books about dark-skinned Americans help toward understanding and appreciating each other more and to hold very dear the land for which so many have toiled, suffered, and died.

* * *

Miss Graham received both her bachelor of arts and master of arts degrees at Oberlin College. She was a Julius Rosenwald Fellow at Yale University Drama School, and has done graduate work toward her doctor of philosophy degree at New York University. She taught music and literature at Morgan College, Baltimore, and at Tennessee State College, in Nashville. She was director of the Negro unit of the Chicago Federal Theater, the unit that brought *The Swing Mikado* to Broadway, and during 1941-1943 was a YWCA—USO Director. She was a Guggenheim Fellow in 1946-1947, and in 1947 won the Julian Messner Award for "the best book combatting intolerance in America" with *There Was Once a Slave*. In 1949, she received the *Saturday Review* Anisfield-Wolf Award for *Your Most Humble Servant* as the best creative work published the previous year in the field of race relations, and the National Institute of Arts and Letters Award for "contributions to American literature."

René Guillot

1900-

AUTHOR OF

The Wind of Chance; Grishka and the Bear; Sama; Sirga: Queen of the African Bush; Etc.

Autobiographical sketch of René Guillot:

I WAS born in the district of Saintonge, between La Rochelle, France, and Royan, in a small marshland village of the Seugne. At the beginning of World War I, I was fourteen years old; I spent my time working the vines and gathering the wheat and corn with the help of my grandfather's two oxen. The name of my village was Courcoury. It means "running, running streams," because the community is surrounded on all sides by water—from the Charente, the Seugne, and the marshes.

After completing my studies at the Collège (i.e. high school) des Saintes and at the University of Bordeaux, where I took my degree in mathematics, I married and went to Senegal in Africa. There, at the beginning, I was the only professor at the lycée (public high school) of Dakar, which I had just established. There I taught mathematics for twenty-five years, until World War II. I was a volunteer in that war, and became a lieutenant in a battery of American 155 howitzers, participating in the landing at Toulon and the campaigns in France and Germany, the Rhine and the Danube. I received two battle citations: the Legion of Honor and the Bronze Star.

Returning from the war, I went back to Senegal until 1950. Then I asked to be transferred to Paris, where I have since been a professor at the Lycée Condorcet. During more than twenty-five years lived outside of France, I have utilized my vacations to travel through Black Africa—the Sudan, in Chad, Guinea, Nigeria, Dahomey, Gabon and the Ubangi country, where I encountered many wild animals, as I am a rabid hunter (lions, panthers, elephants, etc.). I used this time also to collect legends and native stories in

René Guillot: *ruh NAY ghee YO*

RENÉ GUILLOT

the villages. I have written about forty books for children.

I have won numerous literary prizes: Prix Jeunesse for *Sama, prince des éléphants* (published in English under the title *Sama*); Prix Prouhmen for juvenile literature (a Belgian award) for *The Wind of Chance*; a Jugendbuchpreis (German) for *Sirga: Queen of the African Bush*; Le Prix Enfance du Monde for *Grishka and the Bear*. I edited a series of juvenile novels for Éditions Magnard, called Fauves et Jungles, in which appeared a number of books (twelve or so) about animals: *Sirga, la lionne* (*Sirga: Queen of the African Bush*); *Ouoro le chimpanzé* (*Ouoro the Chimpanzee*); *Kpo la panthère* (*Kpo, the Leopard*); etc.

My juvenile novels have been translated into many languages, including Czech, Israeli, and Japanese. More than twenty of my books have been published in England. Late in 1959 a sequel to *Grishka and the Bear* was published, *Grishka and the Wolves*, and a collection of stories to be read to prereaders at home or in kindergarten.

In addition to my novels, I have written a great deal for radio, and also detective stories. In 1946 I was awarded the Grand Prix du Roman d'Adventures for a detective novel—*Les équipages de Peter Hill*, published by Masque.

Rosalys Haskell Hall
1914-
AUTHOR OF
Young Fancy; Green as Spring; The Tailor's Trick; The Merry Miller; Etc.

Autobiographical sketch of Rosalys Haskell Hall:

WHEN I was born we lived in a house off Sheridan Square in New York City with eighteen window boxes made by my father. My mother loved to travel and he knew wonderful tales about the places they went, as well as all about the birds. Julia and Frances read to me and were as generous to their sister as the storybook princesses they resembled. My sharp bones shoved into their laps and my head thrust between them and the pages, until I found reading an easy art. Thanks to my reading family I met *Uncle Remus* and *The Tempest, The Wonder Clock* and *A Dissertation on Roast Pig* all at the same time. Henry, my brother, introduced me to marbles, a game for which I had always a special passion.

We moved to the National Arts Club on old Gramercy Park and there I grew up, attending Scoville School, opposite the Metropolitan Museum. When I was thirteen, I went to France and to Tunisia, calling in briefly at Spain, Italy, and England. My adventures and affections for the Pyrenees and the Basque people were written long years after into *The Merry Miller* and *No Ducks for Dinner*. Eventually I led the Scoville seniors, rather tremblingly, down the marble staircase—leading simply because I was the smallest.

In college I enrolled as a science major because I liked to make fudge. I came to grief and I want to mention this because sometimes reading about people it sounds as if they never made mistakes. I learned a great deal at this time and very fast. With a teaching certificate, for several years I taught nursery school and French. I still have the stories my children told me—and I began to tell them my own. After a course in writing for children at Columbia University under May Lamberton Becker, I sold my first book. As an assistant to Lena Barksdale, in a most creative children's book department (in a Doubleday Book Shop), I

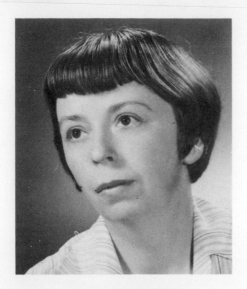

ROSALYS HASKELL HALL

learned some more. After five years I took a
position in publishing—a long-cherished
dream that I had not thought possible. I
have been associate editor since 1944, in the
juvenile book department of Longmans,
Green & Company, which became David
McKay Company in 1961.

An ancestor of mine had the friendship of
the Narragansetts, and because of it democracy took a step forward. In tribute to the
colonists and to these generous Indians, I
wrote *The Tailor's Trick*, based in part on
a bit of New England folklore handed down
in my own family.

I Iike to polish my stories down and down,
until, like the cutter with his stones, I keep
only the deepest color. But love and sympathy and affection for childhood and youth
may be best presented after all by the
simplest and most plain terms, by remembering just how it was in the greening years.
To make people laugh with just a little
catch is what I like to try to do. *Green as
Spring* is an example of this.

I live now with my cats within a pebble's
throw of Sheridan Square.

* * *

Miss Hall has also written *The Baker's
Man* for the picture-book age, while *Bertie
and Eddie* is for slightly older children.

Philip Harkins
1912-
AUTHOR OF
*Young Skin Diver; Road Race; Southpaw from
San Francisco; Etc.*

Autobiographical sketch of Philip Harkins:

DOWN the street from the grammar
school I attended in Boston, Massachusetts (where I was born in 1912), was a
large body of water called, by New England
understatement, a pond. Every schoolboy on
that street would yearn for the day when the
"pond" would freeze over. Then onto it we
would go—and sometimes into it. The game
we played was called ice hockey.

Our enthusiasm was never dampened despite freezing swims when the ice gave way
and excruciating whacks on the shins from
hockey sticks and pucks, the hard-as-rock
rubber missiles that fly through the air with
the speed—so it seems—of a satellite. Two
books on ice hockey paid me back for winters of painful knocks and icy immersions.
Lightning on Ice was one of them.

Later I attended Boston Latin School, the
oldest public school in the country, founded
in 1635. Harvard was started a year later to
give the Latin School graduates an institute
of higher learning. (I use the word *attended*
advisedly, for I did very little studying.)
Boston Latin played its big football game
Thanksgiving Day and from the stands I
watched a friend of mine decline to run back
a punt. From that incident came a book
called *Punt Formation*.

At the age of seventeen I found myself on
the water front in Marseilles and took deck
passage on a leaky tub bound for Algiers. I
got seasick but no book. In Algiers I boarded
an Arab bus for Bou Saada, Biskra, and the
desert. The bus would leave one oasis at
dawn and arrive at another by sunset. As
the Arabs were fasting, it stopped only for
hygienic emergencies. Anyway, there were
no motels or hot-dog stands. At sundown in
the oases the muezzins would come out on
the minarets and shout something that
sounded like "All y all y in free." Fasting
was over for the day. We would rush to the
restaurants for the North African dish called
couscous. I got fleas and dysentery from

this safari but no book. Years later I wrote a book about the Philippines from a friend's diary, *Blackburn's Headhunters*. That's the way things seem to work out for me—I ship to Africa and write about Luzon.

Back in France I studied at the University of Grenoble and then at the School of Political Science in Paris. Then I got a job with a Paris news agency and covered all kinds of stories—politics, spies, wild riots in the capital. But no books.

At home again I began writing for magazines and my subjects seemed to include about everything under the sun—legal medicine, eye surgery, admiralty law. Once in a while a personal adventure would get into print like a story I did for *This Week* about a convoy to England, the soldiers we took over and the thousands of German prisoners we brought back. Merchant marine work subsequently took me to ports like Cristobal in the Canal Zone and Carapito up the Orinoco in Venezuela. Stories came out of these and got into print in magazines mostly.

Just before leaving the country I had done a book with the Air Force called *Bomber Pilot*. That was the one that really got me started writing for the younger generation. I used to wonder why some experiences turned into stories and others didn't. That was before I included in my analysis several other people essential to a writer—the editor and the publisher, and a public.

Marion Havighurst

AUTHOR OF

Strange Island; Etc.

CO-AUTHOR OF

High Prairie; Song of the Pines; Climb a Lofty Ladder

Autobiographical sketch of Marion Margaret Boyd Havighurst:

I WAS born in Marietta, Ohio, but did not live there long. My father was in educational work and we lived also in Painesville, Columbus, and Oxford, all in Ohio. Most of my life has been spent in Oxford, where my father was for seventeen years president of Western College for Women, and where my husband, Walter Havighurst, is research professor of English at Miami University.

MARION HAVIGHURST

Although we moved from Marietta when I was four years old, I often returned there to visit relatives. It has always been a beautiful town, and, as the first settlement in the Northwest Territory, it has a fascinating history. All my growing-up years I heard stories of romantic Blennerhassett Island, fourteen miles down the Ohio River from Marietta. There the famous Burr-Blennerhassett conspiracy was planned. I had always thought the story would make an interesting book for young people, but it was not until the summer of 1955 that I finally wrote it. That book, published in 1957, is called *Strange Island*. Most of the characters in this story were real people, and the events that took place are historically true. I had, however, to introduce a few fictitious young people from whose point of view the story is told. Just for fun, I named them for some of my ancestors.

Despite the fact that my father was president of a girls' college, I wanted to go away to school. So I chose Smith College and later earned a master's degree at Yale University. After that I taught English at Miami University where I met my husband. I continued to teach for five years after we were married. I was fortunate in marrying a man whose interests were the same as my own. He has written a great many more books than I have, but we have collaborated on three teen-age books—*High Prairie, Song of the Pines*, and *Climb a Lofty Ladder*.

My earliest interest in writing was poetry. That seems to be the way many writers start out. My first book, *Silver Wands*, contained some of my youthful poetry and was published in the Yale Series of Younger Poets. Later I thought it would be fun to try a detective story, so I wrote *Murder in the Stacks*, a mystery story, the setting of which was the Miami University library.

During the years we have done a good deal of traveling, both in the United States and Canada and in Europe and the Mediterranean countries. In two of our books, *Song of the Pines* and *Climb a Lofty Ladder*, we used background material from Norway and Sweden.

When my husband and I collaborate, we work out the story together, usually when we are on long automobile trips. Then we name the characters and divide the chapters, so that each of us writes about half of them. Then my husband reads my chapters and I read his to see if all the incidents fit together well. That part of the work is a little like a jigsaw puzzle. I always think my husband's chapters sound much better than my own.

Walter Havighurst

1901-

AUTHOR OF

Annie Oakley of the Wild West; Buffalo Bill's Great Wild West Show; George Rogers Clark: Soldier in the West; Etc.

Autobiographical sketch of Walter Havighurst:

MY earliest memories are of the Fox River, just below the house where I was born in Appleton, Wisconsin, on November 28, 1901. The river was exciting, frozen solid during the winter months and coming alive in spring. When I learned that the first French explorers and missionaries paddled up the Fox on their way to the portage which led them to the Mississippi, the river took on the added excitement of history. My father was a professor of history at Lawrence College, in Appleton, and so I had other reminders of the past. Later, I wrote about the Wisconsin woods and waters in both adult and teen-age books.

My later boyhood was spent in a series of towns in Illinois—Rantoul, Tuscola, Bloom-

WALTER HAVIGHURST

ington, Decatur. On the Rantoul prairie my brothers and I flew kites in the April sky where now the big military airplanes soar. When Rantoul became the site of Chanute Field, it changed past recognition.

One thing I missed in Illinois was water, and so I read a good many sea stories—Stevenson, Jack London, Kipling, Conrad, Masefield. After finishing high school I worked as a deck hand on a Great Lakes freighter. We cruised between Lake Erie and Lake Superior, carrying coal to the north and bringing down iron ore to the lower lakes. There were still a few whitesailed schooners on Lake Superior and I found myself wondering about early trade and travel on the lakes. Twenty years later I wrote, in *The Long Ships Passing*, an account of the development of Great Lakes transportation.

After two years at Ohio Wesleyan University, I transferred to the University of Denver, interrupting my college course for a year in the merchant marine. I sailed out of Seattle and San Francisco, making trips to Japan, China, the Philippines, Alaska, and South America. After graduation from college I shipped out again, later leaving a Leyland Line vessel at Liverpool in order to study in England. Between terms at King's College, London, I rode a bicycle through Scotland, Ireland, and France.

In 1928 I began teaching English at Miami University in the village of Oxford,

Ohio, where I have remained. With my wife, Marion Boyd, I share a five-windowed study that looks through the woods to Four Mile Run, where the Miami Indians used to camp. We have written three teen-age books together, besides other books and stories written separately. When we collaborate, as in *Song of the Pines* and *Climb a Lofty Ladder*, we talk the story out before we do much writing. Then we divide up the chapters; usually my wife writes the indoor and family episodes and I write the outdoor ones. Hers are generally the better. Most of our writing ideas come to us when we are traveling, either in America or abroad.

Elizabeth Headley

See *Cavanna, Betty*

Robert A. Heinlein

1907-

AUTHOR OF

Red Planet; Rocket Ship Galileo; Time for the Stars; Citizen of the Galaxy; Etc.

Autobiographical sketch of Robert A. Heinlein:

I WAS born in 1907 in Butler, a small farm town in southern Missouri. I grew up in Kansas City, Missouri, and attended public schools there. Science of all sorts and astronomy in particular were my hobby as a boy and I planned to become an astronomer; however, I received an appointment to the United States Naval Academy at Annapolis and became a naval officer instead. I graduated from the Academy in 1929 and served as a line officer in the United States Fleet. I was retired for physical disability in 1934. After various activities—real estate, silver mining, politics, graduate schooling—I started writing in 1939. Except for time out for World War II, which I spent as an engineer in the United States Naval Air Material Center at Philadelphia, I have been writing ever since.

As a child and as a young man I had never had any intention of becoming a writer; I had neither the inclination nor any reason to think I had any talent for it. As is the case with many writers, leisure imposed by ill health gave me the opportunity. The rest was mostly chance—I saw a house ad

ROBERT A. HEINLEIN

in a magazine, announcing a "giant prize contest" for amateur writers. I wrote a short story under this stimulus, then decided to send it to the open market rather than to the contest. It sold and so did the next several dozen. I was a writer.

That first story was science fiction. Although I have written in many fields of fiction and nonfiction, I prefer to write speculative stories about the future and have continued to do so; I like the ample elbowroom offered by this field and its challenge to the imagination. As a youngster I was addicted to the stories of Jules Verne and H. G. Wells; as an oldster I try to emulate them.

About fifteen years ago I was invited to try a boys' story. I hesitated because most stories for children had offended me as a child. I attempted that first book for boys with a solemn vow to myself never to "write down" nor to adopt a patronizing attitude toward the reader in any other fashion. I have held to that rule and my books for boys differ only slightly from my books for adults—the books for boys are somewhat harder to read because younger readers relish tough ideas they have to chew and don't mind big words—and the boys' books are slightly limited by taboos and conventions imposed by their elders. Nevertheless the so-called boys' books are usually published in serial form as adult novels and are invariably published as "adult" in other countries. I feel that my experience in this field has justified my belief that kids want tough books, chewy books—not pap.

My wife is the former Virginia Gerstenfeld, chemist and biochemist, a former WAVE lieutenant, whom I met during the war through being assigned to engineering projects with her in naval aviation. We have no children. We share mutual interests in cats, gardening, figure skating, and travel. We live in Colorado, where we stay about half of each year, while I write. The rest of the time we spend on our favorite hobby, travel. We have been in forty-four countries in the past few years and are now planning our next trip around the world.

So far I have published twenty-two trade books in the United States, about a hundred book editions of all sorts in fourteen languages and eighteen countries, and an unknown number of magazine items. I have shared responsibility for two motion pictures and several hundred radio and television shows.

* * *

Mr. Heinlein has been the recipient of the Hugo Award three times for his science fiction, for *Double Star* in 1956, for *Starship Trooper* in 1960, and for *Stranger in a Strange Land* in 1962.

INEZ HOGAN

Inez Hogan

1895-

AUTHOR AND ILLUSTRATOR OF
Nicodemus and His Little Sister; Bear Twins; The Big Ones; Etc.

Autobiographical sketch of Inez Hogan:

I BEGAN writing and illustrating on a blackboard in a first grade classroom in Washington, D.C. I was the teacher. Rows of upturned faces waited for me to start something.

"Can you run?" I asked.

"Yes," came a chorus of childish voices.

"I can run, too," I said, putting myself on their level. "Let's do it!"

We ran around the room. Then, putting myself on a higher level, I announced, "I can write *run* too, and I can draw *run*." I demonstrated on the blackboard.

I have been writing and drawing ever since. In 1926, quite accidentally, I discovered that this ability was negotiable. My

first book was published in 1927. Since then, I have written and illustrated about sixty books for children. And never a book without a child, sometimes several, to inspire me and keep me on their level. I dedicate my books to these children, calling them my co-authors. A book of verse, titled *Me,* is dedicated to eighteen children.

My co-author also plays a part in the delivery of manuscript and illustrations. My publishers are used to seeing me enter with a child by the hand, invading all departments to show how a book gets from the author to the child. E. P. Dutton, with whom I have been associated for over thirty years, have forty of my books now in print. The first, *Nicodemus and His Little Sister,* is still selling. *Bear Twins,* published soon after, has been the all-time favorite.

The Big Ones is about dinosaurs, and between me, my co-author (eight-year-old Steven), and Dr. Colbert, curator, the American Museum of Natural History—we think it's authentic.

I was born in Washington, D.C., and there I went to public school until I entered the Wilson Teachers College. When I became a teacher, I studied nights and summer vacations to become an artist. I attended Corcoran Art School, the National Art School, the Berkshire Summer School of Art, the art schools of Paris, and Cape Cod School of Art, in Provincetown, Massachusetts (which is now my home). I supervised art in the public schools of Washington, D.C., and later in New York City.

Painting is now my hobby and children's books are my sole means of support. And I can think of no happier way to earn a living.

Dorothy Hosford
1900-1952

AUTHOR OF

Sons of the Volsungs; By His Own Might; Thunder of the Gods

DOROTHY G. Hosford was born in Pittsburgh, Pennsylvania, shortly after her parents had come to this country from Scotland. She was educated in the public schools of Pittsburgh, and worked for a brief period in the advertising department of a large department store in that city. During World War I, when her brother was in the service overseas, she rented a typewriter, taught herself typing, and qualified for a position with the War Risk Insurance Board in Washington, D.C. She remained there for the duration of the war, saving enough money to enter the Margaret Morrison School of Carnegie Institute of Technology in her native Pittsburgh. Supporting herself with scholarships and part-time work, she graduated in 1923. She took part in school activities and was student government president for a term.

She served as a secretary for the Pittsburgh branch of the Pennsylvania State extension courses, and in 1924 became secretary for the Carnegie Library School. She was married about this time to Raymond F. Hosford, and they had twin sons, Frederick Duff and Hugh Malcolm. In 1929 the Hosfords moved to Bradford, Pennsylvania, where Mr. Hosford was superintendent of the Bradford Hospital. In the twenty-two years they lived there, Mrs. Hosford was active in civic affairs and various clubs. She also began to write, and her three books were published during this time.

Louise P. Latimer wrote of Mrs. Hosford in *The Horn Book* in February 1953:

"She naturally gravitated to places where children's books were to be found. From this interest doubtless stemmed her desire to bring to children some of the beauty and vigor of folklore not already available to them. She made exhaustive research in the confusing sources, soaking herself with them

DOROTHY HOSFORD

before beginning to write. Sifting this wealth and maze of material, she followed the trail of the particular story, enhancing its interest without losing the setting and atmosphere. She was a rare person and this rareness was translated into the tales she told. Her integrity, her nice feeling for words, her love of beauty, her warmth and her restraint shine through them. . . . She was a modest person but she had a sureness in her work. This sure modesty had real value, for if she asked an opinion, the queried person could feel safe in advising since she would not be swayed against her own judgment."

Mrs. Hosford died unexpectedly in London, June 28, 1952, while on a tour of Europe. She was buried there.

Elizabeth Howard
1907-

AUTHOR OF

The Courage of Bethea; Candle in the Night; North Winds Blow Free; Peddler's Girl; Etc.

Autobiographical sketch of Elizabeth Howard:

ALL but three of my books have been stories set in that section of the United States which lies around the Great Lakes, for I have lived in that part of the country all my life. On August 24, 1907, I was born in Detroit, Michigan, and it has been my

ELIZABETH HOWARD

home ever since, with the exception of a few years in Chicago. We moved there when I was five and came back home to Detroit when I was twelve.

During the years in Chicago we lived in an apartment overlooking Lake Michigan and I could always see the lake, blue or stormy or glittering with ice. In spring and fall I played on the beach and in winter I clambered over the ice piled high along the shore. Each summer we went to Detroit to visit my mother's mother and sisters. There I would listen in the night to the boats whistling as they passed on the river, and the best days of the summer were the ones spent on the excursion steamers which used to sail from Detroit in such numbers. Later we went each summer to a cottage in northern Michigan on the shore of Lake Michigan. We still do. So the lakes were woven into the pattern of my growing up, and so they have come into my books.

When I was a child and that eternal question of childhood was asked, "What would you wish for if you could have it?" my wishes were always the same, a house and a garden and a dog. They all came true when I was in high school and we built a house in Grosse Pointe, a suburb of Detroit, where we still live. But two things I shall never have enough of—flowers and dogs.

I graduated from the University of Michigan with an A.B. in education and then decided not to teach and studied at Wayne

University to be a school librarian. When I had finished that course, I changed my mind again and went back to the University of Michigan for my A.M. in history. Next, I taught history for two years at a girls' college in Georgia. Then, at last, after all my false starts, I settled down to writing books—the thing that had always been in the back of my mind ever since as a very small girl I started to write stories and plays —the thing that I had always intended to do someday. I wrote, for the most part, of my own section of the country which I love and where my roots are deep, and I wrote of long ago because I have always loved the old days and felt a close tie to them, and I wanted to share the pleasure, and the richness, and the value that are there in the past waiting for us to draw upon them.

Perhaps I should make some explanations about my name. My full name is Elizabeth Howard Mizner. My father's mother was Eliza Howard and so the Howard is a family name. When I wrote my first book I thought that Mizner is so often mispronounced and misspelled that I would use my middle name, for there could be no mistakes made about Howard. Since then, I have regretted that decision. It has often led to confusion. When, however, I wanted to use Mizner instead of Howard on the fourth book, the publisher was strongly against the change, and so I shall continue to be Elizabeth Howard.

Harriet E. Huntington

1909-

AUTHOR OF
Let's Go to the Seashore; Let's Go to the Brook; Let's Go Outdoors; Let's Go to the Desert; Etc.

Autobiographical sketch of Harriet Huntington:

I WAS born in Ormond Beach, Florida, in 1909. My mother came from Massachusetts and my father from Connecticut. I suppose the winters we spent in Florida started me in my love of nature. Certainly, they influenced me to write *Let's Go to the Seashore.*

We moved to California when I was ten, and I went to my first school. Up until then I had had a governess. As for formal schooling, I never graduated from high school but went around the world instead. I suppose the trips in Europe, looking at the famous paintings, gave me a sense of and for good composition, and as I can't draw I used a camera when I wished to illustrate a book. I took a few piano lessons, then studied the harp, but as I did not like to practice I can't play. I did enjoy going to the symphonies—hence my book *Tune-Up*. Listening to classical records is my favorite pastime and inspiration.

I went for six weeks to a class at Whittier College in child psychology and nursery school training. It was one of my assignments to write what a child did and said for a period of an hour. Naturally, I chose my two sons as subjects and found out that they loved "bugs." I also found out that there was no book on the subject. So, with the aid of the encyclopedia, I wrote one, *Let's Go Outdoors*. The two boys on the jackets of my nature books are my sons. *Aircraft U.S.A.* is the outcome of my older son's going into the Air Force. My younger son is in the Navy, and at present, a great help in answering questions about the harbor, the subject of my current book. My daughter was a guinea pig for *Let's Go to the Brook*, but now that she is in her teens I shall have to look to my two sons' daughters for more inspiration.

You might say that I "come by" writing naturally. Both my father and grandfather wrote religious books. They were clergymen. My mother's mother was a Beecher, related to Harriet Beecher Stowe. I use my maiden name, Huntington, as a pen name, and also legally since my divorce.

Clement Hurd

1908-

AUTHOR AND ILLUSTRATOR OF
The Race; Run, Run, Run; The Merry Chase
ILLUSTRATOR OF
The Runaway Bunny; Caboose; Etc.

Autobiographical sketch of Clement Hurd:

IN looking back over my childhood, it always surprises me that I didn't start painting and drawing until I was about fifteen. I started at boarding school under the influence of a new master who was a recognized water colorist. From then on painting and drawing have always played a vital part in my life.

Sometimes I wonder if I wouldn't have responded sooner if, in my childhood, I had had the enlightened opportunities for free painting at school and at home that children have today. My only memory of "art class" was at a private school in New York, where, at the age of about eight, we modeled a lion rampant from a cast about six inches high. The whole class worked on it for several months and the teacher would correct each boy's work each day so that when the finished product was cast and proudly taken home, every lion was "perfect."

However, looking back in general I believe I had a happy and certainly a very secure childhood in New York City. I was born there and grew up on Sixty-eighth Street until I was sent off to boarding school at the age of thirteen. In the summers we stayed near the seashore in New Jersey and led a free, gregarious life as there were five children in my family and four double first cousins next door.

After five years at St. Paul's School, I progressed to Yale and while there decided to head for architecture, viewing it as a practical compromise between painting and business. However, after one postgraduate year at the Yale School of Architecture I decided to shoot the works and become an artist, so I went abroad to study painting in Paris. There in two years I learned a lot about art and life, particularly from the painting classes under Fernand Léger and partly from being exposed to French civilization and the wealth of European art treasures. In fact, I sincerely believe that I absorbed more education in those two years than in all my prior formal training.

In the autumn of 1933, the depression having hit home, I returned to New York and set out to be a self-supporting artist. I painted murals in bathrooms and once in a while even murals in dining rooms. I designed needlework to order for a wool shop called the Knit-a-Bit! I even hand-painted a few lampshades. In fact, I was doing what is known as free-lancing or executing any art work that anyone wanted. I even hand-hooked two stair carpets. One of my pleasantest jobs was painting the inside of an octagonal bathhouse in Greenwich, Connecticut. On the ceiling I portrayed "The Perils of Bathing," such as crabs and octo-

CLEMENT AND EDITH THACHER HURD

puses, and even foreign Lotharios that pinched under water.

Margaret Wise Brown saw some of the studies for these "Perils" and suggested that I try my hand at illustrating for children. At that time she was acting as editor for the publisher William R. Scott and just getting into high gear in her own writing. My first book was *Bumble Bugs and Elephants*, which was said to be the youngest book then in existence. The next year I won a very informal competition to illustrate Gertrude Stein's only published book for children, *The World Is Round*. All the illustrators who were working for the Scotts at that time wanted the privilege of illustrating this book. It was decided therefore that sample illustrations should be sent to Miss Stein in Paris. Fortunately she chose mine! Fortunately not only for the privilege of doing the work but also because the advance helped to finance my marriage to Edith Thacher in June 1939.

Since then I have illustrated more than thirty books, the majority of which have been written by my wife. I have also been active in the decorative arts and painting. However, the illustration of children's books has been the major line except for the three years that I spent in the South Pacific trying to camouflage a war that didn't want to take time or trouble to be camouflaged.

My wife and I lived for many years in Vermont, where our son was born in 1949. Since then we have gradually gravitated away from the long winters there until now we are permanent residents of Mill Valley, California, near the beautiful bay of San Francisco.

Edith Thacher Hurd

1910-

AUTHOR OF
Caboose; Galleon from Manila; Benny, the Bulldozer; Engine, Engine, No. 9; Etc.

Autobiographical sketch of Edith Thacher Hurd:

WRITING has always been fun for me. It was lucky that I went to a wonderfully progressive school in Kansas City, Missouri, where we were given lots of time to write and to act and do all sorts of creative things. I loved it when we were given the writing of a story as homework. This was particularly true when we studied the Middle Ages. I must have been about twelve at the time. My stories were full of knights in armor who lived in great castles and my favorite author, of course, was Howard Pyle. I guess this makes me rather a strange twelve-year-old girl by modern standards for I gather the young today care more for knights with hot rods than jousting sticks. Nevertheless, I had two friends who must have been equally strange for we shared our love of writing and reading and the three of us seemed to live in our own world and a very delightful and creative one it was.

Both my mother and father were great readers. Meals were always a time for some member of the family to share the book he was reading at the time. When my father was away on business, my mother often read out loud to my two brothers and myself at the dinner table. We went through most of *The Pickwick Papers* in this way. Why my mother did not gradually starve to death I have never quite understood.

On leaving school I went to Switzerland to study for one year. Here we were not encouraged to do anything creative. Nevertheless, I was fortunate enough to have as a teacher a person so creative herself that this quality could not help spilling over a bit despite the rigid school pattern. She filled me with excitement for painting, the history of art, European history, and French literature. I was unconscious of learning anything. I just absorbed and this contact became the background for my choosing fine arts as my chief study at Radcliffe College.

To write as a profession was not an idea that had ever entered my wildest dreams. I had never met an author and the fact that one could make a living out of anything that seemed so close to just having fun seemed incredible. So, on leaving college in the depths of the Depression (1933), I took the first opening I could find and accepted a scholarship at the Bank Street College of Education in New York City to prepare myself to be a teacher.

Here again luck was with me for I found that the Bank Street College was full of exciting and creative people. This was no humdrum teachers' college, filling its students with dust-dry facts. We were made to listen to and look at real live children. Then we were told to use our heads in thinking about teaching them. We were not given stacks of books but whatever creative possibilities we had, be they ever so slight, were encouraged and nurtured. At last, to my amazement, mine flowered when I had my first book accepted by a publisher while I was still studying at the Writers' Laboratory at the Bank Street School.

This was exciting. With the idea of the fun and the possibilities very much in my mind, I kept on teaching but now combined it with writing. I began to write books that I felt children wanted at certain ages. They were not whimsical tales but tough old streamlined-train stories, stories about bulldozers, and fire engines, the stuff that a six-year-old boy's imaginative play is made of.

Then one day I met a young artist who had just come back from studying art in Paris for two years. He too was interested in children's books, as an illustrator. Even before we were married, in 1939, we were already writing and illustrating children's books together. Since then we have created many, over forty now, I guess, and we seem to do more and more each year. Our house is full of the young, friends of our son, and that makes it fun for we gear our books to their interests, except of course when we take time off for a teen-age novel or a purely fanciful tale such as *The Cat from Telegraph Hill*. We wrote this when nostalgic for the city we both love best in all the world, San Francisco.

We live very close to this beautiful city now, in Mill Valley, but each summer we return to Vermont which was our home for many years. We go back to a very small house in the foothills of the Green Mountains because it's hard to break the Vermont habit.

Moritz Adolf Jagendorf

1888-

AUTHOR OF

New England Bean-Pot; Tyll Ulenspiegel's Merry Pranks; The Merry Men of Gotham; Sand in the Bag; Etc.

Autobiographical sketch of Moritz Jagendorf:

THERE was a golden literary spoon in my mouth when I was born in Austria. At nine I wrote nine-year-old love poems to my sweethearts, and read everything in print that came into my hands, from Grimm to Max Stirner. Whether I understood it or not, it was sunshine to my mind and helped me create my own marvelous world.

At eleven I ran off with a circus where I had acted in a pantomime, only to be brought back the very next day ignominiously, but it resulted in writing a fairy play which was performed in our horse stable. Mother took me often to plays and I was bitten by the theater bug and decided to go on the stage. With a peasant boy's costume under my arm I waited at the stage door for Mr. Maurer, the leading actor, and offered my services for juvenile parts. He promised to engage me but never did. Between daydreaming and hounding the theater and theatrical ventures in the stable, there was little time for studying. I was a very plague to my mother.

I had a strange love for flowers (there will be soon a book about this) and robbed nearly every garden every summer. When my poor mother could not stand the shame any longer, she shipped me off to my father who was in New York. At first I hated the city. I missed the open green country, the sleighing on steep hills, the mountain climbing, but one day I found a free library where I could get all the books I wanted.

Jagendorf: *YEA ghen dorf*

MORITZ ADOLF JAGENDORF

My father took me to the theater often and teachers in public school were more than nice to me. I could do almost anything I liked, something unheard of in Austria. I spent my time drawing on the blackboard, producing plays, and playing basketball, and we won the championship of the United States. Of course, I was a good student. America was paradise.

In the year and a half at the Townsend Harris High School, I had the same happy experiences with literary work playing a major part. I wrote for the magazine and won some prizes. Then, one day, I decided I had to get married in a hurry. Since Yale had a three-year law course, I went there. How I was accepted is one of the great sagas of America. But I couldn't get away from writing. Instead of studying law, I wrote a most unoriginal novel. Professor William Lyon Phelps read it and said it had promise and that I should continue writing. So I left law and the girl, wisely, left me.

Then to Columbia University. I wanted the city with theaters and concerts and ballets. At Columbia I came in contact with men who shaped my life's work, Professor Brander Matthews, Odell, Erskine, and others. Writing came first. One of the plays I adapted for one of the courses was published and is still produced all over the world. Articles and stories were published. Some of the plays were produced in the small theaters. Off-Broadway, if you want to sound snooty. Notes set down developed into plays and stories as the years went by.

I headed the Free Theatre where unusual plays were produced; then the Children's Playhouse, which gave productions on Broadway and up. I was director of the Washington Square Players, which became the Theatre Guild. Book after book of plays were published and produced. Then came a great change. It was soon after the Tyll Ulenspiegel tales were published.

One day, while traveling, I heard my first American folktale. It fascinated me. A New Englander, who knew slews of them, told them to me. I lost my interest in plays. Here was a vibrant American life, a thrilling folk life, more colorful than the Arabian Nights. *New England Bean-Pot* was the first result. Every one of the stories was told to me by New Englanders. I remembered the tales of Johnny Darling when I went summer after summer to the Catskill Mountains and they went into a book. Others followed. It was a great new world, full of excitement and pleasure. I dug deeply into this (new to me) field, both in America and Europe. I have penetrated a little, but I hope to go into it deeper and deeper.

Eleanore M. Jewett

1890-

AUTHOR OF

The Hidden Treasure of Glaston; Mystery at Boulder Point; Cobblers' Knob; Which Was Which? Etc.

Autobiographical sketch of Eleanore M. Jewett:

IT was natural I should be born in New York City. I always felt that I practically owned the place because one side of my family had been there ever since it was the little Dutch village of New Amsterdam. I lived there until I married, but I can't say it is a particularly happy place for children to grow up in. Being an only child, I rarely had anyone to play with. Instead, I had imaginary playmates and an imaginary brother who did everything with me. At one time we had a literary club. All the other members were book people: the four Little Women, of course; Hortense, who came out of a book called *Hortense, a Difficult Child;*

ELEANORE M. JEWETT

As to formal education, I went to Horace Mann School, then Barnard College for my A.B. After that I taught in a private school and at the same time took my master's degree at Columbia University, in comparative literature. There I became more deeply interested in the medieval period which had fascinated me ever since I first heard a King Arthur story down in the grades. And since then I have written two books with a twelfth century background.

I married Charles Harvey Jewett, a doctor with a long medical heritage, and we moved to a lovely old town in upstate New York. We have two daughters and now three grandchildren. These are too young yet to be helpful critics of my stories, which are usually slanted to the ten-to-twelve-year group, or older. But if they don't grow up too fast, I am hoping to write a book just for them!

and several others. The object of the club was to write stories but, as my brother could not help me in that, I had to do them all myself and it proved too arduous (I was about nine), so the club disintegrated. But from then on I can't remember a time when I did not intend to write for children.

My next venture was scarcely more successful. I was eleven then and had another child to collaborate with me. We decided that the school history book was too dull so we would write another that would be really interesting. Armed with a notebook, I went to the public library and entered the field of research, my subject being Columbus. I found there was a discouraging amount of knowledge in the world not contained in our school textbooks. But I wrote one chapter before we wilted under the weight of our ambitious project.

In the summers my mother, who was an artist, took me to the Massachusetts coast, Plymouth and East Gloucester, where she painted. She was a widow and her art work meant our "board and keep"—and also her great joy—so it was very important. Happily for me she forgot my existence (almost) while she was out sketching and that left me free to play with other children or wander by myself on the shore. Out of those days grew a tremendous love for the sea, a sense of the beauty and terror and wonder of it, and I find the sea keeps washing into my stories whether I want it or not!

Mary Alice Jones

1898-

AUTHOR OF

Tell Me About God; Tell Me About the Bible; First Prayers for Little Children; Stories of the Christ Child; Etc.

MARY Alice Jones was born in Dallas, Texas, "on a Sunday night," she recalled once, "*after* Mother got home from church." She joined the Methodist Church at the age of ten, and while attending the University of Texas worked in the University Methodist Church.

She received her master's degree in religious education from Northwestern University, was director of children's work for the South Carolina Conference and children's editor for the Methodist periodicals, and then received her Ph.D. from Yale University. For sixteen years she was director of children's work for the International Council of Religious Education, where she taught in leadership training schools and did field work of all sorts. She was the first woman to be asked to teach at the Yale Divinity School, and she has been visiting professor at numerous seminaries. She has also done a good deal with religious programs for children in radio.

In 1945 Miss Jones became children's book editor for Rand McNally & Company. At her suggestion Marguerite Henry and Wes-

MARY ALICE JONES

ley Dennis, the well-known author-illustrator team, went to Chincoteague to see a roundup take place. Out of this experience came *Misty of Chincoteague*, which was published in 1947 and later filmed. Soon Miss Jones' books began appearing on the Rand McNally list. While *Prayers for Little Children* has sold well over two million copies, perhaps her best-known title is *Tell Me About God*. Two recent ones are *Tell Me About Heaven* and *Tell Me About Christmas*. This latter book, she says, is "an attempt to interpret the Incarnation rather than to retell the Christmas stories."

Miss Jones left Rand McNally in 1951, and at present is director of children's work for the General Board of Education of the Methodist Church.

Virginia Kahl

1919-

AUTHOR AND ILLUSTRATOR OF
Away Went Wolfgang; The Duchess Bakes a Cake; Maxie; Plum Pudding for Christmas; Etc.

Autobiographical sketch of Virginia Kahl:

MY love of Europe, and especially Austria, belies my Middle Western roots. I was born in Milwaukee, Wisconsin, in 1919, and grew up there. After graduating from Milwaukee-Downer College with a major in art, I worked for the Milwaukee Public Library, both as library assistant and as a commercial artist.

In 1948 I went to Berlin as a librarian for the Army. It was a strange and exciting time. The blockade had already begun and the airlift brought in all of our supplies. Although streetcars ran once an hour, planes landed every minute. And although there were many shortages, we had two mayors, two police forces, even two kinds of money. In all that time, I was able to leave the city only once, for a week end in Switzerland.

I was not sorry to be transferred to Salzburg, Austria, where I spent the next six years. My work took me throughout Austria and into Italy, and my vacation trips took me to most of the other countries in Europe; but I was always happy to return to Salzburg. It is a beautiful little city that nestles in the mountains. There are narrow, crooked streets; and in the center of the city, on a small mountain, there is a castle nearly a thousand years old. The people are cheerful, easygoing, and friendly. Each year, for the whole month of August, there is the great music festival for which Salzburg is world-renowned. Then visitors crowd into the little city; banners fly from the bridge; everyone wears quaint costumes; and each day is filled with concerts. It seems as if no one can be serious then— there are parades, band concerts in the gardens, and laughter and music everywhere.

This is what I should like to get into my picture books—all of the color and gaiety and humor which I found in Austria. It was there that I began to write and illustrate children's books. It is truly a fairytale country.

I'd like, too, to have my pictures reflect another of my enthusiasms—my love of Romanesque and early Gothic art. I admire the simplicity, sincerity, humor and boldness of work of that period. I try to give my pictures the same qualities.

Although I visited many museums, walked through countless ancient towns, climbed the narrow stairs of every castle I could find, and was awed by work in numerous cathedrals and churches, I'll never have enough.

VIRGINIA KAHL

I hope to be able to go back and live for long periods in Europe. As I continue to travel and write, I hope I can bring to American children the joyous spirit of European people. And I hope that children get as much pleasure out of reading my stories as I do creating them.

Nicholas Kalashnikoff

1888-1961

AUTHOR OF
Jumper; Toyon; The Defender;
My Friend Yakub; Etc.

Autobiographical sketch of Nicholas Kalashnikoff, written for MORE JUNIOR AUTHORS shortly before his death:

I WAS born on May 17, 1888, in Minusinsk, Siberia. My father, who was a farmer, died when I was very young. My mother was part Tartar. From her father I heard as a boy many stories of his adventures as a soldier under Nicholas I at the siege of Sevastopol, and no doubt these stories influenced me in thinking of a military career. My early schooling was received in Irkutsk; then I spent two years at the Moscow University as a student of history and philosophy. When I was sixteen, like many idealistic youths of that time who hoped to liberalize conditions under which the Russian masses lived, I joined the revolutionary movement, participating in the 1905 rebellion. For this I was later exiled by the czarist government to the arctic, which put an end to my studies.

This period of my childhood and youth is background for my book *My Friend Yakub*, and it forms part of my autobiographical novel, *They That Take the Sword*.

After four years in the polar region, during which time I took part in an expedition to the Anadir Peninsula, I was released by a general amnesty on the outbreak of World War I and volunteered for service with the Russian army. I was captain when the war ended and civil war broke out. Appointed commander of the People's Army of Siberia, I led the forces which in 1919 defeated the notorious Ataman Semenoff and his allies at Irkutsk. But soon after this the Bolshevik victory destroyed the hope of a moderate democratic regime in Russia and I was forced to flee to China. From there I came to the United States in 1924, to become a citizen in 1930. Like many other newcomers here, I have worked at many trades besides that of writing.

From my experiences of war and life in the polar region came the material for my other books, *Jumper, Toyon,* and *The Defender*. I am married to Elizabeth Lawrence, an editor.

NICHOLAS KALASHNIKOFF

Kalashnikoff: *kuh LASH nick off*

Ezra Jack Keats

1916-

AUTHOR AND ILLUSTRATOR OF
The Snowy Day

ILLUSTRATOR OF
*Wonder Tales of Dogs and Cats; The Rice
Bowl Pet; What Good Is a Tail? Etc.*

EZRA Jack Keats, who was awarded the Caldecott Medal in 1963 for *The Snowy Day*, was born and brought up in Brooklyn, New York. His parents ostensibly disapproved of his ambition to be a painter, but his father, a Greenwich Village waiter, provided him with painting materials (which had supposedly been acquired from artists in return for free meals, but had in reality been purchased), and his mother would wake him to see the colors of dawn over the city.

Mr. Keats had no formal art training. Although he was awarded three scholarships on his graduation from high school, he preferred to work at manual jobs. In the late 1930's he worked as a mural painter on WPA projects, but with the advent of World War II he became a member of the United States Air Corps and served as a camouflage expert. After the war he decided to become an illustrator and in 1947 he received his first assignment, a full-color editorial illustration for *Collier's*. The next year he traveled through Europe, painting, and on his return he exhibited his work in the Associated American Artists Galleries in New York.

EZRA JACK KEATS

Over the years, Mr. Keats has illustrated many children's books, in particular *Wonder Tales of Dogs and Cats* by Frances Carpenter, *In the Night* by Paul Showers, *The Rice Bowl Pet* by Patricia Miles Martin, and *What Good Is a Tail?* by S. P. Russell. *My Dog Is Lost*, written and illustrated by Mr. Keats and Pat Cherr, was published in 1960.

The Snowy Day, published by Viking in 1962, is the first book written and illustrated by Mr. Keats without a collaborator. To show the delight of a small boy upon waking one morning to find snow on the ground, Mr. Keats used simple text, collages, and bright-colored drawings. In reviewing this book in the *Saturday Review*, Alice Dalgliesh praised Mr. Keats as "a gifted illustrator; he shows in pictures and story that he has a sympathetic feeling that is rapidly going out of picture books for young children."

Harold Keith

1903-

AUTHOR OF
*Rifles for Watie; Oklahoma Kickoff;
Shotgun Shaw; A Pair of Captains;
Etc.*

HAROLD Verne Keith was born April 8, 1903, in Lambert, Oklahoma, of Scotch-Irish ancestry. He spent his childhood in Kansas, Missouri, and Texas, as well as his native state, and he and his brother and sister went to school in nine towns. In 1921 he graduated from high school, where he had been busy as cartoonist, sports editor, and co-editor of the school news magazine, and went on to Northwestern State Teachers College, at Alva, Oklahoma, where he won the Scroll Scholarship in his freshman year. He then spent four years at the University of Oklahoma, with an additional seven summers, three of them at the professional writing school, earning his bachelor's and master's degrees.

Mr. Keith has long been sports publicity director for his alma mater. In his free time he writes, chiefly boys' books. His first, *A Boys' Life of Will Rogers* (1937), grew out of his master's thesis, about the father of Will Rogers—"Clem Rogers and His Influence on Oklahoma History." *Sports and Games*, published in 1941, was a Junior Literary Guild selection. *Okla-*

home Kickoff (1948) was an early history of Oklahoma University football.

On March 31, 1958, Mr. Keith was awarded the thirty-seventh Newbery Medal for *Rifles for Watie,* published the preceding year. It tells of a boy who served four years with the Union forces in the western campaign in the Civil War. It took five years to write, not to mention the time spent in preliminary research. He spent two summers (1940 and 1941) traveling in Oklahoma, seeking out Civil War veterans. He found and interviewed twenty-two, all nearly a hundred years old. Mr. Keith's comments on how he applied this research and used it in the writing of the book are illuminating:

"In my interviews I looked mainly for suggestions out of which I might build believable characters and dramatic scenes. I rarely found them in complete form. Usually I had to blend traits of several people to get the one character I wanted. I would take two parts of some Civil War character and mix with an individual trait of some athlete, cowpuncher, or newspaperman I know today, add a pinch of imagination, stir vigorously and out came the characters. The plot was easier. Characters and scenes are far more important and harder to come by."

Mr. Keith grew up in a family that loved books. Among his favorites were those by H. Rider Haggard, the sea stories of Morgan Robertson, and novels of the postbellum South. He has written fiction and nonfiction for numerous magazines. His prime interest is the history of his home state. Mr. Keith feels that writing is like long-distance running—you keep on going even after you are dead tired. He is married, the father of a boy and girl, and his hobbies are quail hunting and trout fishing, as well as barbershop singing.

Alice Geer Kelsey

1896-

AUTHOR OF

*I Give You My Colt; Once the Mullah;
Many Hands in Many Lands; Tino
and the Typhoon; Etc.*

Autobiographical sketch of Alice Geer Kelsey:

CHILDREN have always been more important to me than writing. Being busy with them saved me from writing before

ALICE GEER KELSEY

the education of living and working with them. In Connecticut school days it was my small neighbors, my sister's children, my Sunday school class. After Mount Holyoke College, it was Polish and Italian children of a settlement house in Hartford. After marriage to Lincoln Kelsey it was Greek, Armenian, and Turkish orphans in Turkey. Then for fourteen years in upstate New York our own four children and their friends filled days too full for writing the stories they liked to hear.

When our youngest child entered kindergarten I tried writing stories I had been telling from our experiences in Turkey, from our children's own days, from my happy New England childhood. (Born in Danvers, Massachusetts. Learned to talk in Lewiston, Maine. Kindergarten through high school in West Hartford, Connecticut.) The stories I made up to drive home a point in church school also went over my typewriter for publication.

One of my greatest concerns has been that children have sympathetic understanding of people who are different. A favorite bedtime prayer asked God's blessing for "other children far away." Whenever possible we had friends of other lands in our home. Our first "Fresh Air" guest came when our children were so small that our neighbors thought us demented. Naturally this concern for world friendship has shown in my writing.

Though my stories are not limited to this type, I feel most satisfaction when I show how children of other races, creeds, or background can be different and delightful without being queer. In retelling folk tales, such as the Nasr-ed-Din stories, I hope appreciation of another culture is increased through shared laughter. In writing on assignment, I sometimes get material from reading or merciless questioning of people who know. Sometimes I can go where the assignment calls—Puerto Rico, or camps for migrant laborers.

Since our honeymoon in Turkey after World War I, I have three times found story material while following my husband on leave from Cornell University for overseas work. Before the close of World War II, we were in Greece where he was agricultural chief for UNRRA. In 1953, we were in Iran while he trained extension workers. Now we are at Los Banos, Philippines, where he advises in training community development workers. My ambition for our two years in the Philippines is greater than turning out a book or two. Working as a volunteer on the curriculum committee of the Philippine Federation of Christian Churches, I hope to help a few Filipinos become writers of good stories with local settings for Filipino children.

The hardship of separation from fourteen fast-developing grandchildren has its compensations: a fourth grader announcing to his class that the story in their reader is by his grandmother, or a kindergartner invited to a room of "big kids" to show a toy Filipino house sent by "the Grandpa and Grandma that live way across the ocean on an island."

Lee Kingman

1919-

AUTHOR OF

Peter's Long Walk; The Quarry Adventure; The Magic Christmas Tree; Pierre Pidgeon; Etc.

Autobiographical sketch of Lee Kingman:

LEARNING to read was just doing what came naturally, and my happiest hours as a child were spent in sharing the lively adventures of book children. As I was an only child, my favorite stories were about

LEE KINGMAN

large families! Growing up in a small town, Reading, Massachusetts, a trip to Boston was a big event.

It was in Boston at the famous Bookshop for Boys and Girls, when I was nine, that I chose ten books, the prize in a reading contest conducted by *The Horn Book* magazine (imagine a prize for your favorite occupation!) and first met Bertha Mahoney Miller. Later, *The Horn Book* used an article and picture of the hand-painted paper dolls I made to illustrate operas and books. This was an enticing introduction to seeing my own work in print!

From junior high school on, I wanted to write as well as read, and I knew I would never conquer mathematics. After Reading High School, I attended Colby Junior College, and was graduated from Smith in 1940. As a college junior, I wrote a novel and sent it to a contest which it did not win but the comments on it encouraged me. Senior year, *Vogue* magazine printed my Prix de Paris contest essay on Mary Ellen Chase. I left college convinced I would be a best-selling novelist!

Four months later I had a job as receptionist and switchboard operator in a huge insurance company. By a horrible quirk of fate, I ended up in the investment department. For relief, I wrote children's plays, and several appeared in *Plays* magazine.

In 1942, by a happy chance I went to Houghton Mifflin in the juvenile book department, and in 1945 I became children's book editor, a position I held until I resigned in 1946. I worked with writers and illustrators, and learned every phase of bookmaking from editing to writing jacket blurbs, from choosing illustration techniques to laying out books. The most difficult thing was estimating costs, as I never did conquer mathematics.

One summer I went to Cape Ann, Massachusetts, to study drawing and met Robert Natti, who came from a wonderfully large Finnish-American family of twelve children. We were married in 1945 and have lived on the edge of a large water-filled quarry near Gloucester since 1947. Susanna Matilda was born in 1948 (she spends most of her time reading, and she is very good at math!), and Peter Eino was born in 1950. My husband is a schoolteacher and we often have lots of boys and girls visit us. He also makes pottery and raises sheep and trees. For a change from writing, I make linoleum blocks for hand-printed textiles. It is very busy, but any time my husband remembers something funny that happened while he was growing up, it is apt to turn up somewhere in one of my books.

Ruth Adams Knight

1898-

AUTHOR OF
Queen of Roses; Halfway to Heaven; Top of the Mountain; The Land Beyond;
Etc.

Autobiographical sketch of Ruth Adams Knight:

I WAS born in Defiance, Ohio. My mother's ancestors were among the earliest settlers in New England and my father's in Pennsylvania. One of my first recollections is being taken to the old fort ground on the Maumee River, where there were reproductions of the blockhouses used by "Mad Anthony" Wayne during the Indian wars. Next to the swing under the apple tree in the back yard, the fort ground was my favorite spot, first as a place for picnics and later as the site of the public library. By the time we moved from Defiance to Toledo, I had read everything in the juvenile department, as well as all the volumes in the adult stacks the librarian would permit a pig-tailed youngster to check out.

RUTH ADAMS KNIGHT

From the time I became the proud eight-year-old author of a story in a magazine called *Little Sunbeam,* I knew I would be a writer. But while during my school years my accumulation of literary awards pleased my parents, they took a dim view of any career for a woman. They regarded the "finishing school" routine, with eventual marriage and homemaking, as the only desirable feminine pattern.

Today I suppose my urge to write would be termed "compulsive." Then my determination to study journalism was regarded as stubbornly perverse. But, the "finishing" completed, I enrolled at Toledo University and took every writing course possible. When a shortage of experienced reporters caused the Toledo *Times,* the morning and Sunday newspaper, to ask the university for student journalists, I was among those selected.

Because of the emergency, I was assigned to a "run" usually barred to women. Once I had written Page One news stories, my fate was sealed. Later, I became a feature writer, and eventually dramatic and literary editor for both papers, doing a daily column and editing a Sunday section. I doubt there ever was a more rigorous training school than the editorial room of the twenties, with its emphasis on deadlines and scoops. But sustained by the smell of printer's ink, I worked happily from 1:00 P.M. to 1:00 A.M., and in the mornings I wrote verse, which was published in the poetry journals of that period.

Challenged by the new arrival, radio, I came to New York as managing editor of a radio-script syndicate, then for years wrote network dramatic scripts and documentaries. I also wrote two novels, and short stories for national magazines, one of which was included in the O. Henry prize award collection of best stories of the year.

In 1942 I wrote the first of a dozen books for teen-age readers, *Valiant Comrades: A Story of Our Dogs of War*. Several of these books have been dog stories. One, *It Might Be You*, dealt with intolerance. Others have told of the life of young people in other lands. *Halfway to Heaven* took me to Switzerland to cross the Alps in winter and write of the famous Hospice of St. Bernard. Another, *Search for the Galleon's Gold,* was based on the Duke of Argyll's scrapbook about the sunken treasure ship of the Spanish Armada, for which he is still searching. Since understanding among the young people of the world seems particularly important at this time, it has pleased me that several of these books have been translated and published in European countries.

While I greatly value a teen-age audience, I use no special technique in writing for it, other than to keep subject matter from becoming overly complex or sophisticated. I would no more slant or write down than I would speak down in conversation with young people. I find them so keen and well informed that writing for them is a challenge as well as a pleasure. I have little sense of age limits in literature. The books I enjoyed with my own two children ranged from Mother Goose to Shakespeare; we read together at many levels and always with a shared joy. This experience I am now repeating with my grandchildren, and it continues to be an infinitely enriching and rewarding one.

I like to write about the things I know well and about which I feel deeply—things which come out of my love of travel, my love of animals, my love of people. I enjoy the stimulation of New York and often work there, but home to me means a farm in New England.

Ursula Koering
1921-

ILLUSTRATOR OF
The Picture Story of the Philippines; The Picture Story of Hawaii; Holly River Secret; The Strange Man and the Stork; Etc.

Autobiographical sketch of Ursula Koering:

I WAS born in Vineland, New Jersey, and am still living in the same town, though we moved about while I was small. I have always loved to draw and work with clay. It seems to me that for years I drew only horses and more horses.

Both of my parents have artistic leanings. My father has worked in glass blowing and my grandfather made wagons and carved figures in wood. My mother paints in oils and on china and her father was also a glass blower. My brother, Karl, and I spent most of our childhood on a small farm where there were many dogs, cats, goats, pigs, pigeons, chickens, even canaries and parakeets at one time, and best of all a horse.

I attended Sacred Heart grammar and high school and during my school years I was given the lovely task of drawing with colored chalks decorations for the different seasons on the huge blackboard in the hall. During my grade school years my mother took me to Philadelphia every Saturday to attend the children's drawing class at the Philadelphia Museum School of Art. When I graduated from high school, I took the illustration course there, and later postgraduate courses in clay modeling and ceramic work.

My first drawing assignment on leaving art school was a story for *Jack and Jill* magazine. I have been doing work for them ever since. I was going along illustrating books for several years, when there came a wonderful opportunity. I had illustrated two Picture Story books, Hawaii and the Philippines, when it was decided for the author, Hester O'Neill, and me to do *Picture Story of Norway*. To do it we flew to Norway and traveled all over that beautiful rugged country, she with her notebook and I with my sketchbook and camera. We traveled up and down fjords, climbed mountains, walked in the snow in June, and saw

Koering: *CARE ing*

the midnight sun. We saw whaling ships bring in the catch of huge whales and traveled for miles through desolate country to see and speak to the nomadic Laplanders.

I enjoyed doing the Picture Story books very much. Later, we did picture stories on Sweden, Denmark, and Alaska.

My favorite subjects are people, people in action, especially people in costume, any kind of costume, from caveman days on up to the nineteen hundreds; and animals, any kind of animals.

I hope I may always be able to illustrate books for children and I hope boys and girls will always like to see my drawings.

PHYLLIS KRASILOVSKY

Phyllis Krasilovsky

1926-

AUTHOR OF

The Man Who Didn't Wash His Dishes;
The Very Little Girl; The Cow Who
Fell in the Canal; Etc.

Autobiographical sketch of Phyllis Krasilovsky:

I WAS born and brought up in Brooklyn, New York, where I lived a dual childhood—torn between the lively games and roller skating on our street and the quiet, cultural life of museums, theater, and ballet which my mother, an avid bookworm, fostered. My mother was not a writer but she had a writer's eye for everything she saw or read. Writer's and artist's eye, actually, for she recognized color and beauty in places hidden to average awareness—in the design of clothing strung on back-yard clotheslines, in the flowers she grew in the tiniest patch of earth we had (she taught us to see that pansies had faces, that lilies of the valley were little white bells, etc.)—all this besides her more arty leanings. She always insisted that we "be original" and not go along with the crowd whether in feelings towards people or in simple school compositions that we wrote for homework. I think her instinct for genuine self-thought has helped me a great deal in my writing.

I didn't always want to be a writer. I had all the usual aspirations of young girls, I suppose—to be a dancer, an actress, a poet, etc.—but I did always write whenever I could from the time I was eight, so I suppose the subconscious wish was there, at any rate! I wrote my first children's book, *The Man Who Didn't Wash His Dishes*, at nineteen. It was just a letter for a little boy who was dying of cancer. I'd written him a whole stack of funny letters to amuse him and then his mother said he loved this one so much he had to hear it over and over again. That's what really started me off. Since then I've written for several children's magazines and just for the fun of amusing my two little girls and their friends.

I have worked at all sorts of jobs, from page girl at the New York Stock Exchange to secretary at the *New Yorker*. Graduated from high school at seventeen and plunged right into the subway bedlam. Attended evening session at Brooklyn College for three years and then took courses at Cornell University when my husband was finishing his degree at Cornell Law School. After graduation we moved to Alaska, where we lived for three years, and where our older daughter, Alexis, was born. Now we are back East. My husband practices law in New York City.

We live in Mamaroneck in a small house on the edge of a wood and are continuously busy gardening, writing, reading, learning to play instruments. We are a great family for arts and crafts and like to make all kinds of things, from mobiles to furniture, to wood carving to collages. We like best of all to

Krasilovsky: *kraz uh LOVE ski*

travel and manage a few weeks each summer with the children to a new area. The love of travel stems for both my husband and myself from high school days when we were avid hostelers and explored every inch of New England and Canada. (For two summers I was an American Youth Hostel leader and led large groups of teen-agers.) *The Cow Who Fell in the Canal* was written while my husband and I were on a hitchhiking hosteling trip through Europe in 1953. I noticed the cows grazing along the peaceful canals and wondered what would happen if one of them fell in.

Besides writing and speaking for children, I write travel articles, do-it-yourself articles for magazines and newspapers. Also do short stories but am not very successful with them, alas. I do think that writing for children is most rewarding, though. It is good to know that you are enriching a child's imagination, that you are adding laughter to his life, that you are giving some measure of happiness, and that you may be creating a steppingstone to his further love of literature. And literature gives our lives that much more beauty.

RUTH KRAUSS

Ruth Krauss

1901-

AUTHOR OF

The Carrot Seed; A Hole Is To Dig; I'll Be You and You Be Me; Charlotte and the White Horse; Etc.

Autobiographical sketch of Ruth Krauss:

I HAVE had no special training in writing books for children, nor in writing in general. I feel that much of my writing is tied in with training in the graphic arts—I am a graduate of an art school—and also with the study of music. I played both the piano and the violin—rather, I studied to play both of these instruments at various times.

I have also had some education in anthropology, which, although not undertaken too seriously by me at the time at Columbia University, extended over a period of four years and broadened my understanding to the point where it fused with the understanding of many other things, including (I hope it includes) that branch of people categorized as "children." I have also "undergone" a personal analysis which has been, as far as I can judge now, a kind of final

touch in making me aware of things I formerly was not aware of about myself and other people. Because, as I always say, "After all, I am a people too," which grammar is not too fine but I think it is clear.

I am naturally illiterate in my language and I sometimes wonder if this isn't simply a continuation of the way I talked as a child. My formal education stopped after two years of public high school. The Columbia anthropology studying was done on an extension level, although the courses were in the regular department.

My own, I guess, favorite books are *The Carrot Seed, A Hole Is To Dig, I'll Be You and You Be Me, Charlotte and the White Horse,* but I feel my best or rather most comprehensive book is *Somebody Else's Nut Tree, and Other Tales from Children.*

I live with my husband, Crockett Johnson, in Rowayton, Connecticut, on the water front. I've had published about sixteen or seventeen books. But I have written at least one thousand more, including a couple of bad novels, an anthropology "first book," poetry, and an experimental-type very long book (according to my usual standards) which seems to be just growing by itself.

Part of my hobbies, although definitely related to their use in writing books for children, is making collections of material, such as "new words for old," humor (children's), children's poems, dreams, etc., etc., and many other facets of what people give forth with.

Fritz Kredel

1900-

ILLUSTRATOR OF
*Grimm's Fairy Tales; The Complete Ander-
sen; All About the Sea; Silent Night; Etc.*

Autobiographical sketch of Fritz Kredel:

FRITZ KREDEL

BORN in wooded mountain country in Germany, I had never thought I would sometime make the trip across the ocean and stay here, happily, in America for the rest of my life.

I started drawing very early, sitting on my father's lap. "Draw me a railroad where the smoke comes out," I used to urge him. This done, I wanted one "where the none-smoke comes out." And then I grabbed the pencil and added the smoke. Other things had to be drawn for me, too, of course—horses, carriages, soldiers, and God knows what. My father, having studied art in his younger years, was a fine instructor.

When I went to school I got myself into trouble, because I was and still am what is called over here a southpaw. My teacher spanked me several times with a cane when he caught me drawing with my left hand and he predicted that I would never be able to draw. Finally my father stepped in and I was allowed to draw the way I wanted.

Up to my sixteenth year I could go to the school in my home town. Then I had to go to the *Realgymnasium* in the capital, Darmstadt, to finish my education and get my diploma of "maturity." Meanwhile the war had broken out and I joined the army in 1918.

After the end of the war I came home with no great hopes for the future. I became an apprentice to an apothecary, but this was never to my liking. I broke a lot of bottles and made out wrong prescriptions so in the end I was allowed to quit. I went to Pomerania to become a *Gutsinspektor*, which means a supervisor of a farm. But this also did not work out too well. It had always been my dream to be an artist and to that my father finally agreed, after having consulted some experts and shown them some of my sketches.

I went to Offenbach in Germany, where at that time the famous Rudolf Koch was teaching. After a short time I became his master student and a great and lasting friendship developed. It was an exciting time. Things were not going too smoothly. There was the great inflation and we all became millionaires and even billionaires. In 1924 I went to Italy and Austria to study art with Victor Hammer, a friend of Koch, now also living here in the States. Later, I returned to Offenbach to finish the big *Blumenbuch* (book of flowers) which Koch and I had started. In 1926 I did one very intelligent thing—I got married. Meanwhile, the late George Macy of the Limited Editions Club had come to Europe and he gave me, much to my surprise, my first assignment in the U.S.A.—*Grimm's Fairy Tales*. After that, almost every year I got a book to illustrate for him.

I left Germany after Hitler had taken over and went to Austria in 1936. In 1937 M. B. Cary, Jr., visited us in Vienna on Christmas and, leaving, asked me if I would like to come to the States. I did not take his question too seriously, but promised to come if Hitler invaded Austria. He did so, as everybody knows, in 1938, whereupon Mr. Cary sent me the affidavit for the whole family. (We were four!) That's how I came to this country and I can say I never felt sorry for it and I have illustrated literally hundreds of books. I still think it is one of the most interesting and rewarding professions there is. Unless you want to become rich—then you'd better look for something else to do.

Kredel: *pronounced "cradle"*

Joseph Krumgold

1908-

AUTHOR OF

Sweeney's Adventure; . . . And Now Miguel

Autobiographical sketch of Joseph Krumgold:

WHEN most authors list the titles of their books, they usually end up with the word *etc.* I've never written any *etc.* All I have been able to manage are the two stories listed above. And the reason is that I am not really a full-fledged actual author.

What I actually do is make movies. For instance, both the titles listed up top were motion pictures before they ever got written into books.

All this started back in Jersey City where I was born. My father was an exhibitor; he owned and operated movie houses. My big brother was an organist who played in the great motion picture palaces in New York City, to accompany the silent pictures which were all we had at the time.

So around our house there was always a good deal of talk about movies. And by the time I was twelve years old, I decided that what I wanted to do when I grew up was to make movies. So that during most of my schooling I kept my eye out for the things that would help me when it came time to go to work.

I became interested in chemistry when I saw it had to do with developing film, and in physics when we studied optics and lenses. History and English were important, too, on account of the stories they suggested that could be turned into pictures. That's the way I went to school, to Dickinson High School in Jersey City and to New York University. When I graduated from college I went to work for Metro-Goldwyn-Mayer. I started making pictures and I've been at it ever since.

At first, most of this work was in Hollywood because that's where most pictures are made. I spent a good many years in California as a writer in the big studios there, and then as a producer. Then along about World War II, I left off making studio pictures. I became interested in films about actual people in actual places, the kind of pictures they call documentary. This way of making a movie seemed more exciting, working with facts—the real thing—instead of actors and fake scenery. Part of the excitement, anyway, is that you have to go where the story is happening. And that involves a lot of travel. I've made pictures all over the United States and in Europe and in the Middle East. For a while I ran a company with studios in Jerusalem.

And some years ago I made a picture in New Mexico about a boy named Miguel Chavez. After it was all finished I found there was a lot more I wanted to say about Miguel than I could get into a picture. And so I wrote a book called . . . *And Now Miguel.*

It was a real surprise for me when the book was given the Newbery Medal for "the most distinguished contribution to American literature for children" of the year. The medal gave me a new ambition, the first new one I have had since I was twelve years old. And that is to become a full-fledged author of children's books.

I'm trying very hard. So that one day, I hope, I'll be able to add to the stories above the tiny word that is the mark of the true professional—*etc.*

* * *

With the publication of *Onion John* in 1959, Mr. Krumgold acquired "the mark of the true professional—*etc.*"

JOSEPH KRUMGOLD

Beth and Joe Krush

ILLUSTRATORS OF
*The Borrowers; The Borrowers Afield;
Gone-Away Lake; The Magic Circle;
Etc.*

Biographical sketch of Beth and Joe Krush,
by Beth Krush:

JOE and I both grew up in typical row-house neighborhoods of the 1920's, Joe in Camden, New Jersey, where the busy Delaware River and the local airport (which had a real Ford Tri-Motor!) were major attractions; and I in Washington, D.C., where my favorite attraction was the Smithsonian Institute.

Though Joe denies any childhood ambition to be an artist, he filled notebooks with drawings of ships and won prizes for his model planes and boats. I always loved to draw; my parents kept me supplied with paper and pencils and my home town supplied subject material.

Joe and I met at the Philadelphia Museum School of Art. Art school was a joy after years of being sent to the principal's office for drawing in study hall! I won the illustration prize for the girls and Joe won the illustration prize for the boys. (He also won an assortment of other prizes for water color and graphics drawings.) We were married during World War II when it began to look as if it would be a long war. Joe

JOE KRUSH

was with the Office of Strategic Services and attended the original meeting of the United Nations as a graphics designer, and the war guilt trials in Nuremberg, Germany.

Since then we've worked at the business of making pictures together and separately. People often ask, "How can you both work on the same illustration?" Usually we pick the incidents and talk over the staging together. Then Joe does the first composition and perspective sketch; then I rework that, adding my two cents and looking up costumes, furniture, plants, animals, people. Most often Joe does the final rendering in his own decorative line. But we have our individual pride and each likes to do work that is all his or hers. My favorites are some of the books we've done together—*The Borrowers Afield,* and *Gone-Away Lake.*

I enjoy drawing the things women are interested in—children, plants, animals, clothes, and people.

Joe likes to draw people too, but feels his characterizations are more biting, and he "builds" his drawings of machinery, vehicles, and buildings with a masculine love for all the gadgets. I always marvel that he can impart such character and decorativeness to anything as hard and cold as a machine.

Joe has done a great variety of work in many mediums—posters, album covers, advertising and magazine illustration, storybooks and textbooks. He teaches illustration

BETH KRUSH

one day a week at the Philadelphia Museum School of Art.

We bought an old Victorian summer house on a hill near Valley Forge and we're forever redoing it. Our studio is the attic, and on a clear day we can see from here to Reading, forty miles away. At our house we have a red-haired little boy. He draws, too, and this place bulges with the prolific output of three busy "drawers."

We have a plump, patient beagle named Duffy. Her sisters Annie and Missie live in the neighborhood and they come to see her, push open the screen door and they all sit on the sofa. We also have a procession of stray cats I am always trying to place in a happy home other than mine.

If we had any time we'd like to improve our house and garden, piano and violin playing, and learn some more figures to do on our ice skates. I'd like to do "loops"; Joe is up to "brackets" and "counters."

ELISABETH KYLE

Elisabeth Kyle

Holly Hotel; West Wind; Lost Karin; The Provost's Jewel; Etc.

Autobiographical sketch of Agnes Mary Robertson Dunlop, who writes under the pseudonym Elisabeth Kyle:

I WAS born in Ayr, Scotland, a rather delicate child who liked to make up stories to pass the time. My father, a lawyer, had been forced to enter into partnership in the family firm instead of embracing literature, as he longed to do. Perhaps to console himself, he tried to form my own taste at a very early age by paraphrasing the classics to me by word of mouth, and by vetting every book that came into the nursery. Many, which he thought badly written or otherwise undesirable, were quietly suppressed.

I fear this has not helped to form my style as much as it should. But after all, he died when I was only nine, so he had little time to work upon his material. I had no conscious wish to become a writer when I grew up, but was encouraged by an editor friend of the family to have a shot at it. I found I could sell little stories for children, but soon got sidetracked into newspaper work. This was useful discipline, as it taught me to use the blue pencil and not resent others doing so.

Between the wars, I traveled a good deal through Central and Eastern Europe in search of material for the *Manchester Guardian,* and other newspapers. I also published one or two novels. But I came back to writing for children through a request from my British publisher for full-length adventure stories to suit the twelve-to-fourteen-year-old group, which was little catered for then.

In doing so, I made a curious discovery. My adult books I could place anywhere, giving them a foreign or an English background. My books for children had to be placed amongst real scenes I remembered; and the children in them had to be mostly Scotch, such as I had played with myself as a child. Since Scotland is a democratic country, I had been allowed to play with the village children when visiting country parts; and in writing dialogue, the old "broad Scotch" rose far more naturally to my lips than did the more correct English. (I still have to prune this carefully, out of consideration for my English and American readers.) This too, in spite of the fact that we never spoke it at home, and that I had had an English governess.

I have written more than fifteen adventure stories for young people, most of which have appeared in America as well as in Britain. I think the most popular seem to be *Holly Hotel, The Captain's House, The Reiver's Road,* and *The House of the Pelican.*

Evelyn Sibley Lampman

1907-

AUTHOR OF

Treasure Mountain; Tree Wagon; Rusty's Space Ship; The Shy Stegosaurus of Cricket Creek; Etc.

Autobiographical sketch of Evelyn Sibley Lampman:

I WAS born and grew up in Dallas, Oregon, which is a small town in the midst of the Willamette Valley. My great-grandparents had come there in a covered wagon, and when I was a little girl the stories of their trip and of the pioneer days were those that I heard over and over again. I wish now that I had paid even more attention than I did, for although I made up my mind in the first grade that I would be an author eventually, my early writings were exclusively concerned with little girls who had closets filled with many dresses, all pink. While these may have given me practice in writing, it would have been much better had I put down on paper the firsthand stories of my grandmother and her friends. Some of them I do remember, however, and I use them whenever I can. In *The Bounces of Cynthiann'*, for instance, the townspeople are all real. They died before I was born, but my father had told me about them so often I felt that I knew them personally.

After I was graduated from Oregon State College, I found a job as a continuity writer for a radio station. Continuity is everything that an announcer says, and because he says so much in the course of a day, there wasn't time for any other form of writing. I was married to a newspaperman and we had two little girls, Linda and Anne, but when my husband died I went back to radio.

Eventually I became educational director of a station which broadcast six dramatized in-school listening programs a week, which were tied in with the regular course of study of the Portland public schools. We covered everything from history to hygiene, and they were lots of fun to write and produce. I used to check the broadcasts in the classrooms with the children, because we wanted to make them interesting as well as educational, and I found that I liked working for, and with, the children most of all. Tapes were made of our programs, and they are still being used in our local schools.

EVELYN SIBLEY LAMPMAN

One day my daughter Linda, who was then in the fourth grade, came home and told me she had read everything in the library. She said there was a shortage of children's books, and why didn't I write one? It seemed like a good idea, so I wrote *Crazy Creek*, which was accepted by Doubleday. I've been writing books ever since, and because I write two a year, one under my own name and one under the pseudonym of "Lynn Bronson," it's become a full-time job.

Anne and I live in a gray stone house in Portland's Mt. Tabor, which is an extinct volcano, together with an Irish terrier named Miss Clancy, and Ugly-Pooh, a black-and-white tomcat, while Linda spends her vacations with us.

Jean Lee Latham

1902-

AUTHOR OF

Carry On, Mr. Bowditch; The Story of Eli Whitney; This Dear-Bought Land; Trail Blazer of the Seas; Etc.

Autobiographical sketch of Jean Lee Latham:

I WAS born in Buckhannon, a small college town in West Virginia, and was never out of the state until after I was graduated from West Virginia Wesleyan College. I spent quite a few years in a house right on the edge of town, with a patch of

Charles Copeland
JEAN LEE LATHAM

woods almost next door, and a farmer's fields just down the road, so it was almost like living in the country. We went barefoot in the summer, played in the woods, climbed hills, built a house high up in an oak tree, went blackberrying in the summer, and always enjoyed the rain because the dirt road turned into puddles, and we could squoosh the mud through our toes.

I never was a very serious student. I liked to be out of doors too well. As soon as I could read, I read everything I could lay my hands on, but I generally did my reading under a tree or up in one. The only thing I liked to read indoors was Poe; I'd read his complete works by the time I was ten, and somehow I always wanted a solid wall behind my back for that.

I started making up stories long before I started writing, and for a very good reason. I had to wash the dishes, and I found if I made up stories my brother George would dry the dishes. I tried once or twice writing them, but that took too long; it was easier to make them up. The first writing-down writing I did was poetry; that didn't take so long. I wrote reams of it.

When I was a freshman in high school I read my first modern plays; I liked them so well that I decided I would write plays even if it was a tedious business. Through high school, through Wesleyan College, through Ithaca College, where I took a degree in drama, through Cornell University, where I took my M.A., I wrote plays and more plays. By then I liked writing so well that I was beginning to get over being impatient about how long it took. After Cornell, I was editor-in-chief for six years at the Dramatic Publishing Company in Chicago. All those years I wrote stage and radio plays at night and over week ends.

I never stopped writing until World War II, when I decided I wanted to do something with my hands to help win the war. I took a course to train me to repair radio equipment for the Signal Corps; I learned to handle a soldering iron, to wind coils, to make holes with an electric drill . . . and then what happened? All at once I was writing again—directions for inspecting radio equipment, lectures to train new inspectors, and finally a course for the advanced training of women inspectors.

After the war, I reconverted to peacetime writing, and I'm still at it. Besides writing—which I like to do better than anything else —I like dogs, and people, and cooking, and any kind of fun that is in motion—dancing, swimming, hiking, biking—all such things. I also like to try something new at least every six months.

Since 1952 I've been writing books with historical background. It seems to me I'm back where I started so many years ago, spinning yarns to my brother. The only difference now is that I don't mind how much work it is to write them down.

* * *

In 1956 Miss Latham was awarded the Newbery Medal for *Carry On, Mr. Bowditch*, a fictional biography of the famous American astronomer, mathematician, and authority on navigation.

Mildred Lawrence

1907-

AUTHOR OF

Peachtree Island; Sand in Her Shoes; Indigo Magic; One Hundred White Horses; Etc.

Autobiographical sketch of Mildred Lawrence:

I HAVE led what I consider a most satisfying life—never a minute of boredom— and almost all the unusual places where my husband and I have lived and the things we have enjoyed the most pop up sooner or later in my books. Although fundamentally newspaper people, we are always trying something new that sounds interesting, whether we know anything about it or not— all probably the result of the newspaper business, which does develop a diverse and curious mind.

I was born in Charleston, Illinois, on November 10, 1907, and lived the first ten years of my life in a small-town aura of high-laced shoes, the Ben Greet Players giving Shakespeare at the Normal School, and much reading aloud under the glass-shaded table lamp. When I was eleven, my parents brought me to Flint, Michigan, an industrial town which was beginning to burst its seams as people flooded in to work in the automobile factories.

I went to high school and junior college in Flint, then was graduated from Lawrence College in Appleton, Wisconsin, returning to Flint to become society editor of the Flint *Journal*, where I had been working summers all through college. After a year there, I went on to Yale for an M.A. degree in English literature, emerging in 1931 in the depths of the Depression to a city-desk job on the *Journal*, where I stayed until shortly after my marriage to C. A. Lawrence, the new state editor.

My husband and I have raised peaches on an island in Lake Erie, operated a motel in Chambersburg, Pennsylvania, and run weekly newspapers in Florida, all of which activities have eventually reappeared in children's books. I began writing in college, after abandoning a much-too-optimistic dream of being a concert pianist, and stubbornly kept it up from then on. When our daughter, Leora Mary, was small, I tried writing stories for children instead of adults and, later still, I turned to books for children and young people. I like to write about unusual places—in fact, places are the starting points for practically all my books—and I like to do historical books now and then, too, because I think children need to learn that history is not just dates but people doing things and having much the same emotions that their present-day readers do.

My husband is now retired, and we live on the shore of a lake in Orlando, Florida, surrounded by orange trees and mockingbirds. Our daughter attended the University

MILDRED LAWRENCE

of Florida. Our family is passionately devoted to travel—we will leave for almost anywhere at the drop of a hat—and my daughter and I love to sew in our spare time. And we all read endlessly, on everything from the Battle of Gettysburg to the architecture of the basilica.

Manning de V. Lee

1894-

ILLUSTRATOR OF
*Smoke Jumper; From Star to Star; Cadmus
Henry; Prairie Printer; Etc.*

Autobiographical sketch of Manning de V. Lee:

I WAS born in the South Carolina coast country—a romantic land of moss-hung oaks, camellias and ghost stories. When I was four years old the Spanish-American War broke out. Near our place there was an encampment of troops waiting to go to Cuba and since my father was the commanding general of the National Guard, our house was always full of clanking sabers and jingling spurs. In the background was a goggle-eyed small boy aquiver with excitement. Small wonder that my first efforts at drawing should be of rearing horses and cannons belching flame. There was such a nice flame color in my box of wax crayons!

MANNING DE V. LEE

My childhood was like that of many a boy of that day. There were horses to ride, boats to row, fish to catch, books to read, and the companionship of Sam Stanyard, our faithful old Negro man-of-all-work, who was a master of all homely skills and a truly unforgettable character. His wife was Sarah, the younger children's nurse, known to them as Dada. But it wasn't all play. There were chores to do, too. I went to public schools and to Porter Military Academy in Charleston. But I think the best schooling I ever got was in our own library. With no more selectivity than a vacuum cleaner, I read everything in it and even started in on my father's law books.

In 1914 we had moved to Virginia and from there I entered the Pennsylvania Academy of the Fine Arts in Philadelphia. There was just no help for it, I was going to be an artist, although none of us had any clear ideas of how I was to make a living at it. A year or so later I had to lay down my brushes. Pancho Villa was raising a ruckus down in Mexico and my outfit, the First Virginia Field Artillery, was ordered to Texas. When all was quiet on the Rio Grande we came home and were mustered out. Two weeks later we were called back into service. The First World War had caught up with us. Then followed officers' training camp, a commission as second lieutenant, and orders to leave for France.

Christmas was spent aboard an English passenger liner bound for Liverpool. We were in convoy. Not a glimmer of light was allowed to show outside. Heavy curtains at every door and porthole. It was a pretty dismal day for one who had never spent a Christmas away from the home fires. And not even a friend near by. Nowhere a familiar face.

It was almost a year and a half before I saw my home again. I went to three artillery schools in France, saw service with troops both at the front and in training areas, and spent many a week end in Paris. The old Academy seemed rather tame after an absence of four years. In 1921 I won a Cresson scholarship for travel and study in Europe, so back I went for a summer of gallery-hopping, sketching and sightseeing in England, France, Switzerland and Italy. The following year I was awarded the Academy's second Toppan Prize.

While at school it had become evident that illustration was my field. It offered an outlet for the kind of pictures I liked to do— historic subjects, horses, ships, adventure. Now it was time to begin storming the editorial citadels. The first visit brought me a story to do. It was a modest little job but it was the start of a busy career. Since that long-ago time there has not been a day without work waiting to be done.

Next came the sale of some decorative spot drawings to the *Ladies' Home Journal*. It was a thrill to see my work in a national magazine even if the drawings were in the back pages and no bigger than postage stamps. Then followed work from *Country Gentleman, American Boy, Redbook, Blue Book, Liberty, World's Work*, and *Maclean's* of Toronto. No longer postage stamps! There were books to be illustrated too. I've stopped counting, but by now it must be well over two hundred. They deal with every kind of adventure in all parts of the world and every period in history. Those hours spent in our library have paid rich dividends. And speaking of postage stamps, I have done a series of commemorative stamps for Liberia and Indonesia.

Some of the latest books are *Buffalo Trace, Out of the Wilderness*, and *With a Task Before Me*, by Virginia S. Eifert. All three books are about Abraham Lincoln and his ancestors. And there's *Manners To Grow*

On, written by my wife, Tina Lee, with illustrations by me, the fourth of her books on which we have worked together. It is quite a departure from the Lincoln biographies, since it is a book on how to behave yourself for the junior pony-tail and spaceman set. Judging by its popularity it must have been needed.

Tina and I live in a big old eighteenth century stone house, twenty miles from Philadelphia, with fifteen acres of woods, fields and thickets. There's a three-acre lake at the foot of the lawn with woods behind it. Sometimes deer come out of the woods to nibble the lily pads. There's a boxwood garden too.

Tina Lee

AUTHOR OF
Fun with Paper Dolls; What To Do Now;
Manners To Grow On; How To Make
Dolls and Doll Houses; Etc.

TINA LEE

Autobiographical sketch of Tina Lee:

I WAS born in St. Louis, Missouri, the youngest of seven Sandoval children. My four sisters and two brothers were a source of constant wonder to me for they all seemed glamorous and able to do most remarkable things. I thought each one exactly perfect and tagged along trying to imitate first one, then the other. My efforts at imitation were not rewarded for I turned out exactly like myself, different from any one of them.

The fact that I now write children's books often gives me pause. This I feel can be none of I, for certainly I can't say that I wrote from the time I was six, nor do I have boxes of stories, verse or other early literary efforts. Of course I loved to read and did it endlessly. Being read to I enjoyed even more.

I can't remember a time when I didn't draw, mostly pictures of things going on around me, my playmates, family and animals. Later on I concentrated on paper dolls, whole families of them and their wonderful clothes. I did write little plays in which I could make them act. When anyone asked me what I wanted to be when I grew up, the answer was always the same: "I want to be an artist and design clothes and rooms."

The decision between attending college or design school was not hard for me to make, though I remember having the feeling that I shouldn't make it look too easy out of deference to those who loved me and felt that I was wasting my life by not going to college. September of 1919 found me living with a married sister in New York and working happily in the costume-design class at Parsons, which is also well known as the New York School of Fine and Applied Art. I knew I had started on my way, but the way led into an unexpected road when my brother-in-law's business moved his department to Philadelphia and I was considered too young to be left alone in New York. So I moved to Philadelphia, too, without having finished my work at Parsons. Fortunately I had covered enough ground to have had no difficulty in finding work as a fashion artist.

My first job was with an advertising agency, small and comfortable. I had an idea that I'd be helping around the art department, sharpening pencils for the artists, cutting drawing paper to needed sizes, perhaps being allowed to do some inking and now and then a very unimportant drawing, so I was overwhelmed and no little frightened when I discovered that I was to be in complete charge of a speciality shop account. After muddling through two or three weeks, my work seemed to satisfy and I relaxed into enjoying my job. This was my work for two years until the shop was taken over to become part of a large department store which had actually owned it all the time. I moved to the department store along with my advertising manager, who was given a rather impressive job under the new arrangement.

By this time I had met and married Manning Lee and now with a house to run it seemed a good time to start free-lancing. This led to the Curtis Publishing Company, where I did, among other things, a fashion feature for one of its magazines. Who could know that this was my first step toward writing children's books? In 1938 when Curtis planned to publish a children's magazine, *Jack and Jill*, I was offered the job of art director. I had a son of my own, but that didn't mean that I knew what other children would like or need in a magazine.

Starting *Jack and Jill* with Ada Rose, the first editor, was a rewarding experience. It led us right into the hearts of American children, for after the first few issues had got into their hands they began to write to us. Their confidence was touching—they told us everything. My nine years at *Jack and Jill*, plus those revealing letters, taught me much about children and made me want to work for them. Fashion and design seemed unimportant by contrast.

Jack and Jill started as a fifty-two-page magazine and we devoted two pages each month to things the children could make and do. Demands for more such material flooded the mail. Why, I wondered, wouldn't a publisher be pleased to know of such a ready market? Before long we were signing the contract for a sixty-eight-page book. We called it *What To Do Now* and it became a Junior Literary Guild selection. There have, since then, been other books. *Manners To Grow On* is my special pet.

What, I often wonder, would today be had I finished my work at Parsons? I'm happy with things as they are. We have a lovely, big, early-American country house. My husband and I work happily together surrounded by garden and animals, and our little grandson lives down the road. What more can I ask?

Margaret Leighton

1896-

AUTHOR OF
Journey for a Princess; Judith of France; Comanche of the Seventh; The Sword and the Compass; Etc.

Autobiographical sketch of Margaret Leighton:

I WAS born in Oberlin, Ohio, where my father, Thomas Nixon Carver, was professor of economics at the college. Very soon after that he moved to Harvard, and my earliest memories are of the then elm-shaded streets of Cambridge.

Reading was always my greatest pleasure and I often tried my hand at writing, also. I even illustrated my folded-paper volumes, which ranged from fairy tales to what now seems a startling facsimile of *A Tale of Two Cities* (with different names for the hero and heroine, of course!). Movies were still in their awkward infancy when I was small, but I was taken often to the theater, to the local stock companies, to Maude Adams, and to those pinnacles of glory and glamour, Southern and Marlowe.

I attended schools in Cambridge and, during my father's sabbaticals, in France and Switzerland. I graduated from Radcliffe College near the end of World War I and worked for a short time nursing in an Army hospital. Then, with the war over, I got a job in a publishing house where I set type, read proof, and was working in the advertising department when I left to marry Herbert Leighton.

As a child I had said that my future family should consist of "a boy and a girl and a boy and a girl and a baby." I achieved the first four but not the perpetual and indefinite "baby." We were a gay and lively household until the untimely death of my husband in the splendid prime of his youth and vigor. At that time we were living in an old house in Virginia, a place which seemed utterly charming to us and for which we had made many happy plans. Later, after I had brought my children to California, I pictured that house and my own four youngsters in it in a "might-have-been" tale which turned out to be my first published book, *The Secret of the Old House*.

Madeleine L'Engle
1918-

AUTHOR OF
*A Wrinkle in Time; Meet the Austins;
And Both Were Young; Etc.*

Autobiographical sketch of Madeleine Franklin, who writes under the name Madeleine L'Engle:

MARGARET LEIGHTON

I WAS born in New York City on the snowy night of November 29, 1918, and lived in New York for the next twelve years, with a jaunt or two to Europe. My father, Charles Wadsworth Camp, was a writer and my mother, Madeleine Hall Barnett Camp, a pianist, and the house was always full of artists of one kind or another. When I was twelve we moved to Europe, where we lived mostly in France and Switzerland, and I went to a Swiss boarding school. Then followed school in South Carolina and Smith College.

After graduating from Smith in 1941, I took an apartment in Greenwich Village with three other girls, two of whom were aspiring actresses. Because I wanted to be a writer, I was the lucky one to get jobs in the theater (I thought it an excellent school for writers and it is). When I was in Chekhov's *The Cherry Orchard* I met the actor Hugh Franklin, and I married him a year later. At his request I withdrew from Actor's Equity and in 1952 he also retired from the theater "forever."

We had an old white farmhouse in northwestern Connecticut, and he wanted to settle down, put down roots, and get away from the tensions of the city and the theater. In order to earn a living, we acquired a defunct general store. I must honestly admit that helping to build up a dead general store, participate in the life of a small, but very active community, run a large old farmhouse, and raise three small children, is the perfect "way not" to write a book. However, I did manage to write at night. I have written since I could hold a pencil, much less a pen, and writing is for me an essential function, like sleeping and breathing.

The store was a smashing success, and then suddenly the fun and the challenge were gone. So we decided to move back to the quiet life of New York and the theater. Although here, too, we are drawn into civic and church affairs, we find that the life of

My other books followed in what was really a logical sequence in spite of the variety of their themes and settings. *Twelve Bright Trumpets* was suggested by a publisher who had seen but not wished to use *The Secret of the Old House. The Secret of the Closed Gate* and *The Secret of Bucky Moran* were sequels to *The Secret of the Old House*, requested by letters from youngsters. *Judith of France* grew out of research done for *Twelve Bright Trumpets; The Sword and the Compass* from research for a shorter, requested biography of Captain John Smith. Two other biographies, of Florence Nightingale and General Custer, although of entirely different characters, were nevertheless outgrowths of that one. *The Singing Cave* came from a journey my children and I made during a spring vacation in California, while *Who Rides By?* grew slowly from a very small seed planted many years ago on another journey. *Comanche of the Seventh*, is, of course, plainly derived from my earlier *Story of General Custer*.

I live in California in a vine-covered house near the edge of cliffs overlooking the booming surf of the Pacific. My four children are grown but I have nine grandchildren. Two other stories are jockeying for priority in my mind now. Which will be my next book? I don't know yet, and that is part of what makes writing such fun.

MADELEINE L'ENGLE

theater and New York is infinitely more peaceful than that of a tiny village, and there is nothing more exciting than seeing a magnolia burst into bloom in the middle of Broadway!

* * *

Madeleine L'Engle was the recipient of the 1963 Newbery Medal for *A Wrinkle in Time*, a mystery which relates the adventures in time and space of three children and a missing scientist. Her earlier books include *And Both Were Young*, the story of the fifteen-year-old daughter of a widowed artist, spending her first year at a Swiss boarding school she is determined to dislike; and *Meet the Austins*, in which a spoiled young orphan comes to live with the family of a country doctor. *The Moon by Night*, published in 1963, is "a continuation of (though not a sequel to)" *Meet the Austins*, according to Miss L'Engle.

Meridel Le Sueur

AUTHOR OF

Chanticleer of Wilderness Road; Little Brother of the Wilderness; Sparrow Hawk; Nancy Hanks of Wilderness Road; Etc.

Autobiographical sketch of Meridel Le Sueur:

I WAS born at the beginning of the century in a little town in Iowa. I was always very interested to find out what had

happened, what history had taken place in whatever place I happened to be. I was in many places in my youth, as my family moved often, and I thus saw most of the Middle West, lived in the Lincoln country, and in the John Brown country, and saw often the apple trees that were brought as little seedlings by that lovely one, Johnny Appleseed.

So I became very interested in history and especially the history that throws light upon our own lives, and our own place and our own time. Most of all on those who helped to build our democracy and brought light to what kind of people we are when we are together building and not destroying. So I wanted to write about Abraham Lincoln, especially in his youth, and of his mother, Nancy Hanks, because she is little known.

When I had children and grandchildren of my own I also felt that many children's books choked you when you had to read them aloud, so I felt I wanted to write books that would be alive rhythmically and would read aloud like poetry, and give you a strong emotional feeling and memory as well as factual truth.

So this is what I have tried to do.

I live in the Middle West because it is my native land and I love it. I know what the people are thinking and doing and hoping for. I love writing about them in everything that they are doing.

John Lewellen

1910-1956

AUTHOR OF

You and Space Travel; You and Atomic Energy; You and Your Amazing Mind; You and American Life Lines; Etc.

JOHN Lewellen was born March 30, 1910, in Gaston, Indiana. He ran his father's farm, where he had grown up, during his last year in high school, and for the year following; then attended Ball State Teachers College at Muncie, Indiana, for two years. His work on the college newspaper attracted attention and he went to the Muncie *Evening Press*, where he remained eight years. He left there to go to Chicago, where he worked for *Time, Life*, and *Fortune* for a year. During that time he met Louis G. Cowan, a public relations man. The field of publicity appealed to Mr. Lewellen and he joined Cowan. When the two of them originated the "Quiz Kids," he found he was fascinated by radio and, later, television. He remained with Louis G. Cowan Associates, as vice president and also vice president of the Quiz Kids, until 1955, when he left the organization to concentrate on free-lance writing.

A charming, unassuming man, Mr. Lewellen was interested in many things, particularly in science. He met his wife when both were thirteen, and they dated then, although she admits that she kept this fact from her daughter until recently! They were married when they were nineteen, and in those early days he was torn between the desire to be a doctor, to do research in some field of science, or to write a book—the Great American Novel, of course. He found radio and television time-consuming but managed to spend his week ends on books for children. "Those were his happiest days," Mrs. Lewellen says, "and I can truthfully say that the last year of his life, where his more relaxed time was spent fully in the writing field, was his fullest and happiest."

Mr. Lewellen's first effort in the educational recording field was *The Atomic Bomb* and *Peacetime Use of Atomic Energy.* These recordings caught the attention of the Children's Press and the idea for his first book, *You and Atomic Energy,* was born. For this book Mr. Lewellen received a Boys' Clubs of America award in 1950. He received a second Boys' Clubs award for *The Earth Satellite* in 1958 (posthumously). *The True Book of Airports and Airplanes* was a Junior Literary Guild selection, while *Tee Vee Humphrey* was a choice of the Weekly Reader Children's Book Club.

When he turned to free-lance writing in 1955, three manuscripts submitted to the *Saturday Evening Post* resulted in three published stories. His first attempt at writing for television, aside from the scripts for the shows he had produced, was "Good Friday—1865," bought by the producer Robert Montgomery, on February 6, 1956. On the same day Mr. Lewellen was given the Thomas Alva Edison award for the best book on science published in the children's field in 1955, *The Boy Scientist.*

Mrs. Lewellen says of her husband: "He recognized that complex subjects, such as math and the various sciences, could be in-

Pan-American Photo Service
JOHN LEWELLEN

teresting and fascinating to young minds if they were properly presented. He loved the job of taking a so-called complex subject and reducing it to an easy-to-read book. He often said, 'If I can understand it, anyone can.' He meant if he could understand it, he could tell it so that all could understand."

Mrs. Lewellen adds that as a boy her husband could never get enough to read, and that perhaps the recognition of the lack of books in his youth may have been a contributing factor to his final direction in writing. He first attempted a scientific story when he was on the Muncie newspaper and wrote feature stories about the local Ball Hospital laboratory. This gave him experience in writing simply about complicated subjects.

Mrs. Lewellen feels that the books her husband wrote reflected his wide interests. "His is the only mind that I have known which found everything interesting," she comments. "His interest in people and things was not a surface interest. This, plus a retentive mind, made him a great reporter. This, in turn, was his great asset as a writer of books for children."

Mr. Lewellen learned to pilot a plane, and the entire family—wife, daughter Lu Ann, and son Tom—flew all over the country. The book he had nearly finished at the time of his death was published in January

1959, *The Story of Flight*. Perhaps the best summation of his career was made by his wife:

"To me and to John, the knowledge that one of his books could help one child to a better understanding and a better life, made all the effort worth while."

C. S. Lewis

1898-

AUTHOR OF
The Magician's Nephew; The Silver Chair; Prince Caspian; The Horse and His Boy; Etc.

CLIVE Staples Lewis was born in Belfast, in November 1898. His father, Albert James Lewis, was a lawyer there; his mother, Flora Augusta Hamilton Lewis, was the daughter of a naval chaplain. His paternal great-grandfather, the son of a Welsh farmer, was an amateur preacher, while his grandfather eventually became co-owner of a small shipyard in Belfast.

In his autobiography, *Surprised by Joy*, Dr. Lewis tells of his early years. His mother died when he was quite small, and his childhood and youth were spent in various boarding schools, all of which he detested. In 1917 he entered Oxford University, but enlisted soon after in the British Army. He was commissioned a second lieutenant and served in France, where he was

C. S. LEWIS

wounded. He returned to Oxford, and later settled down as a don at Magdalen College.

He was well established as a distinguished Anglican theologian and as a literary scholar, the best-known of his many books being *The Screwtape Letters*, but it was not until 1950 that his first book for children was published, *The Lion, the Witch and the Wardrobe*. In this book four children enter another world right in their own house, something like the children in the E. Nesbit books. In this and succeeding books Dr. Lewis created the mysterious land of Narnia. *The Horn Book* commented: "Beautifully written, . . . it is reminiscent of George Macdonald in its allegorical quality." A sequel, *Prince Caspian; The Return to Narnia*, was hailed by *The Horn Book* as "convincing fantasy unusually well written."

There are seven books about Narnia, and one of them, *The Last Battle*, was selected in 1957 to receive the Carnegie Medal, the English counterpart of the Newbery Medal.

Mina Lewiton

1904-

AUTHOR OF
The Divided Heart; A Cup of Courage; Beasts of Burden; Penny's Acres; Etc.

Autobiographical sketch of Mina Lewiton:

ONE day of early spring I discovered that I am, and must always have been, a country person, although I was born in New York City (on March 22, 1904) and grew up there, went to school there, and married there. In about 1945, when gasoline was scarce, my husband, Howard Simon, and I took a train for Poughkeepsie. A real-estate agent drove us out twenty-five miles to a cluster of small neat houses named the Town of Stanford. A few miles beyond the town there stood a once-white house with fluted pillars. It was as unpainted inside as out. It was unheated and had been untenanted for many years. All the land about it was overgrown and looked to us forlornly lovely and as if waiting for a pair of people who would recognize it for the enchanting place it was.

We knew at once we were that pair of people. We bought the house (and brought

MINA LEWITON

that Uptown did not possess the positive and desirable virtues of Downtown, such as the public library, my beloved public school and teacher, the familiar crowded streets and the pleasant sights and sounds and smells of pushcarts. I told this story in *Rachel* and the Uptown adventures are related in *Rachel and Herman,* both illustrated by my husband.

If I have a credo it is that writers for children must be, besides being good writers and entertaining ones, educators as well, for their readers are at their most impressionable and educable. It is a high responsibility. It is important for writers to remember and all children to know that despite differences of alphabets, customs, skins, and clothing, the children of the world are a family of nine hundred million.

an assistant caretaker with us in the person of our then small daughter, Bettina). Ever since, we have been restoring our house to itself. We uncovered neglected gardens and we planted an orchard. We built a tennis court and we moved about a lilac grove, making it into a hedge, and then set out a pine plantation. The house and the land are enormously grateful and are forever rewarding us by unexpected bursts of beauty in the landscape.

We still live in New York City part of the year—the smaller part—in a double-height studio of the old-fashioned kind on West Sixty-seventh Street.

I have tried to set down my love for the country in *Penny's Acres* and *First Love* and, in fact, in all my books, but perhaps I must write many more books—I have written ten—before I can possibly sum up all that I feel about the goodness and the rightness of living on the land.

To come back to New York City, all my youngest childhood was spent in the most crowded part of it, the Lower East Side of Manhattan, known then to my parents and our relatives and friends as Downtown. I was astonished and grief-stricken one day when I learned—I was about ten—that my parents ambitiously contemplated leaving the crowded neighborhoods of Downtown for the uncrowded Uptown. This seemed a far country full of unknown dangers and known ones too. The known ones were

Astrid Lindgren

1907-

AUTHOR OF

Pippi Longstocking; Bill Bergson, Master Detective; Bill Bergson Lives Dangerously; Mio, My Son; Etc.

Autobiographical sketch of Astrid Lindgren:

I WAS born in Vimmerby, Sweden, as a farmer's daughter. I was number two among four children and I cannot imagine any children having more fun than we had. In those days there were no automobiles,

ASTRID LINDGREN

no radios, no films, no television, no nothing —but there were people, lots of interesting people and there was a lot of room for imagination.

I was a very happy child. I loved people, I loved nature, and I loved books. In high school everybody kept telling me that I was going to be an author someday, and I very stubbornly decided *never* to write any books. I finished school, went to Stockholm to learn how to be a secretary, married, had two children, was still very sure I would never write any books.

But I had two children always pestering me to tell them stories and so I did. One day in March 1944, when snow had fallen in Stockholm, I went for a walk. It was very slippery. I fell, broke my ankle, and had to stay in bed for a week with nothing to do but write. Actually I became an author just because it snowed in Stockholm one day in March 1944.

And now it is very hard to stop me. I go on and on. Up to now I have published nineteen books. My own childhood is in whatever I write.

JENNIE D. LINDQUIST

Jennie D. Lindquist

1899-

AUTHOR OF
The Golden Name Day;
The Little Silver House

Autobiographical sketch of Jennie D. Lindquist:

I WAS born and grew up in Manchester, New Hampshire. My mother died when I was born and I lived with my father, grandmother, and aunt. Although I had no brothers or sisters to play with, I was fortunate in having many cousins. *The Golden Name Day* is based on recollections of some of our happy times together.

When I was in the eighth grade in grammar school, I was taken to hear a young woman talk on children's librarianship as a vocation. Perhaps it was because library books meant so much to my cousins and me that I decided at once that there couldn't be anything more fun to do than library work with children. And I never changed my mind. I have been a children's librarian in New Hampshire and in Albany, New York; and editor of *The Horn Book,* a magazine about children's books, in Boston. For many summers I have taught courses in appreciation of children's books to teachers and librarians studying at the University of New Hampshire. I am now living in Albany.

My grandparents were born in Sweden and came to this country when their children were very little. They brought with them, of course, many of their Swedish customs, and we always celebrated two sets of holidays. At Christmas, for instance, we did the things American people do, and the things Swedish people do. We celebrated American holidays like the Fourth of July, and those distinctly Swedish, such as name days, just as the children do in *The Golden Name Day.* The grownups in the book are based on the grownups of my childhood. The children do many of the things we used to do as children. The animals are real and were all friends of mine.

I cannot write about *The Golden Name Day* without paying a tribute to its editor, Ursula Nordstrom of Harper's. Until I had the privilege of working with her, I did not realize how much of a creative children's editor's thought and time and understanding encouragement goes into every book on her list. Garth Williams, who illustrated mine, never saw the people or animals in it, but he must somehow have known just how they looked. I cannot now even imagine the book without his pictures.

Willis Lindquist

1908-

AUTHOR OF
*Burma Boy; Call of the White Fox; The
Red Drum's Warning; Alaska, the
Forty-ninth State; Etc.*

Autobiographical sketch of Willis Lindquist:

I WAS born on June 5, 1908, in Winthrop, Minnesota, a small town surrounded by prairie farms of wheat and corn. There were no hills—only the endless, sunny plains and small groves of cottonwood with crows flapping above them. Our wooden frame house stood at the edge of town, overlooking a large marshy pond. To me, it was as beautiful as any lake, and it brought all the mysteries and moods of nature right to our back door. There the frogs sang to the stars on summer nights. Great blue herons, wild ducks, rails, sandpipers, mud hens, snipe, turtles, muskrats, carp, and minnows—all these were an intimate part of my childhood. Great flocks of red-winged blackbirds settled among the reeds and cattails each spring and fall.

In the summer, my friends and I explored the open pond on a raft. It served at times as a pirate ship, or a Spanish galleon, or the *Mayflower,* sailing on our own private ocean. And in winter, we had a mile-long rink for skating.

As a child, I remember seeing Indians. The last of a great tribe lived only forty miles away, and they always brought to mind one of my great-aunts who had been very friendly with the Indians. My mother told me many stories about my great-aunt's Indian friends, and how one of these Indians came to warn her of the Sioux uprising led by Little Crow. She and her family fled in their farm wagon, but before they were out of sight the Indians had set fire to the farm buildings. These stories, and the frontier tales told to me by my grandfather, one of the early settlers, stirred me more deeply than any of the books I read as a child.

My childhood animal pets included dogs, cats, rabbits, pigeons, and a screech owl—which reflects a love for pets that always creeps into my books. During my years in high school I had three hives of bees, and sold honey to the neighbors for spending

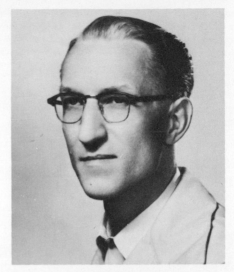

Atelier von Behr
WILLIS LINDQUIST

money. I was once offered a dollar to take a swarm of bees out of a farmer's shed. Twenty-two stings later I earned the money and took the bees home. The stings put me to sleep for a day but my interest in bees continued until I left home to study at the University of Minnesota.

After studying law at George Washington University in Washington, D.C., I passed the bar and became a tax lawyer with the United States Internal Revenue Service. During my vacations I traveled in foreign countries and wrote articles and took pictures for *National Geographic.* My longest sea voyage, made on a four-masted bark, started at Copenhagen, Denmark, and ended a hundred and two days later in Australia. I continued on around the world for two years, visiting some thirty-odd foreign countries. During this time I wrote many articles for newspapers and magazines. During World War II, I sailed with the Merchant Marine for almost three years. Since then I have lived in New York, earning my living as a writer of articles and fiction.

In *Burma Boy,* my first book, I wrote about life on the fringe of the Burmese jungles as I saw it when I visited Burma. My second book, *Call of the White Fox,* has to do with life on the tundra along the northern coast of Alaska. I have never been to Alaska. Yet, oddly enough, I became acquainted with many of the arctic birds of that region within a few miles of New York City, for the snowy owl, the arctic tern, the snow goose, the loon, and the eider duck, as well as many others, spend the winter months on the bays and ponds of Long Island. One of my favorite hobbies during the winter is to search for these arctic visitors and study them through my binoculars.

William Lipkind

1904-

AUTHOR OF

Finders Keepers; The Two Reds; The Magic Feather Duster; Days to Remember; Etc.

WILLIAM Lipkind was born in New York on December 17, 1904. He was educated in the New York public schools and received his degree of bachelor of arts from the College of the City of New York in 1927. A year at the Columbia Law School followed, then some study of history and literature while working in a number of business fields. Systematic study was resumed at Columbia University in 1934—in the English department—with a year of work on the seventeenth century, at the end of which he transferred to anthropology. His first field trip to the Winnebago in the summer of 1936 provided the material for his

doctor's dissertation. Work for the degree was completed in 1937. The next two years were spent in central Brazil in the study of the Carajá and Javahé Indians under the auspices of the Social Science Research Council of Columbia University.

Mr. Lipkind taught for a time at Ohio State University, and served in England during World War II, in the Office of War Information. After the war he made a study of Bavarian society, in Germany, for the American Military Government.

Mr. Lipkind has written the text for a number of picture books illustrated by Nicolas Mordvinoff. One of them, *Finders Keepers,* was awarded the Caldecott Medal in 1952. He has also written three books for older children: *Boy with a Harpoon* and *Boy of the Islands,* which Mr. Mordvinoff illustrated, and *Days To Remember,* illustrated by Jerome Snyder.

Mr. Lipkind is a poet and painter, deeply interested in music. He is at present adjunct assistant professor of anthropology at New York University and also teaches a class in writing at Hunter College. He is at work on a new theory of the arts based on his investigations in primitive culture.

Mr. Lipkind is married to Maria Cimino, librarian, Central Children's Room, The New York Public Library.

William Vandivert

WILLIAM LIPKIND

Joseph Wharton Lippincott

1887-

AUTHOR OF

Wilderness Champion; The Phantom Deer; The Red Roan Pony; Wahoo Bobcat; Etc.

JOSEPH Wharton Lippincott was born in Philadelphia, February 28, 1887, in his family's old colonial home. He was graduated from the University of Pennsylvania's Wharton School in 1908, and went into his family's publishing firm, J. B. Lippincott Company, founded in 1792. During World War I he served in the United States Naval Reserve Forces.

Mr. Lippincott has many interests—nature, wild animals, birds, plants, hunting, polo, yacht racing, riding and horse racing. He has been master of fox hounds of the Huntington Valley Hunt, and also of the

JOSEPH WHARTON LIPPINCOTT AND OPOSSUM

Oak Hill Beagles. He has collected and written about the seashells of Florida and Cuba. He has written articles on hunting for national magazines and has lectured widely, using his own motion pictures. He has collected animals for museums and organized big-game-hunting expeditions into Alaska, parts of Canada, Mexico, Scotland, Bavaria, and Austria. In this country he has hunted, fished, and explored his way from Washington and Oregon to the Florida Keys, with a number of narrow escapes.

Mr. Lippincott's books have grown logically out of his many interests. He writes: "When a boy, I nearly always had whole bunches of puppies and dogs around me. . . . Since I lived in the country where there were many interesting wild animals, such as foxes, raccoons, opossums, squirrels, weasels, rabbits, and even rats, it was only natural that hounds, which are hunters by nature and could help me in seeing and capturing these furtive creatures, became my first choice among breeds. . . . When I was hunting in the mountains of the western states, of Yukon Territory, of Alberta, and of Mexico, my hair tingled when I heard the wolf packs running furiously at night and when I saw wolves loping single file in the daytime. . . . How natural it seemed to unite in a story a big, fine hound with the wonderful, wild wolf packs of Canada!"

Mr. Lippincott adds that the more he hunted and trapped wild animals for mu-

seums, the more he admired their ways and their ability to survive. "They seemed almost human at times. This led to a number of books, such as *Chisel-Tooth, the Beaver; Red Ben, the Fox of Oak Ridge;* and *Animal Neighbors of the Countryside.* The one I enjoyed writing the most was *The Wolf King,* the story of one of the grandest wolves in Alberta, who naturally appears again in *Wilderness Champion.*"

Mr. Lippincott retired in 1958 as chairman of the board of his publishing company, and now devotes himself entirely to writing and to his many hobbies.

T. Morris Longstreth

1886-

AUTHOR OF
Elephant Toast; Doorway in the Dark; Time Flight; The MacQuarrie Boys; Etc.

Autobiographical sketch of T. Morris Longstreth:

I WAS born a Philadelphia Quaker in the midst of a February blizzard. This so entranced me that weather has been one of my prime interests ever since. My first book welled up from this delight in weather and, with revisions, is still selling at the age of forty-nine.

I got my second wind at thirteen, when Back Log Camp introduced me to the Adirondacks and the wilderness which I loved at first smell. Thanks to its founder, Thomas K. Brown, I shifted to Westtown Boarding School, where I discovered friendship, first love, poetry, and the joys of freedom. Music was then banned by the Quakers and so my intoxication by it grew. I planned to become a composer, Beethoven's successor, to speak frankly. But my father's death routed me out of dreamland and I taught school instead.

Meanwhile I had benefited by the fact that rich boys had parents who were only too happy to have their sons travel. I saw some of the Czar's Russia, watched the Panama Canal deepen, chartered a private car on the railroad and took a dozen lively young males around this country and Canada. Teaching was fun, but I found writing at night fun, too. My second book, *The*

T. MORRIS LONGSTRETH

of adult novels, provided that we kept the same proportion of goodness to badness and grace to unrefinement that the youngsters' lives keep. In my latest book, a boy, intent on a certain purpose, wishes the same thing and sighs, "When will the world grow up and no longer need to be shielded from its children's conversations?" On the other hand, writing to a discipline provides its own incitements, as do school rules and sonnets, and there's still lots of room for a juvenile *War and Peace.*

Robert M. McClung

1916-

AUTHOR AND ILLUSTRATOR OF
Wings in the Woods; Bufo, the Story of a Toad; Major, the Story of a Black Bear; Leaper, the Story of an Atlantic Salmon; Etc.

Adirondacks, contained a chapter on the Lake Placid Club that ended my teaching. I was invited to be the Club's guest for a year—and stayed ten.

Then the Royal Canadian Mounted Police took over. I became their historian and had a desk at Headquarters. I traveled to the places where history had been made throughout the Canadian West and the Northwest Territories. My life so far had been steeped in masculine youth, and gradually this influence preponderated in my writing. For the last twenty years I've been viewing boyhood from different angles. History gives sound footing to interest. My boys' history of the Mounties, *The Scarlet Force,* and *The Force Carries On* have been my best sellers. I tried another sort of history in *Hideout,* by showing what happened to a boy in Henry Thoreau's Concord, and still another sort in *Time Flight,* where two boys are wafted by mistake to Salem at the time of the witch purge.

Another mistake was responsible for *Elephant Toast,* where a boy at a summer camp inadvertently becomes owner of an elephant. Humor is the most fun to do, and comes pretty close to being the truest to the teens. I live now next door to my old school and there are more laughs in the dorms in one day than get into all the juvenile literature of any year. I do wish that we junior authors could be as realistic as the authors

Autobiographical sketch of Robert M. McClung:

THE second oldest of a family of three boys and a girl, I was born and brought up in Butler, a small city in western Pennsylvania. Both of my parents were active leaders in community affairs, and our family enjoyed a very happy and always interesting life together.

Ever since I can remember I have been interested in the out of doors, and in animals of all kinds. Hiking was—and still is —one of my favorite pastimes. As a boy I explored the countryside for miles around, collecting everything I found of special interest—frogs and toads, garter snakes, rabbits, chipmunks, turtles, hornets' and birds' nests, to mention only a few of the things I brought home. I became especially interested in insects after I took a big cocoon which I had found to school. Luckily, my third-grade teacher knew about such things and appreciated them. When a spectacular big moth emerged from the cocoon, she showed me how to mount and preserve it. From then on I was an enthusiastic butterfly and moth collector, and pursued the hobby tirelessly, especially during summer vacations at my grandfather's farm. These interests and activities, as well as the old-fashioned farm background, are described in my first book, *Wings in the Woods.*

ROBERT M. McCLUNG

I was interested in writing and drawing from the beginning, too. As soon as I was able to hold a pencil I was drawing pictures of animals, and from the age of eight on I was writing stories—mostly wild and woolly epics of adventure.

After high school I went to Princeton. There I took all the zoology I could, as well as lots of history and literature. I found that I was interested in such a wide variety of things that it was difficult for me to decide exactly what I wanted to do. In turn I considered being a doctor, a teacher, an advertising man, a writer, and a zoo man. While in school I worked at a variety of jobs to earn money. I drew cartoons for the campus humor magazine, and wrote the book for the annual college musical show.

Soon after I had graduated and worked a brief stint in an advertising agency, World War II came along. For five years I was in the Navy, first as a crew member of a destroyer, and then as a flier and landing signal officer on aircraft carriers. After the war I went to Cornell and took my master's degree in natural history and science education. From there I went to New York's famous Bronx Zoo, where I worked for seven years, starting as an assistant in the animal departments, and finally becoming curator of mammals and birds.

I got married soon after I went to the zoo. It was at this time, too, that I started to write my series of books about animals for young people. My aim has been to show how different kinds of animals live, by relating the story of one individual animal in each book. In 1955 I left the zoo to devote my full time to writing and illustrating. I live in Harrison, New York, with my wife, Gale, and our two boys, William and Thomas.

Eloise Jarvis McGraw

1915-

AUTHOR OF
Moccasin Trail; Crown Fire; Sawdust in His Shoes; Mara, Daughter of the Nile; Etc.

Autobiographical sketch of Eloise Jarvis McGraw:

I WAS born in Houston, Texas, but after five years my parents moved to Oklahoma City, and it was there I grew up. I began to write early—I believe my first story occurred when I was eight years old and was written in school, when I should have been doing arithmetic. It was called "The Cedar Pencil Boys" and I remember nothing about it except that its heroes were two animated cedarwood pencils. I had just acquired such a pencil, the first I had even seen, and it struck me as fascinatingly exotic—so different from the ordinary yellow affairs with red erasers. I have always loved pencils, notebooks, paper, pens—all the tools of writing—and hang over that counter in the dime store to this day, wanting to buy everything.

I wrote other stories, once I'd begun, all highly fanciful, all mercifully perished long ago. I was entranced by the Oz books and had no higher ambition than to write such things someday. I have wondered since if my intense interest in imaginative stories as against realistic ones could have been a first indication of my strong tendency now to write about colorful eras of the past rather than modern-day fiction. At any rate, even then I was determined to be a writer if I possibly could, though I held such an exaggerated and reverent view of writers that I never really believed I might someday join their rarefied company.

During high school in Oklahoma City I wrote much poetry, crammed with adjectives

ELOISE JARVIS McGRAW

and descriptions. I was madly in love with words and my poems were scarcely more than excuses to string together words like "purple" and "scintillating" and "dusk"— or, in the case of the better ones, to describe a mood or scene which had affected me deeply. Since almost everything affected me deeply at that time, I wrote a great deal of terrible poetry, and have adjectivitis to this day unless I watch myself closely.

The strongest influence on me during this time and, indeed, during my whole life, was the summers we spent on my uncle's Oregon farm. The Oregon country is beautiful and its forests and streams a real foretaste of heaven; moreover, the farm and country living were a constant delight to me. (Later, I made use of my stored-up memories in my first three books, all of which were laid in Oregon. Shortly after completing the third of these, I actually enticed my own family up here to live, and I think they love it as much as I.)

In college I went on for a while with writing, then suddenly turned to oil painting instead, and changed my ambition. I became proficient enough to earn several commissions for portraits and murals, and had no idea I would ever return to writing. But after a bit of postgraduate work at the Universities of Oklahoma and Colorado—in sculpture and painting—and after teaching oil painting a couple of years at Oklahoma City University, I married a newspaperman

from Des Moines, Iowa, William Corbin McGraw. His work took us to Athens and Cleveland, Ohio; to Oklahoma City again; and finally to La Jolla, California. By this time we had two children, a boy, Peter, and a girl, Laurie. I had dropped painting for theater work, puppet work, a little radio, and a great deal of modern dance, and was becoming interested in ceramics. However, I was possessed of a conviction that my husband should write books, not newspaper stories.

Since he was slow about doing this, I wrote one myself, to nudge him a little. To my astonishment, it was accepted by Coward-McCann and published. I was a writer after all. My husband looked at the book thoughtfully and sat down at *his* typewriter. The following year he had his first young people's novel published and I had my second.

At length we moved to Oregon, bought a filbert orchard and an old farmhouse to remodel, acquired two or three saddle horses, two dogs, and innumerable cats, and are now both settled firmly into our chosen trade. I work with copper and enamel now instead of ceramics and would go back to painting as a hobby if only I had time. But my decision at the age of eight was obviously the right one—I am not really a painter, a dancer, or any of those other things. I am a writer, just as I suspected when I first saw that cedar pencil. And though it is not so glamorous as I thought it would be, it is even more satisfying.

William Corbin McGraw

See *Corbin, William*

Ellen MacGregor

1906-1954

AUTHOR OF
Miss Pickerell Goes to Mars; Miss Pickerell and the Geiger Counter; Miss Pickerell Goes Undersea; Tommy and the Telephone; Etc.

ELLEN MacGregor was born in Baltimore, Maryland, on May 15, 1906, the daughter of George and Charlotte Noble MacGregor. Her parents had met when both were teachers at a small Wisconsin high school. George MacGregor left teaching to attend the Johns Hopkins Medical School and Charlotte Noble traveled from one Wisconsin town to another, setting up libraries. They were married shortly before his graduation.

From Baltimore, the family moved to Wisconsin, and then to the state of Washington, where their daughter and two sons were educated. Ellen MacGregor spent many happy summers on Puget Sound. She majored in science at the University of Washington, received her B.S. in 1926, and did postgraduate work at the University of California in 1931.

Her parents influenced her career. She wrote once that they "had an exquisite sense of fun, with a lovely feeling for the ridiculous. There was much laughter in our home. Also there was much, much reading aloud. . . . Nevertheless, it was with a slight lack of personal enthusiasm that I fell in with their plans for my career. . . . What I didn't know then, was that my training as a librarian was to be the key to many interesting jobs, to many enriching experiences, and to many happy associations."

She was a librarian in Hawaii, in Key West, in Chicago, and other places. She did research in children's literature for a Chicago publisher. And then, in 1946, she began to write. A story she turned in at a workshop at the Midwestern Writers Conference was published as a book, *Tommy and the Telephone.* The old *Liberty* published her first story on Miss Pickerell, "Swept Her into Space," in 1950. The following year this story became *Miss Pickerell Goes to Mars,* and was instantly popular as a science-fiction fantasy. When the Weekly Reader Children's Book Club was started in 1952, this book was an early selection.

While writing many short stories for various magazines, Miss MacGregor continued the adventures of Miss Pickerell. Her last book, *Miss Pickerell Goes to the Arctic,* was a selection of the Junior Literary Guild. All her books have been uniformly popular.

The old *Peterkin Papers* was a prime favorite with her. The humor in this classic may have given her the initial impulse in her own writing. She wrote to a friend once about her feeling on science fiction:

"It's such a satisfying form of literature, isn't it? And interesting, that being scientifically logical actually frees our imagina-

ELLEN MacGREGOR

tions, rather than acting as a constraint. Of course my preference is for the scientific fantasy. . . . Stories like that are so refreshing with their combination of delightful absurdity and utter logic, aren't they?"

This friend's estimate of her is probably as fine an epitaph as anyone could have: "An understanding, kind, friendly, intelligent woman with a fine sense of humor and a fertile imagination. More than that, she could write and planned to go into the adult fiction field. The depth and breadth of her talents had been no more than tapped. There is no telling what excellent writing lay ahead of her."

At her death, March 29, 1954, Miss MacGregor was librarian for the Research Division of the International Harvester Company in Chicago.

Elizabeth MacKinstry

d. 1956

AUTHOR AND ILLUSTRATOR OF
Puck in Pasture; The Fairy Alphabet

ILLUSTRATOR OF
*The White Cat; Andersen's Fairy
Tales; Etc.*

ELIZABETH MacKinstry, an artist and poet, was born in America but grew up in France from the age of four. She was born, she often said, with a pencil in her mouth, but her earliest training was in music. A child prodigy violinist, she studied with the celebrated Ysaye. After a brief season of concerts in France and England, which established her as a violinist with the promise of a brilliant career, she suffered a severe back injury and this ended all playing. She was forced to lie flat on her back for months at a time, but she could draw, and to drawing she turned and to the making of poetry. Later, she studied sculpture with the great Rodin.

Returning to this country, Miss MacKinstry lived for some years in Buffalo, New York, both teaching in the art schools there and being associated with the Albright Art Gallery. She moved to New York and in 1924 wrote in her journal: "First delicious discovery of Reed Pen, Claud Lovat Fraser, Crawhall, Gordon Craig, and definite turning from Sculpture to illustration." Her creed was that of Walter Crane—that a book decoration should be for a book, fit the shape of its page and stay flat on it. Her book of poems, *Puck in Pasture*, published in 1925, won for her much distinction as an illustrator. Bruce Rogers said of it that he was glad to see the first book in America that showed a really modern feeling in its design. Her illustrations for books by Rachel Field, Alfred Noyes, Percy Mackaye, and many others are well known. Those for *The White Cat*, by Countess d'Aulnoy, won for it acclaim as one of the notable books of the year (1928).

May Massee thus described Miss MacKinstry in *The Horn Book*: "Elizabeth was about five feet four, stoutish and sturdy but quick motioned. A large round head topped by an unruly thatch of darkish gray hair, cut short in tufts—she just chopped it off now and then. Big round eyes, blue or gray or green and piercing, though they could be bland as a child's. A good-sized nose, not classic, and a generous mobile mouth shaped to speak exquisite French and to make English beautiful too. Her voice was husky but with bright tones now and then. Most of the time she was happy in her painter's smock but she could look very impressive dressed up in black silk with a bit of lace and old gold about. There was the look in her eyes of one who has lived with pain but never been conquered."

In the spring of 1957 the Central Children's Room of the New York Public Library held a memorial exhibit of Miss MacKinstry's work. In commenting on it, Maria Cimino, then assistant librarian in charge, now librarian in charge, had this to say:

"One sees here a passionate, tireless and courageous spirit reacting to her time and expressing herself in a style recalling the eighteenth century, a style she made her own after her discovery of Claud Lovat Fraser and the use of reed pens. . . . Miss MacKinstry was a sensitive draftsman with sure feeling and taste in decorative design, but mainly she had the illustrator's gift of entering into the heart of the text. Her sympathetic imagination could throw on a story vivid flashes of insight; her illustrations bring scenes and characters to life. And the range of feeling is not limited, turning from the most delicate suggestion to pungent wit, humor and satire. Her drawing has an individual elegance and charm which separates it from all the book illustration of the twenties. Gifted poet that she was, she turned each thing she touched into a kind of poetry. Her illustrations for Andersen, for *The White Cat, The Fairy Alphabet*, and *Puck in Pasture*, are among her best work, which constitutes an invaluable and lasting contribution to the illustrations of children's books." *

Isabel McLennan McMeekin

1895-

AUTHOR OF

Journey Cake; Kentucky Derby Winner; The First Book of Horses; The Postman's Pony; Etc.

Autobiographical sketch of Isabel McLennan McMeekin:

I WAS born in Louisville, Kentucky, and have lived here all of my life, although my father, who died when I was a baby, came from Montreal. My grandfather was an outwardly stern Victorian, complete with high silk hat and long white beard. Inwardly, he was just my age. When I wanted a pair of blue satin "stays" for a fifth birthday present, he converted me with unsmiling diplomacy to a pony—a double pair of little black hoofs, silvery gray fur,

* This comment and the preceding quotation from May Massee, appeared in the April 1957 issue of *The Horn Book*.

even prettier than blue satin, and a doe-skin saddle with silver bells!

And then there was the matter of mid-night fires. Understandably, my mother frowned on our attendance and, unfortu-nately, my room was on the third floor and there were several squeaky steps in the stairs. But there was also a banister which was irresistible. . . .

In Gran's roll-top desk there was a tin strong box. It contained a suitable number of stocks and bonds—plus a supply of stale ladyfingers, delicious when dipped in his silver tooth mug filled with tepid water.

These punctuated our reading sessions which ranged from the Brothers Grimm through a twenty-volume encyclopaedic dic-tionary, via the Shorter Catechism and *Struwwelpeter*. . . .

Gran gave me a golden heritage which stayed in my subconscious treasury during my growing-up years and the typical educa-tion of those World War I days—private school, boarding school, a year of college, and a debut with-all-the-frills.

I married Sam H. McMeekin, then sports editor of the Louisville *Courier-Journal* and learned a little about historic Churchill Downs and the background of bluegrass horse racing from him. We have three chil-dren, a son and two daughters, all born within three years. My pleasure in reading aloud to them began early and lasted until they were old enough to have had enough. Then I became a volunteer reader at the Children's Hospital and have kept up this rewarding job ever since. I find the old favorites are still popular.

All Kentuckians are sentimental about their state, and believe that "the sun shines bright," whether or not it does. Even Davy Crockett, à la Disney, couldn't steal the thunder from Daniel Boone and his Long Hunters, and so my first children's book, *Journey Cake*, told about our settlin' folk. This book was lucky enough to win the Julia Ellsworth Ford Award and that in-comparable editor, Helen Hoke Watts, en-couraged me to go on from there. Several years ago I taught the course in juvenile writing at the summer writers' conference at Indiana University. It was a challenging

ISABEL McLENNAN McMEEKIN

experience which I'd like to repeat. (Four pupils won contracts!)

In my adult books, historical novels and nonfiction, I've been fortunate enough to share the fun of collaboration with Dorothy Park Clark, under the pen name of Clark McMeekin, one of our latest books being one of the Folkways Series, called *Old Ken-tucky Country*. But books for young people are my first, best love. With six grand-children to read to, and write for, I think I'm in the driver's seat and . . . "Once upon a time. . . ."

Marie McSwigan

1907-1962

AUTHOR OF
*Snow Treasure; Three's a Crowd; Our
Town Has a Circus; Binnie
Latches On; Etc.*

Autobiographical sketch of Marie McSwigan,
written for MORE JUNIOR AUTHORS shortly before her death:

SOME of my books have factual bases, are fictionalized accounts of real hap-penings. *Snow Treasure, Juan of Manila, All Aboard for Freedom!* and some others were suggested by events that actually oc-curred. This absorption in the real stems, I think, from my background, the newspaper world. My father was a cub reporter at the Johnstown flood and later became city edi-

MARIE McSWIGAN

tor. One uncle was a highly revered managing editor and another a rather flashy reporter. In my generation, a sister was a woman's-page writer and I was a news reporter.

A lifelong, nay, prenatal affiliation, it had many fruits. I was forced to become a reader of newsprint. Always I was intrigued with the printed word and could read telephone books and timetables with interest. More, I became involved with what was beneath a published account, what of interest had not been told. Then, in turning to fiction, I found confidence in knowing that events so bizarre as those I read of in the newspapers were possible and had only to be presented plausibly to become story material. Journalism, moreover, developed in me a healthy respect for facts. I try to present an imaginary event as it would have taken place and I refuse to take even small flights into the extravagant.

To be as exact as I want to be, I must do considerable research. For *All Aboard for Freedom!* the narrative of the train that broke the Iron Curtain, I visited a railroad yard to learn how the air brake is operated. For *Snow Treasure,* wherein Norwegian children during the German occupation sledded thirteen tons of gold down a mountain, I had to know about both the packaging of gold bullion and the arctic night. For the one I found information at the Federal Reserve Bank, and for the other, at the Allegheny Observatory.

My newspaper work had taught me where to go for what I wanted to know. It had also taught immediacy. For good results, or for lesser ones, I had learned to sit down and write the story regardless of reasons for delay. For the writer of fiction, however, the press as a training school has one most serious drawback. The reporter must be objective, must write without personal interpretation. But unless an author sympathetically interprets his characters, he will have no readers.

Besides being a working newspaperwoman, I was publicist for organizations as varied as an amusement park and a fine arts gallery. My last such assignment was public relations chief of the University of Pittsburgh, my alma mater.

I was born and have lived all my life in Pittsburgh. It has been my joy to see my city emerge from a blight of mill dust and a consequent apathy into a bright prideful place, which during the past decade has undergone vast renovation. One of the most dynamic of cities, in 1958 it celebrated its bicentennial, commemorating the capture of Fort Duquesne and the establishment of Fort Pitt. As a place to live and write in, it has the advantages of friendly cooperative people, excellent research and educational facilities and now a favorable climate. Although I am only a spectator of the widely hailed Pittsburgh Renaissance, I am grateful to witness so thrilling a sight and I wear my sidewalk superintendent badge with the same pride as do so many others.

Anne Malcolmson

1910-

AUTHOR OF
Yankee Doodle's Cousins; The Song of Robin Hood; Mr. Stormalong

Autobiographical sketch of Anne Malcolmson:

I WAS born in St. Louis, Missouri, in 1910. I went to the public schools for the first eight grades and then to the John Burroughs Country Day School. At Bryn Mawr College I majored in English literature.

The summer after our graduation from Bryn Mawr, a friend and I went as counselors to a girls' camp in New Hampshire.

We drove up to camp early, to help make it ready for the campers. On our arrival we were assigned to Angus, the camp handyman, as his helpers. The first job he gave us was to take down the boards that covered the windows of the lodge. His instructions seemed a little odd. We were to take out the nails very carefully, put the straight ones in one box and the crooked ones in another. We struggled hard to save all those crooked nails, and finally presented them proudly to Angus, expecting him to approve our work. Instead, he looked disappointed.

"Where are the holes?" he asked. He insisted that he had asked us to save the nail holes in a third box.

That was the first of Angus' tall tales that I had met. He claimed to be the first cousin of Paul Bunyan. In his youth he had been a lumberjack in the Maine woods. Often, during our summer, when the girls were gathered around the campfire, Angus joined us and reminisced about his days as a logger in Paul's camp. As a Middle Westerner I had never heard of Paul Bunyan. At first I swallowed Angus' yarns, "hook, line and sinker." Later, however, I discovered that Paul was a great legendary character, well known to many Americans.

Some years after this, I was teaching American geography to a fifth grade class in Chicago. I kept wishing that I could find a book about Paul Bunyan and other American folk heroes for the youngsters to read. There were numerous books and magazine articles on the subject, but at that time there was no collection suitable for the reading capacities of the fifth grade. Consequently, as an experiment, I wrote a few stories, had them mimeographed, and used them as supplementary reading. The children seemed to enjoy them, so I kept at it. Eventually, these stories were collected and published as a book, *Yankee Doodle's Cousins*.

Since those days I have taught school off and on during most of my adult life. At one time I had a seventh grade. The children all knew the fine Howard Pyle retelling of the adventures of Robin Hood. We were reading English ballads, and it occurred to me that they might enjoy knowing the Robin Hood tales as they were originally sung in ballad form many cen-

turies ago. Unfortunately, the originals were sung in Early Modern English, a little difficult for my "Sevens" to follow. It was not too hard, however, to change the spelling and some of the words to make them comprehensible. I was able to find a number of the old ballad tunes, or airs. Eventually these early ballads became another book, *The Song of Robin Hood*.

My third book, *Mr. Stormalong*, really grew out of the first. I had included a chapter about Captain A. B. Stormalong, the Paul Bunyan of the China trade. Some years afterward, Dell McCormick, a writer from the Far West, started to do a whole book about the legendary sailor. He collected the bulk of his material, but was unable to pull it together before his sudden death. Since I knew the story, the publisher asked me to complete his book.

At the present time, I am married and living in Washington, D.C.

Miriam E. Mason

1900-

AUTHOR OF
Happy Jack; Little Jonathan; Matilda and Her Family; Smiling Hill Farm; Etc.

Autobiographical sketch of Miram E. Mason:

I WAS the second child and the "story-telling sister" of a family of seven children, living on an isolated backwoods farm in Indiana. My father had dreams of changing the great tract of hilly woodland into a paradise of orchards. In our house were many books which my parents had brought from town. There was a piano, played beautifully by my older sister who taught me also to play the piano and to appreciate music. We had cats, dogs, and equine animals, including mules, Shetland ponies, and horses.

I wrote and told stories while we children washed dishes or stemmed strawberries. I wrote plays which we produced in a woodland theater on the side of a hill. I read most of the many books on our shelves, though I did not understand everything in them. In early childhood I learned to love books—not just what was in them but the bodies of books. The one-room rural school which I attended gave a yearly box supper to raise money to buy a box of "reading

MIRIAM E. MASON

circle" books. It was a wonderful day when those books arrived and the box was opened. It was then, too, that I got my first ambition—to be an author when I grew up and to see a whole shelf of books all "by Miriam E. Mason."

I was never inside a public library until I started high school in town. I can never forget how wonderful that whole building of bookshelves seemed! I wrote from the time I was eight years old, mostly stories about cats, for children's columns in magazines and won a number of prizes. My first moneyed writing was a story sent to the Methodist Book Concern for which I received twenty-five dollars and felt that I had really arrived.

I had had brief periods of wishing to be a circus performer, and became very adept at high jumping and tightwire walking. Then I wished very much to be a doctor or a nurse, but what I really loved was writing. Any other work I did was only supplementary to my true ambition to be a writer. I went to Indiana University and the University of Missouri, taught school, wrote advertising for a city department store, edited readers in a textbook publishing house. Off and on I would write short stories for magazines. I wrote and sold nearly four hundred of them before writing my very first book, *The Little Story House*.

By the time I had written my second book, *Smiling Hill Farm* (a Junior Literary Guild selection), I had a definite idea of what I wanted to contribute to the body of children's literature. I wanted to write books which would allure the young and beginning reader, and would give him an appetite for reading just as I had.

My early work in the textbook house helped me understand the technicalities of vocabulary and similar problems. But my life as a storytelling sister on the old farm taught me the magic that lives in words and what can be done with words. My first books were written in words that would be found in their potential reader's school vocabulary, though I soon discarded the use of the graded vocabulary except in my textbooks which require it. I found that the children of the world were exactly as I had been—longing for books which they could read, which stirred their emotions, which made the work of learning to read worth while. Each of my books (about forty by the time this volume is published) has its roots in my own childhood. The cats and dogs I loved, the ponies we rode, the loud-voiced mule, and the Indiana farm life all appear in my stories. I write of nothing I do not love or of no biographical character who does not appeal to me.

Now, of course, having written so many books, I get dozens and dozens of letters from children all over the United States and from foreign countries, too. They convince me again that times may change but children's hearts remain the same. I am also convinced that a love of reading is terribly important, and that the writer who can manage to produce books that will make people love reading in childhood is doing a worth-while thing.

My one child is now married and has five children of her own. Several of my books are dedicated to them and they help me to understand modern children. *Katie Kittenheart* is drawn from my granddaughter Kathy, and the book jacket portrait is a reproduction of her school picture. I am so glad now that I did not become a tightrope dancer, a patent-medicine manufacturer, or even an advertising writer, praising cigarettes and hair spray! I live in a large house in a small town, have cats and a dog and many birds in the trees, and go driving every day in lieu of the childhood pony rides.

Rutherford Montgomery

1896-

AUTHOR OF
*Beaver Water; Mountain Man; Jets Away;
The Golden Stallion's Victory; Etc.*

Autobiographical sketch of Rutherford G.
Montgomery:

MY home is in Los Gatos, California, but
I was born in North Dakota. After
high school, I had three years of college,
mostly at Western State in Colorado. Then
I taught school, served as a judge, and as
Colorado State Budget Commissioner. Since
1938 I have devoted all of my time to
writing. I have had sixty-nine books published, fifteen of them adult novels.

My father and mother were farmers. Up
until I finished grade school we lived in
the hill country near Velva, North Dakota.
Our farm was not far from the Canadian
border. As soon as I was big enough to set
a steel trap, I ran trap lines along the creek
which flowed through the farm. In order
to catch animals I had to learn about them.
They fascinated me and I kept on studying
them. I also quit trapping them and killing
them. But I didn't start writing about them
until my second year in high school. My
first story published in a national magazine
was written as an assignment for sophomore
English.

The folks moved to a Montana ranch but
I finished high school at Velva, then joined
them on the ranch. Again I was out in the
country where I could study animals, this
time with a mountain background.

In 1932 I wrote my first book, a story
about three cub bears. It found a publisher
and I was off. I would listen to lawyers
argue cases during the day, but I have to
admit that on warm summer days my mind
wasn't always upon the evidence or the
arguments, and at night I would write. The
day arrived when I had to decide whether
I was to be a writer or hold down a job. I
could not do both successfully. I decided to
write and have never had a job since 1938.

I always use backgrounds I know and
write about things I know about, wildlife,
ranch stories, and books about airplanes.
This last interest came from my serving in
the Air Corps of the Army. One of my most
recent books is about the B-47 stratojet
bomber. Before I wrote it, I was the guest
of the Strategic Air Command for four weeks
and flew with a bomber crew. I take my
research very seriously and never use anything as fact unless I am sure it is true. I
wanted to know how it felt to be without
oxygen at forty thousand feet altitude, so I
entered a decompression chamber and found
out. One of my characters in the book faces
this test and I had to know just what a man
could do with only fifteen seconds of con-
sciousness granted him.

Nicolas Mordvinoff

1911-

AUTHOR AND ILLUSTRATOR OF
Bear's Land and *Coral Island*

ILLUSTRATOR OF
Just So Stories; Finders Keepers; Etc.

Autobiographical sketch of Nicolas Mordvinoff:

I WAS born on September 27, 1911, in
what was then called Petrograd; St.
Petersburg in my father's day; and Leningrad now; perhaps Khrushchevgrad tomor-
row! If I cannot recall my very first days,
I cannot remember any when I was not
drawing. Writing came a little later. At
the age of five I was editing a newspaper of
sorts, written phonetically, and making illustrations for it. As I grew older I was
constantly scolded for doing my "silly drawings" instead of studying mathematics, but
thanks to those "silly drawings" and not to
mathematics, I make my living today.

After graduating from the University of
Paris, where I studied Latin languages and
philosophy, I attended the studios of Léger,
Ozenfant, and Lhote. The only thing I
learned from them was self-criticism. In
the meantime, I was drawing cartoons for
newspapers and magazines and writing a
three-hundred-page novel which I threw into the fireplace one year after its completion.

In 1934 I went to the islands of the South
Pacific where I spent thirteen years painting
and writing. If I did more painting than
writing, it was because I could sell pictures
and could not spend two or three years
writing a book. I will not speak of the real

or fictional charms of these faraway lands, but I loved the simple life and the natives. Most of my time was divided among writing, doing horrible pictures for the tourists, and studying painting. I spent two years on one of the most remote islands—Manga Reva. There I painted all of the time, studying nature, eating fish and breadfruit and manioc. It was delicious food even though it lacked variety. One day my next-door neighbor ate his dog. Somehow this didn't appeal to me and I declined his invitation for dinner.

I remember one day in Tahiti when, coming home to my coconut-leaf and bamboo hut, I found a manuscript on the floor. A few days later I discovered it had been left there by William Stone, whom I had never met. He had published several books in New York and at this time was specializing in writing for children. The book was *Thunder Island,* the first book I illustrated.

I had never thought of illustrating books, but it seemed a logical solution to my dilemma: drawing or writing. Drawing for writing was one answer; writing for drawing was still to come.

I illustrated several other books for William Stone and somehow my next move was to come to New York where these books were published. It was quite a change of pace after the islands and of course it was not as easy at first as it seemed from far away, but since I did not know how to do anything else, I kept on doing the same thing and had a one-man show of my paintings in a gallery on Fifty-seventh Street. It was at this time that I met Will Lipkind and during a game of checkers we had the idea of making a picture book for children together. It was the first of a series.

Now that I live on a farm in New Jersey, I plan to do many more books for children, and I hope to have time to paint, as well. A farm in New Jersey is a long way from the South Pacific, but my book, *Coral Island,* combines writing and drawing with some of the charm I remember of those islands.

* * *

In 1952 *Finders Keepers*, with illustrations by Mr. Mordvinoff, was awarded the Caldecott Medal.

Alfred P. Morgan

1889-

AUTHOR AND ILLUSTRATOR OF
*The Boy Electrician; A Pet Book for Boys
and Girls; A First Electrical Book for
Boys; The Boys' First Book of Radio
and Electronics; Etc.*

Autobiographical sketch of Alfred Powell Morgan:

I WAS born in Brooklyn, New York, before it became part of New York City. Some of the streetcars were drawn by horses and there were no automobiles. Streets paved with cobblestones and vacant lots were the children's playgrounds in those days. My father owned a glass factory and it was fun to visit there and watch the men blowing lamp chimneys and bottles. The factory was near Erie Basin and I watched many famous ships go into drydock for repairs, including several of the United States men-of-war which fought in the Spanish-American War.

When I was eight years old my family moved to Upper Montclair, New Jersey, a suburban country village. Here a boy's activities were very different from those in the city and very different from what they are today. There were ponds and a canal near by which provided swimming, fishing and skating. Some boys hunted rabbits, squirrels and ducks with air rifles or twenty-two caliber rifles.

I was very much interested in science but there were no books for young people about chemistry, electricity, etc. I tried to read and understand grown-up people's books about engineering and science and decided that when I grew older I would write books which young people could understand. In my search for information I visited many famous scientists and engineers and asked them questions, among them Thomas A. Edison, Nikola Tesla and Santos-Dumont.

I graduated from the Montclair High School and taught physics and chemistry as a paid student instructor while I was still a senior at high school. I attended the Massachusetts Institute of Technology. I started writing books and magazine articles while at college in order to earn money.

I have written more than fifty books and a couple of hundred magazine articles. An

ALFRED P. MORGAN

electrical book for boys written nearly fifty years ago still sells well. Writing was not my only activity after leaving college. For many years I also manufactured electronic and electrical equipment. When I am not writing or illustrating my books, I enjoy raising flowers in the back yard, and week ends on my small cruiser.

My wife was Ruth W. Shackleford and we have three sons, now grown up and married. One is a doctor, one a salesman, and the third an officer in the United States Air Force.

E. Nesbit
1858-1924
AUTHOR OF
*The Bastable Children; The Five Children
and It; The Phoenix and the Carpet;
The Wouldbegoods; Etc.*

WROTE Edgar Eager in the October 1958 issue of *The Horn Book:* "Just as Beatrix Potter is the genius of the picture book, so I believe E. Nesbit to be the one truly 'great' writer for the ten-, eleven- and twelve-year-old." Miss Nesbit's two biographers, Doris Langley Moore in her *E. Nesbit,* and Noel Streatfeild in her *Magic and the Magician,* concur in this opinion. The hold of this author on her readers today is as strong as it was half a century ago.

"One reason why E. Nesbit's books are not dated," Miss Streatfeild declares, "is that she understood the essence of childhood. . . . She wrote about intelligent children for intelligent children."

Edith Nesbit was one of six children in a London family. She was a tomboy and loved all kinds of practical jokes and frolics. Her father died when she was four, and her mother took her to France and Germany to be educated. Her teens were spent in a village in Kent, where she told exciting stories to the neighbor children and wrote verse. At seventeen, she had a poem published in a magazine. At twenty-one she married Hubert Bland but the marriage was not happy. She had five children and also found time to write a great deal and was published.

When E. Nesbit was forty she began to write the stories that brought her fame, the stories of the Bastable children. They were based on her own happy childhood and her escapades with her brothers and sisters. Three books—*The Treasure Seekers, The Wouldbegoods,* and *The New Treasure Seekers*—were published in this country in 1928 by Coward-McCann as one volume, *The Bastable Children.* They are probably the best known of her books.

Miss Nesbit's "magic" books are the ones that remain timeless, ageless. Mr. Eager feels a child should read these books first. "For if there is one thing that makes E. Nesbit's magic books more enchanting than any others," he remarks, "it is not that they are funny, or exciting, or beautifully written, or full of wonderfully alive and endearing children, all of which they are. It is the *dailiness* of the magic. . . . The world of E. Nesbit is the ordinary or garden world we all know, with just the right pinch of magic added."

It is pleasant to know that Miss Nesbit earned a great deal of money from her books while she lived, something not always true of writers, either in the adult or juvenile fields. For twenty-three years she lived in a large house in Kent, which appears as the Moat House in the Bastable stories. It actually had a moat, a relic of the eighteenth century, and she would float on it in a flat-bottomed boat for hours at a time, a pad of writing paper on her knee. She wrote in the mornings and late afternoons, always on glossy, colored paper.

Newell

E. NESBIT

After the death of her husband, shortly before World War I, Miss Nesbit remarried. This time the marriage was a happy one. Probably her best epitaph was written by Miss Streatfeild:

"Perhaps nothing shows E. Nesbit's gift for writing for children more clearly than the ability she has for making her children live. . . . She never wrote a word of the Bastables until she knew them better than the children around her, for only by knowing everything about her characters, infinitely more than she had any intention of using, could she have made them live and breathe. . . . To be able to do this is a quality possessed by the very few, and so it is no wonder that E. Nesbit's books still live and will live for countless children yet unborn."

Hope Newell

1896-

AUTHOR OF
The Little Old Woman Who Used Her Head; Steppin and Family; A Cap for Mary Ellis; Penny's Best Summer; Etc.

Autobiographical sketch of Hope Newell:

I WAS born in Bradford, Pennsylvania, and lived there until I finished high school. From September to June I spent about one half of my waking hours in school and the other half at the Carnegie Public Library. I should have liked to spend more time at the library and less at school, which I'm sorry to say I didn't like at all. Nothing very exciting happened in Bradford, so even a little thing like getting up at four in the morning to watch the circus come to town and following after gypsy vans and having our fortunes told by one of them, seemed exciting to us.

My parents, my two sisters and I spent our summers in a rural spot called Moody Hollow, where our father had a small oil lease. There the most exciting day of the week was Tuesday when the rural free delivery postman came by with his horse and buggy and brought us all the Sunday newspapers that had funny papers—"Little Nemo," "Buster Brown," "Foxy Grandpa," and many others. An elderly man who was a great friend of our family sent them, and in all the summers we spent in Moody Hollow they always arrived on Tuesday.

From Bradford I went to Cincinnati to study nursing. Soon after I completed my course, World War I was under way. I enlisted in the United States Army Nurse Corps and served ten months in France. After I was discharged I got married, had a baby, and received a B.S. degree from Columbia University. I spent five years with my family on a fruit ranch in Napas Valley, California, and since then have lived in New York City. I was in public health nursing until 1943, when I took a position with the National Nursing Council for War Service. Since then, I have spent most of my time writing books for young people.

My father told me the Little Old Woman stories as he had heard them when he was a boy. They are from the Dutch, and evidently have been passed along to each new generation. The first one was about her making blankets for her geese. The stories have a sort of backward logic that a child understands instantly and that makes him feel superior. My son Jim used to try to help me with the stories when he was small. I remember when a maniac shot a dentist at the Medical Center through the heart, Jim exclaimed, "Mother, wouldn't that make a nice Little Old Woman story!"

I started *Steppin and Family* when I was living in Harlem and was a public health nurse. The children there have always amazed me. I wore a mask all night and

HOPE NEWELL

they used to ask, "Do you bite?" The books about Mary Ellis, Steppin's sister, grew out of that same experience. She becomes a public health nurse. *A Cap for Mary Ellis,* which followed *Mary Ellis: Student Nurse,* has been translated into Swedish. *Penny's Best Summer* came out of the Pennsylvania oil country, where I grew up. I like to write fantasy, and *Cinder Ike* is one of my favorite books.

Andre Norton

AUTHOR OF
Star Man's Son; Time Traders; Stand to Horse; Follow the Drum; Etc.

Autobiographical sketch of Alice Mary Norton, who writes under the pseudonym "Andre Norton":

MY involvement with the future began while I was still in high school, but then it was a reader's interest rather than a writer's preoccupation. Working on the *Collinwood Spotlight,* writing short adventure stories for the once-a-term literary magazine of that paper, belonging to a keen-minded Quill and Scroll chapter, all led to stringing words together on paper. Though, at that time, I had every intention of becoming a history teacher rather than a professional writer. However, I wrote my first book, an adventure-mystery, the year I graduated from high school. Some four years later, having learned a little more of my craft, I rewrote that same manuscript and sold it. But in the meantime I had already marketed my first book, a Graustarkian romance for teen-agers.

During World War II, I was introduced to the fine work being done by the Cleveland *Press'* World Friends Club, and was given access by members to some exciting letters from the Netherlands. From this contact developed my three espionage novels— *The Sword Is Drawn, Sword in Sheath,* and *At Swords' Points. The Sword Is Drawn* was awarded a plaque by the Netherlands government for its sympathetic portrayal of that nation at war.

Since history and legend led me to explore, via books, odd byways of the past, I came to translate and adapt two cycles of legends, telling the tales aloud first in special story hours at branches of the Cleveland Public Library, where I was then an assistant in the children's department. These cycle stories, having proved popular with listening groups, were eventually published as *Rogue Reynard* and *Huon of the Horn.* And in addition, scattered through my working years, I have written four historical novels for young people—*Follow the Drum,* a story of the settlement of Maryland; *Scarface,* about pirate action in the West Indies; *Yankee Privateer,* concerning a Marine during the Revolution; and *Stand to Horse,* a chronicle of the Apache wars during the late 1850's. All of these required long months of research and delving into old records, volumes of letters, Army reports, and much revision.

Then, in 1951, I had published my first science-fiction adventure—*Star Man's Son.* Having long collected and read science fiction for my own pleasure, I had a liking for what is termed "space opera," the science-fiction adventure story, which is the type I wanted to write. Since that time I have written the other Star titles in a loose arrangement of future history—*Star Rangers, Star Born, Star Guard, Star Gate, The Stars Are Ours!*

There is also the Solar Queen series, dealing with the exploits of the crew of a tramp space freighter of the far future—*Sargasso of Space* and *Plague Ship.* And I have two unrelated volumes—*Time Traders* and *Sea Siege.* In addition, I was asked to choose the stories for and edit four anthologies—*Bullard of the Space Patrol, Space Service, Space Pioneers,* and *Space Police.*

ANDRE NORTON

Several of the Star books and one of the Solar Queen adventures have been translated into German, Italian, and Spanish, as the demand for such stories of our "might bes" has spread around the world. And so I have become used to living in the future with a reference shelf of spaceship projects and speculations at hand. A good knowledge of history is also a fine tool for a writer of science fiction, for history repeats itself, and the colonies of a mother planet revolt in an "American Revolution" of some future time.

Having served as a library assistant until 1950, I am now a free-lance writer. My home is in Cleveland, where I was born, as my family has been Ohio rooted since the land-grant days just after the Revolution. In addition to library work, I have managed a bookshop and served as juvenile editor for Gnome Press.

Jack O'Brien

1898-1938

AUTHOR OF

Silver Chief, Dog of the North; Valiant Dog of the Timberline; Corporal Corey of the Royal Canadian Mounted; Spike of Swift River; Etc.

JOHN S. O'Brien, better known to young readers as Jack O'Brien, was born on August 18, 1898, in Duluth, Minnesota.

After public school there, he attended the University of Minnesota for two years, then went to Fordham University, where he played on the football team, as he had at Minnesota.

During World War I, he enlisted in the Army and saw action on the Mexican border, later going overseas as an airplane mechanic. He found all the things he sought—excitement, hardship, danger, and romance. When the late Admiral Byrd was planning his first antarctic expedition, O'Brien took the job of chief surveyor. He had a way with dogs, so he was given the added task of assuming charge of the dogs of the expedition.

When the expedition returned to the United States, O'Brien went to northern Canada, where he spent a number of months driving huskies on long prospecting trips. He lived with the sled dogs until he knew them as few do. One of his trips was traveling alone seven hundred miles by dog sled, to reach a man who was lost in the ice regions of the Far North. O'Brien nearly lost his life several times on this trip, but he rescued the man and brought him back safely.

Jack O'Brien loved all kinds of dogs. In addition, he had the gift of storytelling, so it was natural that he should turn to writing. Four of his books were about Silver Chief, a dog that was a composite of all the brave dogs he had known in his wilderness adventures. He wrote of this composite dog as follows:

"All the splendid characteristics that are to be found in every dog, regardless of color, breed, or size and shape of tail, I found in Silver Chief. He was a husky and I knew him well. When I wrote of him, I wrote of all dogs and gave him the job of carrying my mite of praise for all dogs across the printed page. I came to know him first in Canada. There I saw him and one other stand off three ravenous wolves in a desperate, running fight. They were slashed to ribbons, but their courage enabled us to reach our cabin, where fresh ammunition soon ended the uneven battle.

"I knew him again in the antarctic, when, as a member of Larry Gould's geological party, we slogged sixteen hundred miles across the dreary, frozen wastes, with the

JACK O'BRIEN

Scott O'Dell

1902-

AUTHOR OF
Island of the Blue Dolphins; Etc.

SCOTT O'Dell, whose first book for young people, *Island of the Blue Dolphins*, won the Newbery Medal and the Rupert Hughes Award in 1961, was born in Los Angeles on May 23, 1902. His father, Bennett Mason O'Dell, was an official of the Union Pacific Railroad and the horizons of his mother, May Elizabeth Gabriel O'Dell, were, he says, "bounded by the walls of her home." He was brought up in Los Angeles, San Pedro, and Long Beach, California, and "was never far from the sound of the sea."

After graduating from Long Beach Polytechnic High School, Mr. O'Dell attended Occidental College, the University of Wisconsin, and Stanford University. For several years he worked in the motion picture industry, first as a technical director for Paramount, and then as a Technicolor cameraman for Metro-Goldwyn-Mayer on the filming of the first *Ben Hur* in Rome. While in Italy, he attended the University of Rome and wrote a first novel which he never published.

Returning to the United States, Mr. O'Dell became a newspaperman, a book re-

weary dogs dragging our heavy sleds every step of the way. Time and again they saved us, swerving aside as the treacherous sea ice cracked wide open and the oily water licked the jagged edges hungrily. Often it was 35° below zero and the tears that streamed down our cheeks froze in icy masks. When the grub was scarce and the marches long, and all there was for them at the end of a grueling day was a bitter bed on a hard-packed drift, even then those fine eyes would seek ours beseechingly and they'd laugh up at us in the manner a dog has of laughing, when we thumped their sides, rubbed their ears, and tried to show them what they meant to us."

Jack O'Brien's last book, *Royal Red*, was published posthumously, as it was not found until several years after the author's death. His heir was going through some personal property left by O'Brien and found the manuscript of the story of a sorrel horse belonging to the Royal Canadian Mounted Police. It needed only a little work to make it ready for publication. *Silver Chief's Revenge* was also published posthumously, developed from notes and ideas found in the author's papers.

Jack O'Brien was a member of the famous Adventurers' Club, and an honorary member of the National Geographic Society. He died in 1938 in New York City.

Robert C. Frampton
SCOTT O'DELL

viewer, a frequent contributor to West Coast periodicals, and an author of both fiction and nonfiction for adults. While doing research for an informal history of California, *Country in the Sun,* he found an article about a young Indian girl, Karana, who spent eighteen years alone on the island of San Nicolas off the California coast. This article led Mr. O'Dell to further research and eventually to write *Island of the Blue Dolphins,* a fictional reconstruction of Karana's years on the island, narrated in the first person.

Mr. O'Dell now lives on a farm in Julian, California, an 1880's gold-mining town east of San Diego. He was married in 1949 to Dorsa Rattenbury, who types his manuscripts and offers him editorial advice. He devotes his time to writing and growing apples and oranges, and to his hobbies, book collecting and fishing.

ADRIAN A. PARADIS

Adrian A. Paradis

1912-

AUTHOR OF
Librarians Wanted; The New Look in Banking; Americans at Work; Never Too Young To Earn; Etc.

Autobiographical sketch of Adrian Alexis Paradis:

MY birthplace was a distinguished one— the first apartment house in Brooklyn, New York, to have an elevator. Before I was old enough to enjoy using it, the family moved out to what were then the suburbs, Flatbush, where I lived until I entered Dartmouth College in 1930. Because I had hoped to go to the Yale School of Drama after graduating from college, I majored in English. The Depression changed my plans, however, for it had become so bad by the time I graduated from Dartmouth in 1934 that I had to go to work.

After several jobs at fifteen dollars a week, the then going pay for beginners, I entered the hotel business with a friend and helped manage a small inn up in the White Mountains of New Hampshire. When Grace Dennis came up from New Jersey to work for us, I fell in love with her at first sight and a year later we were married. Soon we left the inn because it offered no opportunity

for family life. Promised a job in the Dartmouth College Library if I obtained a degree in library service, we returned to New York. Here I studied nights at Columbia University for three years, while I worked in a law library from nine to six.

But the war started before I graduated and instead of going back to Dartmouth I joined American Airlines to start an economic research library for the company. I did not remain a librarian long, for I became office manager of the economic research department; then, an economic analyst; next, assistant to the corporate secretary; and finally, assistant secretary of the corporation, which is still my main occupation.

My mother is a writer and perhaps that is why I have always had an interest in writing. My career as an author started one night in 1949 with a dream. I dreamed that I had written a book for boys on how to earn money. It seemed like such a good idea when I woke up next morning that I hurried to the library that noon and was delighted to find that there was no such book in print. A year later a publisher accepted my manuscript. Since then I have published eight other books.

I write about four hours a day—an hour on my way to work, an hour on the return trip, and two hours in the evening. Week ends I may spend four, eight, twelve or

Paradis: *pronounced "parody"*

fifteen hours at my desk. I like young people—we have three children—and enjoy writing books that suggest how they should prepare themselves for and choose the right career. Perhaps my interest in career guidance was stimulated by the fact that I didn't know what I wanted to do until I was almost forty. I know how important it is that young people choose and prepare for their life work as soon as possible.

We live in Westport, Connecticut, and when our youngest child, our daughter, graduates from high school, we plan to move closer to New York City so I can spend more time writing at home!

Bertha M. Parker

1890-

AUTHOR OF
Beyond the Solar System; Seeds and Seed Travels; The Golden Treasury of Natural History; The Golden Book of Science; Etc.

BERTHA Morris Parker was born February 7, 1890, in Rochester, Illinois, the daughter of Homer Darius and Margaret Elizabeth (Lawrence) Parker. She was a student for a year at Oberlin College, and at Columbia University summer school, but took her bachelor's degree in 1914, and her master's degree in 1923 at the University of Chicago.

Miss Parker taught science in the Springfield, Illinois, public schools for five years, and then for many years was a teacher of science in the Laboratory Schools of the University of Chicago. From 1934 to 1938 Miss Parker edited *Science News Notes*, the publication of the National Council on Elementary Science. Since 1938 she has been associate editor of *Science Education*.

Of her *Science Experiences*, published in 1952, the *The Booklist* said: "Although designed primarily for teachers and for use in the classroom, this book of nearly two hundred simple experiments, chiefly in physical science, can be used by children at home by making some substitutions in equipment and by purchasing some materials. Clearly illustrated directions tell what to do, what will happen, and why." The *Library Journal* recommended her *Golden Treasury of Natural History*, published the same year: "Concise, authoritative

information on the prehistoric period on the earth through the beginning of life. . . . Really remarkable book . . . a worthy addition to books on natural history."

Miss Parker has written seventy-two books, including a good many textbooks. She has served on committees of numerous scientific organizations in the educational field, and is a past president of the National Council on Elementary Science. She lives in Chicago and is unmarried.

Catherine Owens Peare

1911-

AUTHOR OF
Mahatma Gandhi; Mary McLeod Bethune; Rosa Bonheur; Washington Irving; Etc.

Autobiographical sketch of Catherine Owens Peare:

FROM early childhood the ambition to write has created the basic story line of my life. It followed its unbroken way through the tangle of fantastically plotted novels at grammar school level, the love poems of adolescence, and the double-meaning mystical dramas of the college years. But because no one since the invention of the printing press, with a rare few dazzling exceptions, has ever earned an adequate living at writing, I always knew that I would have to train for some other occupation. I chose teaching, because I knew I would like the work, and its scholastic atmosphere, and because I love young people. But I came out of teachers' college in the 1930's when there were no teaching posts, and found a position in a Wall Street house. Investments became my area of work for many years. I wrote all the while in my spare time, working toward the day when I could at last turn to free-lancing as a full-time occupation.

After World War II, I felt, like so many others, that there was something which very much needed saying. If war had become global, then so must peace. If peace was global, then every kind and variety of race, culture, and creed must share it. They could share it only if they knew each other. My teacher training convinced me that this could most appropriately be said to children and young people, and my two interests—teaching and writing—combined into books for them.

Peare: *PEER*

CATHERINE OWENS PEARE

My first major writing project for young people was thus interracial—a biography of the most outstanding individual of each of the world's kinds. First came Albert Einstein, then Gandhi, then Mary McLeod Bethune. By the time I had finished and published Mrs. Bethune's story, I was able to leave my position and free-lance full time. And that is what I am doing now—devoting all my time to writing, which includes a great deal of traveling (I've been to ten foreign countries so far) and meeting a great many interesting personalities.

The next series of books for young people that I launched, and which is still going strong, was in the arts: biographies of outstanding writers, painters, poets, and composers, whose forms are understandable to youngsters. I've done quite a few in this group so far, including Stephen Foster, Mark Twain, Henry W. Longfellow, Rosa Bonheur, and Washington Irving.

Whenever I visit a school assembly or a classroom, or talk to young readers under whatever circumstances, the profound satisfaction and happiness that I draw from my work is renewed again and again by their candid admiration, their ardent enthusiasm, their love of books.

* * *

Catherine Peare was the recipient of the 1962 Sequoyah Children's Book Award for *The Helen Keller Story.*

Henry C. Pitz
1895-

AUTHOR OF
*A Treasury of American Book
Illustration*

ILLUSTRATOR OF
*Razzberry Jamboree; Mysterious Island;
Valley of Rebellion; Etc.*

Autobiographical sketch of Henry C. Pitz:

I WAS born and grew up in the city of Philadelphia but we always lived close to the great Fairmount Park or to the fringes of the city where the fields began. My father had a house full of books. He had no idea that children should have any special kind of books given them; he brought home histories, biographies, many magazines and, best of all, books crammed with pictures. So reading seemed as pleasant to me as playing ball. My closest friend had two grandfathers who were artists, so pencils and brushes seemed natural to me.

By the time I reached high school I was deeply interested in history and under the urging of my history teachers I thought that it might be pleasant to spend my life teaching that subject. But I also had two kindly and helpful art teachers who managed a scholarship for me to the Philadelphia Museum School of Art. As it turned out, I didn't really abandon history; for a great deal of the illustration I have done has centered around historical subjects.

While I was still in art school, I picked up odds and ends of illustration to do, but World War I came along and I spent a year in France with the Army. Upon my return, I tucked my portfolio under my arm and made the rounds of the New York editors. My first jobs were with *Boys' Life* and the old *St. Nicholas* magazine. Then the Century Company gave me my first book to illustrate, *Master Skylark,* and now my latest book is about my one hundred and sixtieth.

For a good many years I have spent part of my time teaching illustration at my old school, the Philadelphia Museum School of Art. I am proud that a great many of the younger book illustrators have been in my classes. In my spare time I have enjoyed writing articles and books about illustration and picture-making in general. In between

HENRY C. PITZ

there has been a little time for painting in water color and oil and for etching and lithography.

We—my wife and our son and daughter—live in an old house in Plymouth Meeting. This was, until very recent years, a small Quaker village in a very historic part of Pennsylvania between Germantown and Valley Forge. The Germantown Pike, on which we live, is an old highway over which the Continental soldiers tramped many times. My wife is a painter and musician; our daughter is studying art at the old school we both attended; and our son, fortunately, shows no signs of this family weakness.

Lynn Poole

1910-

AUTHOR OF
*Your Trip into Space; Frontiers of Science;
Ballooning in the Space Age; Diving
for Science; Etc.*

Autobiographical sketch of Lynn Poole:

I WAS born with three characteristics for which I am now grateful: curiosity, imagination, and a great desire to tell things to other people. As a child in Iowa, I was curious about everything in country and town. At an Indian reservation near my home, I played with children and talked to their parents. What I learned from the Indians, young and adults, I talked about to my family and school friends.

Roaming in the woods, swimming in the river, skating on an ice pond, watching the clear sky at night, sleeping in a tent, building a tree house, gathering a zoo in my own back yard were activities which excited my curiosity about things I saw on the earth and in the sky. I was thrilled by what I learned, puzzled by facts I couldn't understand.

When I didn't understand things, my curiosity led me to our own family library and the public library. In books I found answers to some of my puzzles. I also found a new world in books and magazines. Reading with enthusiasm, I was carried by my imagination to distant continents where, in my mind, I lived with foreign people and enjoyed a life quite unlike the one in our town.

How well I remember the excitement of the news about the discovery of the tomb of the ancient Egyptian king Tutankhamen! Our newspaper reported the details about the excavation and every morning I got up early and raced to the front walk to pick up the newspaper, which I read while the rest of my family still slept. At breakfast I told everyone what had happened in Egypt, at the tomb, the very day before.

As a teen-ager, I lived in many cities and traveled in many states. During this time, amazing new events took place. Radio was being developed, so I built a crystal set. Airplanes were being flown from city to city and whenever possible I hung around small landing fields, hoping to hitch a ride. My curiosity led me to new knowledge, my imagination led me to daydreams about the world and its people, about the space beyond our earth. Excitedly I told everyone who would listen about the fascinating facts I learned, the events that thrilled me.

As an adult, I began to travel to foreign countries which I had read about when I was a child. I was fortunate enough to meet men and women who worked in the fields of science, literature, music and the theater. Naturally, I kept telling friends about my experiences.

Then I began to reach more people through my network television program. I demonstrated and told about all kinds of

LYNN POOLE

people, about many kinds of events, discoveries, and achievements. Soon I was writing books, again telling about things I had learned because of my curiosity and imagination. Happily, I married a girl with a lively curiosity, a gay imagination, and a desire to pass on her experiences to other people. She is a writer, too. Together we now collaborate in writing, always guided by curiosity.

Christine Price

1928-

AUTHOR AND ILLUSTRATOR OF
Three Golden Nobles; The Dragon and the Book; Song of the Wheels; Etc.

Autobiographical sketch of Christine Price:

I WAS born in London, England, but my family soon moved to Gerrards Cross, in Buckinghamshire, where we lived until I was twelve. This was a small place, set in rolling farmland, and my early memories are of long walks and picnics in fields and woods, picking primroses in the spring and gathering holly from the hedges at Christmastime. When I was old enough to ride a bicycle, we made longer trips to the villages round about, and I soon caught my mother's enthusiasm for exploring ancient churches and ruined medieval castles where the people of the past came alive for me, as

they never did in my history lessons at school.

My father is American, and when he brought the family to New York in 1940, I carried with me this feeling for history, together with a love of nature and the out-of-doors, and these, I think, are the roots of my later work.

I have always enjoyed writing and drawing. My first drawings were mostly of horses, wildly galloping horses; my first literary effort, an ode to the family parakeet. By the time I reached high school, at Scarborough School on the Hudson, I was determined to become an illustrator of children's books as quickly as possible. After a year at Vassar and a year at the Art Students League in New York, I began making the rounds of publishers' offices with a portfolio of sample drawings under my arm. I was lucky in finding work that first summer when I was eighteen, and I was busy illustrating children's books until 1949. By then, I had so much work that I felt I was getting into a rut and broke off to return to England for two years' study at the Central School of Arts and Crafts in London.

I had also started working on a book of my own, and while in London I finished writing and illustrating *Three Golden Nobles*, a children's story set in fourteenth century England. My second book, *The Dragon and the Book*, a story of King Alfred's time, was begun in London and

CHRISTINE PRICE

inspired by my stay there. During my summer holidays at the Central School, I traveled in England and France and took walking tours in the Scottish Highlands and the Dolomites in Italy.

Since my return to the States in 1951, my family has moved to Vermont where the beautiful countryside and exciting pioneer history provided part of the background for my third book, *Song of the Wheels,* most of which is laid in the Hudson Valley during the Farmers' Rebellion of 1766. While Vermont is now my home, I spend a good deal of time in New York. My favorite summer hobby in the country is gardening; in town, I like to play chamber music with my friends. My instrument is the recorder, ancestor of the modern flute, and music enters my illustrating and stories wherever possible.

ISABEL PROUDFIT

Isabel Proudfit

1898-

AUTHOR OF

The Treasure Hunter: The Story of Robert Louis Stevenson; River Boy: The Story of Mark Twain; Noah Webster: The Father of the Dictionary; The Ugly Duckling; Etc.

Autobiographical sketch of Isabel Boyd Proudfit:

I WAS born in Evanston, Illinois, went to college in Boston, and alighted in New York City for my adult life. Here I did newspaper work and publicity until I married, and then turned to writing children's stories and books in the gaps between babies. My original plan was to write a book one year, have a baby the next year, write a book the third year, etc., but the books outstripped the babies—twelve books to only three babies. (This was long ago; the babies are now hearty, independent adults.)

In the meantime, I have had a lot of fun. The books were fun because they took me to far places—Scotland (for research on Robert Louis Stevenson), Missouri (for research on Mark Twain), etc. The other fun has included many things: a farm in Connecticut for many years, where I collected books and information on early American ways (also for the books); a good bit of travel (I like primitive countries best, but have seen England, France, Italy, Spain, Greece, etc.,

too); some adult fiction published here and in England; gardening (with the other fellow doing the digging); raising canaries until everyone I knew had one, goldfinches in all shades of the rainbow, African violets, because they are so hard to make bloom in New York City. The last few years I have spent the summers on Nantucket Island, which has a charm all its own.

I mention the writing again last, because it is *hard work*—especially research writing. This work must never show in the finished product, which should move effortlessly and gracefully in beautiful sentences at all times. I have done this hard work in attics and furnished rooms with a sign on the door— "Do not disturb unless someone is bleeding or the house is on fire." One puts in the manuscript, say, in speaking of the year 1790, that "the man spit on the stove." Then one has to run and find out if they had stoves in 1790 and if they spit on them. It is a great temptation to cut out the particular phrase, instead of doing the research, but enough of this lazy writing and one has destroyed the Local Color in the manuscript —a serious error with publishers. As I like Local Color, I have tried to write honestly and carefully most times. A writer's life is an ideal life anyway, so why cheat on the details? The fact that one is writing for the young and eager also encourages a juvenile writer to do her best.

Charles Henry Bourne Quennell
1872-1935
and
Marjorie Quennell
1884-

AUTHORS AND ILLUSTRATORS OF
A History of Everyday Things in England;
Everyday Life in the Old Stone Age;
Everyday Life in Roman Britain;
Everyday Things in Ancient
Greece; Etc.

MARJORIE Courtney Quennell was born in Bromley Common, Kent, England, the daughter of Allen Courtney. She attended private schools and then studied at the Crystal Palace Art School, the Beckenham Technical Art School, and the Westminster Art School. In 1904 she married Charles Henry Bourne Quennell, and they had two sons and a daughter, one of whom, Peter Quennell, is a well-known poet, novelist, biographer, and literary critic.

The Quennells lived first in Bickley, Kent, and then moved to Berkhamstead, Hertfordshire. Mr. Quennell was an architect, a writer, and an authority on housing. He was a fellow of the Royal Institute of British Architects and a member of its Council for three years. (Mrs. Quennell is an honorary associate of this organization.) He was also a member of the Town Planning Committee and the editorial board of *Architectural Education.* "With the idea of trying to give children some background to their study of history," so Mrs. Quennell says, the Quennells wrote and illustrated a series of books dealing with everyday life and things in different eras.

Upon the death of her husband in 1935, Mrs. Quennell moved to London where she became the curator of the Geffrye Museum, a position she held until 1941. In 1939 she visited the United States to study museums and education, and she returned in 1951 to live in Melrose, Massachusetts, for a year. Since 1941 she has done some work as an illustrator, including the art work for *Builders of the Old World* by Gertrude Hartman. At present she lives in Lewes, Sussex, England. She has not exhibited her paintings for many years, although she still paints for recreation.

Louise S. Rankin
1897?-1951

AUTHOR OF
Daughter of the Mountains;
Gentling of Jonathan

Autobiographical sketch of Louise Rankin, written for her publishers in 1948:

IT was my great good fortune to be born into the home of a professor (at Johns Hopkins University), for he had long summer holidays and had married a western girl whose family wanted to see her as often as possible. So, though we lived in Baltimore, at least every other June my parents took my two brothers and me on the long train trip to San Francisco, and thence up to Nevada, for a rapturous summer of ranching and camping at Lake Tahoe. If we did not go West, we spent the summers on a Maryland farm.

We swam in Lake Tahoe, fished for mountain brook trout in its tributary streams, and with a lunch tied to our saddles went on all-day rides over the mountains. My mother was one of three devoted sisters, who brought their children, six in all, to their old home for these summer vacations. The "ladies," as we called them, had the courage to turn us loose both in the dry foothills around Carson City, my grandfather's home, and the pine-swept mountains of Lake Tahoe.

One of our great joys was to go, all six, on climbing expeditions. As nimble as mountain goats we scaled all the peaks within reach of us; and then, after hours of hard climbing, and eating our lunch on a wind-swept rocky summit, in how short a time we went leaping down the steep mountainsides! A sport not entirely without dangers, as we learned once when, grasping for support to pull ourselves to the summit of a mountain, we found ourselves looking into the face of a mountain lioness, who looked out at us from her cave. That was one peak whose summit we left unscaled— and quickly. Another time the granite ledge on which I stood broke from under me, and I started a rapid coast down toward the canyon hundreds of feet below. But thanks to the guardian angel who watches over foolhardy children, the seat of my overalls tore, caught on a rocky point, and for a breathless moment I felt myself suspended in space. Then my brothers hauled me back to safety. Such moments were our greatest delight—in retrospect, at any rate—for danger met and overcome was the dearest of our young adventures.

As a child I was an omnivorous reader with a catholic taste for stories. Hans Christian Andersen and the Brothers Grimm; *Little Women* and *Little Men; Treasure Island* and *The Secret Garden;* Scott and Dickens and *Alice in Wonderland;* Conan Doyle and *Huckleberry Finn*—these were among the favorites which I felt I'd want to read till I died. But I swallowed everything printable that came before my eyes. During the winters I was a bookworm first, my happiest hours being those when I was blissfully immersed in a good story; but in summer I was a tomboy, the inseparable companion of a cousin almost my age.

The public schools of Baltimore and Goucher College gave me my formal education, but equally important were our large library at home, the interests of my scholarly father, and our pilgrimages to the West Coast. Each time our parents took us by a different route, stopping off now and again to teach us history, a love of nature and of beauty, and to give us some sense of American industry and agriculture. My father was a keen traveler, and took us on long walks in the country and around Baltimore; he went with us too about the city of our birth, to show us the sights of historic importance.

Within this inheritance it was natural for me to step from college back into the classroom, to teach English in secondary schools. But even before I had learned to write, I had begun to tell myself stories, and had told and written them for myself all through my schooldays. One day this urge to write won out over my love of children and of teaching, and I went to New York convinced that the road to successful writing lay in the training of publishing-house work. Instead of a publisher, however, I found a professor who wanted assistance in studying publicly owned enterprises, both here and abroad. This diverted me, and I made my second trip to Europe, with him and his wife, remaining there for a year of travel and study.

On my return, and the end of that project, I got a position on the editorial staff of the *Reader's Digest,* which I held until I met and married my husband. He was a Standard Oil man, home on leave from their offices in India. For nine years I lived in India—all too short a time to study and see and enjoy that wonderful land—but years which I used to the best of my powers. We lived in Calcutta, Bengal, but my husband occasionally toured the whole of India, Burma, and Ceylon, to visit his territory—a rare opportunity for one so travel mad as I. Furloughs to America gave us the chance, which we eagerly took, of exploring the Far East and Europe before the destruction of World War II. And on our local holidays it was our delight to go on treks into the Himalayas. *Daughter of the Mountains* grew out of one of these treks into Tibet, and my meeting there a little girl and her dog.

In 1942 we were returned to America, where my husband bought a farm near his birthplace, Ithaca, New York. Different as this Finger Lake farm is from India, we have given it an Indian name—*Nahananda,* or Great Happiness. And there we now live, close enough to Cornell University to inquire into whatever we wish to learn, absorbed in watching gardens grow, and enjoying the lives of chickens and pigs, dogs and cats and cows. The best of having a farm in the north is that when nature puts it to sleep in the winter, we can take a long holiday!

* * *

Mrs. Rankin's *Daughter of the Mountains* won a prize in the New York *Herald Tribune* Spring Book Festival in 1948. Her second book, *Gentling of Jonathan* was published by Viking a year before her death in 1951.

Laura Cooper Rendina
1902-
AUTHOR OF
Roommates; Summer for Two; My Love for One; Lolly Touchberry; Etc.

"HAS she any children?" the editor asked, when I submitted my first manuscript, and that sounded very funny to me, because without children how could I have written my story? If it weren't for my five children

Rendina: *RENN din uh*

and our adventures as a family, I would never have become a writer at all. So they do come first in any story of my life.

I had always loved to write. At seven years I was turning out short stories; I gave three of them to my mother for her birthday, tied up in blue ribbon. The next year I lost my mother. My father had died when I was a baby, and now my family life was broken up. I went to live with friends of my mother. I was to spend a number of my growing-up years in Northampton, Massachusetts, where I was born, the rest of them in the Boston suburbs. During my high school years I was lucky to live in Cambridge, to go to Cambridge Latin School with its fine teachers. As a sophomore I first saw my printed work in the school magazine, encouraged to submit it by my English teacher, a small, ugly, crippled man who blazed enthusiasm. A year later I was chosen head editor of the magazine, and my career seemed to have begun.

But after two years at Smith College I married, and three babies kept me too busy to write. Then my husband died and I took my three tiny children to Europe. We spent much of the 1930's abroad—in England, in North Africa, and in Italy—although home was in the little village of Wayland, Massachusetts. In Capri, where at one time and another we have spent several delightful years, I met and married Mario Rendina, an artist.

The war came, and no more traveling. My family increased by two babies. The older children were teen-agers. During all the years I had done no real writing but now I began—because at last I had something to say. More than enough, really. Adolescence was popping around me like the breakfast cereal. As most teen-agers know, those years are hard on all members of the family, not just themselves. My daughter Judy, in particular, interested me, fascinated me, and annoyed me. I admired her and could barely live with her. So as a safety valve I began writing—about a girl something like Judy in a family somewhat like ours, growing up in a New England village.

Although my first three are grown up with children of their own, I'm still writing about teen-agers. And living with them. My last two children are furnishing plenty of ma-

LAURA COOPER RENDINA

terial for new books. But the locale has changed. After the war we moved to Sarasota, Florida. Our cottage was on the Gulf of Mexico until, one stormy night in 1950, it was *in* the Gulf of Mexico. So, the way people do here, we picked it off its pilings and moved it a block inland. The gulls and pelicans still fly over, but we can no longer watch the porpoises from our front windows. We spend summers in New England, and although the children love this circus city with its water sports and open-air life, they are planning on college in the North.

Marion Renick

1905-

AUTHOR OF

Young Mr. Football; Seven Simpsons on Six Bikes; The Heart for Baseball; Swimming Fever; Etc.

Autobiographical sketch of Marion Renick:

EVER since I can remember, I have been excited about this world around us. At the age of five I was trying to express my excitement in words because I was excited about them too. I started to school in Springfield, Ohio, where I was born and grew up, and as soon as I could spell I began recording in passionate childish rhyme everything of personal significance, such as the first spring beauties, falling leaves, Easter baskets, and summers on the Great Lakes.

MARION RENICK

Through my mother's fond treachery those verses sometimes appeared in our morning paper with the invariable introduction: "From the pen of little Miss Marion Comfort Lewis, Springfield's youngest writer. . . ." Whenever this happened I lost status with my playmates, most of whom were of the age and sex to regard the ball bat as more important than the pen. Many a time little Miss Marion Comfort Lewis had to win back acceptance among her peers by proving she was no effete intellectual but still a good man in the clutch.

In high school I edited the school paper and thus had my first enchanting whiff of printer's ink. I have been under the spell of deadlines ever since. I went to Wittenberg College and did part-time reporting on a daily paper, becoming editor of the home-makers' page in my senior year. After graduation and a few years in Community Chest publicity, I married James Renick, a sports writer for the Associated Press. We were divorced later, but for thirteen years we attended most of the major Midwest, and many national, sports events. During that period I spent a great deal of time listening to the fascinating shoptalk of famous coaches, athletes, and sports writers, some of whom have been kind enough to continue over the years as sources of research material for my books. Several of the football coaches suggested I write some authentic instructions

for younger boys. The result was *Tommy Carries the Ball,* published in 1940 by Charles Scribner's Sons. The book was brought out in both my name and my husband's, because in those days nobody would have bought a football story authored by a woman. In a few years the situation changed and my books were published in my name alone.

After World War II, I became an editor of *My Weekly Reader,* a newspaper used in many American schools. Later I went into education by radio and television at Ohio State University, where I also occasionally teach a journalism class.

I live in a neighborhood full of boys and girls, a few of whom are perennially at the right age to read my books. In summer this group sometimes plays beneath my work-room window, calling up to me above the clatter of my typewriter, "Haven't you finished that chapter yet?" When I do finish the chapter and read it to them, I always suspect they hear nothing but their own names, which I often use in my stories. Yet I keep hoping that they and all other boys and girls will somehow find and take into their own lives the lessons of courage, perseverance, self-mastery, and good will that are to be learned from sports.

Keith Robertson

1914

AUTHOR OF
Ticktock and Jim; Outlaws of the Sourland; Wreck of the Saginaw; The Pilgrim Goose; Etc.

Autobiographical sketch of Keith Robertson:

I CAN truly say that I grew up in the Midwest. I was born in Iowa but my father had wanderlust. At various times I lived in Minnesota, Kansas, Wisconsin, Oklahoma, Missouri, and Iowa. During most of these early years I lived on a farm or in a small town in a farming community. My first book, *Ticktock and Jim,* is a reasonably accurate picture of my life on a Missouri farm.

Writing interested me at an early age and throughout high school I sent short stories to all the national magazines. The only ones that were ever printed were in our high

KEITH ROBERTSON

school paper. No doubt I inherited my father's wanderlust and when I graduated from high school in 1931, I joined the Navy. I was a radioman on a battleship for two years and then I went to the United States Naval Academy at Annapolis. After graduating, I returned to civilian life for several years and worked as a refrigeration engineer. I was writing all this time but with little success.

From 1941 until late in 1945 I was in the Navy again. I spent most of the war aboard destroyers, both in the Atlantic and the Pacific. There was often excitement but more often there were long days at sea when there was little to do but watch the ocean and think. I decided that once the war was over I would do what I had always wanted to do—write. Surprisingly enough, I was able to carry out my plans.

For the first two years after the war, I worked for a publishing firm which publishes many fine books for children. This was fortunate because I rediscovered the world of books for young people. I wrote my first book for children and when it was accepted I quit my job. I have done nothing but write since.

I live on a farm near Hopewell, New Jersey. My wife runs an old- and rare-book business, and naturally I love books. The house and several barns are filled and each year there are more. Building bookshelves is

my second occupation. I have three children, two girls and one boy, and the entire family loves animals. As a result, we are almost as surrounded by animals as books. At the moment we have sheep, horses, dogs, cats, goats, rabbits, ducks, geese, chickens, and parakeets.

We live in a lovely section of New Jersey with wooded hills and tumbling streams. Although our farm is on the edge of town, deer frequently come up to our barnyard. Naturally a number of my books have been about this area.

Ann Roos

AUTHOR OF
Man of Molokai; The Royal Road

Autobiographical sketch of Ann Roos:

I WAS born in Brooklyn, New York, in an old-fashioned, three-story-and-basement brick house with a back garden full of peach trees. These so titillated my parents' love for the country that we moved to Long Island before I could walk.

In my childhood I was probably the most omnivorous reader of all time, due partly to the fact that my baseball pitching skill was below par in our neighborhood and partly because the new branch public library was located in one wing of our village schoolhouse and its delicious smell of leather and furniture polish and glue mixed with the librarian's Parma violet sachet was irresistible. All of this led to irremediable difficulties with arithmetic and to gold-rimmed eyeglasses at the age of ten.

Later it seemed important to be the best jackknife diver in Girl Scout camp, so reading took a slump while I devoted myself to preparing for the life of a pioneer woman, which lay, I hoped, just around the corner. A new world dawned with college. I became versed in the study of dramatic art, with just enough science, sociology and mathematics to sneak through to an arts degree. History courses were a necessary nuisance, and I dreamed through the classes, a fact which appalled me many years later when the whole panorama of history burst on me like a bomb, through the simple expedient of traveling all over the United States in the course of my job.

Rappoport Studios

ANN ROOS

houses, on shipboard and in odds and ends of time in Girl Scout camps. Reference books were lugged in an extra suitcase, often got rained upon and ended up dog-eared and dilapidated. Until the book reached its latter stages, there rarely was a time when the complete manuscript was together, bits of it having been parked here and there in luggage or in the houses of tolerant friends.

So now I feel that I am leading a double life. One half of me is a writer whose task it is to make great figures of the past come alive for boys and girls of the nineteen sixties. The other half is a busy executive in the International Division of the Girl Scouts of the U.S.A., whose work is involved in international friendship through an exchange-of-persons program between American girls and those from countries all over the world. So far I haven't felt schizophrenic because inspiration for the first has so often grown out of the second.

But my first book-length writing project had nothing to do with the history of our country. I had become interested in Father Damien through a biography for adults, and, since my work for some years had been with girls' activities, I decided to try to write a book about this inspiring man which might appeal to young people. The result was *Man of Molokai*, the life story of a Belgian boy, Joseph de Veuster, who was to become one of the greatest humanitarians of all time, Father Damien of Molokai, one of the Hawaiian Islands.

The Royal Road began to stir in my mind one sunny afternoon in 1935 when I sat on a prickly hill behind San Carlos Mission in Carmel and tried to translate it into water color. But it wasn't until ten years and one book later—*Man of Molokai*, of course—that the idea took sufficient form to send me scuttling on vacation to the Stanford University library. The books of Dr. Herbert Bolton were one more windfall and from that time on I itched for leisure to find a way to bring that glorious phase of the history of our country between the pages of a book that young America would want to read. The leisure never came but somehow the book, in the course of the next five years, got written.

Much of both books was written "on the run," as it were—on trains, in hotels, and in strange cities, on week ends in country

Constance Rourke

1885-1941

AUTHOR OF
Audubon; Davy Crockett; American Humor; Etc.

CONSTANCE Mayfield Rourke was born November 14, 1885, in Cleveland, but grew up in Grand Rapids, which was her home throughout her life. After graduating from Vassar, she taught there for a number of years, but left her post to go abroad for travel and study. She studied at the Sorbonne, and eventually returned to America for more travel and research.

Her best-known biographies are *Davy Crockett* and *Audubon*. Most of her work dealt with early American history, in which she was an undisputed authority. She brought new material and hitherto undisclosed facts to her books. Her *Troupers of the Gold Coast*, published in 1928, was the first study of the American theater in the California gold rush.

Miss Rourke had a genius for discovering new material in out-of-the-way places—diaries, almanacs, prints, and the like. She traveled the length and breadth of the West, doing what someone has called "living research." She talked to old-time lumberjacks, heard them sing songs and tell stories. She

CONSTANCE ROURKE

knew the men who had acted in the old minstrel shows, vaudeville actors, stagecoach drivers and miners of the West. She has been saluted as the foremost research scholar of the American frontier. Her *Trumpets of Jubilee*, published in 1927, was the social history of an epoch. Lewis Mumford called her *American Humor*, published in 1931, brilliant.

Although the number of her books is comparatively few, she wrote countless magazine articles on all phases of American folklore, literature, and art, and many book reviews. Her *Davy Crockett* was foreshadowed in *American Humor*, one critic felt, and Davy's own exuberance spills over into Miss Rourke's book. She brought him to life some twenty years before the mania for this frontiersman swept America's small fry in the late 1950's.

Julia L. Sauer

1891-

AUTHOR OF

Mike's House; The Light at Tern Rock; Fog Magic; Radio Roads to Reading; Etc.

Autobiographical sketch of Julia L. Sauer:

ROCHESTER, New York, has always been my home. Here I was born, went to grammar and high school and to the University of Rochester. If our city had pro-

vided a library school I should undoubtedly have gone to it but since there was none nearer than Albany I succeeded in eluding my family and getting all of two hundred miles away from home for one year at the New York State Library School.

Although I was an only child I cannot remember being a lonely one. Our house had no porches, only "stoops." It dwindled away at the back in a series of steps, and over a one-story addition my father built a great platform the width of the house, railed in and with a canvas roof. It lacked only secrecy to be the tree house every child dreams of but it offered all the desirable hazards and it served the entire neighborhood. Here through the long hot summer afternoons we read everything we could get out hands on—current and bound volumes of *St. Nicholas*, the Alcotts, the Stoddards, and Joel Chandler Harris. Then, in the absence of a public library, we fell back on Dickens, *Jane Eyre, Scottish Chiefs*, and all the other treasures our homes could provide. My enjoyment of children's books as such came only after I was a children's librarian. At that time in our lives none of my "best friends" nor I ever considered any future except authorship. Jo March in her attic wanted to be an author so naturally *we* had no choice. Jo had decided it for us too.

The Rochester Public Library was established while I was in college. It offered an unexpected new career, and one with some pioneer glamour, to those who looked upon teaching reluctantly. During my senior year I worked in the library's first children's room and knew almost instantly that I wanted to be a children's librarian. Except for one hectic year as playground librarian and storyteller, I have held no position outside of the Rochester Public Library and I am still there.

The tree house of childhood dreams has been replaced by a small vacation cabin on the top of North Mountain in Nova Scotia, where each spruce tree has individuality and wears its fog with a difference. Fundy roars at its back. The view from the front is across St. Mary's Bay to the French shore where the windows of the cathedral at St. Bernard's are truly golden in the afternoon sun.

Nova Scotia is a land where sea and rocks and spruces and fog are woven together to

JULIA L. SAUER

make magic. My first story came into being almost without effort. It was appropriate that it should be called *Fog Magic* because into it went all the love and feeling for a very special place and its people that has brought a kind of continuing magic to me.

Miriam Schlein

1926-

AUTHOR OF

Fast Is Not a Ladybug; Big Talk; Elephant Herd; Little Rabbit, the High Jumper; Etc.

Autobiographical sketch of Miriam Schlein:

I WAS born and grew up in Brooklyn, New York, where I followed the usual childhood pursuits—roller skating, riding about on my bicycle, sledding in Prospect Park in winter, and playing city games—hopscotch, jump rope, and the like.

There were never any writers in our family. But there was always a lot of reading going on, and I was included in this activity when I was old enough to be read to. I remember how I loved the Doctor Dolittle books, with the amiable doctor and his entourage of talking animals. Then too, my literary teeth were cut on Grimm and Andersen's fairy tales. No other book in the Harvard Classics became so dog-eared as that one called *Folklore and Fable*.

I never did specifically dare to say to myself, "I want to become a writer." But as I got older, I did know I would like my work to have something to do with books. I attended Brooklyn College, where for a short vigorous period I was a member of the girls' swimming team. I was diver for the team. I practiced and practiced, but I never seemed to improve. Finally I got tired of catapulting through the air, landing smack on my back half of the time.

I spent some time on the college newspaper, but then, as now, I did not care for reporting. Rather than write about things that happen without, I like to write about ideas that come from within. I received my bachelor of arts degree in English and psychology.

After that, I had a fair miscellany of jobs —always having to do vaguely with writing. Secretary to a magazine publisher; assistant in a radio continuity department. Then I got a job writing advertising copy for a local Sears, Roebuck. How proud I was of my first few ads—for at last I was earning my living by *writing!* I felt justified in buying a new typewriter—at Sears, of course—and kept on writing stories and poems in the evenings. In six months I was not quite so keen on what I had to write about—camisoles, birdbaths, refrigerators, and the like.

I then took a job as secretary to the editor of a juvenile publishing house. No disenchantment here. After three years of working hard, and reading all the children's books I could lay my hands on, my enthusiasm for the field, my appreciation of its worth, was even greater. My spare-time writing was now confined to juvenile manuscripts. I didn't sell anything; but still, in 1951, I decided to strike out on my own. I stayed home, and wrote, and submitted stories, eliciting what could not be called wild enthusiasm on the part of any editor. Doggedly I kept on. And lo, finally a completely unconventional manuscript of mine called *Shapes* caught the eye of the editors at William R. Scott. That was the beginning, more than ten years ago. Now, my enthusiasm and devotion to this kind of writing is as strong as ever.

At present I live in New York City with my husband, Harvey Weiss, the sculptor, who is also author and illustrator of *Clay,*

MIRIAM SCHLEIN

Wood and Wire, and a number of other children's books. We both enjoy tennis, skiing, sailing, and being outdoors in general. We have a daughter, Elizabeth, born in April 1957.

Herman Schneider

1905-

AUTHOR OF
Everyday Weather and How It Works

CO-AUTHOR OF
How Your Body Works; Science Fun with Milk Cartons; You Among the Stars; Etc.

Autobiographical sketch of Herman Schneider:

MAKE up your mind what you want to do and then stick to it.

I suppose this is good advice, but what if you can't make up your mind? Ever since I can remember, I've wanted to do almost everything I saw anyone else doing. In the little village in Poland where I was born I saw a coachman driving a shiny blue carriage pulled by four proud prancing horses. This was surely the most glamorous job in the world! Then on the steamship to America I watched the radio operator working at his clicking, flashing machines and changed my mind. Then, in New York City, I envied a fireman skillfully steering a hook-and-ladder truck through a narrow street. . . .

There were many other changes, but finally in the eighth grade the field narrowed down to a mere three: I would be a scientist, or a teacher, or a writer. I managed to hold on to these ambitions all through high school. In college I worked my way through, sometimes by writing greeting card verses and short stories, sometimes by teaching English to foreigners, sometimes by repairing cars and installing electric wiring.

Finally I became a teacher—first in elementary school, then in junior and senior high school. Most of the time I taught science—biology, general science, physics, chemistry, photography, meteorology, and aviation theory among others.

During this period I took up flying and had a glorious accident. I came gliding in for a landing—just as another airplane was taxiing up the runway, where it had no business to be. The result was a splendid crash, two utterly demolished airplanes, and a three-week stay in the hospital, during which time I was wrapped up like a mummy. I'm still alive, whole, and as fond as ever of flying.

To get back to careers—as a result of teaching science I became convinced of the need for a different kind of science book: one that dealt with the everyday experiences of children, with easy, simple experiments that could be done with ordinary materials such as tin cans, tea kettles, and milk cartons. My wife, Nina (yes, I'm married, with two sons and two daughters), and I set to work on *Let's Find Out*, which was published in 1946. Since then we have written over twenty children's books, six teachers' manuals, and dozens of articles for *American Home, Parents' Magazine, Life*, and other magazines. The books have been translated into Japanese, Arabic, Swedish, French, and about a dozen more languages.

During this time I became supervisor of science for the New York City elementary schools. This was very interesting work, but after several years I decided to spend my full time at writing. Still, I couldn't stay away from teaching altogether, so at present I give two courses on methods of teaching science at the City College of New York. In between the writing and teaching I make flying trips (*not* in my own plane!) to various parts of the country, to lecture on science teaching. My family and I also spent a fascinating six-month vacation in a little

HERMAN SCHNEIDER

Indian village in Mexico, where we dug for mastodon fossils, explored extinct volcanoes, and rode burros.

As you can see, I never did make up my mind as to whether I would choose teaching, writing, or science as a career. I chose all three!

Nina Schneider

1913-

AUTHOR OF

David Comes Home—a Hanukkah Story of Today; While Susie Sleeps; Hercules, the Gentle Giant; Etc.

CO-AUTHOR OF

Let's Find Out; Etc.

Autobiographical sketch of Nina Schneider:

A BIG ship, small boats rocking in the harbor, tugs hooting, a noisy confusion of people, and the sharp smell, color and taste of an orange. These are my first memories of arriving in New York from Belgium where I was born on January 29, 1913. My family came to New York when I was not quite two years old, and I have lived in or near this city ever since. I've gone to school there, been married, and raised a family there.

Although I have traveled in the United States, Europe, Mexico, and other parts of the world, I secretly feel that Central Park is my home view. I know its cherry trees in bloom, rowboats on its crowded lake, Belvedere Tower like a play castle, ragged Shakespeare garden, the wonderful museums on its east and west sides, its shaded flat rocks on which I have sat reading all through balmy afternoons, glancing up to watch its picture-book riders cantering by on gleaming brown horses. I have laughed at the honking wet seals by myself, with friends, and then over the years with each of our four children. The zoo café terrace on a sunny spring afternoon is to me one of the most intimate places in the world.

As a child, I enjoyed other things about New York, although life was not filled with the kind of amusements our children enjoy today. There was a rare ride on the elevated train, a visit to the Battery Aquarium, or a day in Bronx Park. But I was a shy and lonely child and I spent most of my free time reading. I trudged back and forth from the library like a loaded shaggy pony. Yet I was quite grown-up, in my teens, before I thought of a book as written by *a* real person. I had the impression that a book happened, like a child or a storm. To me, *Jane Eyre* appeared on earth one day as a giant or a talking toad or a princess in a secret garden might appear. Though I have worked on quite a number of books since then, some of that fairy-tale feeling is with me. When I begin to write anything, I still feel the need for fairy godmothers and magical powers.

I began writing in high school, some poetry and play reviews for the high school paper. I enjoyed working on the paper and loved the companionship it brought, but I was almost permanently discouraged from writing by an acid tongued grade adviser, whose criticism was harsher and more personal than I could bear. After his sneers I kept only scraps of paper notes.

After high school I was married and it was not until I went back to college, when my first child was four years old, that I dared to write again. It was perhaps just that my first college instructor was lavishly encouraging. I wrote short stories which appeared in the college publication, and later I became editor of the magazine.

Then I grew tired of repeating my young son's favorite story and I wrote it down. This became *Hercules, the Gentle Giant*, which was a selection of the Junior Literary Guild. This was very encouraging, of course.

NINA SCHNEIDER

With my husband, Herman Schneider, I have collaborated on more than twenty science books, among them *Let's Find Out; You Among the Stars; Rocks, Rivers & the Changing Earth;* and many others. I have been an editor, librarian, and teacher, and so I have always had the pleasure of being with books in some close way. I have written other children's stories, and for my deepest pleasure I try to write poetry. I would like to be magical enough, someday, to write some very good things.

Jackson V. Scholz

1897-

AUTHOR OF

Man in a Cage; Base Burglar; End Zone; One-Man Team; Etc.

Autobiographical sketch of Jackson V. Scholz:

BUCHANAN, a small town in southern Michigan, was my birthplace. I lived there long enough to complete the first year of grammar school, after which my schooling was continued in Boulder, Colorado, Los Angeles, and St. Louis. The University of Missouri was handy at this stage, so I matriculated there and was graduated in due time, a process interrupted for a while by World War I. I managed to get my wings as a naval aviator but saw no active service.

I suffered the common ailment of collegiate indecision in the choice of a career. I decided on agriculture for some silly reason and was soon disillusioned by the farm work required of me in summers. Cows and crops, I found, were not for me. I switched to journalism, hoping I might find a niche in advertising.

It was discovered, meanwhile, that I was a pretty good sprinter. I preferred football or baseball as a personal sport but I was too small for the former and too fumble-fingered for the latter. So I stuck to the cinders and became a member of the 1920 Olympic team which was sent to the games in Antwerp. I placed fourth in the hundred meters and was on the winning sprint relay team.

On my return to this country I tried vainly to sell real estate in Detroit, and later to become interested in the hosiery business in New York. My degree in journalism from the University of Missouri finally landed me a job with the United Press. I was a most inadequate newsman and they had to fire me.

While this was going on I learned that one of my fraternity brothers had sold his first short story. I reasoned that if he could I could, so I wrote one and sold it too. Then came the blizzard of rejection slips. They would have snowed me under had I not stumbled on the chance to ghostwrite a serialized autobiography for a famous athlete, Mel Sheppard. It put me in the writing business for keeps, mostly pulp stuff, sport stories, flying stories, and westerns.

During this period I competed on two more Olympic teams. In Paris, 1924, I won the two-hundred meters and finished second in the hundred meters. In Amsterdam, 1928, I placed fourth in the two-hundred meters, making me the only sprinter who has reached the finals in three Olympics. In those days, as at present, athletes were in demand throughout the world. I was invited to many European countries as well as to New Zealand and Japan for exhibition competition.

When the pulp magazines began to fold, I started writing sport books for boys, discovering finally the field of work that pleased me best. I like to believe it is a constructive field, because my own experience in ath-

Scholz: SHOALS

JACKSON V. SCHOLZ

letics has convinced me that the moral and physical benefits are virtually unlimited. I like to believe that, in some small way, I can pass on what I have learned. If I am able to achieve this, I shall be happy.

Frank Schoonover

1877-

ILLUSTRATOR OF

Rolling Wheels; Rifles for Washington; Roland the Warrior; Boy Captive of Old Deerfield; Etc.

Autobiographical sketch of Frank Earle Schoonover:

I WAS born August 19, 1877, in Oxford, New Jersey, a mining town. The family eventually settled in Trenton, New Jersey, about two blocks from the Delaware River. I had a boat and some minnow nets and traps. My first business venture was catching minnows and selling them alive to bass fishermen. Part of each summer I spent with my grandmother, who lived in Bushkill, Pike County, Pennsylvania. I spent most of my time along a stream, building tiny raceways and small water wheels. I also built a flat-bottomed boat that leaked.

My grandmother kept asking what I was going to do when I grew up. I told her I was not sure but I would do something that had to do with streams and trees. I really thought I would be a builder of bridges. Of course I know now that this was the beginning of my painting pictures of bridges and trees and streams. I made pen-and-ink drawings and did pretty well with houses, barns, and little buildings but I could not manage trees at all. My father gave me help with the perspective business. We rigged up a pencil and notches and string. One end of the string was held in my mouth so that there was always the same distance from pencil to eye. A building could be two spaces high and a tree four or five; it really worked.

Back in Trenton I got some oil colors and started to paint. I kept on with pen and inks, copying all the Howard Pyle drawings I could find. I went to a preparatory school in Trenton and took entrance examinations for Princeton Theological Seminary. I lacked Greek but studied with a minister all summer, the rest of the time on the Delaware River, in my boat, sketching by day and copying Howard Pyle at night. In 1896, when I finished preparatory school, I was not very happy about going on to seminary. That fall I read about what Drexel Institute had to offer by way of illustration instruction—under Howard Pyle. To enter his class I had to submit original drawings. Mr. Pyle looked at them and said because of the creative thought in them he would admit me to his class, which I entered the day before Christmas, 1897. I won two summer scholarships at Drexel that permitted me to study under Howard Pyle at Chadd's Ford, Pennsylvania (1898, 1899). The second summer, two books were illustrated that Mr. Pyle secured for me, *A Jersey Boy in the Revolution* and *In the Hands of the Redcoats*, published by Houghton Mifflin of Boston.

Other books followed: a long serial for *Collier's, Cardigan,* by Robert W. Chambers, then a set of illustrations for *McClure's.* For *The Lane That Had No Turning,* by Sir Gilbert Parker, I went to Quebec and Cap Rouge. I lived in the latter place and made many sketches in colored crayon, Sir Gilbert approving them.

About this time the first great strike in the coal industry occurred. I lived in the home of one of the workers in Scranton, and made

FRANK SCHOONOVER

many drawings on the spot for *Children of the Coal Shadows*. I've illustrated books by Mary Raymond Shipman Andrews, Ellen Glasgow, and Henry Van Dyke. I also illustrated two of my own stories for *Scribner's Magazine*, "The Edge of the Wilderness," and "The Winter Harvesters."

In 1906 I went to Denver to get the story of Judge Ben B. Lindsey and his juvenile court. Then to Butte, Montana, for pictures of the fight for the Minnie Healey, a copper mine. I worked for *Century, Outing, Harper's Magazine, American*, and from 1908 the *Saturday Evening Post*. For Harper's I did pictures for Elsie Singmaster's story of the Pennsylvania Dutch, and for the same firm did a story about the women and girls who worked in the Scranton silk mills. Later, I assisted Mr. Pyle in painting a mural for the Hudson County Courthouse in Jersey City, New Jersey, of the Indians in canoes paddling out to sniff at the *Half Moon*. I joined with Rex Beach to illustrate his stories, and then one of my own, *In the Haunts of Jean LaFitte*, in 1910. I lived at a small village on the Bay of Barataria, Louisiana.

So all I have written and drawn goes back to the early days in Bushkill when my grandmother wanted to know just what I was going to do with myself. Woods, streams, bridges—they are all in my work.

Françoise Seignobosc

See *Françoise*

Millicent E. Selsam

1912-

AUTHOR OF
Play with Plants; Microbes at Work; All About Eggs and How They Change into Animals; See Through the Sea; Etc.

Autobiographical sketch of Millicent E. Selsam:

I WAS born and brought up in New York City and have never lived anywhere else. This often seems strange to my co-workers in the field of nature books. But I came to my interest in nature through the study of biology in high school and college. The field trips I took grew out of course work and were my first contact with the world of nature. Perhaps this is one reason why I so strongly try to interest very young people in the subject now. I feel their lives will be richer and fuller if they become and stay curious about the world around us.

I took a B.A. degree at Brooklyn College as a major in biology. All this time I was interested in dancing and the theater and therefore was not as enthusiastic as I might have been when I was offered a teaching fellowship at the college. While I taught there, I continued with graduate work at Columbia University. I completed an M.A. degree in botany, and did everything for the Ph.D. degree but write the dissertation. After the fellowship ended, I taught biology in New York City high schools for quite a number of years. But my hankering for the theater finally exploded in my trying for and getting a job as assistant stage manager in the Broadway show *Lute Song*, in which Mary Martin starred. My flier into show business convinced me that I was not for it, and I settled down to finding some avenue other than teaching in which I could use my knowledge of biology. The writing of children's books on the subject seemed the perfect idea. Since then I have written some sixteen books on natural science subjects. A lot of the books include experiments with plants. I do many of these on sunny window sills in my New York apartment. But lots of them require an outdoor garden. In

MILLICENT E. SELSAM

order to have one, I have turned the back of a Fire Island sand dune into fertile ground. For the purpose I have imported bales of manure and peat moss, collected fish off the beach and buried them in the sand, and gathered seaweed from the shores of the bay. Flowers grew and flourished, but once in a while, a strong wind would blow in from the ocean and turn everything brown. Now we have a fine windbreak, and I no longer shudder when the strong winds blow.

I have an enduring love for the sea, and a great admiration for Rachel Carson, who so beautifully described it in *The Sea Around Us*. The best compliment I've ever received in a review is one in which it said that I "was leading the children as Rachel Carson has led their elders to observe and to understand."

Maurice Sendak

1928-

AUTHOR AND ILLUSTRATOR OF
Kenny's Window; Very Far Away
ILLUSTRATOR OF
The Wheel on the School; The Giant Story; Etc.

Autobiographical sketch of Maurice Sendak:

PAPA gave us two plums apiece and sent us out to play—and then you were born." That is the story of my birth, as told to me by my sister and brother. They re-

member the plums very clearly—but me hardly at all. The date was June 10, 1928. The place—Brooklyn, New York. I think that four juicy plums is perhaps too high a price to pay for a new squalling little brother. They still rejoice in telling me what a little nuisance I was.

I know just what they mean. I remember tagging after an angry sister. I remember copying with all my might every picture my brother drew (and I remember signing my name to his drawings, and presenting them at school as my work). Perhaps it was hard on them, but I feel that all the "youngest of the world" will be on my side—it is so hard being the littlest. It's good too. Copying my brother's pictures was a way of fighting, I suppose—a way of showing I was as good as the "big people" all around me. It also (and this is the best) started me drawing at a very early age—loving pictures and books with a child's boundless passion.

And then there was my father. He had the rare gift of storytelling. He disliked reading us stories; he much preferred making them up. And it was marvelous—listening to him weave and mold magic words out of thin air.

I knew I wanted to be a writer and illustrator before I even went to school. I set my goal at the age of four or five and happily reached it. I practically drew my way through school—worked for *All American Comics* after school (drawing backgrounds for *Mutt and Jeff*) and illustrated my first book in high school, for my biology teacher, called *Atomics for the Millions*. I didn't illustrate any books for four years after graduation. I went to the Art Students League and worked in window display (F. A. O. Schwarz toy shop).

Then came the happiest time of my life. I did my first children's book for Harper & Brothers. It was Marcel Aymé's *Wonderful Farm*. Then came *A Hole Is To Dig*, by Ruth Krauss, and other Krauss books. Working with Ruth Krauss has been an inspiration. I learned more than how to illustrate a book—I learned the *meaning* of the book, the sense of the book, how text and pictures work *with* each other and not against.

After some years of illustrating, I finally wrote and illustrated my own book, *Kenny's Window*, and in 1957 my second, *Very Far*

MAURICE SENDAK

Away. I have also collaborated with Meindert DeJong, and it has been a tremendous thrill working with such a sincere and fervent artist. One of our books was *The Wheel on the School.* Other books are *I'll Be You and You Be Me,* by Ruth Krauss, *The Giant Story,* by Beatrice Schenk de Regniers, and *The Happy Rain,* by Jack Sendak, my brother.

Dr. Seuss

1904-

Author and Illustrator of
And To Think That I Saw It on Mulberry Street; The Cat in the Hat; How the Grinch Stole Christmas; Sleep Book; Etc.

THEODOR Seuss Geisel, better known as Dr. Seuss, in 1962 celebrated his twenty-fifth anniversary as an author-illustrator, having produced nearly two dozen books for children, all of them enormously popular. Written in lively verse, they are illustrated with broadly fanciful drawings, mostly of imaginary animals.

Mr. Geisel was born on March 2, 1904, in Springfield, Massachusetts, where his German ancestors had settled and where his father later became the superintendent of parks—this latter, unfortunately, not until the young Geisel had grown up. Mr. Geisel attended Dartmouth College, where he edited the college humor magazine, contributing many cartoons with bizarre animals as subjects. After his graduation in 1925, he became a graduate student at Oxford University. There he met a young woman who had planned to be a teacher, Helen Palmer, and they were married in 1927. She encouraged him to follow his artistic bent.

When Mr. Geisel sold a cartoon to the *Saturday Evening Post,* he signed it "Dr. Seuss," deciding to save his real name for more serious work. Very soon he was using his new name often. One of his cartoons, concerning an insecticide named Flit, caught the eye of its manufacturer's advertising man. That began Mr. Geisel's long association with the Standard Oil Company of New Jersey and also was the beginning of the catch phrase of the era "Quick, Henry, the Flit."

In 1937 Vanguard Press published Mr. Geisel's first book for children, *And To Think That I Saw It on Mulberry Street.* This was followed by *The 500 Hats of Bartholomew Cubbins,* and many other titles, all received with joy by boys and girls and their parents. With the advent of World War II, however, Mr. Geisel turned to drawing editorial cartoons and later became a lieutenant colonel in the Army Signal Corps. He also did publicity work for numerous Government agencies, including the Treasury Department. He was awarded the Legion of Merit for the educational films he wrote and directed during this period.

After the war, Mr. Geisel continued writing films for several years. With his wife he wrote a screenplay about the rise of the Japanese war lords, *Design for Death.* This won an Academy Award in 1947. His most famous film was *Gerald McBoing-Boing,* which won an Academy Award for the best motion picture cartoon of 1950.

Mr. Geisel's greatest success was still to come. In 1957 Random House, which has been his publisher since his third book, published *The Cat in the Hat.* Mr. Geisel says that he wrote it because of an article in *Life* by John Hersey, objecting to the supplementary readers used in schools. He thought it would take a week or two to write; it took a year and a half. This book launched not only a new venture, Beginner Books, but started a new trend in children's books. These books are written expressly for the child who is just beginning to read. To be able to read a Beginner Book gives him a

Seuss: *rhymes with "moose"*

DR. SEUSS

sense of having achieved a goal. All of a sudden reading becomes wonderful, a marvelous thing to do! Mr. Geisel, who besides writing several more books in this series is one of its editors, says that he has written as many as twenty versions of a Beginner Book before he is satisfied. All of his Beginner Books have not less than eleven drafts, some of them more.

In 1955 Dartmouth College awarded Mr. Geisel the honorary degree of doctor of human letters, as the "creator of fanciful beasts" who has "stood as St. George between a generation of exhausted parents and the demon dragon of unexhausted children on a rainy day."

The Geisels live on a mountaintop in La Jolla, California, where Mr. Geisel works, although they make frequent trips to New York to oversee their Beginner Books.

Ernest Shepard

1879-

ILLUSTRATOR OF
The Wind in the Willows; When We Were Very Young; At the Back of the North Wind; Winnie the Pooh; Etc.

Autobiographical sketch of Ernest Shepard:

I WAS born on December 10, 1879, at Number 55 Springfield Road, St. John's Wood, London. My father was an archi-tect. My mother was the daughter of William Lee, R.W.S., the water-color painter. I was the youngest of our family and, with my sister, Ethel, and my brother, Cyril, went to school at the Church of England School in Baker Street. We moved house to Kent Terrace, Regents Park, when I was about four years old. It was there that my mother died in 1890. I was always fond of drawing and was encouraged by my father. My pictures were mostly battle scenes.

In 1891 we moved to a house in Hammersmith and lived there for seven years, moving in 1898 to a house at Blackheath, near Greenwich. My brother and I studied at St. Paul's School, as day boys, and I left there at the age of sixteen to take up the study of art. I spent a year at Heatherleys Art School and then won a scholarship at the Royal Academy Schools. There I met Florence Chaplin to whom I became engaged; she was also studying painting. My father died in 1903 and we were left very poorly off.

I exhibited my first painting, a portrait of my sister, at the Royal Academy in 1902 and two years later was fortunate enough to sell a picture in the exhibition. My fiancée was, at this time, commissioned to paint a large mural in the nurses' home of Guy's Hospital. On the strength of our united earnings we were married in September 1904. We lived in a tiny cottage at Shamley Green, Guildford, and there my son was born in 1907, and my daughter, Mary, in 1909.

In 1906 I had my first drawing accepted by *Punch* and worked at oil painting and black and white, exhibiting at the Royal Academy and the Paris Salon. During the First World War I was given a commission in the Royal Artillery and served through the battles of the Somme, Arras and third Ypres and finally went to Italy, finishing my service there (Major, M.C.) in 1919. My brother was killed in 1916, at the battle of the Somme.

On returning home I resumed work for *Punch* and also for *The Sketch*, and was elected to the *Punch* "round table" in 1921. In 1924 I was commissioned to illustrate *When We Were Very Young*, by A. A. Milne. This was followed by *Winnie the Pooh, Now We Are Six*, and *The House at Pooh Corner*, by the same author.

ERNEST SHEPARD

In 1927 my wife died and I moved, with my son and daughter, to a house on Longdown, Guildford. During the following years I illustrated *Everybody's Pepys* and *Everybody's Boswell*. Then followed *The Wind in the Willows*, by Kenneth Grahame; *Bevis*, by Richard Jeffreys; and the three books by Laurence Housman, *Victoria Regina*, *Golden Sovereign*, and *Gracious Majesty*, besides several others.

In 1932 my son, Graham, married Ann Gibbon and a daughter, Minette, was born in 1937. At the outbreak of World War II my son joined the Royal Naval Volunteer Reserve and served on a corvette. His ship was sunk with all hands in the Atlantic in 1943. My daughter married E. V. Knox, the editor of *Punch,* in 1937. In 1944 I married Norah Carrol, who was a nurse at St. Mary's Hospital and in 1955 we moved to my present home, Woodmancote, Lodsworth, Sussex.

Since the war, besides continuing my work for *Punch,* I have illustrated a number of books, including *The Silver Curlew* and *The Glass Slipper*, by Eleanor Farjeon; *The Brownies, and Other Stories, The Cuckoo Clock, Frogmorton, At the Back of the North Wind, The Secret Garden*, and others; also *Bertie's Escapade*, by Kenneth Grahame. I have written and illustrated a story of my own boyhood, *Drawn from Memory*.

Katherine B. Shippen
1892-

AUTHOR OF
Portals to the Past; New Found World; The Great Heritage; The Bright Design; Etc.

KATHERINE Shippen's ancestors came to America from Yorkshire, in 1669. One of her direct ancestors, Dr. William Shippen, was a member of the Continental Congress and one of the founders of the College of New Jersey, later Princeton University. She attended a school in Hoboken, New Jersey, that had been founded by men who escaped from Germany in the Revolution of 1848, and among other subjects, she studied German and French. At Bryn Mawr she earned her bachelor of arts degree and played water polo. She received her master's degree from Columbia University.

Miss Shippen's mother read to her and her sisters all of Dickens' novels, the works of Dante, and many other books. Later, she and her sisters traveled in Scotland and England, and on the Continent. They lived in China for a year, studying Chinese, and then returned home through the Indian Ocean and the Red Sea. Miss Shippen found there was nothing so thrilling as discovering new worlds. The title of her first book was *New Found World*, a story of six centuries in South America. *The Horn Book* called it "highly informative and much needed."

Miss Shippen tried social work but did not care for it. Then she taught history in Orange, New Jersey, and found she did not like that. She taught at the Brearley School in New York City for six years, and for another five she was headmistress of Miss Fine's School in Princeton, New Jersey. Then she became Curator of the Social Studies Division at the Brooklyn Children's Museum. She lives in a house in the country.

Miss Shippen's second book, *The Great Heritage*, was on the taming of the North American wilderness. Again she and her sisters traveled, and she gathered material in many states. Her other books have grown out of her talks to groups at the Brooklyn Children's Museum. *The Bright Design*, a book on electrical energy, was called "vivid and luminous" by *The Horn Book*. Its title

KATHERINE B. SHIPPEN

came from the lines in the old hymn by Cowper, "God moves in a mysterious way, His wonders to perform."

Katherine Shippen's contribution to children's literature has been significant. *The Booklist* called her *Miracle in Motion* a "brief but meaningful survey of three centuries of American industry." Her *Pool of Knowledge* was about the United Nations, and the New York *Herald Tribune* termed it "inspiring." Her 1963 book has a delightful title, *Portals to the Past*. It is the story of archaeology. She is at present working on a book about music.

Nicolas Sidjakov

1924-

ILLUSTRATOR OF
*The Friendly Beasts; Baboushka
and the Three Kings*

Autobiographical sketch of Nicolas Sidjakov:

I WAS born in Riga, Latvia, of Russian émigré parents. At the end of World War II, I was alone in Paris, my parents having died during the war. Here I studied painting at the École des Beaux Arts; later, free-lanced as an illustrator and designer, mainly for the reviving postwar French motion picture industry.

Then followed a period of exciting growth and experience for me—exploring and experimenting in the graphic arts. With Paris

as a hub, I traveled, lived and worked in Italy, Switzerland, and Germany. This also provided the opportunity to learn five languages. In Paris I met a young American girl attached to the United States Embassy, who soon became my wife. We came to the United States in 1954 and settled on the West Coast. We now live, with our young son, Nicolas, Jr., in Sausalito, California. My studio is in San Francisco. Here I have established myself as a designer in the field of advertising art. My award-winning work has been shown in exhibitions in New York Chicago, Los Angeles, Detroit and San Francisco.

My first children's book illustrations appeared in *The Friendly Beasts*, by Laura N. Baker, published in 1957. The book was very warmly received. The experience of creating the illustrations had been a stimulating one for me. I was eager to illustrate another picture book. The perfect opportunity came in the story, *Baboushka and the Three Kings*, by Ruth Robbins. With my Russian background, I was able to give full expression to this old Christmas folk tale. I visualized the old woman, Baboushka, as a warm and friendly person. The landscape, I felt, must reflect the primitive country, its strong colors, its early bold architecture. An appropriate type face had to be selected, which would lend dignity and a "special feeling" to the book. Finally, all of these elements, including endpapers and cover,

NICOLAS SIDJAKOV

Sidjakov: *SIDGE uh koff*

had to be blended into a book that would be a complete art form. The result of all this work can be seen in *Baboushka and the Three Kings,* which, I am happy to say, was awarded the Caldecott Medal in 1961.

Howard Simon

1903-

AUTHOR AND ILLUSTRATOR OF
*A Primer of Drawing for Adults;
500 Years of Art in Illustration*

ILLUSTRATOR OF
The Prince and the Pauper; Christmas Stories; Upstate, Downstate; Etc.

Autobiographical sketch of Howard Simon:

I HAVE lived in Paris and in New York City, homesteaded in Arkansas for six years and again returned from the Ozark wilderness to great cities. My wife, Mina Lewiton, and I now live in Dutchess County in New York State. In a modern city I am deeply aware of pulsating vitality. I cannot keep myself from translating its mood and color and excitement into pictorial form on canvas and drawings. But when I get into deep country and wilderness, I begin to feel that these—racing clouds and gnarled trunks of trees, swift-moving or leisurely animal life—these are the best. The truth is each place has its own enchantment for an artist.

I love to draw people because their faces and figures have the greatest range of emotional expression. I keep remembering the look of a tired man walking alone, for instance, or a running happy boy, or a woman bending concernedly over a child in a city street, or farm workers going home from the fields along a country road. These, too, are irresistible subject matter. I love animals, too, with their unconscious grace or swift power or delicacy of movement. I try to put into my pictures and drawings my feeling about all that I see, especially the particular characteristics of what I see, whether it is a place or object, human being or animal. In illustrating books, I try to learn the individualized quality of the young or old people, the places or things the author is describing, projecting these into what I hope are vibrant lines.

HOWARD SIMON

I cannot remember when I wasn't drawing. I felt the need, however, for formal instruction and went to the National Academy of Design in New York for drawing and then studied at the Académie Julien in Paris for five years.

I have illustrated over a hundred books but my favorite of them all is Mark Twain's *The Prince and the Pauper* as a story and as material which encourages the very best in an illustrator. I have also illustrated Dickens' *Christmas Stories.* Others are *Johnny Darling* and *Upstate, Downstate,* both of which are collections of folklore.

When I am not drawing I am painting, and when I am not doing either of these I love above all else the real satisfactions of gardening.

Marc Simont

1915-

ILLUSTRATOR OF
*The Happy Day; The 13 Clocks;
A Tree Is Nice; Etc.*

AUTHOR AND ILLUSTRATOR OF
Polly's Cats; Etc.

Autobiographical sketch of Marc Simont:

IT has always seemed inevitable that I should have become an artist. You could say it is a family trade, what with my father, two uncles, and a sister all artists.

Simont: *sih MONT (as in Vermont)*

I was born in Paris in 1915 of Spanish parents. At the end of World War I my father, who was an illustrator on the staff of *L'Illustration*, made a trip to the United States. It was to be an exploratory trip, but he was so impressed with what he saw he decided to bring the family over. In the meantime, the immigration laws had stiffened, and before the rest of the family could join him he had to become a citizen, which took five years. During that period my mother and two sisters and I moved to Barcelona to live with my grandfather. During the years when most American boys are making pictures of cowboys and Indians I was drawing bullfighters. It was also in that period that, while recuperating from chicken pox, I learned to write by going over and over the text of a picture book called *El Ginesillo*.

All through my school years, which were divided between both sides of the Atlantic, drawing remained my chief interest. I was always more concerned with what a teacher looked like than in what he said, which didn't do my algebra any good.

In 1932 my family moved back to Paris and at that time I made the study of art a full-time project. I attended various schools, among them the Académie Julien, Académie Ranson, and the André Lhote School. In 1935 I made the fledgling's traditional gesture of leaving the nest, which gesture was made easier by the fact that my father would continue to support me. I came back to the United States. But after being in New York for some time, during which I attended the National Academy of Design, this false-fronted gesture began to weigh on me. So, one day when I sold a portrait for thirty-five dollars I cabled my father to discontinue my allowance. In regard to the time that elapsed between this sale and my finally getting regular work I'll just say that I made some very good friends.

My regular work started with an illustration job of a collection of Scandinavian fairy tales by Ruth Bryan Owen. From that time on I have worked mostly with children's books, though I've also done portraits, caricatures, worked as an assistant mural painter, taught a little, illustrated for magazines, and while in service for the United States Army designed visual aids.

MARC SIMONT

It was while in the Army that I met and married a social worker named Sara Dalton. We have a teen-age son. Our home is in West Cornwall, Connecticut, though we are at present spending half our time in New York City.

Constance Lindsay Skinner

1882-1939

AUTHOR OF

Rob Roy: The Frontier Twins; Andy Breaks Trail; Silent Scot: Frontier Scout; Beaver, Kings and Cabins; Etc.

CONSTANCE Lindsay Skinner was born at a Hudson's Bay Trading Post on the Peace River, in northern British Columbia, five hundred miles from a railroad. Her father, Robert James Skinner, was a factor there, and her mother was Annie Lindsay Skinner, of the Lindsay family of Scotland. Her schooling was unorthodox. She was tutored and attended a private school in Vancouver. She said later her childhood was "spent among fur traders, Indians and mounted policemen."

When she was sixteen Miss Skinner was writing for newspapers in British Columbia. Two years later she was a reporter on the Los Angeles *Times*, then on the *Examiner* there, finally leaving the West Coast for Chicago and the *American*. Trekking farther east, she settled in New York and turned to writing books. Oddly enough, she began writing for *Boys' Life*, the Boy Scout magazine. One of her *Boys' Life* serials was *Silent Scot: Frontier Scout*. Helen Ferris, then editor of the *American Girl*, the Girl Scout magazine, believed in sharing the wealth, so she and Miss Skinner had lunch with the end in view of her writing for the *American Girl*. According to Miss Ferris, Miss Skinner looked her in the eye and asked, "Miss Ferris, do you actually want stories with guts in them?" Laughing, Miss Ferris said the more guts the better. So Miss Skinner wrote *Becky Landers,* a story of pioneer Kentucky, and other stories for girls. One of her heroines was the daughter of Daniel Boone. These books are credited with starting the trend to historical fiction for older girls.

What Miss Skinner will be best remembered for, perhaps, is the great Rivers of America series. She went with the idea to the publisher, Stanley Rinehart, and the series was inaugurated in 1937 with *The Kennebec*, by Robert P. Tristram Coffin. Miss Skinner served as the first editor of the series and she lived to see four of the Rivers books published. She was looking at the most recent book in the series, Carl Carmer's *The Hudson,* at the time of her death. There are fifty-two of these books, most of which are still in print, now under the banner of Holt, Rinehart and Winston. In 1961 that firm published a version of *The Hudson*, especially for young people, beginning a juvenile series taken from the original books.

The Constance Lindsay Skinner Medal was founded in 1939 by the Women's National Book Association, in memory of this great-hearted woman who did so much for American writers. Miss Skinner had been a vice president of the Association and had originated its teas for visiting bookwomen. Until her death the teas were held in her home. The medal, designed by Frances O'Brien Garfield, is really a bronze plaque that can be used as a paperweight. On one side is a head of Miss Skinner in bas-relief and on the reverse side is the legend "For merit in the realm of books," with a spray of laurel. The first medal was awarded to Anne Carroll Moore in 1940.

In appearance Miss Skinner was impressive. She was a large woman with a majestic carriage, lovely eyes, and a rich voice. She was literally awe-inspiring. Something she wrote over a quarter of a century ago is worth rereading:

"Your most splendid adventure, and mine, is that we belong to this land and have the right to uphold its ideals of character *now,* as the pioneers did in their different day."

Virginia Sorensen
1912-

AUTHOR OF
Curious Missie; Plain Girl; The House Next Door; Miracles on Maple Hill

Autobiographical sketch of Virginia Sorensen:

THOUGH I was born in Provo, Utah, most of my childhood was spent in a tiny town called Manti, which is in Sanpete Valley, almost exactly in the center of the state. My father, C. E. Eggertsen, was agent on a branch of the Denver and Rio Grande Railroad, and my mother was Helen ElDeva Blackett. There were six children in our family, three boys and three girls.

I can't imagine a better place to grow up than "down in Sanpete," as Utah people know it. The valley is called "Little Denmark" sometimes, because it was settled almost entirely by Danes a hundred years ago. They were good farmers and good carpenters, so we inherited a very substantial life in the valley; we also got from them a great love for celebrations or "festivals," our favorite being the 24th of July. That's Utah's birthday, the day Brigham Young first saw Salt Lake Valley and said, 'This is the place." The whole town helped with parades and programs and fireworks, and I've never seen them surpassed anywhere. In the hot summers we often climbed the mountains, which took us quickly into cool weather, or waded and paddled wherever there was a dam in the irrigation ditches that ran down both sides of every street.

My fifth-grade teacher, Miss Kunzler, provided my first real "literary thrill," telling the whole class one day that she suspected I might grow up to be a poet. Later, my best friend sent a poem of mine to a magazine in Salt Lake, and when I saw it in print my fate seemed sealed. I would be a writer and nothing else. In high school most of my activities had to do with newspapers and yearbooks and I was always being elected to be reporter of everything.

In 1933 I was married to Frederick Sorensen and we went off to Palo Alto, California, where we lived while he studied for his Ph.D. in English literature. I had finished my work at Brigham Young University by then, but missed the graduation ceremony; my diploma was sent to me in California—the very week my daughter Beth was born. Two years later my son was born, and I remember how surprised my friends were that I should spend most of my ten days in the hospital writing a three-act verse play. To me it seemed a good use of the time, perhaps because I had been enjoying an evening class in the writing of poetry. I often wonder if this is why my son wants to be a poet!

Very early, my husband and I decided that we might as well live and work in as many parts of the country as possible. So we have lived, teaching and writing, in Utah and California and Indiana and Michigan and Colorado and Alabama and Pennsylvania, in that order. Two Guggenheim Fellowships have taken me to Mexico and to Denmark. In Mexico I studied a tribe of Indians that has always fascinated me, and in Denmark I searched out the backgrounds of some of the people who had settled "Little Denmark."

I published my first novel for adults in 1942. It was not until the early 1950's, down in Alabama, that I began to think about writing for children. *Curious Missie* was published in 1953. Since then I have written two other books for children, both set in Pennsylvania, and one for teen-agers about how Utah came into the Union. One of the Pennsylvania stories, *Miracles on Maple Hill,* received the Newbery Medal in 1957.

Everywhere I go, it seems as if stories are there before me, waiting to be told. I am only sorry I can't write them all or live in every lovely place. Certainly I plan to live in as many as possible and tell every story I can find time to tell.

Elizabeth George Speare
1908-

AUTHOR OF
Calico Captive; The Witch of Blackbird Pond; The Bronze Bow

Autobiographical sketch of Elizabeth George Speare:

I WAS born in Melrose, Massachusetts, which seems to me an ideal place in which to have grown up, close to fields and woods where we hiked and picnicked, and near to Boston where we frequently had family treats of theaters and concerts. Every summer we went to the shore, where we stayed on a hill with a breathtaking view of the ocean, with fields and daisies and blueberries, and lovely secret paths through the woods, but, except for my small brother, not another young person anywhere. As I grew older I realized that those lonely summers had been a special gift for which I would always be grateful. I had endless golden days to read and think and dream, and it was then that I discovered the absorbing occupation of writing stories.

I went on writing stories all through high school, but I never again had much time to be alone. I went to Boston University and on to graduate school, and then I taught in Massachusetts high schools. I very much enjoyed teaching English because it was a wonderful opportunity to share the books that I loved and because it was always a thrill to watch some girl or boy discover for the first time the enchantment of reading and writing. I spent vacations as a camp counselor and traveled for one summer in Europe.

In 1936 I married Alden Speare and came to live in Connecticut. Alden, Jr., was born in 1939, and Mary in 1942, and for a good many years I was absorbed in camping in summer and skiing in winter, in dressing dolls and making costumes and being a den mother and a Brownie leader. One of the happiest things I did was to introduce to my children the stories I had loved in my own childhood. Once in a while I would catch a story of my own peeking out of a corner of my mind, but before I found time to sit down with a pencil and paper it would have scurried back out of sight. When both chil-

ELIZABETH GEORGE SPEARE

Elizabeth C. Spykman

AUTHOR OF

*A Lemon and a Star; The Wild Angel;
Terrible, Horrible Edie*

Autobiographical sketch of Elizabeth S. Spykman:

I AM not sure anyone will want to hear anything about me, as I was brought up in the country in New England exactly like a little English girl. There were six of us, four boys and two girls. We spoke more English than American, had tea in the afternoons, and kept stiff upper lips like anything. My father's family lived on one side of the road in our village and my mother's on the other, and as there were very nearly ten of each kind, with land and houses to match, the children who lived among them had a kind of enormous park to use as their own.

All the roads were dirt roads and there were no cars, no telephones, television, radio, or movies for quite a while. We had ponies instead. Each child had one, and my father had a furious black horse called The Moor. Our stable caught fire once and no one but my father was able to get a blanket over The Moor's head and lead him out. My father saved the stable, too, by making a bucket brigade of the cook, the parlor maid, our nurse, and the coachman. No one else would have been able to do that with the cook, either. But alas, we were not allowed to see it. We were sent to a maternal aunt across the road where we howled until the flames died down. There were lots of barn fires in those days and dog fights, too, which the farm hands enjoyed but which we thought tragic.

My father was a lawyer in Boston and the relations were businessmen and farmers. What they liked best was to grow things, the best flowers, the biggest vegetables, the most milk-giving cows, the tallest hay, shrubs and trees. I think they grew the biggest weeds too because we were all urged to pull them to show we were not afraid of hard work. Dock weeds from the hayfields brought a penny apiece and they were worth it.

Very often in the summers we went to Cape Cod. I have lived all over Cape Cod

dren were in junior high I found myself alone again for long hours of the day, and gradually the ideas began to come creeping out of the corners. I wrote articles for women's magazines about the things our family had done together, and I experimented with one-act plays.

A few years ago I discovered a wonderful little book written in 1807 by a woman who had been captured by Indians in the French and Indian War. With her had been her younger sister Miriam, about the age of my own daughter, and I began to dream about the adventures this girl might have had. My first long novel, *Calico Captive*, published in 1957, was the result.

The second book, *The Witch of Blackbird Pond*, was written about an imaginary girl who lived in my own town of Wethersfield, Connecticut, in 1687 when people believed in witches. In the year and a half that I spent in writing this book Kit Tyler and her imaginary family and friends came to seem very real to me, and when this book won the Newbery Medal in 1959 I was happy to know that they had made so many friends for themselves.

* * *

In 1962 Mrs. Speare was awarded the Newbery Medal a second time for her third book, *The Bronze Bow*, published in 1961.

Spykman: *SPEAK man*

and swum all over a lot of its bay and harbors too, but I am no sailor and never liked lying on the weather rail soaked to the skin at the command of a younger sister, though more often than not she won the race.

In the winter we skated, coasted, and punged behind sleighs and often we sat on our sleds and longed for someone to invent a machine to pull us back uphill. Presently someone did and so there is no more punging and little coasting either, but the machine took some bad things away too. Runaway horses, dust, and not being able to get the doctor quickly when you had cut off the end of your finger in the corn chopper.

I went to two or three schools but none of them seemed to me to be as valuable as living in the country until I was sent to a boarding school called Westover where there was a set of very remarkable women in charge. I was told there that one ought to read books and although I did not take advantage of this valuable information right away, I began to see it might be possible and perhaps worth while for the future. Also, I made a great friend and later she and I traveled all over the world. After a trip to New Zealand in a cargo boat by way of the Canal and on through the South Seas, I wrote a piece about going to visit Robert Louis Stevenson's grave at Samoa, which was accepted by the *Atlantic Monthly*. The *Atlantic* then printed some more of my things. Later, I fell in love with a fascinating Dutchman and had two fascinating children, Angelica and Patricia. My husband was Nicholas Spykman, the man who started the Department and Institute of International Relations at Yale University which, since his death, has been lured to Princeton University.

I wrote my two books for no other reason than that I wanted to. I am doing another about the same family who are mostly us.

My name is pronounced "Speakman," but is written the Dutch way with the *ij* turned to *y* which is very easy to slip into if you are writing by hand.

I now live outside New Haven, Connecticut, and grow things just as my relations used to do. I have a large house and lots of land and a lot of books. I learned quite a while ago what they were for. I have a

ELIZABETH C. SPYKMAN

dog called Jingle, after the bad character in *Pickwick Papers* who told lies and stole things. My Jingle would tell lies if he could, especially about the things he steals off the kitchen table. But my younger daughter calls him Beautiful One. He is a Dalmatian and can run with the speed of light.

I guess that's all.

* * *

The third book which Mrs. Spykman mentioned in her autobiographical sketch has since been published under the title *Terrible, Horrible Edie*.

Arthur D. Stapp

1906-

AUTHOR OF
Mountain Tamer, Escape on Skis, Captive of the Mountains

Autobiographical sketch of Arthur D. Stapp:

I WAS born in Seattle. It is outdoor country, and I saw the sun rise over the Cascade Mountains and set over the Olympics, while off to the southwest was Mount Rainier with its perpetual snow. I camped out often, and climbed a mile-high snow peak while in high school. Usually we were in groups of three or four or half a dozen, but once I made a lone trip for a week and saw no one for several days while I climbed

ARTHUR D. STAPP

high up a peak, an ill-advised and irresistible venture. Later, I joined the Washington Alpine Club and became an advocate of mountain safety, with strong disapproval of lone trips.

My family had a weekly community newspaper, and at one time or another I did everything from setting type to writing editorials and a humorous column. I sold ads, struggled with a Depression budget, and as a reporter exposed a fraudulent inventor who was taking the public for thousands of dollars. We knew the young man in charge of short-wave communication for the Byrd expedition to the South Pole, and were proud that we printed the message forms he took on the Wilkins expedition to the North Pole.

For some time I was manager of the newspaper. Eventually, because I wanted to concentrate on writing and felt business responsibilities would keep me from it, I sold my interest in favor of going to New York to study and write. The Second World War intervened. I spent two and a half years in Brazil as a propeller mechanic in the United States Air Force. The base was the jumping-off place for thousands of our planes, mostly bombers, which crossed the South Atlantic. Because of an interest in technical and scientific things, I enjoyed my work and developed a strong interest in planes.

After the war I came to New York and at New York University took writing courses in half a dozen fields. I wrote my first book in a hotel room and the close walls and excessive steam heat helped me write feelingly of mountains and wide-open spaces. When I was tempted to gloss over the toil of climbing, I took the stairs instead of the elevator to the fifth floor.

I began work as a linotype operator on a New York newspaper, taking time off when needed for writing. A two-foot snowfall inspired me to renew my skiing and start my second book, and a few months' residence on the tough Lower East Side contributed some philosophy to it.

My wife, Eleanor, is a former children's librarian. Our daughter, Marilyn, often says, "Tell me a story about when you were a little boy." This is much quicker than writing a book, and what an audience! I think, however, that the required background for a writer for children is not so much to be a parent, but to have been a child.

William O. Steele

1917-

AUTHOR OF
*Wilderness Journey; Winter Danger; Davy
Crockett's Earthquake; The Lone
Hunt; Etc.*

Autobiographical sketch of William O. Steele:

I LIKE to tell that I was born in a hollow sycamore tree, deep in the canebrakes of Tennessee with catamounts howling all around. And sometimes I say I was born in a log fort under attack by savages, the stockade fence burned away and flaming arrows everywhere. But it isn't true. I just lie to enjoy myself and the truth is that I was born in the quiet little middle Tennessee town of Franklin with not an Indian closer than a hundred miles. Not a warwhoop sounded, not a muzzle-loading rifle cracked when I arrived.

As I grew up, I felt bitterly cheated that the frontier had come and gone before my day. Yet I found that it was not entirely gone. The past was all around Franklin, in the old log cabins now used as smokehouses, in the Indian arrowheads found in

WILLIAM O. STEELE

the plowed fields, and in the Minié balls washed up by heavy rains. In the back country and the mountains of Tennessee, in many places the old pioneer speech is still preserved, the old superstitions are still believed, and the old methods of farming and manufacturing are still used. It still takes three men to see to the top of a tall Tennessee tulip poplar on a clear day, and often two men are required to hunt deer when the mosquitoes are so thick one man has to shoot a hole in the mosquitoes so the other can shoot through the hole at the deer. All my materials were available and I was anxious to use them in books and stories.

But first I went to college at Cumberland University; then I spent a five-year period with the Army and the Air Force in World War II. Before I went overseas I was married. My wife was herself the daughter of two authors, Gilbert and Christine Noble Govan, who have always helped and encouraged me to write. After my discharge, I took a clerical job, for by 1948 my wife and I had three children, two girls and a boy, and they needed clothes and food. But I still wanted to write, and I still wanted to write about Tennessee history.

It took an allergic child to get me between hard covers. As my wife rocked this fretful child I read aloud to her about my favorite subject. It wasn't long till she ceased to

listen and I felt I had to tell somebody about the Old Southwest, about the beautiful country and the brave and colorful people who inhabited it. So I wrote a book, *The Buffalo Knife,* followed by *The Golden Root.* Shortly after that I gave up my job to devote all my time to writing stories and tall tales about pioneer Tennessee.

Now I live on Lookout Mountain in a somewhat dilapidated house, heated by a huge stone fireplace like those the pioneers often had. My children are sometimes uneasy that their father does not work like other fathers, but loafs at home all day. However, they are getting used to it and I would not change places with anybody. For it is pleasant to study and write about the past and to keep one's eye on one's books published in New York, which I can see on a clear day from the mountaintop here.

Emma Gelders Sterne

1894-

AUTHOR OF

Loud Sing Cuckoo; Drums of Monmouth; The Long Black Schooner; Mary McLeod Bethune; Etc.

Autobiographical sketch of Emma Gelders Sterne:

I WAS born in Birmingham, Alabama, on May 13, 1894, the eldest of a family of three. Birmingham, now a large industrial city, was still boasting of its pioneer days. The surrounding hills were all blackberry patches and hickory and persimmon groves. The tall pines and wooded trails of Red Mountain were much more my home than the tall white house we lived in. I rode horseback wherever I had to go, or on a funny bouncing streetcar. I roamed the woods, hours on end, alone or with my two brothers, four and ten years younger than I. I read my way through our own bookshelves and through the small public library.

At eight I "wished on a star" that I could be a writer, although at that time I had never seen an author in the flesh. Under the influence of Jo March, I concocted very bad plays which I cajoled the neighborhood children into acting in our attic. Through high school I wrote bad poetry, too—in English, French, or Latin—when I was

EMMA GELDERS STERNE

supposed to be learning cases and tenses and other oddments of grammar.

New England, where I went to college, was full of writers and the memory of writers. I visited Concord and Cambridge and the homes of Hawthorne and Thoreau and the Alcotts, and smuggled a green apple to eat on the horsehair sofa Louisa Alcott wrote about in *Little Women*. That was for luck. For the hard training in communication of ideas every day, year in and year out for four years, I bless the head of the English Department at Smith College, Mary Augusta Jordan.

I took an A.B. degree at Smith in 1916 and lived only one year in Alabama after college. In 1917, Roy M. Sterne, a Birmingham lawyer, and I were married. In 1918, our first daughter was born. Three months later we moved to New York and to the new life that was to fill the next forty years. Before our second daughter was born, I had collected a red-flowered candy box of rejection slips. Then in 1926 my first full-length book for children was published, an Indian story. Since then, I have written mainly but not exclusively for young people, wanting to share with them the things and people I care most about. My second published book was about Socrates and the ancient Greeks; the third, about Chaucer. After that, my subjects were drawn chiefly from the American scene. Usually there is a poet among the characters of my books;

always there is the struggle for a more decent world, and always, from my own experience, the changing miracle of the natural world.

Drums of Monmouth (1932) has for its hero a poet of the American Revolution. *The Long Black Schooner* (1952) is the account of the Negroes on the slave ship *Amistad*, who freed themselves and after two years in the United States were able to return to their homes in Africa. In 1957 I completed *Mary McLeod Bethune*, the biography of a great Negro woman. Though Mrs. Bethune and I were both from the South, though we had both taken part in the struggle for woman suffrage, I had grown up without knowing of her and, like most white Southerners, without any real knowledge of half of my fellow citizens—the Negro people of the South. I feel strongly that the two halves of the South must become one strong whole. As a writer, I feel it my responsibility and my privilege to hack away at the wall of ignorance. The story of a Negro scientist, Charles Richard Drew, is included in *Blood Brothers* (1959). I am now at work on a full-length biography of Drew.

Altogther I have had about twenty-five books published. In between writing, I have taught and edited and enjoyed the companionship of nine grandchildren. My husband and I now live in San Jose, California, where I have been collaborating with my daughter, Barbara Lindsay.

Augusta Stevenson

AUTHOR OF

Abe Lincoln: Frontier Boy; Buffalo Bill: Boy of the Plains; Clara Barton: Girl Nurse; Sitting Bull: Dakota Boy; Etc.

Autobiographical sketch of Augusta Stevenson:

WITH my patriot parents and my birthplace in the village of Patriot, on the Ohio River in southern Indiana, I could hardly escape being a patriot myself. In fact, I didn't escape. Patriotism became the background of my plays for children, and also of my books in the Childhood of Famous Americans series.

My desire to write and my interest in all things literary and dramatic can be traced back again to my parents—to my mother's love for Shakespeare's plays and to my Scotch father's absorption in such poems as "The Lady of the Lake." My father was related to a famous storyteller, Robert Louis Stevenson. My first interest was in plays. When I was ten or so, I was getting up plays for the neighborhood children. I was writing plays for a local dramatic club soon after I graduated from an Indiana college.

Still later, when I became a teacher, I wrote little plays for reading lessons. The children enjoyed the stories in their readers and history books much more when I dramatized them or they could act them out. This gave me new insight into the juvenile mind. I found that every child in the room, without exception, had an innate love of drama. This prompted me to write my six volumes of *Plays for Children and Young People.* They were to be used in school for reading, and only incidentally for acting.

It was only one more step from plays to stories. My parents had made a young patriot of me, and I had always liked stories about real people. I believed all children should learn to feel patriotic pride in our history and our heroes. To introduce children to America's greatest hero, I wrote my first storybook, *Abe Lincoln: Frontier Boy.* Though it was written over twenty-five years ago, this book is still among my "best sellers." And it set a pattern for a whole series, the Childhood of Famous Americans. *Sitting Bull: Dakota Boy,* was my twenty-first of this kind and the hundredth book in the series. In these stories I tried to show that American heroes and heroines were once children like the boys and girls who read my books. They lived in exciting times and had the kind of adventures a child understands and enjoys.

I believe my various travels have helped me somewhat to create stories of adventure. Besides journeys to Central America, where I lived for two years, I have visited Newfoundland and Hawaii, and have traveled from east coast to west coast, from north to south in the United States. A visit to Williamsburg, Virginia, for instance, furnished an idea for my *Daniel Boone: Boy Hunter.* Daniel's muddy boots just had to walk on the lovely polished floors of the

AUGUSTA STEVENSON

palace! But he was delivering a patriotic message.

A trip to England made it possible for me to write the boyhood story *Myles Standish: Adventurous Boy.* And it gave me some background for another subject that appeals to my patriotic spirit—Virginia Dare, the first girl in American history.

My home now is in Indianapolis, and my present hobby, between books, is making picture scrapbooks for children's hospitals.

Mary Stolz
1920-

AUTHOR OF

In a Mirror; Ready or Not; The Sea Gulls Woke Me; Pray Love, Remember; Etc.

Autobiographical sketch of Mary Stolz:

I WAS born in Boston, educated in New York City—at the Birch Wathen School, New College of Columbia University, and the Katharine Gibbs School. The first two were progressive and permissive and gave me all sorts of encouragement to do the two things in which I was really interested —writing (mainly poetry and fairy tales), and reading anything at all. At the third school I learned to type, which is wonderful because I'm afraid I'd be too lazy to write an entire novel by hand, and would

MARY STOLZ

and I became quite taken with the idea and got a secondhand typewriter, a ream of yellow paper. I wrote a novel, *To Tell Your Love*, about a girl who loses the boy and does not get him back, and sent it to Harper. They took it, and I've been writing ever since.

I'm quite healthy now, but have absolutely no interest in horses, except to look at. I don't write poetry any more (not even in secret), nor fairy tales, but love to read them. I write about and for teen-agers—as I've said somewhere else—not because I think they are more important than other people, but because their time of life, their problems, their climate have the strongest appeal to me as a writer. They're wonderfully responsive readers. I find it a very happy association.

skip words, paragraphs, whole sections, just to have fewer words to pen. Actually, I didn't write again for years, in spite of knowing how to type, and in spite of the recollection of the really tremendous pleasure once taken in an idea, a sheet of paper, and a few words to get started with. (In school I used to love the part where several sentences were put on the board and you selected one and built a theme around it. It was my favorite assignment. My son, Bill, at fifteen, found it the assignment he most loathed. At least we're both positive about the same thing and have discussed it with a great deal of interest. It's nearly as good a bond as baseball, which we like.)

In any case, I didn't consciously think again of writing until about 1949, when I became ill enough to be confined to the house for months. I had a most patient and understanding doctor who asked me what interests I had that might see me through this period. I kept saying that all I cared about was riding horses. This was rather true, at the time, but also out of the question, so he waited until I stopped being silly and asked again. At length I said that in school I'd loved to write. He told me then about a medical student he'd known, who'd been far worse off than I, quite bedridden, for whom he and some other young doctors had constructed a board, to which papers were clamped, which could go above his head. In this position the young man had written a textbook. The moral was clear,

Helen Stone

1904-

ILLUSTRATOR OF

Let It Rain! The Plain Princess; Tell Me Mr. Owl; The Horse Who Lived Upstairs; Etc.

Autobiographical sketch of Helen Stone:

I WAS exposed very early to drawing and painting; that was the preoccupation of one of my parents—so followed the twig. I began to draw. Fixed in their outlandish situations, my paper dolls stared back, long after the age of doing them. Where, by what means they traveled, the rooms they stiffened in, their suitable wardrobes, their scrapes (action!), their families—all this was fascinating to me. Or I would trail after my mother, sketching with her, the summer afternoon long, hearing something of "beauty" and "fall of the light." How children store these things away, never to lose or forget! I remember always a nibbled still life set up somewhere in the house. This I approved without awe and with probably better results than later, in the studio, where reverence or caution slows down one's hand.

I went to art schools in New York and was luckily sent to Europe at a wonderful time to be there. Bohemianism clung to the old streets, the cafés and ateliers—the souls of great artists still lived in the City of Light.

Returning, I taught a little, did some designing, traveled, painted, married, painted.

An old farm horse, gaining Elysian pastures in Connecticut, was the reason for my starting to do pictures for children. We both browsed—I had apples and lunch in my pocket. This intimacy led to lots of studies and drawings, which led back to *The Horse Who Lived Upstairs*, by Phyllis McGinley, and my first illustrations. Followed other books by the two—shall I say three?—of us, among them *The Plain Princess*. So on and on. Came stories to do, mostly picture books, including *The Little Ballet Dancer, Tell Me Mr. Owl, Lucy McLockett*, and *Let It Rain!*

Oh, yes, I was born in Englewood, New Jersey. After many years in New York, I now live in East Hampton, Long Island, a salty, beautiful old town. We love, honor, and have restored a couple of old houses, scorn a power mower, and fall back on evergreens. We are governed by dachshund puppies, the most delightful.

PHIL STONG

Phil Stong

1899-1957

AUTHOR OF

Honk: the Moose; No-Stitch: the Hound; Mississippi Pilot; The Prince and the Porker; Etc.

PHILIP Duffield Stong was born on January 27, 1899, in Keosauqua, Iowa, near a bend in the Des Moines River. His grandfather, George Crawford Duffield, had settled there in 1857. Phil Stong collapsed and died of a heart attack on April 26, 1957, in the workroom of his home in Washington, Connecticut.

Scarcely a week before his death, he wrote the editor of this volume:

"I never thought of myself as a 'junior' writer, though your note startled me into observing that I've published sixteen of the pieces, with one coming up this fall, so I guess I must be. I use the pieces to clear my throat between books, to remind myself that direction, simplicity, and suspense are the *sine qua non* of all narrative writing."

Although Phil Stong will doubtless be remembered longest for his novel *State Fair*, which brought him fame and his first real money, and has been produced three times as a motion picture, younger readers, as well as older ones, will think of *Honk: the Moose* and his other "pieces" with affection.

The phrase "just a moose" was a byword among adults for some time after *Honk* made his appearance. Kurt Wiese's rollicking color illustrations helped, but the story itself is a near classic.

Stong's grandfather was a vivid memory and from the old man's stories of the settling of the Middle West came some of the material for Stong's books. Grandfather Duffield had prospected for gold in California and bought his Iowa farm with it. Linwood Farm was sold but years later, in 1933, Mr. Stong bought back the three hundred and twenty acres, again with California gold, this time from Hollywood. He did this after writing the scenario for *State Fair*. (This movie was remade as a musical in 1945, with songs by Rodgers and Hammerstein, among them "It Might As Well Be Spring," which won an Academy Award.) At the time of his death, Mr. Stong still owned Linwood, raising cattle and crops there, although his residence was in New England.

After graduating from Drake University in 1919, Phil Stong began his career as a working newspaperman. From 1923 to 1925, he wrote editorials for the Des Moines *Register*, then was a wire editor in New York for the Associated Press for two years, after which he was a copy editor for the North American Newspaper Alliance. In 1928 he went to *Liberty*, and the following year to *Editor and Publisher*. He was with the New York

World from 1929 to 1931. He also did graduate work at Columbia University and the University of Kansas, and in later years received two honorary degrees—a Litt.D. from Parsons College, in Iowa, and a doctor of laws in 1947 from his alma mater.

On November 8, 1925, he married Virginia Maude Swain, also a newspaper reporter. She encouraged him in his writing and it was her faith in him that led to his first successful novel. He had written twelve books, none of them published, when his thirteenth, *State Fair*, the story of a prize boar, soared to fame. Appearing in 1932, the worst year of the Depression, it was a relief from the somber aspects of life and literature, and readers seized it joyously. Other adult titles were *Week-End, Village Tale, Iron Mountain, Stranger's Return,* and *If School Keeps,* described as autobiographical.

Among his juvenile titles were *High Water, Young Settler, Captain Kidd's Cow,* and *Way Down Cellar. The Hired Man's Elephant* won the New York *Herald Tribune* Spring Festival award in 1939.

Stephen Deutch

SUSANNE SUBA

Susanne Suba

1913-

ILLUSTRATOR OF

Sonny-Boy Sim; Dancing Star; Homemade Year; Jaime and His Hen Pollita; Etc.

Autobiographical sketch of Susanne Suba:

THE story told me is that I started drawing at the age of three, lying under my father's drafting table in his architectural office. That was in Budapest, Hungary, where I was born. I begged the head draftsman to teach me oil painting but when he wouldn't I took up pencil on penny post cards. I drew families and ladies with wonderful bows on their shoes.

When I was six my mother, who was American and a pianist, brought me back to her native Brooklyn. And there we stayed. I graduated from Brooklyn Friends' School and Pratt Institute there. My first job after that was decorating the walls of a corset shop. The first book I illustrated was Thoreau's *Life Without Principle.*

About this time, too, I felt the need of some typographical knowledge. I set type and studied the design of books. The first book I designed, *Here Comes the Circus,* was chosen one of the Fifty Best Books of the Year. I also illustrated this book and being on my favorite subject, it has remained one of my favorite books. My father painted all his life, and was also a circus fan. In fact, we three used to spend as much time as possible at the circus when it came to Brooklyn under a tent pitched where Brooklyn College now stands.

My father's paintings have been exhibited at the Museum of Modern Art, M. H. De Young Memorial Museum, the Art Institute of Chicago, Brooklyn Museum, Museum of the City of New York, and many other galleries. He is in the permanent collections of the Art Institute of Chicago, Metropolitan Museum in New York, and private collections. My drawings are in the collections of the Brooklyn Museum, Museum of the City of New York, and private collections.

After that first book, there have been many which were included in the Fifty Best Books of the Year and have won other honors. Chief among the sixty-odd I have illustrated are *Dancing Star,* a biography of Anna Pavlova; *A Rocket in My Pocket,* a delightful collection of folk verses; *Gabriel and the Creatures,* the story of evolution, imaginatively told by Gerald Heard.

Sonny-Boy Sim, The Elegant Elephant, The Gentle Giraffe all vie in my heart as favorites. And there is *The Hobo Hound,* written by my mother. Beside the books, I have done hundreds of "spots" for the *New Yorker* and several covers. A collection of these drawings came out as *Spots by Suba*. A recent book laid in Majorca is *Jaime and His Hen Pollita*.

Beside working, I have traveled all over the United States, and spent five enjoyable years in Chicago. I spent a wonderful sojourn of over two years in Europe. Paris, Italy and Austria all live in beautiful memories and beckon to call me back. My dog, Suzy Beagle, traveled with me and was my interested and constant companion. She, just like me, loved to arrive in a new city, eat new food and go to the museums. Poor Suzy with her gay little heart died in Vienna, but lives in all the animals I love to draw.

JAMES L. SUMMERS

James L. Summers

1910-

AUTHOR OF

Girl Trouble; Prom Trouble; Off the Beam; The Wonderful Time; Etc.

Autobiographical sketch of James L. Summers:

BOTH my mother and father were artists but Father was trying to do something practical so I was born at a summer resort he had invented and built on the shores of Lake Winnebago in Wisconsin. I think I was the only guest that summer; the harder Father tried the more unprofitable his ventures became and the farther west we went.

I developed my interest in writing for young people either when Father was managing the school for bad boys in Oregon, or when we were in the Hawaiian Islands, or when I was a Tenderfoot Scout in Tucson, Arizona, or in high school at Redondo Beach—I can't remember. It could have been in Milwaukee, where I was graduated from South Division High. I was in a sort of daze, I recall, and belonged to a gang called the Greenfield Lancers devoted to sand-lot athletics and evil doings. I was a mediocre ball carrier so I wrote poetry, especially dedicated to certain young ladies. I submitted a poem in a contest conducted by the Milwaukee *Journal* and won a dollar, the first money paid to me for writing. For a long time it also seemed to be the last.

Unhappily both my parents died when I was quite young. I started to work my way around the world but only got as far as Puerto Rico where I became ill. I chased the cure for tuberculosis at St. Luke's in the desert in Tucson for a year or so and then I went back to college at UCLA where I met a girl. We were married—at a rather young age, too. I hadn't bothered to graduate from college which was a pity because behind my back the Great Depression had seeped in, so I became employed in a wide variety of jobs which were all boring and low paid.

Meanwhile Julie and Richard, my children, had arrived and they stirred my distressing economic lethargy into working by night and going to UCLA by day. Finally I had a teaching credential and in various California high schools taught woodshop, English, public speaking, printing, United States history, mechanical drawing, physical education, senior problems and driver education, to mention a few of the subjects. Gradually I became familiar with the fanciful lore of public education and the nature of the young. Besides, my own children were now teen-agers and suffering enormous pain and sorrow.

Of course I had been writing like mad all the while. Suddenly Daisy Bacon paid me another dollar for a love story which I published under my wife's name because I was teaching welding at the time and it could

give the townspeople a wrong impression of
the acetylene torch. So there I was on the
merry-go-round, and because an author must
write what he knows it was natural that my
stories concerned youth.

Still, I wasn't as flippant about youth's
problems as I appeared. In the late forties,
the American press began to give the
younger generation a terrible pounding and
I couldn't see it that way. I had the exotic
idea that the boys and girls I knew constituted the finest generation in our national
history and I decided that writing sympathetically about the young had become in
my time a great calling. I left teaching and
began to write full time.

Critics have said my books were "zany"
and it is true that I have tried to make
them light and amusing, but in the background I have also dealt with themes as
serious as any written about today, I think.
I work in deadly earnest because I am trying
to tell my young readers that we do believe
in them; that the brilliance of free choice is
still theirs to grasp; that their way is the
broad mainstream of history; that to me and
many another free man they shine as may
only the young, the brave, and the true; and
that out of the murk and muddle of their
discouraging and awesome times they will
surely emerge triumphant—as did their fathers before them, according to the books
the children study. For myself, I like to see
a well-worn book in the hands of a fresh
kid, and the laughter of children in so
solemn a matter as H-bombs is music to a
guy who likes the solid beat.

Rosemary Sutcliff

1920-

AUTHOR OF

*The Shield Ring; The Eagle of the Ninth;
The Queen Elizabeth Story; Brother
Dusty-Feet; Etc.*

Autobiographical sketch of Rosemary Sutcliff:

I WAS born in Surrey, England, but during the first ten years of my life, I don't
think we were ever two years in the same
place. My father was a naval officer, and
when he moved from one ship or dockyard to
another, of course my mother and I followed

ROSEMARY SUTCLIFF

him. When I was two we went to Malta, and
when I was four we came home again. I can
remember Malta, not in long connected
memories, but in little bright pictures. I
remember the tall, cool stone-floored rooms
of our house, and the little garden that had
just space for a wellhead in it, a lemon tree
and a frangipani and nothing more. I wish
I could say that I remember the ships in the
Grand Harbour, but I don't; all that I remember about them is a party on board
H.M.S. *Benbow*, when I made my tea exclusively of crystallized orange slices.

I suppose I must have been about five
when I began my career, not as a writer, but
as an artist. I took, for no apparent reason,
to drawing robins, very fat robins sitting on
logs, and I continued to draw robins with
great singleness of purpose for years.

When I was ten, my father retired, and we
settled in Devonshire, and I went to a private school in the near-by town. Four years
later it had become painfully clear to my
family that I was "Educationally Sub-
normal," or else just plain incurably lazy
where the three R's were concerned. On the
other hand, I really could draw—other
things beside robins by that time—so they
allowed me to leave and go to art school.
At art school I did well, and took to miniature painting. I was eighteen when I had
my first miniature hung in the Royal Acad-

emy, and about ten years later I was elected a member of the Royal Miniaturist Society. But before that time I had started to write.

The beginning of *that* story goes back, I think, as far as my first robin, for it was at about that time my mother began seriously to read aloud to me. She read aloud most beautifully, and her choice of books, which besides *Peter Rabbit* and *Winnie the Pooh* included, even in those early days, most of Dickens and Trollope, *Beowulf,* and Lord Lytton's *Last Days of Pompeii,* gave me a feeling for good writing that stood me in most useful stead when my own urge came upon me. Certainly the three Roman stories in Rudyard Kipling's *Puck of Pook's Hill,* which she read me many times, were the start of my feeling for Roman Britain, which I later put into *The Eagle of the Ninth,* my favorite so far among my own books.

Nowadays I have given up painting entirely. It was my first love, but writing has come to mean more to me than ever painting did. And I live in Sussex, just half the county away from the place where *Puck of Pook's Hill* was written.

Ronald Syme

1910-

<small>AUTHOR OF</small>

Balboa, Finder of the Pacific; Henry Hudson; John Smith of Virginia; Magellan, First Around the World; Etc.

RONALD Syme was born "down under," and spent his boyhood sailing off the New Zealand coast or hunting wild boars in the North Island bush country. At sixteen he left school and until he was twenty spent his time on a Pacific cargo steamer, trading between Australia, New Zealand, San Francisco, and the South Sea Islands.

During these years at sea, Mr. Syme began to write, chiefly short stories. When he was thirty-one, he left the sea to become a professional writer. Until the outbreak of World War II in 1939, he lived in many places—Rome, Vienna, Paris. With the war, he joined the British Merchant Service as a gunner and saw action in the North Atlantic until the end of 1940. Twice the ship he was

RONALD SYME

on was sunk. As he could speak four languages, he was transferred to the British Army Intelligence Corps. He fought with the Eighth Army in Africa, then became a paratrooper during the Italian campaign.

After the war, he settled in England and devoted himself to writing. In 1957 he sailed 1,660 miles in a twenty-ton schooner from New Zealand to Rarotonga in the Cook Islands. He now lives in the South Seas, and in the spring of 1960 married a Polynesian princess, Ngamarama. Her name means "Queen Star of the Moon." Mrs. Syme was women's tennis champion of Rarotonga and according to her husband can "deftly throw a steel-tipped spear and hit a drowsing fish ten or fifteen yards away, three times out of five."

Other titles by Mr. Syme published in the United States are: *Bay of the North; Cortes of Mexico; Champlain of the St. Lawrence; Columbus, Finder of the New World;* and *La Salle of the Mississippi.*

Mr. Syme is not to be confused with Sir Ronald Syme, Camden Professor of Ancient History at Oxford University.

Campbell Tatham

See *Elting, Mary*

Sydney Taylor

1904-

AUTHOR OF

*All-of-a-Kind Family; More All-of-a-Kind
Family; All-of-a-Kind Family
Uptown; Etc.*

Autobiographical sketch of Sydney Taylor:

WHEN I was a little girl and people asked, "What would you like to be when you grow up?" I used to answer, "An author." But when I grew up, life had so many other attractions, I forgot about my first ambition.

I went to work right after graduating from high school. I married early and continued to work as a secretary. Nights were devoted to the Lenox Hill Players, one of the aspiring Little Theater groups of the period. Once, when the leading lady took sick, I had the glorious opportunity of playing her role for two successive nights on Broadway!

As part of our training, our director, Lee Strasberg, introduced dance technique, and I found myself increasingly drawn to this medium. I began the study of the dance in earnest, first with a disciple of Mary Wigman, and then with Martha Graham. After several years I became a member of her concert group. I was fortunate to participate in the excitement of those early years when the modern dance was in active revolt against the ballet.

SYDNEY TAYLOR

I left the company to have a baby. When my daughter, Jo, was born, I found I had a new job—housewife and mother. When Jo was seven, I resumed some of my former activities in a new way. Since 1942 I have been in charge of dance and dramatics at a nonprofit summer camp. Not satisfied with available play material, I write my own scripts, which I direct and choreograph.

Jo, being an only child, would listen avidly as I'd tell her about my mama, papa, and the five little sisters who lived on New York's Lower East Side. This was in the early 1900's, when streams of immigrants poured into the narrow streets, their hearts aflame with hope for a better life in the new land. In the retelling, I suddenly felt a great compulsion to write it all down. After writing the story, I was satisfied. I promptly put the manuscript away and the years rolled over it.

In 1950, when I was in my children's world at camp, my husband chanced to read the announcement of a contest for juvenile literature. He disinterred the manuscript and sent it off without telling me. When I heard from the Follett Publishing Company that I had won the prize, I did not know what they were talking about. I showed the letter to my husband—and the secret was out! That's how I became a recognized author.

Since then I have published short stories in magazines and books. My second book appeared in 1954, my third in 1958. I owe it all to my husband, Ralph Taylor, president of a firm of chemists and perfumers. Sometimes, when my writing is not going well, I feel like throttling him. But when the story or book is out, I think how lucky for me I have his help, encouragement, and love.

Gustaf Tenggren

1896-

ILLUSTRATOR OF

*Mother Goose Story Book; The Tenggren
Tell-It-Again Book; Etc.*

Autobiographical sketch of Gustaf Tenggren:

MY family lived in Gothenburg, Sweden, where I attended school with my brother and four sisters. I was born in Magra Socken in the home of my paternal grandparents. Summers were happily spent in the country, tagging along with my grandfather, who was a woodcarver and painter, and also a fine companion for a small boy. I never tired of watching him carve or mix the colors he used when commissioned to decorate, with typical primitive designs, churches and public buildings in the community.

Aware of my keen interest in drawing, a kind and understanding teacher, Anton Kellner, provided stuffed animals and other interesting subjects from which to draw and paint. When I was thirteen I passed a scholarship test in art and enrolled in evening classes. The following year I received a three-year scholarship and became a full-fledged art student attending day classes. This was the same school from which my father, also an artist, had graduated.

During vacations and spare time I painted portraits, illustrated for periodicals, but the most exciting work was painting scenery and helping to design settings for the theater in Gothenburg.

Again a scholarship entitled me to three more years of study at the Valand School of Fine Arts. While still in school I was commissioned to illustrate my first book, *Bland Tomtar o' Troll*.

I arrived in the United States in the early spring of 1920 and settled in Cleveland. Those were busy days, drawing for the Cleveland *Plain Dealer*, painting six posters weekly for Keith's Palace Theater, fashion drawings for a department store, and at the same time working full time for an art studio. After two years of this heavy schedule I was ready for a change and decided to try my luck in New York. For many years my studio was in this great city. Work was plentiful and during this period I illustrated a number of children's books.

My work at the Disney Studio (1936-1939) was an interesting experience. There I designed backgrounds, settings, characters, and worked out sequences for such pictures as *Snow White, The Old Mill, Pinocchio*, etc.

Since 1940, I have devoted my time to illustrating juvenile books. I find this work very rewarding as it seems to give so much pleasure to so many children.

Self-portrait

GUSTAF TENGGREN

Traveling in Europe, Mexico, and the width and breadth of the United States, sketching and painting, is my way of relaxing and having fun. Then back to the coast of Maine, where my wife and I have made our home in West Southport for the past twenty years and where living seems to be just right for us.

Louise Hall Tharp

1898-

AUTHOR OF

Tory Hole; Champlain, Northwest Voyager; Company of Adventurers; Etc.

Autobiographical sketch of Louise Hall Tharp:

I WAS born in Oneonta, New York, June 19, 1898, the daughter of Newton Marshall Hall, D.D., a Congregationalist minister, and Louise Buffum Varney, a State-of-Maine Quaker. My parents moved to Springfield, Massachusetts, when I was about a year old. My father was pastor of the North Congregational Church in Springfield for over twenty years. I graduated from Classical High School, Springfield, and went to the School of Fine Arts, Crafts and Decorative Design in Boston, with the idea of becoming an illustrator. I traveled for two years in Europe with my father, studying art

LOUISE HALL THARP

and working with him on a series of travel articles.

On my return from Europe I went into Girl Scouting. I served as captain, field captain, camp counselor, assistant camp director, and editor of the *Trailmaker*, the magazine for Girl Scout leaders of Region I. I became a nationally accredited speaker on Girl Scouting and served on the National Brownie Committee.

I married Carey Edwin Tharp in 1925. Subsequently we lived in Cambridge, Massachusetts, and in various parts of New York State. We moved to Darien, Connecticut, in 1932.

In 1940 I began writing children's books for my two sons, then aged six and nine. The problem was to provide them with reading which would compete with entertainment offered by radio and moving pictures. My books for young people were written to my sons' specifications, true stories based on American history. They had become intrigued with the drama behind the many historical markers along the roadsides and my first book, *Tory Hole*, told of Darien, our home town, during the Revolution. As my boys grew, my books were pointed toward successively older age groups.

When my sons went to college I transferred my attention to the adult biographical field. The first of these biographies was *The Peabody Sisters of Salem*. This includes the story of Sophia, wife of Nathaniel Haw-

thorne; Mary, wife of Horace Mann, the educator; and Elizabeth, founder of the kindergarten in America. This was followed by *Until Victory*, the life of Horace Mann, and *Three Saints and a Sinner*, which includes the life of Julia Ward Howe, author of "The Battle Hymn of the Republic." These books prove of interest to high school students.

Now that both our sons are married and have homes of their own, I devote most of my time to writing, research and lecturing.

Jane Thayer

See *Woolley, Catherine*

James Thurber
1894-1961
AUTHOR OF
The 13 Clocks; The Great Quillow; Many Moons; The White Deer; Etc.

JAMES Grover Thurber was born in Columbus, Ohio, December 8, 1894. After studying at Ohio State University, he became a code clerk in the United States State Department for two years. In 1920 he went into newspaper work, first as a reporter with the Columbus *Dispatch* for four years, then on the Paris edition of the Chicago *Tribune* for a year. During 1925 he was on the staff of the New York *Evening Post*.

His long association with the *New Yorker* began early in 1927, the year after the magazine was founded. There his "casuals"—humorous articles on personal misadventures—and his off-beat cartoons, with their equally amazing and amusing captions, and sometimes without captions at all, immediately captured the readers. His drawings first appeared in *Is Sex Necessary?* a book written in collaboration with E. B. White and published in 1929. Many other stories and books have added to his fame—*My Life and Hard Times*, hilariously funny anecdotes about his boyhood and early youth; "The Secret Life of Walter Mitty," a classic story of the valiant daydreams of a timid man, later made into a movie with Danny Kaye; *Fables for Our Time; The Last Flower; The Seal in the Bedroom; The Owl in the Attic.*

JAMES THURBER

A selection of his stories and sketches was put on the stage in *A Thurber Carnival*, in which he had the fun of acting a little while before his death. Perhaps the best of his later books is *The Years with Ross*. Published in 1959, it is a candid-camera account of the *New Yorker* and its brilliant but eccentric editor, Harold Ross. It also sheds a good deal of light on Mr. Thurber himself. It was read eagerly when it appeared in installments in the *Atlantic Monthly* in 1958 and later in book form with illustrations by the author.

Mr. Thurber lost the vision of one of his eyes in boyhood as the result of an accident. In his mature years the vision of the other eye deteriorated steadily, and in his last years he was almost totally blind. As total blindness approached, he gradually ceased to draw. He continued to be as active as ever in other ways, dictating his articles and books, and, as was noted above, he even performed briefly on the stage.

James Thurber's first book for children, *Many Moons*, was published in 1943. It was awarded the Caldecott Medal in 1944. A fantasy of a little princess who wanted the moon, it became popular immediately. *The Great Quillow* was published the following year, the story of a toymaker who saved his town from a plundering giant. The *Saturday Review* wrote glowingly of it and said Mr. Thurber had brought to the

story "grace and humor and a phrasing that is an unending delight."

In 1945 *The White Deer* appeared, again a fairy tale full of enchantment. This time the author was co-illustrator (with Don Freeman). *The 13 Clocks* was published in 1950, about the castle of a gloomy duke. This has been presented successfully on television. Marc Simont illustrated this book, as he did *The Wonderful O*, published in 1957.

Mr. Thurber was married to Althea Adams in 1922 and they had one daughter, Rosemary. His second wife, whom he married in 1935, was Helen Wismer.

Ruthven Todd

1914-

AUTHOR OF
Tan's Fish; The Space Cat; The Space Cat Visits Venus; Etc.

Autobiographical sketch of Ruthven Todd:

I WAS born in Edinburgh, Scotland, June 14, 1914, the oldest of ten children. My father was an architect and, when she had time for it, my mother cultivated a most elaborate rock garden, and kept bees. The bees were, I think, rather more successful than the rock garden, even though Mother was a friend of the Hippopotamus, as we called the professor of botany who lived in the Royal Botanical Gardens opposite our house. The bees could go for a longer time without attention.

I started life with the idea that I was going to be a doctor, another Dr. Dolittle, able to talk to animals and cure everything. My natural laziness, however, soon made it clear to me that I would not be keen on the long hours, and regularity, of a doctor's life. Father, who had wanted to be a naval officer, wanted me to become an architect. So I spent a lot of time in his office, learning something of the rudiments of the profession. The only house I ever designed (with much help from Father) was a villa for a Mr. Peacock. I wanted to be an artist. The life of an artist seemed to me to be admirable as, although it might mean hard work, I would not be tied to set hours and an office. I went through school with this intention and won prizes for drawing and then went to the Edinburgh College of Art.

Ruthven: *rhymes with "given"*

Judy Tennyson
RUTHVEN TODD

After a year there, however, the slump hit Father. Banks and insurance offices no longer wanted new buildings. So I moved to the Island of Mull, off the west coast of Scotland, where I worked as a shepherd and farm laborer on a small holding. I painted my last oil painting there, a large portrait of a Clydesdale stallion with its groom.

The expenses of painting were too great for me, so I took up another passion of mine. I had always written poetry, so now I devoted all my spare time, and there was not too much of it on a farm, to writing poems. After two years of farming I became the assistant to a man who was running a picture gallery, a literary agency, and a magazine, in Edinburgh. Then I moved to London where I did all the usual things, teaching, running a pottery gallery, helping out at the Surrealist Exhibition in 1936, working as a copywriter, and so on.

During the war I worked in the Civil Defense until I was thrown out as unfit. Then I worked for a London bookseller until a flying bomb knocked down the back of my apartment, when I moved to a farm which I had rented in Essex. By this time I had realized that I could not live on poetry and so I was a professional writer. I wrote novels and detective stories and anything else that anyone ordered. At least I was not tied to an office desk.

I discovered, however, that I had a desire to write books which would not sell enough to keep me alive, so I tried to write these in the intervals of potboiling. In 1947 I came to America on a visitor's visa, and went back to England in 1948 to get a proper immigration visa. I visited Martha's Vineyard first in 1947 and after that always managed to spend a week or two on the island. In 1954 I moved to the island to live permanently, all the year round.

Although I had written a couple of children's books in England, I did not think of doing others until William Lipkind suggested that I should write one on space travel, and that started the books about Flyball, the Space Cat. *Tan's Fish* was founded on a true story which I found while doing research for a paperback book on how to keep tropical fish. In 1952 I bought a box of water colors and a sketchbook and started to keep an illustrated natural history diary of life, during the summer, on Martha's Vineyard. It took me a long time to learn to draw again, but now my house and myself are divided into two parts, one of them writing and the other drawing flowers, shells, mushrooms, and the like.

I have fulfilled my ambition of avoiding an office desk and office hours, but I have discovered that I work many more hours than I would do if I had a regular job. But I live in a lovely place and have a lovely time. I became an American citizen in 1959.

J. R. R. Tolkien

1892-

AUTHOR OF
The Hobbit; The Lord of the Rings; Etc.

JOHN Ronald Reuel Tolkien, the Englishman whose imaginative and exciting fantasy, *The Hobbit*, captured an immediate public when published in 1938, was born in South Africa January 3, 1892. His father died when he was four and his mother took him to England with the family. They settled in Birmingham, where his father had been born. When he was twelve, his mother died, and he was reared, with his brother, by a Roman Catholic priest. He was graduated from Exeter College, Oxford University, in 1915 and saw service in World War I

Tolkien: *TALL ken*

J. R. R. TOLKIEN

with the Lancashire Fusiliers. He went back to college after the war and received his M.A. degree in 1919.

After two years as an assistant on the *Oxford English Dictionary*, Mr. Tolkien began his career as a teacher at the University of Leeds. After five years there, he was appointed Professor of Anglo-Saxon at Oxford University and a Fellow of Pembroke College. Since 1945 he has been Merton Professor of English Language and Literature and Fellow of Merton College.

His four children, three boys and one girl, doubtless were the combined reason for Mr. Tolkien's fairy tales, although it has been natural for critics to observe that he has merely followed his illustrious Oxford predecessor Lewis Carroll in this field. His interest in tales of the imagination, however, goes farther back than his children, for he has written that as a child he "desired dragons with a profound desire." He goes on to say he did not want them in the neighborhood, intruding into his safe world, but he yearned for them, nevertheless, the way "the dweller in the quiet and fertile plains may hear of the tormented hills and the unharvested sea and long for them in his heart. For the heart is hard though the body be soft."

In 1950 Mr. Tolkien published a second book for young readers, *Farmer Giles of Ham*, a humorous fantasy about a reluctant conqueror of giants and dragons. This book

was followed by *The Lord of the Rings*, a three-volume sequel to *The Hobbit*, which is a much more complex and serious allegory-fantasy. It was described by the critic Edmund Wilson as "essentially a children's book . . . which has somehow got out of hand."

Marjorie Torrey

1899-

AUTHOR AND ILLUSTRATOR OF
Penny; Artie and the Princess; Three Little Chipmunks; The Merriweathers; Etc.

Autobiographical sketch of Marjorie Torrey Hood Chanslor, who uses her maiden name as her pen name:

I WAS born in New York City, and grew up there and near by. One of my earliest memories is of my father drawing pictures for me of my then not-yet-born baby brother and myself. I was pulling him on a sled, or we picked flowers, climbed trees, built snowmen or houses of blocks, read together. My father was not a professional artist, but the little pencil sketches were charming. Perhaps they started my making pictures. I've done so as long as I can remember.

I had plenty of time for this, as a back injury in childhood kept me from going to school. At thirteen I went to the National Academy of Design, then to the Art Students League. In the summers I painted at home, in a little studio my father had had built for me; and twice a week at the Metropolitan Museum of Art. One winter I went to the Museum in the evenings, with a group of young people drawn together by Vachel Lindsay. We gazed at pictures, sculpture, the reminders of past civilizations—Egyptian, Greek, Roman, medieval—and talked of whatever came into our minds, history, art, poetry, and people. Afterward, we walked through snowy Central Park. Those evenings are a wonderful memory.

At that time Vachel Lindsay begged or borrowed a room in a YMCA building and held exhibitions of amateur paintings. He asked me to contribute. I replied, with a mixture of youthful arrogance and shyness, that I only painted to try and satisfy myself. He said, "Oh, so you just want to *talk to yourself*." I sent several paintings. And have always remembered his remark.

MARJORIE TORREY

I also recall a remark of Jerome Myers (the painter): "Imitate anyone you like. Afterward, if you've anything to say you'll find your own way of saying it." I thought of it later, in London, in a gallery of Turner's pictures. At one end hung two of his earlier paintings; at the other, two by a noted painter he had obviously admired and imitated. He had left instructions that these were always to be shown with his own work. But how his work later differed!

I was influenced by many pictures, but not, I think, by any particular artist or style. (I'm not comparing myself with Turner, of course!) At art school I seldom took advice from the instructors, but used the models to study anatomy, form, light, color in my own way, then went home to experiment from memory and imagination. Soon after leaving art school I stopped "talking to myself." I also wanted to earn my living. So I made many drawings and lugged them around to publishing offices. They were very crude, but got me quite a few assignments for illustrations.

Then I married and had a son. That year I made baby clothes. I was too intent and blissfully content and lazy to paint and draw. I began again during my son's first year, doing mostly magazine illustrations and covers and advertisements. I went to Europe twice on assignments. My "magazine career" extended over quite a period of years. Then I went to live on the West Coast, and wrote several novels, some published, under different names. But I had always most enjoyed picturing children, so I began illustrating and writing books for and about them. This I love.

I never use posed models for my pictures of children—can anyone? I watch them and try to absorb and express *something* of their wonderful charm. I like to watch and talk with grown people too. To work, of course, and to read. Also to dance when I get the chance. For some reason I'm rather addicted to Victorian surroundings, perhaps because my parents were young people in the eighties, and my Grandmother Van Tassel of Sleepy Hollow told me stories of her early life. I loved Europe, especially the cities, and want and hope to see Europe again, and more and different places. I've spent some years on the West Coast, but am essentially an easterner, especially a New Yorker. I live in New York now.

My son and his beautiful wife and four lovely children live—except for summers in Connecticut—in "my" exciting city. I use my maiden name for children's books. Of these I've illustrated too many to name.

Geoffrey Trease

1909-

AUTHOR OF
Web of Traitors; The Seven Queens of England; The Secret Fiord; Message to Hadrian; Etc.

Autobiographical sketch of Geoffrey Trease:

I WAS born on August 11, 1909, in Nottingham, England, son of a wine merchant, and grew up in the center of Robin Hood's ancient city, though as soon as I was old enough to plan my own vacations I went on hiking and camping trips all over the country, often alone. I wanted to be an author even in those days. I edited private magazines and class magazines in single copies; then, for my last three years, the official school magazine. When my father offered me either a bicycle or a cricket bat, I asked for a secondhand typewriter instead. At sixteen I wrote a full-length play which was put on by the school dramatic society. I played games (everyone had to) but my real interest was in books, debates, acting, and attending the theaters in town.

Trease: *TREEZ*

GEOFFREY TREASE

At nineteen I won a scholarship to the Queen's College at Oxford, but, though I liked university life and made plenty of friends, I had had enough of Greek and Latin for the time being. So, after a year, I burned my boats, resigned the scholarship, and went off to London to seek my fortune. For several years I had rather a struggle (but a great deal of fun) making a livelihood as a journalist. Then, almost accidentally, I found I could write for the older boys and girls.

Just before this, I met and married Marian Boyer. We lived in various places—the basement of a Regency house in Bath, a Tudor cottage in the Somerset hills, and a modern house near Oxford. Now we live on the slopes of the Malvern Hills, facing the distant mountains of Wales, in a beautiful region full of literary and historical memories.

We have one daughter, Jocelyn, who has been a great help to me in my work, especially my modern stories. Her own life at school and university has aided me in keeping up to date in my ideas of the present-day girls—and boys.

During World War II, I was in the Army and went to India. Since then my travels have been family trips, usually combined with collecting material for my stories. Thus, we went to Norway for *The Secret Fiord,* and to Greece for *The Young Traveler*

in Greece. I also travel about Britain a good deal, giving talks to schools, universities, teachers' conferences, and such like. This makes a stimulating change from the weeks of quietly writing at home in the heart of the country. A writer's life can be *too* solitary.

I find now that—apart from articles, short stories, and radio plays for both adults and children—I have published more than forty books, mostly for young readers. About fifteen of these have come out in America, including historical and modern fiction, biography, and travel stories, and my first historical novel for adults, *Snared Nightingale,* which I hope will be acceptable also to older boys and girls, was published in 1957. Altogether my work has appeared in eleven foreign languages.

Henry Treece

1911-

AUTHOR OF

Viking's Dawn; The Road to Miklagard; Men of the Hills; Perilous Pilgrimage; Etc.

Autobiographical sketch of Henry Treece:

I WAS born in the town of Wednesbury, once an ancient Saxon settlement named after Woden, in Staffordshire—but spent as much time as I could among the woods and hills of Shropshire and Wales. A member of a large family of cousins, Aunts, Uncles, and dogs, I was much more interested in larking about than in schoolwork. There were hills to slide down on tea trays, pools to skate on or to fall in—a flickering magic-lantern show in our splendidly built, but then disused and whitewashed pigsty. Teachers said I would come to a bad end.

On my father's side, we could trace our descent back to 1573—all Nottinghamshire countrymen, who lived on the same piece of land just south of Sherwood Forest.

On my mother's side, I came from an early iron-founding family which, to turn the tables, had migrated from Wales to set up their furnaces in the English Midlands. I once wrote an adult novel about them, *The Rebels;* a carefree, spendthrift lot. Great-grandfather still smiles wryly down the staircase of my old house in Lincolnshire, holding his precious black beaver hat

HENRY TREECE

which, on pay days, he used to fill with gold guineas for his workmen—until that day the crown fell out, when the ensuing scramble caused some men to go unpaid and others to return home with much more than their share.

He was an appealing character. A young lad at the time of the wars with Napoleon, his mother hid him in a boiler at the iron-works to keep him from the press gangs. He survived to gain a Hall in Worcester-shire and a carriage and pair—true Regency style. But the Wicked Earl of Dudley is reputed to have tricked him out of the lot —otherwise I wouldn't be writing this now! By family agreement, his pair of dueling pistols should have come down to me—but a sly, gipsy-consorting Uncle got in first and took them. I never forgot that—although the loping Uncle and his pack of foraging black dogs has long since gone to join Great-grandfather. As soon as I could afford it, I bought a pair of pistols of my own—but they are not as grand as my whiskered an-cestor's pair of vicious little beauties.

Still, my Wicked Uncle did do one thing for me—he told me all sorts of apocryphal yarns about the highwayman Dick Turpin, and gave me a set of colored prints to prove it. I lost the prints in moving house, but I still remember the harsh feel of the black horsehair sofa on which I sat, bare-legged and wide-eyed, to be chilled to the marrow

each Sunday evening, after the family prayer singing.

Of course, such a background is hope-less for a scholar. I grew up quite violent and unacademic—and *so* impractical! I once built a glider in our barn before I bothered to measure the doors and find they were too narrow for the thing ever to come out and fly.

Slovenly, daydreaming, innocent of all mathematics, I lounged my way through school, held in an old manor house. But somehow I won the senior science prize for two years and then, by some error, no doubt, gained a scholarship to the University of Birmingham, where I read some English and became captain of the University boxing club.

Here I began to write, my early pieces for the University magazine being either in the manner of Auden—who had just exploded in the academic world, and whose father taught me—or that of the Surrealists.

I began to write seriously. As a school-master in a northern boarding establishment I had lots of time for this—when I was not running along hills with hosts of boys, or charging up and down a football field, urging my team on with a tightly rolled umbrella in my hand.

Then T. S. Eliot noticed me, and pub-lished four of my books of verse. I even began a literary Movement, called Apoca-lyptic; at which time I got to know Dylan Thomas rather well and wrote a book about him—the first one to be published on that sadly gifted writer.

When World War II came, I joined the Army; but my unit was destroyed at Dun-kirk before I could get to them. I trans-ferred to the Air Force and went into In-telligence. In slack periods, I edited maga-zines for Gollancz and collections of Air Force poetry for the Bodley Head. Then one day, after the war was over, I tried my hand at a short story, based on an old Scots legend about a man who was murdered and his head put into a bag for delivery to his crazed widow. This story grew and grew, until it became my first novel, *The Dark Island*, set in Celtic Britain. It took four years to write, because I didn't know how one went about writing novels then.

I have learned a bit more since, and have published about fifty books—but we don't have heads in bags any more. I let my characters keep their heads, so that they can talk their way into the next chapter.

My main interest is in the historical novel, especially for children—of whom I have two, Jennifer and Richard—and my pet period is early Britain, New Stone Age to Norman Conquest. My illustrator has almost always been Christine Price, whose drawings always thrill me and my horse-loving children.

One day I may grow into the Tudor period; I should do, if only because there is a feast hall dating back to Henry VIII in my garden. But Tudor folk are so difficult to visualize; I can get on better with my more remote British ancestors at the moment.

ALVIN TRESSELT

Alvin Tresselt

1916-

AUTHOR OF

White Snow, Bright Snow; Little Lost Squirrel; Bonnie Bess, the Weathervane Horse; Etc.

Autobiographical sketch of Alvin Tresselt:

EVERYONE thought I would be a preacher when I grew up. For hours at a time I would stand on a box haranguing my flock, calling down the five-year-old equivalent of damnation on the indifferent heads of the daisies and dandelions that choked our dooryard.

I couldn't decide whether I would be a farmer or an architect. Summers spent on a farm had pretty much convinced me there was nothing better than a fine herd of Jerseys and a fat barn redolent with the evidence of livestock. But to counterbalance this, I had been given one time a box of stone blocks, and my Christmas request for years after was for still another—and larger—box of these wonderful red and white blocks. My constant delight was creating grander and more fabulous buildings with them. Even after I discovered that being an architect entailed an impossible mastery over such things as trigonometry and calculus, I spasmodically drew plans and built buildings with blocks that had long since ceased to be mere toys.

I ended up writing for children, but I was almost thirty before that happened. Knowing Leonard Weisgard and Margaret

Wise Brown at the time they were fighting to gain recognition for their particular contribution to the juvenile field, I heard many of their discussions about what constituted a good children's book. Gradually this talk began to stimulate the deep roots of my love of nature. I remembered my acute childhood reactions to the vagaries of weather and seasons, and the concern I had felt for the farmer and his crops. I remembered so well one of the few children's books I had actually owned, called *Helping the Weatherman,* and the delight with which I had read and reread it. One day, almost as though it were a letter of application to join Leonard's and Margaret's magic circle, I wrote *Rain Drop Splash.* Getting a nod of approval from them, I sent it on to Beatrice Creighton of Lothrop, Lee & Shepard, and her nod of approval was in the form of a contract.

I then discovered that one doesn't just write a book, especially if that book proves to be successful. I soon had Beatrice prodding me for more, and it was *White Snow, Bright Snow* that followed. This marked the beginning of a most happy relationship with Roger Duvoisin, which has continued through some dozen books together.

In 1952, when Parents' Institute was planning a new magazine for three to sevens, I was approached to be the managing editor, and I have been serving in that capacity on

Humpty Dumpty's Magazine ever since. I now live in Redding, Connecticut, with my wife—who writes for children under the name of Blossom Budney—and my daughter, Ellen Victoria, commuting each day to my office in New York. Eventually I hope to live full time in the country, writing, watching the weather, and raising the most beautiful delphiniums in the world.

* * *

Mr. Tresselt was born in Passaic, New Jersey, September 30, 1916, and educated in the public schools there. He moved to New York when he was eighteen. He has had over twenty books published, and is a member of the council of the Authors' Guild. *White Snow, Bright Snow* was awarded the Caldecott Medal in 1948.

EDWIN TUNIS

Edwin Tunis

1897-

AUTHOR AND ILLUSTRATOR OF
*Oars, Sails and Steam; Weapons;
Wheels; Colonial Living; Etc.*

Autobiographical sketch of Edwin Tunis:

THIS person is a "two-legged animal, without feathers," and now seems unlikely to grow any, though he might be excused for a few barnacles, in view of the years that are bracketed by the date above and the one now on the calendar.

The event associated with the earlier date, an important one in any life, occurred at Cold Spring Harbor, New York, in a house that faced a shaded street, a strip of sand, and Long Island Sound. Life on Long Island was simpler in those days; nobody ever went to a hospital merely to be born. The baby was carried up to the attic, to make sure he would rise in life.

Quite early in the life of its eldest son, the Tunis family began to move about. The new electric lighting was in demand in the smaller centers along the East Coast and it was the business of the father of the family to set up the necessary equipment for producing it. The installation of a ponderous Corliss engine belted, with about seventy-five feet of leather, to a generator, took a year or so. When a job was finished, the family moved to the next town.

This footloose existence had its points but its effect on the schooling of your deponent was not all for the best, and there was a certain lack of cooperation on his part that didn't help much. Art school seemed the only kind worth attending and there he went, before the good professors at the Baltimore City College had been able to teach him to read Latin at all readily. This did not, however, interfere with his reading everything in English he could reach, including the directions on labels.

The course at the Maryland Institute of Art and Design was never properly finished either. There was a war on in 1917 and the tyro artist felt he had to become a fledgling flier, which he did without achieving anything spectacular, but the experience was broadening.

There followed years of commercial art at its most commercial, with some illustrating that gradually took on a historical bent. This led to some murals and one of these prompted the first venture at writing. "The History of Spices" was painted for McCormick and Company in Baltimore. There are a lot of ancient ships in it. In seeking for facts about them, it became apparent that there was no one book which covered the development of ships and also had clear pictures of them. So *Oars, Sails and Steam* had to be written. (It was in the 1953 Fifty Best Books of the Year, as well as in the Graphic Arts Club Exhibit, and in the Best Juvenile Books of Twenty Years.)

William Targ, of the World Publishing Company, suggested a book about weapons, a subject which the writer approached with a completely open mind, practically blank in fact, but there was the same sort of niche for such a book that there had been for the first one.

The third, *Wheels*, like the others undertakes to present a panorama of a whole subject without stopping for minor details. It won a gold medal in 1955 from the Boys' Clubs of America. *Colonial Living* is different. It peers into all sorts of holes and corners of the daily life of the American colonists.

John R. Tunis

1889-

AUTHOR OF

Iron Duke; The Kid Comes Back; Rookie of the Year; Schoolboy Johnson; Etc.

JOHN R. Tunis was born in Boston and went to Harvard. At college he played on the tennis team and was a two-miler. He saw service overseas in World War I, and began to write for newspapers and magazines. He was one of the byline sports writers for the New York *Evening Post*, and did stories on major sporting events on both sides of the Atlantic. He saw Tilden be-

JOHN R. TUNIS

come the world's tennis champion, Bobby Jones perform on the golf links, Babe Ruth play for the Yankees, and a host of others.

For radio, Mr. Tunis covered the Davis Cup matches at Wimbledon and Forest Hills. He is a tennis player himself, and has won tennis titles here and abroad.

Mr. Tunis's numerous novels about sports for young people are characterized by realism and a keen sense of social values. Perhaps his best-known title is *Iron Duke*, the story of a track athlete at Harvard. *Highpockets*, the story of a professional baseball player, was given a Junior Book Award of the Boys' Clubs of America in 1949.

Mr. Tunis makes his home in Connecticut but spends his winters in Florida.

Annette Turngren

AUTHOR OF

Mystery Walks the Campus; Mystery Haunts the Fair; Flaxen Braids; The Copper Kettle; Etc.

Autobiographical sketch of Annette Turngren:

MY home when I was a child was a grain and dairy farm near Montrose, Minnesota. My parents had come from Sweden in their youth and settled there, and I was the youngest of their nine children. There were few other children in the neighborhood, but there were so many of us, and always a few cousins or family friends visiting, that we never felt lonely. We did everything together, went swimming in the muddy Crow River, skated on pasture ponds, had a homemade tennis and volley-ball court out under the trees, and on winter evenings a big kitchen table around which we all played games or did our lessons or read our books.

Though libraries were far away, books found their way into our home somehow, and a Christmas without books under the tree would have been no Christmas at all. The loft above the woodshed held a many years' accumulation of reading matter and one of the delights of my childhood was to hide away under the dusty rafters and lose myself in some fascinating book or delve into a stack of old magazines.

ANNETTE TURNGREN

Even at the age of nine, I dreamed of becoming a writer. In spite of her busy life, my mother sometimes wrote poems and sketches which were published in a Swedish magazine, and one of my sisters had begun writing stories and had broken into print. I longed for the same glory, but though I filled the blank pages of my father's discarded old ledgers with one "novel" after another, I always left them half done. Yet I was sure I was going to write books someday. No other future had any appeal for me.

When I was thirteen we moved to Minneapolis. In my senior year in high school, and after some experience on the school paper, I decided that I would become a journalist. Armed with a letter from the dean of girls, I set off for the Minneapolis *Journal* to offer my services to the editor, but though I walked back and forth in front of the building most of the day, I never had the courage to go in. So ended my career in journalism.

That fall I entered the University of Minnesota, where I studied to become an English teacher. Dreams of a writing career were laid aside and might never have been taken out and dusted off except for one of my instructors, who suggested I try writing for children. The more I thought about it, the more I liked the idea, mostly because I have always liked children.

During the years I was teaching, I wrote for young people's magazines, but I never thought of attempting a book. Then one summer when I was listening to some of my mother's recollections of her childhood in Sweden, I thought, "Why not write it down and weave it into a story?" It wasn't until I was hard at work on *Flaxen Braids*, my first book, that I realized this was what I had really wanted to do ever since I was nine—write a book. Only now I was better equipped to do it.

Flaxen Braids, my mother's story, was published in 1937. The following year I visited Sweden and there wrote a second book, *The Copper Kettle*, most of it on the little island of Öland where my father was born, basing the story on his childhood.

Several girls' mysteries followed before I came to New York City to work on teen-age magazines and in a book publishing house. New York is still my home, though I often return to Minnesota, and a number of my books have had that state as their setting.

Yoshiko Uchida

AUTHOR OF
The Dancing Kettle, and Other Japanese Folk Tales; New Friends for Susan; Etc.

AUTHOR AND ILLUSTRATOR OF
The Magic Listening Cap; The Full Circle; Etc.

Autobiographical sketch of Yoshiko Uchida:

ALTHOUGH I was born in California, a good bit of Japan was inside of me all along, for this was the country from which my parents came. Father was a businessman in San Francisco, and we lived—my parents, my older sister and I—in a small house with a large yard, in Berkeley. Our house seemed always to be filled with guests. Many of them were lonely, homesick students from Japan, with flat wallets and enormous appetites, who came to be consoled, to speak Japanese, and to eat vast quantities of Mother's Japanese cooking. But it was not just the food. There were other Japanese touches in our home too.

On the third of March, for instance, we always celebrated Dolls Festival Day. All of Mother's tiny Japanese dolls would emerge from her trunk for the occasion and

Yoshiko Uchida: *yoh shee koh oo chee dah*

often friends would come to see them and have a cup of tea. Sometimes Mother would wear her kimono for a party and occasionally she dressed my sister and me in ours for special programs at school. Then, of course, there were all the fascinating stories read to us from the books that came from Japan. Some of these went into my first collection of folk tales which I was to write many years later.

In spite of all this, most of the time I felt like any other American child and lived a life somewhat similar to Susan's in *New Friends for Susan*. I had a hammock strung between a peach and an apricot tree where I liked to sit and write stories on sheets of wrapping paper. I liked, always, to draw. I had a collie who plagued me by running away several times a year. Some days I adored school, and some days I didn't; and sometimes I quarreled with my sister.

Summers, we often traveled. One year we went to New York City with stops all along the way. Another year we went to Japan, but I was old enough only to grumble about visiting so many relatives and to count the number of bows my parents exchanged with their friends. The record at one meeting was thirteen!

I went to school in Berkeley and probably would have spent most of my life there if it hadn't been for World War II. I was a senior at the University of California when Pearl Harbor was attacked. Before I could finish school, all Japanese were evacuated from the West Coast and my diploma came through the mails in a cardboard roll. My family was sent, with about eight thousand other Japanese, to a relocation center in the midst of a Utah desert, and there I taught second grade in a drafty barracks where snakes and scorpions sometimes came to share the room with us. After a year, a fellowship came from Smith College, and I spent a year there getting my master's degree in education.

My first job was teaching a class of first and second graders in a small Quaker school near Philadelphia. It was fun, but I felt there might be a better way in which I could work with children. The answer came when I moved to New York City, where an

YOSHIKO UCHIDA

artist asked me to work with him on a picture book based on a Japanese folk tale. That book didn't work out, but I kept on working with Japanese folk tales until I had enough for my collection. As soon as I began to write, I knew this was what I wanted most to do. I wrote some stories and articles for adults as well as for children. Some of these were published and some were not, so I worked in an office too.

In 1952, the Ford Foundation granted me a fellowship to Japan, to collect material for more books. I was to stay a year, but I liked it so well I stayed two. This time I did more than count bows. I was happy to be able to retell and illustrate a book of folk tales that Japanese children still read and enjoy. I think it would be such a fine world if we could keep on sharing, not only our stories but our ideas too.

A book of mine, published in 1957, was *The Full Circle*, and curiously, my own life seems to have made a circle too, for I am back once more in California where I am doing a number of things, but enjoying writing most of all.

* * *

Miss Uchida's first story for the picture-book age, *Rokubei and the Thousand Rice Bowls*, with illustrations by Kazue Mizumura, was published in 1962.

Nora S. Unwin

1907-

AUTHOR AND ILLUSTRATOR OF
Doughnuts for Lin; Proud Pumpkin; Etc.

ILLUSTRATOR OF
Once in the Year; A Place for Peter; Etc.

Autobiographical sketch of Nora S. Unwin:

MINE was a very normal, happy childhood. My twin sister and I were the youngest of five children. Our home was a plain suburban house thirteen miles from London (England), but country excursions were frequent. My father was a master printer and a great reader. The house was filled with books; we all loved being read to; the illustrations absorbed me. Many generations of our family have been printers or publishers; thus I've always suspected some printing ink in my blood! Hence, perhaps, my devotion to engraving, printing, lettering and illustrating. I've always loved to draw. The first book I wrote and illustrated—printed (by hand), published (for Mother's birthday), limited edition (one copy)—was entitled "Adventures of a Blade of Grass."

My father greatly loved outdoor life and instilled in me a deep love and observation of nature. He was a craftsman, handling tools expertly, but he was not exactly an artist. Though I remember how he could delight us by drawing mice wearing top hats and other animal antics. Mother's artistic talents blossomed in the creation of attractive clothes for us, a talent which my twin and I in turn lavished upon our dolls. Though we both drew and painted by the hour, I alone continued in art. My twin became a cellist.

Blessed with parents who recognized my consuming passion, and encouraged (while never overpraising) my efforts, I filled every spare moment, and every available space, with people, animals, flowers, fairies, etc. After extra art periods in high school I had two years of life classes at a private studio; two years' general courses at art school; and finally four wonderful years (and my diploma) at the Royal College of Art (London).

At the age of eighteen I received my first book-illustrating commission, and later began exhibiting my wood engravings. In 1937 I met Elizabeth Yates, who was then in London. We became great friends. Soon we began working together, as author and illustrator, for English publishers. World War II came and Elizabeth and her husband, William McGreal, returned to America. To console myself for this loss, and the end (as I thought) of our collaboration, I evolved the first book of my own, *Round the Year.* Soon, however, in spite of war risks, manuscripts and drawings were crossing the Atlantic, and I was illustrating Elizabeth Yates' stories for American publishers.

In 1946, at the McGreals' invitation, I came to America and joined them in their delightful farmstead home in New Hampshire. I fell in love with America and stayed. Since then, over thirty books have been illustrated; two I have written. My engravings have been widely exhibited nationally and internationally. I love New England. Now I have a small abode of my own; and am still absorbed in illustrating, engraving, writing, and a little teaching. Hiking and playing the recorder are happy relaxations.

* * *

Miss Unwin has taught at Wellesley College and is now working and teaching part time in Peterborough, New Hampshire.

NORA S. UNWIN

Mary Urmston

1891-

AUTHOR OF

Mystery of the Old Barn; The Seven and Sam; The New Boy; The Twenty-five and Ann; Etc.

Autobiographical sketch of Mary Urmston:

I WAS born in Tullahoma, Tennessee, on August 27, 1891, but my family moved to Indiana before I was old enough even to say the name of that state. It was in Indiana that my "formal education" began. At the age of five I started to go to school, quite unwillingly. In fact, I was literally dragged there by an older girl. The school was of yellow brick, square and ugly. The teacher, viewed from the eye level of a five-year-old, was very tall and thin. She wore a high starched collar, and she carried a long thin pointer with a red rubber tip. She tried to teach me to read. The lesson was high up on the blackboard, an endless procession of queer shapes which she called letters. I don't know why, but I didn't like them. For a child who would one day want to become a writer, a balky sort of beginning.

Very soon, however, I escaped from those letters. We moved to Massachusetts and there the village schoolteacher was round and ruffly, and the letters were stories in books, with pictures. I learned to read. I was soon reading everything within my reach.

In Massachusetts we lived on an old farm in a house with a huge spooky attic, wonderful for rainy Saturdays. There were barns too, miles of them it seemed, offering all sorts of opportunities for explorations and discoveries. The fact that the barns were empty of animals which had once dwelt there only added to their mystery and adventure, so far as we children were concerned. My father was not a farmer but he wished to make us a home in the country and the old farm was the answer, the perfect answer, we thought. Not only were there the barns and the attic, there was an enormous shadowy cellar with earth floor and rock walls, and there was the out-of-doors, complete with apple orchard, meadows of deep grass, woodlands where mysterious small wild creatures scurried just out of

MARY URMSTON

sight; there were brooks, a swamp where we dared not venture too far, and a pine grove whispering secrets in the wind. This old farm with its special quality of pleasant eeriness—always something just beyond our reach or our sight and needing further exploration—has been the scene of several of my books, the ones about the Arnold family. I think perhaps they are the ones I have most enjoyed writing.

We left the farm eventually and went to live in Somerville, not far from Boston. There I went through high school, and then we moved again, this time to Connecticut. I attended Danbury State Teachers College and, while a student there, had my first and only experience with a "little red schoolhouse." I was sent as a substitute teacher to a country school and there I stayed for two strenuous weeks in March, a cold and muddy month. I found out how to build a fire in the big, pot-bellied stove which occupied the place of honor in the schoolroom, but I did not find out how to keep it burning once I became interested in my teaching. I found out how to range the children around that stove to dry their feet. I also found out that fifteen lively youngsters of assorted ages were just about too many for any one teacher, if that teacher was to be myself, but the walls did hold together and my two weeks did come to an end.

After graduation, I taught in a Danbury grade school for a while, then went to Scarsdale, New York, to teach fifth grade. By that time I had found out that teaching, like reading, can be fun. Many of my books came out of these teaching years. While in Scarsdale, I attended Columbia University, catching up on all the courses I'd missed along the way, including several in writing. It was here that my first book was written (*Forty Faces*) and what a thrill it was to hear that it had actually been accepted for publication!

I am now living in California, in a woodsy hillside spot with a mountain at my window and two lively dogs. Also to keep me busy, I have our very haphazard flower gardens, always needing me and the hose, it seems. And, when dogs and gardens will let me alone, I have my typewriter and "one more book" to write.

MARGUERITE VANCE

Marguerite Vance

1889-

AUTHOR OF

Willie Joe and His Small Change; Windows for Rosemary; Song for a Lute; While Shepherds Watched; Etc.

Autobiographical sketch of Marguerite Vance:

I WAS born in 1889 in Chicago, Illinois, where both Mother and Father were born. Until I was about eight years old, we lived on property which had been my grandfather's land and subsequently became part of the great rolling mill project being gradually developed in Ainsworth Station, later to become South Chicago. So as a very little girl I knew what it was to live in a mill community, and my companions were almost entirely children of foreign (Slovak, Polish, etc.) background. I remember Mother saying I was actually developing a foreign accent, and I guess she was right because I loved my friends, and what they did (or said) was my cup of tea—make no mistake!

But there were drawbacks. After a few years of bliss as a first and then a second grader in the public school—probably with the accent thickening apace—I was sent to a private school in Chicago, Miss Martin's.

The family had moved by that time, too, and just after my fifteenth birthday I went to Europe—Paris, to be exact—where some of the happiest years of my life were spent, where the most lasting friendships were formed.

When I returned, I married William Little Vance and for twenty years we lived in Cleveland, Ohio. Our son died in infancy. My husband died in 1931 and I came to New York where for seven years I had charge of children's books at Dutton's, Inc. Subsequently, I became editor of children's books for E. P. Dutton & Company, Inc., and my work was there until my retirement in 1955. I think that is about all there is to tell about how the years were spent. My two great loves are and always have been the theater and country living.

Now as to why I write books for children: I honestly don't know, unless my consuming interest in people—all people—may have something to do with it. Again, there is the old theater ghost. I wanted the theater almost desperately as a young girl, studied for it so hard under the great Emile Vilemain of the Comédie Française for so long and with such ambitious plans, only to turn my back on it in the end. "Something had to give," and possibly writing for youngsters, dramatizing in story form the lives of great women, was the satisfactory outlet, the answer to a need. If my books can make great characters in history come alive, show themselves to the children as I feel they probably were instead of as they often seem on crowded pages, then I shall be happy. I believe most young people would come to love all history if the people who moved through it could become a little more real to them. I think that is what I am trying to help bring about.

* * *

Mrs. Vance has written over a dozen biographies of famous women—Martha Washington, Patsy Jefferson, Marie Antoinette, Elizabeth of Austria, etc. She was given the 1960 Thomas Alva Edison Award for *Willie Joe and His Small Change.*

VIRGINIA FRANCES VOIGHT

Virginia Frances Voight

1909-

AUTHOR OF

Treasure of Hemlock Mountain; The Girl from Johnnycake Hill; Mystery at Deer Hill; The Black Elephant; Etc.

Autobiographical sketch of Virginia Frances Voight:

I WAS born on March 30, 1909, in New Britain, Connecticut. We lived near the edge of town and I have happy memories of jaunts in the woods with my dog, Pete; of paddling in the brook where the banks were blue with forget-me-nots; and of hearing quail whistling across flowery meadows on a bright June morning.

Later, we moved to New Haven, where I grew up. At present, I am making my home with my sister in the neighboring town of Hamden.

We are a reading family. Our house was always crammed with books. I remember my mother seated in a rocker beside my bed, reading poetry and fairy stories in the soft glow of a kerosene lamp. My two grandmothers were wonderful storytellers. One of them told tales of the rich folklore of Germany, the other stories of her girlhood on a Virginia farm before and during the Civil War.

In school I was an average student, slightly on the tomboy side, enthusiastic about outdoor life, nature lore, and Indian lore. I had a large family of pets which at one time included fourteen assorted cats, two turtles, a salamander, and Pete, the Gordon setter who, years afterwards, was to live again in *Mystery at Deer Hill.*

I began writing back in grammar school days. Urged by a terrific imagination, I scribbled long thrillers in notebooks and passed them to the boy in the next seat at school. He was always flatteringly eager for the next installment. Whenever anyone asked me what I wanted to be when I grew up, I answered promptly, "A writer." But my parents were determined that I should be an artist. I was sent to the Yale School of the Fine Arts and to commercial art school. Through it all I continued with my scribbling.

A friend, who was teaching school in an isolated western community, asked me to write some stories about everyday Pilgrim life for her to use in her school. I responded with enthusiasm, and afterward I decided to try marketing the Pilgrim sketches. They sold promptly. That was the beginning of a gentle rain of short stories and articles sold to children's story papers and magazines, but it was years before I attempted to publish a book.

Walking along a country lane one day, I came upon a deserted house embowered in blossoming apple trees. The place seemed to sing that there was a story awaiting me there, so several days later I went back with a notebook and pencils and started writing *Apple Tree Cottage*. When the story was completed, I rented a box at the post office. If my book was destined to be turned down by the publisher I did not want my family to learn of my disappointment.

It was Christmas Eve when I received the letter telling me that *Apple Tree Cottage* had been accepted for publication. As I walked out of the post office, I saw the lights on the Christmas tree on the New Haven green glittering through the dusk. My heart overflowed with gratitude for the wonderful Christmas gift I had just received.

A great deal of personal experience goes into my books. The nature lore is based on firsthand material. My vacations in the Maine woods have been the source of many stories, as have also some of my girlhood camping adventures. I loved writing *Zeke and the Fishercat* because in it I lived the early Indian history of Connecticut. A love for animals and a sympathetic curiosity about their lives in freedom and in captivity brought about the circus books—*Rolling Show, The Black Elephant*—based on happenings in an old-time American rolling show.

After ten books and many short stories I firsthand material. My vacations in the story, but I have never regretted the impulse that urged me to become an author.

Amelia Elizabeth Walden

1909-

AUTHOR OF

A Girl Called Hank; Three Loves Has Sandy; My Sister Mike; Daystar; Etc.

Autobiographical sketch of Amelia Elizabeth Walden:

VITAL Statistics: Born, New York City, January 16, 1909.

The How and Why of My Joining This Strenuous, Lonely, Sorrow-Ridden Profession:

I think the term "reluctant writer" would be an appropriate epithet for me.

Every professional writer is always running into those well-intentioned people who *want* to write but never manage to get to it. My fate has been the reverse of this. I have

AMELIA ELIZABETH WALDEN

always been a resistant writer, grabbed by the scruff of the neck and dragged to it by

(1) the urgency of things within me that demanded to be said;

(2) the insistence of persons surrounding me who have told me I must write.

"You are a writer," people have been saying to me all my life and I have been both wise and foolish enough to accept their judgment. Several college professors, friends, my husband, and more lately my good friends among the editors have had this faith in me. More faith certainly than I would dare to have in myself! And they have driven me to my trade.

The interesting, and perhaps little-known, fact about my books for young people is that I have never sat down to write a book "for juniors." My first book came to me as a good story about two girls who just happened to be in their late teens. I wrote it as just a good story and was surprised upon finishing it to learn that I had written a book slanted toward the young adult market.

It is always flattering to me to learn that my books are liked by girls throughout the United States. Yet I still continue year after year to write a story that appeals primarily to the author. Letters from girls say much the same thing again and again:

"You don't treat us as if we were imma-ture. You write about us the way we feel about ourselves. We live and suffer and struggle and try to make a go of things in a tough world. We have our daily drama, our joys and sorrows, comedies and tragedies. You seem to understand all about these and you write about them as if you were just one of us."

I think perhaps that it is the other way round. I write about emotions and drama and themes and awareness that I find within myself, urgent things that have to be said. I have an enormous enthusiasm for characters that are young and still have plenty of development ahead of them. The result would naturally be a book that talks to young people on their own level, never talks *down* to them. This would be the secret— if you want to call it that—of the adult and exciting style.

LENORA MATTINGLY WEBER

Lenora Mattingly Weber

1895-

AUTHOR OF

*Meet the Malones; Leave It to Beany!
Beany Has a Secret Life; Make a
Wish for Me; Etc.*

Autobiographical sketch of Lenora Mattingly Weber:

PERHAPS one reason I write for young people is that I have always been surrounded by them. I grew up in a family of six children; we have six of our own.

I barely managed to get born in a little Missouri town before we moved to another small town in Ohio. Then, when I was twelve, we homesteaded on the Colorado plains. Those were hard years, what with trying to wrest crops from dry prairie sod, and yet they were happy and exciting too. I used to follow the big herds of sheep in the spring, and bring home motherless lambs and raise them on a bottle. The mortality rate was high, as I found to my sorrow. I chopped wood, milked cows, herded sheep. One year I rode in the big rodeo at Cheyenne, Wyoming, and won a cup in the ladies' relay race. I have used this ranch and rodeo background in many stories.

Then I came up to Denver to attend high school. My senior year, I was captain of our basketball team and our coach, Al Weber,

used to come home with me to carry the extra balls, score books, and such. So that I didn't go on to college, but married, and we proceeded to have a boys' basketball team of our own (five) and a girl thrown in. But in between repainting the baby bassinet, writing stories, nursing children through measles or mumps, I took classes at our Denver University in literature, psychology, Western history, languages—even clay modeling.

Because of our own six, our house and yard were always overflowing with children. Our back yard was always full of caves. I never knew when I would find a carp in the bathtub, or have a white rat jump out of the shoe I reached for. Then the teen age.

These lovable, hungry, noisy, often troubled, seemingly irresponsible teen-agers have problems of their own to face up to: Uncle Sam's hand on their shoulders as the boys near eighteen; the great urge for cars and speed; and a girl's constant question of whether or not she should be amorous on dates in order to be popular. These are the problems I write about—as honestly as I can —in the Beany Malone books.

When I'm stymied on how a boy or girl would act or react in a situation, I sometimes ask my own children or one of their friends, "What would you do if—?" I'm always sure of an honest answer, though the honesty—"Oh, no, that sounds corny"—may make me flinch.

And now our top three children have grandchildren that are growing into the books I am writing about the Malones. Just the other day, my oldest granddaughter suggested, "Don't you think it's time Beany was cutting off her braids?"

I am taking it under consideration.

Manly Wade Wellman

1903-

AUTHOR OF
The Mystery of Lost Valley; The Last Mammoth; Young Squire Morgan; Rebel Mail Runner; Etc.

Autobiographical sketch of Manly Wade Wellman:

I SUPPOSE my own boyhood was extraordinary. I was born in Portuguese West Africa, where my father was a medical missionary, and I came to America at six, thinking and talking more like one of the Umbundu people than like a boy with three hundred years of American ancestry. I lived almost everywhere—started school in Washington, D.C., went as far west as Utah, and back for my university degree at Columbia in New York, with times between in Kansas, Arkansas, and Minnesota. I harvested wheat, picked fruit, played football, hunted and camped. I was lost once in the Rocky Mountains. I tried to read everything about

MANLY WADE WELLMAN

everything, and thought about writing something for somebody else to read.

After Columbia I worked on newspapers, sold some stories and quit newspapering to write more. First and last, I've published about five hundred stories and articles in magazines. Irving Crump, the wise and helpful editor of *Boys' Life*, urged me to start writing books for young readers. I have written over a dozen and have three more definitely planned for the future, besides books for grownups. These juvenile stories are mostly adventure and mystery, both in the past and the present.

I've found it hard to write these books without the help of the boys and girls who read them. My son and his friends used to listen and suggest. But now my son is growing up, and I have to depend on the sons and daughters of neighbors. They tell me what sort of stories they like, and what sort they don't like, too.

Lots of them have been pleased with giants in my stories. One or two giants have been villains, one or two have been friendly. Those friendly giants, I think, are the best kind, all things considered.

At first I thought I was writing for boys, but I found that girls read the books, too. I'm glad that girls are interested in being lost in the woods without food or fire, or hunting treasure in an old haunted house, or spying during the Civil War, or fighting duels, or solving mysteries about pirates and Indians. Now I put girls into the stories, too; the sort of girls who can square dance and climb mysterious mountains and tell lawyers how to win important cases.

Other writers, and editors, and conductors of reading surveys give you lots of advice about how to write for young readers. Some of the advice is good; but the best advice is from the boys and girls themselves. After all, they know better than anybody what they want to read, and there's no real sense in writing what they don't want to read.

* * *

Mr. Wellman's recent stories are primarily concerned with American history. One trilogy relates the experiences of a young southerner in the Confederate Army.

A second series, comprising four books to date, deals with the life of a young member of the Continental Army.

Kurt Werth

1896-

ILLUSTRATOR OF

The Merry Miller; The Tailor's Trick; One Mitten Lewis; Picnic Pony; Etc.

Autobiographical sketch of Kurt Werth:

I WAS born in Leipzig, Germany. My childhood was one which most of the children enjoyed: playing cops and robbers in empty lots or soccer in the ball fields. Once a year during the time of the fair in a nearby little town, we would race through lanes and places in the twilight, dressed up as Indians and trappers, inspired by Cooper's *Leatherstocking.*

Wintertime attracted me in a strange way. I loved snow, sleigh riding, skating, and building snow fortresses. Even in a city like Leipzig winter was wonderful. At that time I did my first little drawings; they showed children in winter scenes.

When I entered elementary school I used the blackboard in my first bold attempts to draw Easter bunnies and horses, to the delight of my fellow pupils and the teacher. He called my mother in and suggested that she buy as many sketchbooks and crayons for me as I needed. And she did. This was the start of my career.

Education in art could be obtained only in the small municipal art museum and in a few mediocre private galleries. I tried both and found very little inspiration. After graduation from high school, I decided to enter the State Academy for Graphic Arts in Leipzig. My parents, skeptical about this step and always hoping to see me become a postmaster, consented at last. Life in the Academy opened my eyes to the real thing. Here my professor, who was under the influence of Cézanne, taught us how to draw, although the public was not yet aware of the trend of cubism in art. We came under the spell of it. I remember that I repeated the drawing of a skull twenty or thirty times until I was satisfied with the result, which conveyed the impression of an early cubist experiment. We became aquainted with all

KURT WERTH

the graphic techniques and were thrilled to try them out for illustrations of literary works.

This all was interrupted by the First World War, when all the young people left the classes and had to join the army. After the war the undercurrent of the new art movements came into the open and we, who came back to the art academy, profited from them. Soon I began to illustrate books. My first was a limited edition of Shakespeare's *Troilus and Cressida.* It was well received.

I left Leipzig for Munich and continued illustrating German and Russian classics for a number of German publishers. But the American Depression had its repercussions also in Germany. Illustrated books disappeared from the market. On the other hand, new and interesting magazines shot up like mushrooms. I became very busy in this new field. The political climate changed too. The fatal Hitler regime came to power and forced me and my wife to leave the old country. We came to New York, bewildered by the new atmosphere and different conditions but fascinated by the new country.

After some time I got my first jobs in magazines and we rented a little studio on Fourteenth Street. Toward the end of World War II, I made contacts with book publishers and illustrated my first children's books. In 1947 I became an American citizen.

Opal Wheeler

1898-

AUTHOR OF

*Mozart, the Wonder Boy; Stephen Foster, and
His Little Dog Tray; Franz Schubert and
His Merry Friends; Edward MacDowell
and His Cabin in the Pines; Etc.*

Autobiographical sketch of Opal Wheeler:

DURING my early years in Superior,
Wisconsin, my birthday was not antici-
pated with the usual eagerness, because
Halloween was the time when an especially
mischievous brood of four brothers and two
sisters could find a particular outlet for
wildest pranks.

Growing up on the tip end of Lake Superior was rugged, challenging us all in the
fiercely cold winters. But we skated, slid
downhill on our homemade sleds or broken
chunks of Mother's mixing bowl, played
hockey or went iceboating on the lake in
forty-below-zero weather. And never a day
without an exciting adventure, like one I
set down in 1957 in *The Miracle Dish*.

Music was my obsession. By ear I played
for hours on the old upright rosewood piano
("Stars Over Bethlehem"), and always accompanied the hordes of music-loving neighbors and visitors thronging our hospitable
living room. My compositions were endless.
To preserve them, my father slipped a nickel
into my apron pocket for every laborious
note set down. At six, all of the Mother
Goose verses had been set to music and *Sing
Mother Goose* is a product of that childhood
period.

After the usual schooling, higher education
continued at the State Normal School, the
Universities of Wisconsin and Washington,
and, after an interval, Columbia University.
Foreign shores beckoned me to France,
where I studied the piano, and then singing
in Italy.

Years were spent in working with children
of all ages, using music not only as a study,
but as a therapy in ridding them of physical
and mental ills. The lure of strange and
out-of-the-way places has taken me twice
around the globe, and countless times abroad
to collect firsthand material at the birth-
places of composers and authors.

While lecturing on music during four
summers at one of our universities, there
arose a need for material on the lives of
writers of music to put into the hands of
children. And so from necessity I found
myself writing biographies of composers
based on the material gathered through the
years.

* * *

Miss Wheeler has written many books
about the lives of musicians—Chopin, Schu-
mann, Handel, Tchaikovsky, etc. Many
have been translated into more than half-a-
dozen languages and are read by children
around the world.

After ten years of writing books, published
by E. P. Dutton, Miss Wheeler married her
publisher, the late John Macrae, president
of Dutton. She now lives in "a Mother
Goose French house in Belvedere, California, high on a hilltop overlooking the bay
and Golden Gate Bridge."

OPAL WHEELER

Anne Terry White

1896-

AUTHOR OF

*Three Children and Shakespeare; Lost Worlds;
Men Before Adam; George Washington
Carver; Etc.*

ANNE Terry White was born and grew
up in New England. She was graduated from Brown University in 1918, where
she was elected to Phi Beta Kappa. She

ANNE TERRY WHITE

married during her senior year in college, and later began to write for her own children. Her first book, published in 1938, *Three Children and Shakespeare*, grew out of the eager questions asked by her children when she read Shakespeare's plays to them in the evenings and on rainy afternoons. This book makes four plays come alive for youngsters.

One of Mrs. White's finest books is *Lost Worlds*, published in 1941. It is rated as one of the best popular introductions to archaeology for young people, and has been translated into eight languages. *Heroes of the Five Books* does for the first five books of the Bible what her earlier book did for Shakespeare.

In addition to writing and rearing a family, Mrs. White has taught and done social work. She lives in New York City but has a summer home at Blueberry Hill, in New Hampshire, among glacial rocks and blueberries, where she has spent many hours clearing her own woodland and opening up new vistas through the forest. Some of her other titles are *All About the Stars, All About Our Changing Rocks, All About Great Rivers of the World*, and *Prehistoric America*. Her most recent book, *The St. Lawrence, Seaway of North America*, is part of the Rivers of the World series.

E. B. White

1899-

AUTHOR OF

Stuart Little; Charlotte's Web

Autobiographical sketch of Elwyn Brooks White:

WRITING for children is usually regarded as a separate form of madness. I came to it by accident and stayed with it when it proved to be much like other kinds of writing—hard work, followed by pleasing rewards. The character Stuart Little appeared to me in a dream one night when I was traveling by rail. A writer is always grateful for small favors and I recall that I jotted down fragments of the tale next morning. I had no intention of writing a book for children, however, and the thing merely grew, by slow stages, over a period of about twelve years. Storytelling does not come easily or naturally to me; I am more of a commentator than a spinner of yarns.

As for *Charlotte's Web*, it came about as a result of my close association with animals in a barn. This barn, with its creatures and its swallows, has always been a place where I have felt at peace, and I deliberately tried to bring it to life in a story for youngsters. Many of the characters are taken right from life, including the pig and the spider. The tragedy of animal death by murder, which

E. B. WHITE

always haunts a farm, haunted me and I guess I was trying to write my way out of the dilemma in the story of Charlotte, and with her able assistance.

I was born in Mount Vernon, New York, in 1899. My father was a piano manufacturer with a business in New York, and I lived the pleasant life of a boy in the leafy suburbs. After I finished Cornell, I traveled about the country for a while, working at all sorts of jobs. I got as far as the ice pack and then turned around and came back east to Manhattan Island to live. I have spent much of my life in New York, working for the *New Yorker* in a rather loose-footed capacity, with no editorial responsibilities or duties, merely the opportunity to contribute.

I have been writing all my life and see no relief in sight.

* * *

Mr. White's books for adults include *One Man's Meat, The Second Tree from the Corner, Here Is New York,* and (with Katharine S. White as co-editor) *The Subtreasury of American Humor.*

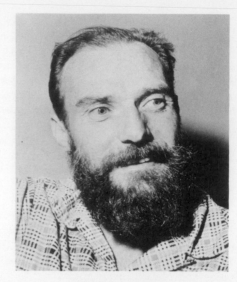

LEONARD WIBBERLEY

Leonard Wibberley

1915-

AUTHOR OF

Epics of Everest; The Wound of Peter Wayne; Deadmen's Cave; Treegate's Raiders; Etc.

Autobiographical sketch of Leonard Wibberley:

IT is my opinion that the desire to become an author is born in childhood and has its birth in childhood reading. That is certainly so in my case. I was born in Dublin, Ireland, in 1915, and got my early education in the Gaelic language. We read, in Gaelic, stories of Irish heroes like Cuchullin who could singlehanded destroy a whole army, and Nuada of the Silver Hand, and my mind was stocked with such fancies. The Irish are great storytellers so when I wasn't reading stories or having them read to me, I was hearing stories from my parents or my nurse and spent a long time living in the glittery world of imagination.

My family moved to England before I was in my teens, and I had to learn then to read and write English. I went to a convent school and can still remember one of the nuns reading *Treasure Island* to us. She read a chapter every class and I was fascinated. She could imitate Long John Silver, Squire Trelawney, and Jim Hawkins to perfection and *Treasure Island* is still my favorite book.

I think it was this book that inspired me to write myself. I spent many years in school, without any firm idea of becoming a writer, and then obtained employment on a newspaper in London. I was a copy boy and then a reporter, and finally went to the British West Indies to edit a newspaper there. All the time I was unconsciously stocking my mind with people and places and sounds and smells and sights which could be used later in books. I looked at fields of sugar cane, and coconut palms, and the pounding surf and gloomy tropical rivers, and tried to impress them on my mind so I could write about them later.

When I came to the United States, in 1943, it was as a newspaperman working as a foreign correspondent for an English newspaper. Then, some years later, while editing a newspaper of small size in California, it suddenly occurred to me that I ought to write a book. The thought occupied but a moment. I picked up a sheet of paper, put it in my typewriter and started writing as follows:

"I have so often told this story of Drake's raid on Cadiz and the part that I played in it. . . ." And so I went on until I had written a book about a boy in England in the reign of Queen Elizabeth I. It was published as *The King's Beard*. Since then I've written twenty or so books—some for adults, some for younger people.

But you can blame it all on Robert Louis Stevenson and childhood reading, and if I could ever write a book half as good as the poorest Stevenson produced, I would be a very happy man.

Ignoring my purely adult books, the children's books I like best (of my own production) are *The Life of Winston Churchill, The Wound of Peter Wayne, Deadmen's Cave*, and *McGillicuddy McGotham*.

My wife was a schoolteacher (as was my mother) and I have four children. The eldest, Kevin, is just learning to read and I've already bought a copy of *Treasure Island* for him.

* * *

Mr. Wibberley's best-known book for adults, also enjoyed by young people, is *The Mouse That Roared*, which was made into a moving picture. Published in 1959, it is a science fantasy written with what the New York *Herald Tribune* described as "beautifully cockeyed humor."

Garth Williams

1912-

AUTHOR AND ILLUSTRATOR OF
*The Adventures of Benjamin Pink;
Rabbits' Wedding; Etc.*

ILLUSTRATOR OF
Stuart Little; Etc.

Autobiographical sketch of Garth Williams:

I WAS born in New York City and then hurried to France to learn French and to be seen by all my aunts and uncles in England. I returned when I was about two. None of this I remember. Then my sister was born which I remember very clearly— and everything since then. We went to Canada when I was six and lived on a lake where I started school. At ten I was taken to England. Both my parents were artists, so I

Berko

GARTH WILLIAMS

decided to be an architect. I worked for architects in my spare time and designed many unusual houses.

When I was seventeen the world was suffering from depression and a future in architecture looked hopeless, so I felt I could not be more hopeless as an artist and I went to art schools in London. I was interested in many things, in theater scenery, in oil painting, poster design, murals, sculpture, and won scholarships which supported me for seven years. Starting as a painting scholar I ended as a sculptor. Then I married and felt I had to be very serious about earning a living. I sculpted portraits and designed textiles. I worked for a new (never published) woman's magazine in London, but World War II began before the magazine could, and I found myself in the Red Cross.

During the war I produced very little indeed until I came back to New York and started drawing for the *New Yorker*. Then E. B. White asked me to try a few sample illustrations for *Stuart Little*, and I finally did them all—and that was my first children's book. I have been illustrating children's books ever since. Now I'm painting and sculpting again too. I live in Aspen, Colorado, with my wife and daughters, where life is as hectic as New York, but different.

Regina J. Woody

1894-

AUTHOR OF

Starlight; Boarding School; Ballet in the Barn; Student Dancer; Etc.

Autobiographical sketch of Regina J. Woody:

I WAS born in Boston but brought up in a big square house on top of a hill six miles away. Horses and dogs were my only play-mates. I rode and read, read and wrote. I sold my first story about my St. Bernard dog Leo to *Our Dumb Animals* for a dollar when I was nine.

Soon, though, I had another love, dancing, for I saw Adeline Genée in *The Soul Kiss*. Not that I lost my heart to a ballerina! Far from it, for I saw her do *La Chasse* dressed in an old-fashioned riding habit, a crop in hand, leather boots, and a derby hat. She pranced and pawed like a mettlesome steed. She tossed her head and I could feel the wind blowing back my horse's mane. I was in the seventh heaven of delight. From then on I rode horseback and pawed the ground in imitation of Genée.

At eleven I was sent to Dana Hall in Wellesley. There I lived an enchanted two years dancing in every class that was given in Dalcroze gymnastics. By the time I was thirteen, I told my English teacher that I wanted two things of life, "to write like Hans Christian Andersen and to dance like

Bradford Bachrach

REGINA J. WOODY

Adeline Genée." She was not amused and suggested that I do one thing at a time.

Off to London I was taken that summer to be disabused of the idea that I could dance professionally. I won a scholarship and two years later made my debut in Paris as *danseuse étoile* at (of all places for a Dana Hall girl) the Folies Bergères. Such success at seventeen indicates great slathers of luck, a moderate amount of talent, and a delight in work that only a born-and-bred New England child could stomach.

Paris, Algiers, Budapest, Broadway, and the Keith-Orpheum circuit as a headliner followed. Then a broken ankle, a meeting with the assistant dean of Harvard Medical School and love at second, third, and fourth sight, for I was his pupil in a class for Red Cross first-aid ambulance drivers who were to go abroad. I never got farther than Rowes Wharf in Boston until after we were mar-ried. Then Washington, as a young lieu-tenant's wife on the Surgeon General's staff.

We have three children and four grand-children. My husband has always encour-aged me to write, as have my children. Writing permits me to relive the sorrows and delights of an exceptionally varied and interesting life. Indeed, I am very grateful to have been permitted for nearly half a century to have a small share in dance, an art which knows no race, creed, or language barrier, but which speaks to all who have eyes to see through flawless technique, beauty, and integrity. I am, at present, edi-tor of the "Young Dancer" section of *Dance Magazine*. I have written for it since 1929. Undoubtedly, I am the oldest "Young Dancer" editor in captivity, but I am still having a perfectly wonderful time writing away and being wife, mother, and grand-mother at one and the same time.

Catherine Woolley

1904-

AUTHOR OF

David's Hundred Dollars; Ginnie and Geneva; Ellie's Problem Dog; A Room for Cathy; Etc.

Autobiographical sketch of Catherine Wool-ley, who sometimes writes under the pen name Jane Thayer:

ON a June day when I was five, we moved into a little white house with a cherry tree in Passaic, New Jersey, and on that day my vivid childhood memories begin, for I had playmates at last.

We had come from Chicago. My father was a writer of magazine articles and books, and my mother later wrote books for girls. Mine was a typical suburban-American childhood, and it is the fabric of every book I have written—especially the Ginnie books. I was Ginnie—shy, sensitive, intense, unsure. I have tried to recreate the security and warmth, yet the passionate problems, too, of that childhood.

I had two years at Barnard College but graduated from the University of California at Los Angeles. Then came copywriting, public relations, and editorial work in New York. Occasionally I wrote a magazine article.

But never did I think of writing for children until my first nephew turned two. Then, using his very words, I wrote a simple picture book script, called it *I Like Trains*, and promptly sold it. That was in 1944. Three years later, *Two Hundred Pennies*, the first of the longer books, appeared, and I have had one to four books published every year since. In 1953 I became Jane Thayer (my grandmother's name) for the purpose of writing picture books. My Jane Thayer picture books include *The Horse with the Easter Bonnet*, *The Popcorn Dragon*, *Sandy and the Seventeen Balloons*, and *The Outside Cat*.

With three books launched I resolved to live by writing. Not for one moment was I tempted to return to business, and the compensations—in freedom and everything else —have been glorious.

I have served as president of the League of Women Voters, on the board of education and citizens' committees. I have worked in local election campaigns and learned about politics from the sidelines. I know almost all there is to know about this tight-packed little industrial city (Passaic), seething with problems, and I love it. Many of these grown-up adventures have found their way into books, for adult affairs have universal themes which can often be translated for children.

Then there are the children, my sister's, who occupy a large segment of my life. Jim was the prototype of David (in *David's Campaign Buttons*, etc.). Susan, Betsy,

CATHERINE WOOLLEY

Stephen, and Allison are never quite sure whether they are reading about themselves, and usually they are.

My mother and I have been here all this time—in the bigger gray house two doors from the little white one. There is always writing to do in the sunny back window or on the old typewriter my father used. I look out on a street full of children playing, but they do not distract me. There are meetings to attend, politics on all levels to talk about. Visits from small fry ("Can I sleep in the front bedroom, Aunt Catherine? I adore that room!"). The business of running a house. And friends and books and friendly bridge games, and spring blossoms or autumn leaves to enjoy in the lovely New Jersey country.

Lee Wyndham

1912-

AUTHOR OF

Slipper Under Glass; A Dance for Susie; Lady Architect; Binkie's Billions; Etc.

Autobiographical sketch of Lee Wyndham:

I WAS born on December 16, 1912, four thousand miles away from where I live today, at the edge of the Sea of Azov, in the Ukraine. My grandfather was a dear scholarly gentleman, and it was he who taught me to read when I was about four or five. It

LEE WYNDHAM

Parade. I haven't stopped scribbling since, but I do it all on the typewriter now.

Over a hundred of my short stories and articles have been published. In 1951 my first book, *Sizzling Pan Ranch,* was published; in 1958, my twentieth, *Dance to My Measure.* In between I have done countless junior book reviews for the Philadelphia *Inquirer* and the Morristown (New Jersey) *Daily Record,* with guest spots in the New York *World-Telegram & Sun,* and several magazines.

One needs to be curious about a great many things in order to write for young people, and the variety of subject matter in my books attests to my own varied interests. *Showboat Holiday* places a group of lively youngsters on a wrecked paddle-wheeler in a New Jersey shore cove. The idea for *The Lost Birthday Present* came from a newspaper clipping about a Sicilian donkey which had chewed up its destination tag. Enchantment with ballet has produced nine books to date—and these, incidentally, have brought me the most fan mail. *Ballet Teacher* is a career romance; *Dance to My Measure* deals with choreography. The Susie books are popular with the younger balletomanes—and their mammas, who write asking for "more about Susie." I have also collaborated on a textbook, *First Steps in Ballet.*

Writing is the joy of my life, and I wish everyone could be as happy in his work as I am. I devote full time to it now—with research, field trips, reviewing (which keeps me up to the minute on what is being published), and free-lance editorial work. I am branching out into the teaching of writing juvenile fiction, with a summer conference class at New York University, and another during the winter term. It's all wonderful fun, with so much to learn constantly, so many lives to sample and places to visit vicariously or otherwise, and to share with my young readers—who make such a delightful audience.

* * *

Lee Wyndham is married to Robert Utley Hyndman, who is also a book critic, writer, and free-lance editor. They live with their two children, Jane and Bill, and a tricolor collie and two cats, in Morristown, New Jersey.

was in his pleasant country home that the first seeds of my own storytelling were planted, for, having no playmates, I made up stories and imaginary friends for my own entertainment. I also fell out of the fruit trees in the orchard, regularly, every summer.

My father was a White Russian and an officer in the Czar's army. In 1919 it became necessary for us to escape from the Bolsheviks. We sailed to Istanbul, and lived there for three years before coming to America in 1923.

My education was resumed in Turkey, and continued in the United States. I spoke English fluently within two years, but was very shy and made few friends, so the making up of stories continued. I wrote for my school papers and magazines, and became editor of one, for which I provided reams of copy. I also kept a journal of my imaginary adventures on a trip around the world. I wish I had it today! But somehow it got lost.

Later on, I studied painting and music, and modeled in New York City, and developed a love for ballet, opera, the theater, and research reading, all of which proved useful when I did turn to writing professionally. I did not begin to write seriously, however, until after I was married and had a son and daughter to enjoy my stories. In 1947 I fell down our back steps and fractured my foot. During the enforced "rest" I scribbled out a story and sold it to *Story*

Taro Yashima

1908-

AUTHOR AND ILLUSTRATOR OF
The Village Tree; Crow Boy; Umbrella; Etc.

Autobiographical sketch of Taro Yashima:

TARO YASHIMA

I WAS born as the last of three sons of a country doctor in a small village on the southern edge of Kyushu Island, Japan. My father was also a collector of Oriental art and he admired the first-class artists of the past as the humans who sat next to God.

I became a student of the provincial high school of Kagoshima City, after graduating from public school. I lost my mother when I was in the first grade and my father three years later. When I decided to be an artist, my father was still alive and gave me encouragement and left me word in his will not to give up my first decision.

I became an art student of the Imperial Art Academy of Tokyo after high school, and gradually moved into the professional field of cartoonists and artists. My wife was also an artist who graduated from the art department of Bunka Gakuin, a cultural college in Tokyo.

My wife and I came to New York as temporary visitors, leaving our little son in Kobe, to study the Western masters' works in museums in the United States. As soon as Japan started the war with the United States, I joined OWI and OSS, later with my wife quitting the Art Students League of New York. My autobiographical picture books, *The New Sun* and *Horizon Is Calling,* which I published in addition to my official work during the war, were also my contribution toward a democratic Japan.

I have had many one-man shows and have exhibited my works at many art exhibitions in Japan and in this country, though it was several years after World War II ended before I stepped into the field of picture books for children. Speaking more specifically, that was after our son joined us, having been separated for ten years, and his sister was born, and I was beaten down by stomach ulcers all at the same time. My intention to start my life anew with our children was the motive.

I believe that one should be able to contribute his best for the growth of the younger generation as long as one lives as a human

being. I would like to continue publishing picture books for children until my life ends. The theme for all those should be, needless to say, "Let children enjoy living on this earth, let children be strong enough not to be beaten or twisted by evil on this earth."

Raymond F. Yates

1895-

AUTHOR OF
*Atomic Experiments for Boys; A Boy and a
Battery; The Boys' Book of Rockets; Fun
with Electronics; Etc.*

Autobiographical sketch of Raymond F. Yates:

I AM but one of a writing family of three. My wife, Marguerite W. Yates, has been on the lists of Harper's and Longmans, Green (now McKay). Our son, Brock W. Yates, of the 1955 class of Hobart College, Geneva, New York, is also on the Harper list.

I was born in Lockport, New York, but spent most of my youth at Niagara Falls, New York. My first published articles appeared while I was in eighth grade. I was contributing feature articles to *Scientific American, Popular Science Monthly,* and lesser magazines before I was eighteen. A prodigious appetite for science was a stimulating factor in this early but modest success.

RAYMOND F. YATES

In 1916 I was called to New York City to edit *Everyday Mechanics,* later purchased by *Popular Mechanics.* A short time after my arrival, the late Waldemar Kaempffert gave me the opportunity of serving as his managing editor on the staff of *Popular Science Monthly.* Following this helpful experience, I became radio editor and columnist on the old New York *Evening Mail.* This newspaper experience was continued on the New York *Tribune,* where I became the world's first radio critic in a column signed "Pioneer." I also served as editor of *Popular Radio.*

My first book was published by the old Century Company in 1916. In 1925 the second book, with Samuel Rothafel (later Roxy of Roxy Theater fame) as co-author, was also published by the Century Company. Since that time, more than seventy other books have followed. Some of them have been published in Spain, Sweden, Holland, France, Iraq, and Norway. I am also the author of the world's first book on television. This was written in 1927. My most successful book, *The Niagara Story,* has sold over seven hundred thousand copies. It has become what almost amounts to the official tourist guide for Niagara Falls. As many as five thousand copies are sold in a single week end during the tourist season.

Aside from my books, I have contributed several million words to a large number of magazines and newspapers, including the *Reader's Digest,* the New York *Times, Life,* and King Features Syndicate. At present I am contributing editor of *Science and Mechanics.* I have lectured at the American Museum of Natural History, in New York City; at the Rochester, New York, Museum of Arts and Sciences; and in many other cities throughout the United States.

Ylla

d. 1955

ILLUSTRATOR OF
The Sleepy Little Lion; Dogs; They All Saw It; Tico-Tico; Etc.

A NIMAL photographer without peer, Ylla, or Camilla Koffler, as she was born in Austria, came to the United States in 1941. She had grown up in Hungary, and had had a photographic studio in Paris. She started out as a sculptor, modeling people, and was successful in catching expressions in marble. However, she could not do animals in this medium.

When Ylla became a photographer, she found that her pictures of people did not satisfy her, but that those she took of animals were just what she saw in her lens. So from then on she was an animal photographer. "They are easier to get in contact with," was the way she expressed it.

Ylla's theory about animals and photographing them led her to go into that work. "Every animal is different from every other animal in the world," she said. When she took a picture of an animal she strove to catch on film just the look or pose that expressed most tellingly the personality of her subject. Of course this presupposed not only an affection for animals but a thorough knowledge of them, and Ylla had both. She also tried to understand the personality of the individual she was photographing, and this helped her to get the best response and the most characteristic expression and pose.

Ylla's favorite position while at work was on her hands and knees. That way she could get the angle she wanted without putting her subject in an awkward or unfamiliar pose. A running accompaniment of sounds served to soothe or arouse the animal. She would cluck, whistle, poke, tackle, and even scream to get the shots she wanted. The results were always amazing. Her books

YLLA

were full of animals wholly alive, with attitudes and expressions as if they were about to step off the page. They have been called living photographs and are well known here and abroad, as she had many exhibitions in Europe as well as in the United States.

This brilliant young woman died March 30, 1955, in India, from injuries received in a jeep accident. She fell from the car while photographing a race between bullock-drawn carts at a fair organized by the Maharaja of Bharatpur, whose guest she was.

Harry Zarchy

1912-

AUTHOR AND ILLUSTRATOR OF
Let's Make Something; Creative Hobbies; Ceramics; Stamp Collector's Guide; Etc.

Autobiographical sketch of Harry Zarchy:

I WAS born in New York City. My parents have told me that as soon as I was old enough to walk, I began to use tools. In fact, I distinctly recall hitting myself on the head with a hammer when I was very young. My father owned tools of every description, and it was only natural that my brother, Rubin, and I should learn to use them. Of course we had to take care of them properly. We built serious things like radios and sidewalk scooters, as well as our own wonderful, secret inventions which whirled around and around and made noise, but which were otherwise completely useless.

There was always something going on at home. My father did beautiful wood carvings, built radios, cabinets, and almost everything else. My brother and I were always busy. If we weren't painting or drawing, we were practicing some musical instrument, experimenting with a chemistry set, doing craft work, reading, or going off on a hike with our Boy Scout troop. We had dozens of hobbies.

Our interest in things out of doors began when we were very young. We used to spend our summers on farms in the Catskill Mountains and we learned to love the country. Ponds and streams were especially fascinating, and it wasn't long before we both became ardent fishermen. We began to spend most of our time on or near the water; if we weren't fishing, we could probably be found lying on the bank just watching the fish. We caught wild trout with rods and reels, and also with our hands, by the age-old practice of "tickling."

My brother had always intended to become an artist, while I spent my younger years preparing for a musical career. Strangely enough, our vocations got switched. Rubin is now one of the country's top-notch trumpet players, while I am the artist. After graduation from high school I attended Pratt Institute, and later New York University. I spent my summer vacations at children's camps, where I organized and conducted crafts programs. I then worked for an animated cartoon studio, designed jewelry, constructed architectural scale models, built window displays, did a little commercial art work, and painted portraits. Then I became an art teacher in the New York City school system, where I teach art, ceramics, and crafts.

Shortly after I began to teach, I decided to write how-to-do-it books for young people. I remembered how difficult it had been for me to find interesting projects when I was young, and I felt there was a serious lack of such material. My first book was well received, so I kept on writing, and have been at it ever since.

I believe everyone should have at least one hobby, and learn as much about it as possi-

HARRY ZARCHY

ble. The saddest thing in the world is someone who has "nothing to do." Hobbyists always have something to do; they seldom have enough time for all the things they would like to do. I still keep busy with my hobbies, which are too numerous to mention, and even find time to operate my amateur radio station, K2RZP. My son, Bill, is a hobbyist, too. He is learning to enjoy the same activities that I did when I was his age. The rest of the family consists of Jeanette, my wife, and my daughter, Sue. We all live in a big house in Freeport, Long Island, not far from New York City.

Gene Zion

1913-

AUTHOR OF

All Falling Down; Dear Garbage Man; Harry the Dirty Dog; The Plant Sitter; Etc.

Autobiographical sketch of Gene Zion:

I WAS born in New York City. Soon after, my family moved to Ridgefield, New Jersey, where life was rural and included a barn with a cow, chickens, and pigeons. My career as an artist started in kindergarten where I received acclaim from the teacher after I had drawn a crayon border around a piece of paper.

I attended grade school in Ridgefield and Fort Lee, where at Thanksgiving and Christ-

mas I decorated blackboards with colored chalk drawings of pumpkins, turkeys, and Santa Claus. I think I resolved to become an artist at this time because I was thrilled and fascinated by the drawings done by a local evangelist who, every Saturday night, collected a spellbound street-corner audience. He drew in colored chalks on a large pad and his routine was always the same—a dramatic pictorial and verbal rendering of the sinking of the *Titanic*, with great emphasis on all the sinners who perished that terrible night.

I loved to read and used to sit on the grass in front of the library trying to finish the books I had just borrowed before I took them home. As a small boy, the first money I earned came from painting pictures to order, in oils, on the backs of my classmates' yellow rain slickers.

I returned to New York City where I went to high school and later graduated from Pratt Institute. While serving my apprenticeship in advertising design, I studied with Alexy Brodovitch at the New School and also with Herbert Bayer. In 1936 I won a national travel poster competition, which resulted in an extended stay and travel in Europe. I visited many fine printing plants abroad and became very interested in the design and printing of books.

I continued in advertising art until I entered the Army in World War II. In 1942 I was assigned to the Antiaircraft Artillery Visual Training Aids Section where I designed filmstrips and training manuals for the instruction of troops. When I became a civilian again, I joined the art department of Columbia Broadcasting System and later the Condé Nast Publications. Eventually, I became a free-lance designer and art director.

Ursula Nordstrom of Harper & Brothers, and my wife, Margaret Bloy Graham, started me writing for children. A sketch of children gathering apples in an orchard, which my wife did years ago in Canada, gave me the idea for our first book, *All Falling Down*. We have been doing books together ever since. Among the books I have done, *Really Spring* was inspired by the drab scene from our studio window one late spring. *Dear Garbage Man* came from watching our Sanitation Department friends saving trash "too good to throw away," and *The Plant*

Sitter stemmed from our eternal problem of what to do with our plants at vacation time. No creative effort has been more gratifying for me than writing picture books for children.

Charlotte Zolotow
1915-
AUTHOR OF
The Park Book; The Storm Book; Not a Little Monkey; One Step, Two; Etc.

Autobiographical sketch of Charlotte Zolotow:

I WAS born in Norfolk, Virginia, and learned to read before I went to school. I loved reading and loved drawing and did both constantly. When grownups asked what I wanted to do when I grew up, I always said I wanted to write books and draw my own pictures for them.

I went to the University of Wisconsin on a writing scholarship, but for some reason did not study art at all and have never really done so. If my books had not been illustrated by such artists as H. A. Rey, Leonard Weisgard, Margaret Bloy Graham, Roger Duvoisin, and Garth Williams, this would be a great regret to me.

After the University of Wisconsin, I married Maurice Zolotow, whom I met there. He is a writer. I worked for Ursula Nordstrom, editor of Harper's children's book department, as her editorial assistant. This brought me into contact not only with her own original and fascinating mind and approach to children's books, but with the books and illustrations as well. I loved it all.

The Park Book grew out of a memo to her suggesting a book about Washington Square

CHARLOTTE ZOLOTOW

Park. She encouraged me to try it myself and that was my first children's book, published in 1944, just before my son, Stephen, was born. Later books took form from bedtime stories I told him, from experiences I had with him, and the revelation his own very individual way of surveying experience was to me. My daughter, Ellen, who is eight years younger than Steve, has again her own way of seeing the world and it is so fresh and poetic a way that she has opened up for me not only the universe in her own terms but—the past recalled—memories of my own childhood that I have otherwise lost.

So it is really out of my contact with Steve and Ellen, with their friends, with the deepened perceptions and awareness children bring to people involved with them, as well as out of my earlier feeling for the spoken and written word, that my children's books have come.